Gender and Sexuality in Modern Japan

Gender and Sexuality in Modern Japan describes the ever-changing manifestations of sexes, genders, and sexualities in Japanese society from the 1860s to the present day. Analyzing a wide range of texts, images, and data, Sabine Frühstück considers the experiences of females, males, and the evolving spectrum of boundary-crossing individuals and identities in Japan. These include the intersexed conscript in the 1880s, the first "out" lesbian war reporter in the 1930s, and pregnancy-vest-wearing male governors in the present day. She interweaves macro views of history with stories about individual actors, highlighting how sexual and gender expression has been negotiated in both the private and the public spheres and continues to wield the power to critique and change society. This lively and accessible survey introduces Japanese ideas about modern manhood, modern womenhood, reproduction, violence and sex during war, the sex trade, LGBTQ identities and activism, women's liberation, feminisms, and visual culture.

Sabine Frühstück is the Koichi Takashima Chair and Professor of Modern Japanese Cultural Studies at the University of California, Santa Barbara.

New Approaches to Asian History

This dynamic new series publishes books on the milestones in Asian history, those that have come to define particular periods or to mark turning points in the political, cultural and social evolution of the region. The books in this series are intended as introductions for students to be used in the classroom. They are written by scholars whose credentials are well established in their particular fields and who have, in many cases, taught the subject across a number of years.

A list of books in the series can be found at the end of the volume.

Gender and Sexuality in Modern Japan

Sabine Frühstück
University of California at Santa Barbara

CAMBRIDGE
UNIVERSITY PRESS

University Printing House, Cambridge CB2 8BS, United Kingdom

One Liberty Plaza, 20th Floor, New York, NY 10006, USA

477 Williamstown Road, Port Melbourne, VIC 3207, Australia

314–321, 3rd Floor, Plot 3, Splendor Forum, Jasola District Centre,
New Delhi – 110025, India

103 Penang Road, #05–06/07, Visioncrest Commercial, Singapore 238467

Cambridge University Press is part of the University of Cambridge.

It furthers the University's mission by disseminating knowledge in the pursuit of
education, learning, and research at the highest international levels of excellence.

www.cambridge.org
Information on this title: www.cambridge.org/9781108420655
DOI: 10.1017/9781108354967

© Sabine Frühstück 2022

This publication is in copyright. Subject to statutory exception
and to the provisions of relevant collective licensing agreements,
no reproduction of any part may take place without the written
permission of Cambridge University Press.

First published 2022

A catalogue record for this publication is available from the British Library.

Library of Congress Cataloging-in-Publication Data
Names: Frühstück, Sabine, author.
Title: Gender and sexuality in modern Japan / Sabine Frühstück, University of
California at Santa Barbara.
Description: Cambridge, United Kingdom; New York, NY : Cambridge
University Press, 2022. | Series: New approaches to Asian history | Includes
bibliographical references and index.
Identifiers: LCCN 2021044710 (print) | LCCN 2021044711 (ebook) |
ISBN 9781108420655 (hardback) | ISBN 9781108430722 (paperback) |
ISBN 9781108354967 (epub)
Subjects: LCSH: Sex role–Japan. | Sex–Japan. | Sexism–Japan. |
Feminism–Japan. | BISAC: HISTORY / Asia / General
Classification: LCC HQ1075.5.J3 F78 2022 (print) | LCC HQ1075.5.J3
(ebook) | DDC 305.30952–dc23/eng/20211022
LC record available at https://lccn.loc.gov/2021044710
LC ebook record available at https://lccn.loc.gov/2021044711

ISBN 978-1-108-42065-5 Hardback
ISBN 978-1-108-43072-2 Paperback

Cambridge University Press has no responsibility for the persistence or accuracy
of URLs for external or third-party internet websites referred to in this publication
and does not guarantee that any content on such websites is, or will remain,
accurate or appropriate.

Contents

List of Figures	*page*	vii
Acknowledgments		ix
Introduction		1
What Is Modern Japan?		2
Families and Households		3
Codes and Laws		6
Words and Concepts		9
Frames and Lenses, or How to Read This Book		12
The Chapters		14
1 Building the Nation and Modern Manhood		19
Measuring Hegemonic Masculinity		21
Is the Company *Man* a Real Man?		32
Manning the Changing Tables		37
2 Controlling Reproduction and Motherhood		47
Revolutionizing Birth		49
Contracepting Imperialism		57
Why Have Babies?		64
3 Redefining Womanhoods		70
Roles and Rights		71
New Women, Modern Girls		79
Suffrage and Pacifism		84
Women's Liberation: *Ūman Ribu*		87
Mainstreaming Feminism and Backlash		90
4 Sex at War		98
Systemic Military Sexual Violence		99
Amnesia and Legacies		106
Global Commemorations		115
5 The Politics of Sexual Labor		121
Liberating Prostitutes		123
Renewing the Oldest Profession		127
The Work of Sex Today		134

vi   Contents

6   Queer Identities and Activisms   141
    Culture and Knowledge   142
    Queer Spaces   149
    Prohibitions and Rights   153
    Does Trans Transform Society?   162

7   Sexing Visual Culture   166
    Laughing at Semi-Naked Truths in Erotic Woodblock Prints   167
    Injurious to Modern Morals   172
    Dangers in the Realm of the Senses   173
    Viewing the Pain of Others with Aida Makoto   176
    Demystifying the Vagina with Rokudenashiko   181
    Silenced Females in Video Gaming   186

8   Epilogue   191
    At the Beginning: The Penis   191
    At Present: Mapping Sexual and Gendered (J-)Humanity   199

    Bibliography   206
    Index   233

Figures

1.1 Photograph of war veteran with child on his back,
Domon Ken, 1950   *page* 30

1.2 Photograph of kabuki and film actor Nakamura Shidō
with baby, *Harper's Bazaar*, May 2018   42

2.1 Fertility graph in supplement to *The Housewife's
Companion* (*Shufu no Tomo*), February 1933   54

2.2 Morinaga Dry Milk advertisement in supplement
to *The Housewife's Companion* (*Shufu no Tomo*),
September 1932   56

3.1 Caricature of a modern woman's woes in *The World
of Women's Learning* (*Jogaku Sekai*), October 1914   77

3.2 Photograph of women and children fishing, 1919   78

3.3 Photograph of Yamada Waka during her visit with Eleanor
Roosevelt, December 7, 1937   80

3.4 Photograph of policewomen's drum corps on the cover
of *Japan*, November 1973   89

3.5 Campaign poster of the conservative Liberal
Democratic Party featuring the slogan, "Your vote
will improve Japan," 1968   91

4.1 Cover of David Hume's comic *Babysan's World:
The Hume'n Slant on Japan*, 1954   109

4.2 Collage titled, "Made in Occupied Japan" by Shimada
Yoshiko and Bubu De la Madeleine   110

4.3 The peace statue of a "comfort woman" in Moabit, Berlin,
September 2020   117

6.1 Kamikawa Aya participating in a Tokyo Pride parade,
2019   155

6.2 Self-styled "unarchitect," actress, artist and drag queen
Vivienne Sato, 2019   164

7.1 A sample of Rokudenashiko's *manko* figurines, 2021   182

viii   List of Figures

8.1 Russian brochure, *606 and Syphilis*, about the discovery
    and development of Salvarsan 606, the first effective
    treatment for syphilis, 1910   196
8.2 Drawing titled, "The Dawn of the East Asian Race,"
    in *Asahi Gurafu*, March 2, 1938   198
8.3 Amateur ethnographer Ella Lurie Wiswell as a child
    with unidentified Japanese girls, summer 1919   200

Acknowledgments

When my daughter was two years old, she sat on the toilet one day with one hand flat on her lower belly. Worried that she might have a bellyache, I asked what she was doing. She answered, "I am holding my penis." (Daycare was useful in this way.) I casually proceeded to tell her that what she had is called "vagina," and that it was boys who had penises. I asked whether she knew whether her father had a penis. She confidently answered in the affirmative. Did I, I probed. She said "yes" to that question too. (Full disclosure: I do not.) I was both amused and intrigued. Had she not just articulated a version of Freud's "phallic stage," associating the penis with power, and adopting the same for herself?

This book is dedicated to all those individuals, in Japan and elsewhere, who have forged their own paths through what has presented itself as modern sex and gender order, those who have, since the late nineteenth century, undermined and challenged the very power that has permeated it – the Fukuzawa Yukichis and Ueki Emoris, Yoshiya Nobukos, Hiratsuka Raichōs, Magnus Hirschfelds, Tōgō Kens, Kamikawa Ayas, Itō Shioris, Vivienne Satōs, and Igarashi Megumis, along with many others who remain unnamed. In the following chapters, I aim to map, to compress and chisel, to provoke, probe, and reshape key questions and problems that have continued to inform and impact that order.

For just one book to see the day of light, numerous institutions devoted to the public good need to provide access to their treasures, many paths need to be explored (and abandoned), and countless creative minds need to intersect. The trajectory of this book was no different. In lieu of a much longer list, I wish to thank the archivists, librarians, and guardians of the National Diet Library (Kokuritsu Kokkai Toshokan), the Ken Domon Museum of Photography (Domon Ken Kinenkan), the Research Institute for National Education Policy (Kokuritsu Kyōiku Seisaku Kenkyūjo), and the Tōsho Bunko, Japan's first library dedicated to textbooks, all in Tokyo; the Magnus-Hirschfeld-Gesellschaft in Berlin; the Library of Congress in Washington, DC; and the Hamilton Library

x Acknowledgments

of the University of Hawai'i at Mānoa. Their and many more collections on three continents plus cyberspace have facilitated my pursuit, over the last twenty-five years or so, of the most important methodology of knowledge production: asking for the way, walking more than one, and doing so countless times. I gratefully acknowledge the companionship of Thomas Ludwig, the mentorship of Jennifer Robertson, the wisdom of Elena Ferrante, and the friendship of Erika Rappaport, Eve Darian-Smith, Fabio Rambelli, Jackie Spafford, Laurie Monahan, Maria Fernanda Acosta, and Songi Han. I cherish the artists whose works have contributed to the collective critique and understanding of the world of sex, gender, and sexuality in modern and contemporary Japan, and I thank them for letting me share their creations: Bubu De la Madeleine, David Hume, Graham Kolbeins, Kurigami Kazumi, Nakamura Shidō, Shimada Yoshiko, and Rokudenashiko – along with a number of anonymous illustrators.

The last bit of research in Japan was facilitated by a University of California–Santa Barbara Academic Senate Faculty Research Grant. My inimitably wonderful editor, Kirsten Janene-Nelson, has again worked her magic. At Cambridge University Press, I am indebted to the fabulous Lucy Rhymer, along with dream team Rachel Blaifeder, Joan Dale Lace, and Emily Plater.

Introduction

On December 18, 2019, a young woman by the name of Itō Shiori stepped outside the Tokyo District Court holding up a banner reading "victory" (*shōso*). The court had ruled that Itō had been assaulted by Yamaguchi Noriyuki, a prominent journalist, who would be punished for his crime. This was a significant result given that Japan's sex crime laws do not consider consent; instead, they require evidence of violence and intimidation – which can be difficult to litigate successfully. But with this case the fact that the court had found her "highly trustworthy" marked new ground, bringing Itō to express the hope that her case would instigate a change in the law.[1] A few months later, *Time* magazine listed her as one of the 100 most influential people in the world for her contribution to Japan's #MeToo movement. While Itō's courage was indeed in part inspired by the global reverberations of what had begun under that hashtag, the critique of sexual and gender relations in Japan has a much longer history.[2]

This book is about experiences of and debates about sex, gender, and sexuality in modern and contemporary Japan. This long period from the 1860s to the 2020s witnessed the uneven transformation of earlier understandings of "sex" into three currently customary categories of inquiry: The term "(biological) sex" concerns chromosomes, genes, genitals, hormones, and other physical markers, some of which have become subject to modification. "Gender" represents masculinity, femininity, and the behaviors commonly associated with them. And "sexuality"

---

[1] Yukiko Tsunoda, "Sexual Harassment in Japan," in *Directions in Sexual Harassment Law*, ed. Catharine A. MacKinnon and Reva B. Siegel (Oxford: Oxford University Press, 2003), 618–33; Motoko Rich and Hisako Ueno, "Woman Wins High-Profile #MeToo Case in Japan against TV Journalist," *New York Times*, December 18, 2019, accessed April 22, 2020, www.nytimes.com/2019/12/18/world/asia/japan-metoo-shiori-ito-rape .html?login=email&auth=login-email.

[2] The hashtag itself was first used by the American activist and founder of the movement, Tarana Burke, in 2006, even though the movement's global prominence was triggered by the revelations of Harvey Weinstein's offenses in 2017; see "Get to Know Us," me too, accessed March 3, 2021, https://metoomvmt.org/get-to-know-us/.

2 Introduction

refers to the erotic, including behaviors and fantasies. This book envisions sex, gender, and sexuality as constructed categories that have been and continue to be redefined while also interconnecting, overlapping, and intertwining in the Japanese and, to varying degrees, global public sphere.[3] It tells of struggles far beyond what the first "womanists" of the late nineteenth century referred to as "sexual morality."[4] It views what current-day law captures as "sexual harassment" as being only the smallest kernel at the core of all the big questions – about life and death, freedom and happiness, and the social contract – and grounds of a range of complex issues related to the continuously evolving arrangements of sex, gender, and sexuality in the archipelago.

In doing so, this book aims to balance descriptions of individual experience (such as Itō's); institutional mechanisms based in law, pedagogy, and statecraft; and the socioculturally inflected politics within which those mechanisms have been embedded and which they have in turn shaped over an extended period that began with the nation- and empire-building of the late nineteenth century. These various elements constellate into distinct themes and categories that are delineated in the following.

What Is Modern Japan?

But when did the archipelago's modernity begin? And what do we mean when we say "Japan"? The political revolution of 1868 that overthrew the Tokugawa shogunate formally marks the foundation of the modern nation-state. This nation-state became almost immediately enmeshed in its first modern anticolonial colonialist project. In 1869, it unilaterally extended its rule over an island – Hokkaido – that the Japanese had for centuries called the "Land of Barbarians" (*Ezo* or *Ezogashima*). And in 1879 it officially annexed Okinawa (formerly the Ryūkyū kingdom), which had been already administratively annexed by the shogunate in 1609. Thus, "Japan" had behaved like an empire long before its formal inception as one – which was marked much later by the acquisition of Taiwan at the end of the Sino-Japanese War (1894–1895). Japan expanded from there, propagating resistance to western colonial powers as it pursued imperialism and war (1868–1945). As a result of the Russo-

---

[3] I adopt Joanne Meyerowitz's descriptions in *How Sex Changed: A History of Transsexuality in the United States* (Cambridge, MA: Harvard University Press, 2009), 3–4.

[4] Marnie S. Anderson proposes the word "womanists" instead of "feminists" for those early activists, since their accomplishment lies less in women's rights than in claiming "woman" as a political and social category; see Marnie S. Anderson, *A Place in Public: Women's Rights in Meiji Japan* (Cambridge, MA: Harvard University Asia Center, 2010).

Japanese War of 1904–1905, the Korean empire, proclaimed such in 1897 by Emperor Gojong of the Joseon dynasty, became a protectorate of Japan; it was annexed in 1910. Subsequently, the Japanese empire aggressively and violently brought under its control vast areas of land and sea. Key moves include the Japanese invasion of Manchuria in 1931; the Battle of Nanking in 1937, which marked the beginning of a full-blown war with China more than two years before the September 1939 start of World War II with Nazi Germany's invasion of Poland; the aerial attack on Pearl Harbor in 1941, after which the United States entered the war; and, finally, the US atomic bomb attacks in 1945 on Hiroshima and Nagasaki, which precipitated the empire's surrender and collapse.[5] This was followed by a largely antimilitarist liberal democracy – a period that has spanned more than five emperors' reigns – Meiji (1868–1912), Taishō (1912–1926), Shōwa (1926–1989), Heisei (1989–2019), and Reiwa (2019–present), with the Shōwa emperor embodying the transition from commander in chief to being a "symbol of the state and of the unity of the people, deriving his position from the will of the people with whom resides sovereign power."[6] Given the instability of the sociopolitical shape and circumstances of the archipelago throughout the modern and contemporary eras, rather than a singular political event, then, a range of changes constitute landmarks of the modern with regard to sex, gender, and sexuality.

Families and Households

The year 1871 saw the establishment of both the family and household system (*ie seido*) and the family registration system (*koseki*), the latter of which required that every individual's family affiliation be registered with the government. Thereafter, the emperor was seen as the symbolic parent of the nation, and the male head of each family was considered his analogue within that family. As such, the husband/father was all-powerful within the household. His dependents were not just expected to defer to him – they were legally compelled to do so. In addition, inheritance became strictly patrilinear. In the absence of a male heir, a son-in-law or male relative was adopted in order to ensure the family headship

---

[5] The phrase "anti-colonial colonialism" was coined by Jennifer Robertson, *Takarazuka: Sexual Politics and Popular Culture in Modern Japan* (Berkeley: University of California Press, 1998).

[6] Article 1 of the constitution of Japan can be found on the government webpage "The Constitution of Japan," Prime Minister of Japan and His Cabinet, accessed February 7, 2021, https://japan.kantei.go.jp/constitution_and_government_of_japan/constitution_e .html.

4   Introduction

would pass from a "father" to a "son." In this system, women were considered nothing more than "items of exchange between families, place markers or 'borrowed wombs' for the production of sons."[7]

A competing notion of the family – the home (*katei*) – took root as well, inspired specifically by the Christian ideology of monogamy and more generally by the western ideal of romantic love. Envisioned as the Japanese version of the modern nuclear family, the home centered on a romantically bonded married couple and their offspring. In contradistinction to the multigenerational households of earlier times, the husband's parents had no place in this new framework. And in both systems – the *ie seido* and the *katei* – women's roles were limited to the home and family. For many women of the lower classes, however, the ideals of the *katei* remained a distant dream until the mid-twentieth century, since they had to work outside the home just as their mothers and grandmothers had.[8] Previous generations of women had primarily been farmers and fishers – until the late nineteenth century onward, when the young increasingly migrated from their villages to work in textile factories, coal mines, brothels, and the households of the rich, both in urban areas in Japan proper and throughout the growing empire.[9] Today, the Japanese nuclear family remains a "stem nuclear" family in that, unlike the western neolocal nuclear families, it can expand to include only one married couple per generation. Not just the absence of offspring, but also the absence of competent biological offspring can be grounds for adopting a successor – even married couples can be adopted in order to insure an *ie*'s continuity. This is why the *koseki* retains its authority even as the postwar constitution recognizes the sovereignty of the individual.

In 1872, just a year after the launch of the family registration system, a host of legislation reconfigured childhood. The Fundamental Code of Education established a mandatory elementary school system, which stratified the child population into age groups by prescribing first five and then six years of basic education for girls and boys from the age of six. In addition, various legislation in the areas of health, welfare, labor, and crime concerned itself with the protection of children as well as the

---

[7] Takie Sugiyama Lebra, *Above the Clouds: Status Culture of the Modern Japanese Nobility* (Berkeley: University of California Press, 1993).

[8] Sharalyn Orbaugh, "Gender, Family, and Sexualities in Modern Literature," in *The Columbia Companion to Modern East Asian Literature*, ed. Joshua S. Mostow, Kirk A. Denton, Bruce Fulton, and Sharalyn Orbaugh (New York: Columbia University Press, 2003), 43–51.

[9] For more on *karayuki-san* see David R. Ambaras, *Japan's Imperial Underworlds: Intimate Encounters at the Borders of Empire* (Cambridge: University of Cambridge Press, 2018).

Families and Households 5

protection of society from any children who might be dangerous. All these efforts gradually replaced class status with age group or grade level as a primary social marker of childhood.[10] Childhood had always been uneven across classes, regions, and communities. After 1872, the end of childhood was in flux, and increasingly differed for girls and boys in various ways. For instance, in 1900 or so about half of the laborers in textile and match factories were children under the age of fourteen, and 60 percent of them were girls.[11] Yet female adulthood remained tied to marriage and motherhood; if a female in her early twenties was unmarried, she was not seen as having reached womanhood. On the other hand, male adulthood was distinctly marked as the age of twenty, when boys had to report for their military physical exam with the prospect, in principle at least, of being drafted for three years of service in the archipelago's new, modern mass army. The 1872 introduction of the mandatory conscription system thus redefined what it meant to be a ("real") man, initiating the militarization of ideal manhood. The subsequent military campaigns and empire-building efforts between the Sino-Japanese War of 1894–1895 and the end of the Asia-Pacific War in 1945 solidified the soldier as the embodiment of the modern nation-state and empire. In the public sphere at least, the forces of militarization increasingly shaped gender roles and sexual lives in decisively binary ways. A range of often class-specific men's roles greatly narrowed to a singular concern: that men be enthusiastic or at least outwardly willing aggressors, a focus that was meant to align their sexual prowess with national military power – in the name of advancing Japan's domination in Asia.

Returning to the roles of women in relation to military men: women needed to be the chief supporters – and later mourners – of their soldier husbands, brothers, and sons. Some of these women were also the victims of sexual violence. Finally, one of the cruel truths of modern militarization concerns the fact that children were elevated to being political actors of sorts. Japanese boys were hailed as future soldiers, and Japanese girls as sisters, girlfriends, and future mothers of such

---

[10] Moriyama Shigeki and Nakae Kazue, *Nihon kodomo-shi* (Tokyo: Heibonsha, 2002), 8–19; see also Michael Kinski, "Japanische Kindheiten und Kindheitsbilder: Zur Einleitung," in *Kindheit in der japanischen Geschichte/Childhood in Japanese History*, ed. Michael Kinski, Harald Salomon, and Eike Grossmann (Wiesbaden: Harrassowitz, 2015), 1–32.

[11] Atsuko Fujino Kakinami, "History of Child Labor in Japan," in *The World of Child Labor*, ed. Hugh D. Hindman (Armonk, NY: M. E. Sharpe, 2009), 881–88; David R. Ambaras, *Bad Youth: Juvenile Delinquency and the Politics of Everyday Life in Modern Japan* (Berkeley: University of California Press, 2006), 41.

6   Introduction

soldiers. Both boys and girls under Japanese imperial rule were expected to be cheerleaders of war – as well as the grateful recipients of soldiers' protection, rescue, and redemption.

Codes and Laws

As far back as in the late nineteenth century, young female activists such as Kishida Toshiko (1863–1901) and Fukuda Hideko (1865–1927) of the Freedom and People's Rights movement of the 1870s and 1880s fought for representative government. They demanded not only "women's rights" but also, rather explicitly, "a single standard of sexual morality."[12] Progressive women and men knew then that the vastly different standards for "sexual morality" were rooted in sexual inequality, which in turn was intrinsically interlinked with other inequalities – of the gender, social, political, and economic sorts – and that power relations were at the heart of them all.

The 1889 Civil Code prevented women from joining political associations or speaking at or even attending public meetings. Furthermore, in line with the primogeniture noted earlier, this law treated wives as minors without property rights, subordinating them under the authority of household heads. While these details all inhibited women, ironically the Code also initiated the recognition of concubines as legal entities. Then, in 1922, the restriction was lifted regarding women attending political meetings – at which point first-wave feminism swept the country, addressing motherhood and reproductive rights, marriage, suffrage, and a range of debates about what it meant to be female. Later, in an act that lagged behind many other countries' similar policies, the right to vote was finally extended to women in 1946. In a separate timeline, reproductive control was embattled throughout the modern era. The struggle to seize it pitched the empire's aggressive pronatalism against eugenics and birth control movements that covered the entire political spectrum – from the anti-imperialist left to the reactionary right, which ultimately imposed forced sterilization of individuals with certain kinds of conditions. The only change in the law to date, in 1996, just emphasized the protection of the maternal body. Ultimately, the dramatic decline in the population has more recently changed the direction of

---

[12] Teruko Craig, "Introduction," in *In the Beginning Woman Was the Sun: The Autobiography of a Japanese Feminist – Hiratsuka Raichō*, trans. Teruko Craig (New York: Columbia University Press), viii. Interestingly, Raichō does not evoke earlier womanists; see Anderson, *A Place in Public*; Anne Walthall, *The Weak Body of a Useless Women: Matsuo Taseko and the Meiji Restoration* (Chicago, IL: University of Chicago Press, 1998).

Codes and Laws 7

the march toward the "world-historical severance of sex from procreation."[13]

The constitution of 1946 signified changes on all sex and gender fronts. Rattling the male-centered order of the preceding period, Article 9 in particular explicitly renounced the state's right of belligerency, which led to the rapid demise of the military man as a masculine ideal.[14] In its stead rose the salaryman – the white-collar middle-class male employee – as the new icon of manhood. According to populist corporate manuals and popular discourse alike, rather than giving his all to nation and emperor in war, this new man instead was to give his all to his company in commerce – with his nuclear family serving as primary support, confirmation of his (idealized middle-)class standing, and reassurance of his sexual and gender normativity. But when the Japanese asset price bubble burst in 1992, the economic and financial crises that followed saw the death of the salaryman as a near-hegemonic masculine ideal. Ever since, social change in the archipelago has been characterized by the diversification of modes of manhood and masculinity – providing a new sense of liberation and freedom for some, while producing considerable anxiety and precarity for others.[15]

The 1946 constitution also recast the family as an egalitarian institution, one based on equality between husband and wife and between male and female siblings. Article 14 declares: "All of the people are equal under the law and there shall be no discrimination in political, economic or social relations because of race, creed, sex, social status or family origin." Article 24 further specifies that "laws shall be enacted from the standpoint of individual dignity and the essential equality of the sexes."[16] Initially, the emphasis on the essential equality of the sexes was

---

[13] Susan Watkins, "Which Feminisms?," *New Left Review* (January–February 2018): 8. According to the World Bank's population statistics, Japan's population is declining at a negative rate of 0.14 percent; see "Population growth (annual %)," Population Pyramid. net, accessed October 1, 2021, www.populationpyramid.net/hnp/population-growth/ 2015; as such, in 2100 Japan might have little more than half of its population in 2010; "Japan 2050," accessed April 23, 2020, www.populationpyramid.net/japan/2050/.

[14] "The Constitution of Japan," Prime Minister of Japan and His Cabinet, accessed June 1, 2021, https://japan.kantei.go.jp/constitution_and_government_of_japan/constitution_e .html.

[15] Annette Schad-Seifert, "Dynamics of Masculinities in Japan – Comparative Perspectives on Men's Studies," in *Gender Dynamics and Globalisation: Perspectives from Japan within Asia*, ed. Claudia Derichs and Susanne Kreitz-Sandberg (Münster: Lit Verlag, 2007), 33–44; and Annette Schad-Seifert, "Väter am Wickeltisch in Japan," *Bildung und Erziehung* 67, no. 2 (June 2014): 203–18.

[16] In addition, Article 21 guarantees "freedom of speech, press and all other forms of expression," and provides that "no censorship shall be maintained." Its rights guarantees are framed in absolute language, without the qualifying clauses that had undermined these in the Meiji constitution. Bret Boyce, "Obscenity and Nationalism: Constitutional

8   Introduction

progressive, radical even. In recent decades, however, two issues have brought an increasing number of progressive individuals and minority communities to deem these constitutional assurances insufficient: They have failed to guide *manifestations* of equality, particularly in government and in the corporate world; and they have also failed to sufficiently protect those with nonnormative sexualities and genders – as well as with differently abled bodies.

In response to the first issue – the viability of the constitution sufficiently shaping and controlling behavior on the ground – in 1986 the Equal Employment Opportunity Law was implemented with the intention of abolishing gender inequality in the workplace. It has since been revised twice: in 1997 to target the discrimination of women in specific areas of recruitment, hiring, and promotion; and in 2006 to make employers responsible for eradicating sexual harassment in the workplace.[17] As for these new laws' efficacy: the World Economic Forum's 2020 Global Gender Gap Report, which surveys and ranks world economies "according to how well they are leveraging their female talent pool, based on economic, educational, health-based and political indicators," has again placed Japan in the bottom third – 121 out of 153 countries, ranking with the United Arab Emirates and Kuwait. (For comparison, the United States is rated 53; Iceland, Norway, and Finland, respectively, score the highest.)[18]

As for the second issue – the marginalization of queer individuals – progress has also been slow and hesitant, and has played out within a curious sphere. Japan has a rich history of ambivalence regarding transgenderism and other gender-related rights and – with the exception of a brief period in the 1870s – Japanese modern law has never criminalized same-sex relations.[19] That said, this legality has not prevented

---

Freedom of Sexual Expression in Comparative Perspective," *Columbia Journal of Transnational Law* 56, no. 4 (2018): 683–749.

[17] An English translation of the law can be found at "Equal Employment Opportunity Law (Japan)," Wikimedia Foundation, last modified December 15, 2020, 17:54, accessed May 31, 2021, https://en.wikipedia.org/wiki/Equal_Employment_Opportunity_Law_(Japan).

[18] *Global Gender Gap Report 2020*, published in 2019, reflects data from 2018; World Economic Forum, accessed August 13, 2020, www3.weforum.org/docs/WEF_GGGR_ 2020.pdf.

[19] Regarding that rich history, Jennifer Robertson points out that "femininity and masculinity have been enacted or lived by *both* female *and* male bodies as epitomized by the 400-year-old all-male Kabuki theater and all-female Takarazuka Revue founded in 1913. Nevertheless, both theaters continue to reproduce not alternative but dominant stereotypes of femininity and masculinity. Moreover, there is a qualitative, socially reinforced – and socially sanctioned – difference between the kind of femininity performed and lived by male bodies and the kind of masculinity performed and lived

institutionalized discrimination from making same-sex marriage a contentious issue – indeed, even the LGBT+ community is of two minds on the subject. On the one hand, proponents have long argued that marriage is an important means of social recognition that many queer individuals aspire to; some hope it would serve as means of making hierarchical social structures more porous. But on the other hand, progressive opponents worry that even same-sex marriage ultimately supports the patriarchal and discriminatory family registration system (*koseki*). Amid that ongoing discussion, in 2015 Shibuya ward in Tokyo made the first step toward the legal recognition of same-sex couples by issuing same-sex partnership certificates. Another curious irony within this contentious environment is the fact that it has been possible since 2003 for Japanese citizens to legally change their sex, namely by changing their entry in the family registration system – but only following sex-reassignment surgery and sterilization.[20]

Adding to the political debate is the fact that, during the last two decades, an ultra-conservative right – which includes former prime minister Abe Shinzō (2006–2007 and 2012–2020) and other members of the conservative ruling Liberal Democratic Party – has been working to "[claim] tolerance and understanding, while simultaneously advocating against legislative reforms" that would address and help prevent such institutionalized discrimination.[21] Altogether, the struggles for equality continue. This book aims to highlight the occasional reconfiguration of the struggle itself. For instance, in the early twentieth century there emerged radical utopian visions of the malleability of sex and gender; at the beginning of the twenty-first, an increasing number of otherwise fairly ordinary individuals now consider, pursue, publicly discuss, and inhabit a great diversity of sexes and genders – while others refuse such distinctions, identities, and fluidities altogether.

Words and Concepts

This book maintains that sex, gender, and sexuality are sociocultural constructs that have historically evolved – perhaps never more dramatically than during the modern era. In the past, the Japanese word for "sex"

---

by female bodies, whether on- or off-stage; see Jennifer Robertson, "Gendering Robots: Post-Human Traditionalism in Japan," in *Recreating Japanese Men*, ed. Sabine Frühstück and Anne Walthall (Berkeley: University of California Press, 2011), 288.

[20] S. P. F. Dale, "Same-Sex Marriage and the Question of Queerness–Institutional Performativity and Marriage in Japan," *Asian Anthropology* 19, no. 2 (2020): 143–59.

[21] Claire Maree, "'LGBT Issues' and the 2020 Games," *Asia-Pacific Journal: Japan Focus* 18, 4, no. 7 (2020): 1–7.

10   Introduction

(*sei*) signified an amalgamation of biology, nature, and culture. Few were invested in separating one meaning from the other, even though a number of other Japanese characters had been used that could variably signify what we today refer to as "sex," "gender," or "sexuality" – or even "character" or "nature."[22] Even in 1929, when a Research Group for Cultural Sources (Bungei Shiryō Kenkyūkai) under the leadership of a certain Satō Koka published a *Dictionary of Japan's Sexual Morals and Customs* (*Nihon Seiteki Fūzoku Jiten*), it included a great many terms that signified sexual relations of one sort or another – from "*aiaigasa*," literally "shared umbrella," referring to lovers, typically involving a prostitute; to "*okefuse*," signifying the Edo-era criminal punishment of a man seeking entertainment-district pleasure without having the money to pay for it.[23] To be sure, the dictionary listed many word composites involving "*iro*" (literally "color" but signifying "erotic") and yet none involved "*sei*" for "sex," "gender," or "sexuality."[24] In Japanese, the almost exclusive meaning of "sex" for the noun "*sei*" crystalized only around the time of the dictionary's publication.

Similarly, previous to the modern period, sexual practice was not necessarily associated with exclusive "sexual orientations" or "identities."[25] Even in contemporary Japan, the self tends to be understood as being "multiple," of which sexual identity is but one malleable component. This is in contrast to what anthropologist Wim Lunsing once described as a mostly US obsession with a singular, wholesome self that neatly aligns with a stable and distinct sexuality.[26] Accordingly, many same-sex individuals who are not out to their families and friends shy away from the "homosexual" label because they do not want to be reduced to what they see as just one aspect of their personhood; to them, coming out would assign superior significance to that one aspect of their personality. When "*gei*" (from the English word "gay") was introduced in

---

[22] Inoue Shōichi, Saitō Hikaru, Shibuya Tomomi, and Hasegawa Kazumi, *Seiteki na kotoba* (Tokyo: Kōdansha, 2010); Furukawa Makoto, "Renai to seiyoku no daisan teikoku," *Gendai Shisō* 21, no. 7 (1993): 110–45.

[23] The punishment for such behavior was intriguing: the man was confined (unable to escape) in a bathtub placed in the middle of Yoshiwara foot traffic; Satō Koka, *Nihon Seiteki Fūzoku Jiten* (Tokyo: Bungei Shiryō Kenkyūkai, 1929), 58.

[24] Satō, *Nihon Seiteki Fūzoku*. On contemporary linguistic/sexual/queer issues, see Claire Maree, *Queerqueen: Linguistic Excess in Japanese Media* (Oxford: Oxford University Press, 2020).

[25] Robertson, *Takarazuka*, 174.

[26] Wim Lunsing, *Beyond Common Sense: Sexuality and Gender in Contemporary Japan* (London: Kegan Paul, 2001), 18; Chikako Ozawa-de Silva, "Beyond the Body/Mind? Japanese Contemporary Thinkers on Alternative Sociologies of the Body," *Body & Society* 8, no. 2 (2002): 21–38; Louella Matsunaga, "Bodies in Question: Narrating the Body in Contemporary Japan," *Contemporary Japan* 27, no. 1 (2015): 1–11.

Words and Concepts

the 1960s, some cultural critics considered it an odd choice because to most Japanese at that time, the word meant "transvestite" or "transsexual." Others were bothered by the term's connotation of "effeminate," or rejected the word because of its foreign origin, which seemed to them to reinforce that being "gay" was foreign. As a result, some gay men resurrected the once-derogatory word "*okama*" (originally "kettle," associated with the anus). For women, two words for "lesbian," "*lezu*" or "*rezubian*," were strongly associated with pornography, and so some appropriated the older term "*onabe*" (literally "pot"). Others have begun to use "*bian*" from "lesbian" to signal a departure from those earlier associations.[27] Today, many Japanese-language publication venues and individuals have adopted the English loanword "queer" (*kuia*) in both writing and speech in order to signify sexual and gender formations that are neither heterosexual nor "cisgender" – persons whose identity and gender correspond with their birth sex – but are instead inclusive, particularly of "transgender" and that term's various inflections in different Japanese communities. In an effort to reflect these complex significations and their continuously evolving character, within this book I use "LGBT +" – short for "LGBTQIA+," the initialism encompassing the words lesbian, gay, bisexual, transgender, queer and/or questioning, intersex, asexual plus) – and "queer," unless a specific community insists on a specific variant.

Scholars, doctors, and other commentators from various fields of expertise – including policymakers, educators, and ordinary men and women around the world – continue to debate the nature of the exact relationship between sex, gender, and sexuality. That said, in the archipelago and elsewhere, "sex" has become widely understood as the biological marker, an inherent characteristic that is distinct from "gender" (*jendā*), a term that has taken on the cultural traits deriving from education, training, self-mastery, and daily performance, and "sexuality."[28] This book recognizes that one of the central games of life is the gender game, or, more specifically, a multiplicity of gender games. After all, the effort to understand the making and unmaking of gender, as well as what gender makes, involves understanding the workings of these games as games – with their inclusions and exclusions, multiple positions, complex rules, forms of bodily activity, structures of feeling and desire, and

---

[27] Wim Lunsing, "Japan: Finding Its Way?" in *Global Emergence of Gay and Lesbian Politics: National Imprints of a Worldwide Movement*, ed. Barry D. Adam, Jan Willem Duyvendak, and André Krouwel (Philadelphia, PA: Temple University Press, 2009), 314–15.

[28] Judith Butler, *Gender Trouble: Feminism and the Subversion of Identity* (London: Routledge, 1990).

12   Introduction

stakes of winning, losing, or simply playing. It involves as well the question of how gender games themselves collide with, encompass, or are bent to the service of other games – for gender is never, as anthropologist Sherry B. Ortner so aptly noted, the only game in town.[29]

Yet the social, historical, and cultural contexts matter – or the social, historical, and cultural contexts in which various categories are invoked (analytically and/or experientially), produced, made meaningful, and deployed matter. After all, as anthropologist Jennifer Robertson reminds us, it is the "composite character of gender" that makes it fundamentally ambivalent and ambiguous. Gender is capable of fluctuating between or being assigned to more than one referent or category and thus is capable of being read or understood in more than one way. Such an excessive semiosis reflects an epistemology of *both/and* rather than *either/or.*[30]

Frames and Lenses, or How to Read This Book

The chapters of *Gender and Sexuality in Modern Japan* are best approached as the petals of a flower subtly held together by the sex/gender/sexuality conundrum at their center. In Japan, female, male, and other individuals have transgressed binaries and boundaries, have refused to be either, or have insisted on being more than both. Collectively positioned between the late nineteenth century and the early twenty-first, each chapter describes key moments, transformations, and individuals without following an even and complete sequence of developments and events. Instead, each chapter dwells on stretches of time particularly relevant to the topic at hand, focusing on instances of contention and change while disrupting the fantasy of linear progress. Accordingly, individual chapters can be read on their own or together with others, and they can be read in any order. At the end of each chapter, a handful of recommendations for pairing the text with literary works, documentaries, and other films are designed to further illustrate or ground the academic text; bridge to other styles of representation; and actively evaluate different modes of truth claims – as well as to enable intellectual, creative, and emotional engagements.

The chapters tell of the movement and reach of peoples, ideas, and things across the bounds of nation, empire, and cyberspace. They share three analytical sensibilities. The first is the transnational historical study that approaches "modernity [as] something that does not simply travel,

[29] Sherry B. Ortner, *Making Gender: The Politics and Erotics of Culture* (Boston, MA: Beacon Press, 1997), 19.
[30] Robertson, *Takarazuka.*

Frames and Lenses

but must be made anew." Within this frame "Japan" is configured as a malleable entity, as both a subject and object of global modernity, and a mediator between a global and a regional East Asian modernity.[31] At the same time, the book as a whole aims to undercut what Jeremy Adelman has described as a key problem of global history, namely the "Anglicizing of intellectual lives around the world," a commonly experienced side effect of or even condition for the drive to overcome Eurocentrism.[32] As such, this book derives from research in several nations' archives and draws from bodies of knowledge in Japanese, German, and English.[33] The second sensibility at work is the interdisciplinary study of sex, gender, and sexuality. This book draws from History, Anthropology, Sociology, and Visual Studies – highlighting and putting into their respective places in the grand archive a wide variety of sources ranging from print media and governmental documents to biographical accounts, from political pamphlets to pulp comics and contemporary art.[34] It also aims to honor the circumstances of the creation (and recreations) of the field of sex, gender, and sexuality studies. Accordingly, the book includes a multiplicity of sources – the voices of a broad range of individuals involved in the field's making – and allows space for the hybridity of theory-making that forever challenges the status quo of what exactly sex, gender, and sexuality mean and are.[35] The third sensibility, which is

---

[31] George Lazopoulos, "Japanese History, Post-Japan.," *Cross-Currents: East Asian History and Culture Review* 3, no. 1 (May 2014): 245–52.

[32] Jeremy Adelman, "What Is Global History Now?," *Aeon*, March 2, 2017, accessed February 1, 2021, https://aeon.co/essays/is-global-history-still-possible-or-has-it-had-its-moment.

[33] Mae M. Ngai, "Promises and Perils of Transnational History," *Perspectives on History* 50, no. 9 (2012): 52–54. For perspectives related to the study of the Japanese archipelago in the wake of the rise of global history, see C. S. Goto-Jones and L. P. Hartley, "If the Past Is a Different Country, Are Different Countries in the Past? On the Place of the Non-European in the History of Philosophy," *Philosophy* 80, no. 311 (January 2005): 29–51; Julia Adeney-Thomas, "Why Do Only Some Places Have History?: Japan, the West, and the Geography of the Past," *Journal of World History* 28, no. 2 (June 2017): 187–218; Martin Dusinberre, "Japan, Global History, and the Great Silence," *History Workshop Journal* 83 (Spring 2017): 130–50; and Sheldon Garon, "Transnational History and Japan's 'Comparative Advantage,'" *Journal of Japanese Studies* 43, no. 1 (Winter 2017): 65–92.

[34] The notion of "intersectionality" was introduced in 1989 by Kimberlé Williams Crenshaw to focus attention on the "vexed dynamics of difference and the solidarities of sameness in the context of antidiscrimination and social movement politics." In this book, it serves as another trans frame, following Sumi Cho, Kimberlé Williams Crenshaw, and Leslie McCall, "Toward a Field of Intersectionality Studies: Theory, Applications, and Praxis," *Signs* 38, no. 4 (Summer 2013): 785–810; see also, Kathy Davis, "Intersectionality as Buzzword: A Sociology of Science Perspective on What Makes a Feminist Theory Successful," *Feminist Theory* 9, no. 1 (2008): 67–85.

[35] Tomomi Yamaguchi, "Feminism, Timelines, and History-Making," in *A Companion to the Anthropology of Japan* (Oxford: Blackwell, 2005), 50–59.

14   Introduction

inspired (but not governed) by Kimberlé Crenshaw's concept of intersectionality, is a "flexible intersectionality," which aims to invite readers to think at the varying levels of structures, dynamics, and subjectivities; take into account minority and majority perspectives and viewpoints; and keep in play the various configurations of often mutually constitutive or contradictory designations of ethnicity, class, gender, and sexuality. For example, consider a figure who does not appear elsewhere in this book, tennis star Naomi Osaka. Born in Osaka to a Haitian father and a Japanese mother, Naomi grew up in the United States from the age of three. Though she plays for Japan, she does not speak much Japanese. On the global scale, she enhances Japan's display of diversity; domestically, her celebrity status paired with her success in the West amplifies and lends authority to the (however mild) criticism she makes of sexism in sports management. In the chapters to follow we can see a similar flexible intersectionality of sex, gender, sexuality, class, and ethnicity – from sixteen-year-old Aboriginal Taiwanese Yayutz who decided sometime around 1900 to marry and run away with a Japanese man whom her Dakekan chief father wanted to have killed, to the steadily increasing number of young Japanese nationals who today embody one configuration or another of Yayutz's or Naomi's complex identitarian trajectory.

The Chapters

Chapter 1, "Building the Nation and Modern Manhood," examines the tense negotiations over different types of men, manhoods, and masculinities – spanning the early processes of nation-state formation and empire-building, through defeat and democratization, to the current challenges of a globalizing society and straining economy. Following the empire's defeat in 1945, the soldier almost immediately lost his status as a hegemonic icon of masculinity. That role was taken on by a dramatically different kind of man: the white-collar, middle-class worker – who for decades was hailed not as the successor of the Imperial Army soldier but as the "modern samurai." Two generations of men strove to embody that ideal manhood, but the heyday of the salaryman came to a crushing end in 1992. A new sense of vulnerability in the wake of the March 11, 2011 triple disaster – earthquake, tsunami, and nuclear meltdown – has fed into the processes of a rapid diversification of masculinity that continues to this day.[36]

---

[36] Tabea Bienek, "Von 'Erziehungsvätern (*ikumen*)' zu 'lokal vernetzten Vätern (*ikimen*)': Japanische Väteraktivitäten für eine bessere Work–Life-Balance," in *Japan in der Krise*, ed. Annette Schad-Seifert and Nora Kottmann (Wiesbaden: Springer, 2019), 195–220.

The Chapters

In the 1870s and 1880s, some of Japan's leading intellectuals and modernizers discussed human rights, reintroduced the binary difference between male and female, and declared motherhood the core principle of women's nature. As gender displaced status as the primary system of social and legal classification, women began adopting the language of rights and representing themselves in public. By the beginning of the twentieth century, women forcefully entered and shaped a range of debates. Chapter 2, "Controlling Reproduction and Motherhood," discusses women's struggle to both define motherhood for themselves and take control of reproduction – the debate about motherhood being closely tied to the quest for legalizing abortions. Notably, this demand was increasingly at odds with the country's advancing imperialism, which relied on rapid population growth. The end of the Japanese empire constituted a major rupture within the question of reproductive control, ultimately leading to today's effects of rapid population decline and the lack of will among the young generation to have babies.

The beginning of the twentieth century was also an experiment in how to be female, male, or something in between – far beyond the matter of reproduction. Chapter 3, "Redefining Womanhoods," examines the new roles some carved out for themselves amid the emerging modern mass culture in the early twentieth century. After a long period of nation- and empire-building – largely characterized by the embrace and adaptation of what became construed somewhat monolithically as "western culture" – the 1910s and 1920s experienced a shift to critical attitudes toward the West that was promoted by both conservative and progressive representatives of the intelligentsia. This chapter focuses on how new women and modern girls (and modern boys) navigated this turbulent time, a period complicated by the dramatically increasing academic interest in knowing and, eventually, controlling women – as well as the politics of gender relations; the antagonistic relationship between nationalism, imperialism, and internationalism; and the multiple inventions of Japanese traditions.[37]

Chapter 4, "Sex at War," describes how violence, sex, and war were linked in numerous and sometimes contradictory ways. The production and circulation of sexual knowledge, as well as of modern ideas about sexual desire and its management, became intimately intertwined with not just nation-building but also overseas expansion – a process that further consolidated nation-building at home. The Japanese imperialist

---

[37] Sarah Frederick, *Turning Pages: Reading and Writing Women's Magazines in Interwar Japan* (Honolulu: University of Hawai'i Press, 2006); Maeda Ai, *Kindai dokusha no seiritsu* (Tokyo: Chikuma Shobō, 1989).

16   Introduction

project spurred the production of new models of citizenship grounded in new sexual regimes often imposed by violence, be it the organized mass rape of women behind the frontlines or the disorganized sexual violence committed by troops. Yet the Asia-Pacific War also constituted an unprecedented vast web of sexual incitement, suppression, and violence – much of which was organized and systematic and most of which victimized women. Given that acknowledgment, commemoration, and reparation for these atrocities remain contested today, the issue of the wartime sexual-slavery system has both "gone overseas" and become a core bargaining chip in the neonationalist revisionist movement.[38]

Chapter 5, "The Politics of Sexual Labor," describes the various manifestations of and shifting attitudes toward sex work in the archipelago, from the "flower and willow world" of bygone times to the proverbial "soaplands" and the range of "new sex industries." Leaving behind centuries of thriving "pleasure quarters" – whose most prominent courtesans and geisha were the object of countless works of art and literature – the modern nation-state increasingly attempted not to suppress the trade but to control and manage it.[39] Though the Anti-Prostitution Law was implemented in 1956, its impact on the sex industry in Japan has remained contested; given the weak legal barriers to what is a segregated prostitution system, customers continue to flock to a range of establishments offering sexual services and catering to a wide range of erotic fantasies and expectations.[40]

At moments of historical shift, the debates about self and society more clearly acknowledge that the boundaries of subjectivity are porous and fragile – and gender, sex, and sexuality are integral parts of these boundaries. While nonheteronormative and nonsexual individuals and relations appear throughout this book, Chapter 6, "Queer Identities and Activisms," conveys their various iterations in modern and contemporary Japanese culture. Regarding such men: no law prohibited or regulated same-sex relations in Japan – with the exception of a brief period from

---

[38] Tomomi Yamaguchi has written widely on the topic, including "The 'Japan Is Great!' Boom, Historical Revisionism, and the Government," *Asia-Pacific Journal: Japan Focus* 15, no. 6 (March 15, 2017), 1–6, accessed April 26, 2020, https://apjjf.org/2017/06/Yamaguchi.html; see also Nogawa Motokazu, Tessa Morris-Suzuki, and Emi Koyama, *Umi o wataru ianfu mondai: Uha no rekishisen o tou* (Tokyo: Iwanami Shoten, 2016), Tomomi Yamaguchi, "The 'History Wars' and the 'Comfort Woman' Issue: The Significance of Nippon Kaigi in the Revisionist Movement in Contemporary Japan," in *Japanese Military Sexual Slavery: The Transnational Redress Movement for the Victims* (Berlin: De Gruyter, 2020); and Lisa Yoneyama, *Cold War Ruins: Transpacific Critique of American Justice and Japanese War Crimes* (Durham, NC: Duke University Press, 2016).

[39] Cecilia Segawa Seigle, *Yoshiwara: The Glittering World of the Japanese Courtesan* (Honolulu: University of Hawai'i Press, 1993).

[40] Gabriele Koch, *Healing Labor: Japanese Sex Work in the Gendered Economy* (Stanford, CA: Stanford University Press, 2020).

The Chapters   17

1872 to 1880. Yet, starting with the rise of new academic disciplines, around 1900 came the modern desire to know the "truth" about sexuality, to several ends: to legitimize knowledge about human sexuality within the academy, to bolster social reform, or, indeed, to use that knowledge for nation-building and nationalist and imperialist agendas. This chapter describes Japanese culture's longstanding embrace of gender ambivalence, covering a range of non-heterosexual and gender-variant identities, practices, and communities that have come into being in Japan throughout the twentieth and early twenty-first centuries: namely, early "gay booms," the more recent "new half" individuals, and the current expressions and activism of LGBT+ communities.

Chapter 7, "Sexing Visual Culture," critically addresses the history of representations of sex and sexuality in visual culture, from erotic woodblock prints to film, contemporary popular art, and video games. The nation-builders of the late nineteenth century considered erotic prints – along with a number of customs, festivals, and rituals that centered on the celebration of fertility, potency, and nudity – as injurious to public morals and thus unfit for the modern civilized nation Japan aspired to become. Later debates regarding "pornography" occasionally pitched both the freedom of sexual expression and "sexual liberation" against aggressive reproductive policies, middle-class morality, and persisting patriarchal conventions. Today, the political and social weight of sexual expression and its social implications continue to be debated. Where some critics see the emergence of the powerful, sexed, ever-transforming, and transformative female in new manga, anime, and popular and digital art, others conceive of such as merely new iterations of the old exploitation of female sexuality designed to fuel and satisfy primarily heteronormative male desire.

The concluding Chapter 8, "Epilogue," provides a critical reflection on the historical study of sex, gender, and sexuality in Japan, highlighting scholarly strongholds, addressing blind spots, and identifying questions yet to be raised. It notes, for instance, that existing sexuality studies question the once implicit, normative, and exclusive gender binary and heterosexuality. It will spin forth anthropologist Jennifer Robertson's observation that, historically, in Japan and elsewhere, sexual practices have not presumed a specific sexual orientation or identity – although today some queer activists and homophobic critics alike tend to fuse the two as some individuals in the new generation refuse both.[41]

---

[41] Jennifer Robertson, ed., *Same-Sex Cultures and Sexualities: An Anthropological Reader* (Oxford: Blackwell, 2004); Jennifer Robertson, "From Tiramisù to #MeToo: Triangulations of Sex, Gender and Sexuality in Heisei Japan," in *Heisei Japan in Retrospect (1989–2019)* (London: Routledge, in press).

18   Introduction

With the Tokyo Olympics – postponed to summer 2021 from the previous year due to the COVID-19 pandemic, issues of sex, gender, and sexuality came to a head. On February 4, 2021, Tokyo Olympics chief Mori Yoshiro publicly apologized for having made comments about "women talking too much during meetings" when explaining why the Japanese Olympic Committee board includes not a single woman. After his eventual resignation, his place was filled by Hashimoto Seiko, a seven-time Olympian and one of Japan's only two female cabinet ministers.[42] The fallout of this particular incident appears to be building momentum for the ratification of the UN International Labor Organization's Convention 111, which would ban employment discrimination based on race, sex, religion, and political opinion.[43] Meanwhile, Human Rights Watch – together with J-ALL (LGBT Hō Rengōkai, Japan Alliance for LGBT Legislation), Athlete Ally, and All Out – pursue new legislation under the hashtag #EqualityActJapan and the slogan "LGBT equality for Japan as well" (*Nihon ni mo LGBT byōdō o*) to explicitly protect LGBT+ people from discrimination. Unlike Yoshiya Nobuko's lone, bold, and ultimately unsuccessful pioneering campaign early in the twentieth century (see Chapter 6) to legalize same-sex marriage, current-day activists aim to capitalize on what they see as a "once-in-a-generation moment" to achieve equal rights while the Olympics attract the bright global media spotlight.[44]

---

[42] Rurika Imahashi and Francesca Regalado, "Tokyo Olympics Chief Mori Declines to Resign over Sexist Remarks," *NikkeiAsia*, February 4, 2021, accessed February 5, 2021, https://asia.nikkei.com/Spotlight/Tokyo-2020-Olympics/Tokyo-Olympics-chief-Mori-declines-to-resign-over-sexist-remarks; Motoko Rich, "After Leader's Sexist Remark, Tokyo Olympics Makes Symbolic Shift," *New York Times*, February 18, 2021, accessed February 19, 2021, www.nytimes.com/2021/02/18/world/asia/yoshiro-mori-tokyo-olympics-seiko-hashimoto.html.

[43] Kuronuma Susumu, "Olympic Sexism Row Pushes Japan toward Work Discrimination Treaty," *NikkeiAsia*, March 10, 2021, accessed March 10, 2021, https://asia.nikkei.com/Politics/International-relations/Olympic-sexism-row-pushes-Japan-toward-work-discrimination-treaty.

[44] Human Rights Watch Japan, "LGBT Equality for Japan as Well (*Nihon ni mo LGBT byōdō o*)," accessed February 5, 2021, www.hrw.org/EqualityActJapan.

1 Building the Nation and Modern Manhood

A young conscript bids an expressionless farewell to his father in front of a gated military base. Clad in the uniform of the Imperial Japanese Army, the young man bows before entering the barracks to begin his mandatory military training. For the next two or three years, he will learn how to kill in a number of different ways and endlessly practice how to move in formation and on command, and he will bathe, sleep, and eat in the continuous company of hundreds if not thousands of young men like him. He will probably struggle to understand his fellow conscripts' dialects, be grateful for the regular and more nutritious meals than those he had been accustomed to from home, and miss his family.

Beginning in the early 1870s, many young men could imagine themselves as the new conscript in the illustration described above and published much later on the back of a publication titled *Japan's Army* (*Nippon no Rikugun*, 1937). Indeed, it was when securely held in the bosom of his family that each future conscript first imagined life in the military. From the Sino-Japanese War in 1894–1895 onward, growing up for boys was envisioned as inevitably leading to soldierhood. This fact is vividly demonstrated in *Japan's Army*, a picture book about the Imperial Army intended for elementary schoolchildren. On each page an image and a few lines of text bring to life an activity that new recruits engage in, thus glorifying a tradition that all boys then dreamed of furthering. But this (pre)occupation also inevitably relegated girls and women to the margins of both the work of war and its glory. The gender order is firmly declared in depictions of girls singing and dancing for soldiers, and women comforting and caring for them. And, of course, keeping to the peculiar logic of a children's picture book, conscripts are shown in battle (or training for battle), but images of women and girls mourning the loss of soldiers are not included.

Decades later, in 1989, Ishihara Shintarō – novelist, and governor of Tokyo from 1999 to 2012 – seized the moment of Japan's economic might in repeatedly expressing his eagerness to turn Japan's Self-Defense Forces (SDF) into a full-blown military in order to restore what he

20   Building the Nation and Modern Manhood

envisioned as a "normal state" with "real men" in charge[1] – not surprising for a right-wing demagogue. A decade later, in April 1999, former prime minister Hashimoto Ryūtarō (1937–2006), born in the same year as *Japan's Army* was published, also proclaimed that Japan was experiencing a crisis of masculinity: Young Japanese men were "incapable" of caring for their families because they had not undergone military training.[2] Hashimoto thus addressed and expressed a nostalgia – shared by (many) men of his (first postwar) generation – that in truth was a caricature of what was considered a responsible man. This call to arms, so to speak, this inclination to capitalize on the older generation's memory of wartime masculinity (or at least the propaganda thereof), echoed across generations into the twenty-first century. It was even more predictable that another conservative former prime minister, Abe Shinzō (prime minister from 2006 to 2007, and again in 2012–2020), would pick up where Ishihara and Hashimoto had left off, pushing for a neonationalist agenda at whose base was his desire to revise the constitution so that the Self-Defense Forces could be deployed in war. For all his reactionary fervor, Abe remained utterly ignorant of the attitudes of his youngest male countrymen in the Japan of today. They no longer look back to Abe's parents' generation for inspiration on how to craft their masculinities, how to situate themselves in relation to the nation or, really, any other aspect of their lives. Outside the rare manga, animated film, or video game, the Asia-Pacific War hero is dead as a model of masculinity. This chapter sketches the tense negotiations regarding these varying types of men, manhoods, and masculinities by examining key moments in different phases leading into the modern era – from the idealization of militarized manhood beginning in the 1870s, to the postwar white-collar, middle-class ideal, to the present, wherein we find multiplying masculinities in lieu of the previous hegemonies.[3]

The history of masculinity before the late nineteenth century is primarily one of maturity envisioned, struggled for, and then either fallen short of or achieved – whether concerning shogun, merchant, farmer, or store clerk.[4] That history includes legal, political, and pedagogical nomenclature concerning grade levels, age groups, and their various

---

[1] Ishihara Shintarō and Morita Akio, *Nō to ieru Nihon* (Tokyo: Kōbunsha, 1989).

[2] See Sabine Frühstück, *Uneasy Warriors: Gender, Memory and Popular Culture in the Japanese Army* (Berkeley: University of California Press, 2007), 89.

[3] R. W. Connell, *Masculinities* (Berkeley: University of California Press, 1995), 76–81; Judith A. Allen, "Men Interminably in Crisis? Historians on Masculinity, Sexual Boundaries, and Manhood," *Radical History Review* 82 (2002): 192.

[4] Sabine Frühstück and Anne Walthall, "Introduction," in *Recreating Japanese Men* (Berkeley: University of California Press, 2011), 1–23.

boundary markers. That nomenclature, once applied nationwide, helped to revamp ideals of masculinity in the modern period. The negotiations about masculinity, which span the early processes of nation-state formation and empire-building, flared anew during the period of defeat and democratization; they appear to have been enormously impacted by the current challenges of a globalizing society and political economy. Medical doctors, scientists, social reformers, and government officials of the emerging modern nation and empire saw sexuality as the natural source of human life, social renewal, and national strength, and thus perceived healthy (male) bodies to be the very basis of the nation's military power. Hence, conscripts and soldiers were of principal concern to the teachers and architects of nation- and empire-building along with the doctors who diagnosed their sexual and psychological illnesses and conditions and the policymakers who sought to fix and contain them.[5] Altogether, massive changes metamorphosed "Japan." From the earliest days of its nation-building project, the boundaries of "Japan" shifted dramatically – as did the composition of its population.[6]

Measuring Hegemonic Masculinity

Promulgated as an Imperial edict on November 28, 1872, the Conscription Decree laid the cornerstone for building a modern mass military charged with the "protection of the nation" via the ability to mobilize forces on a national scale. But work toward that end was already well underway. In 1870, as part of the nation- and empire-building of the late nineteenth century, the Japanese state began to lay the groundwork for the collection and documentation of large-scale statistical population

---

[5] While the nature and level of concern for these different populations were arguably different, my point here is about the obsession with health data (or the meticulously recorded data on illnesses, disabilities, and "insufficient development") of conscripts, on the basis of which normative modern masculinity was crafted. One such prominent doctor's publication is Mori Rintarō's *Rikugun eisei kyōtei* (Tokyo: Rikugun no Igakkō, 1889), which is his translation into German of a fellow physician's findings in Korea, *Zwei Jahre in Korea*. *Rikugun eisei kyōtei* can be found in *Ōgai zenshū dai nijūhachi-kan*, 1889, ed. Midorikawa Takashi (Tokyo: Iwanami Shoten, 1989), 161–213. See also Mori Rintarō's *Eiseigaku daii* (Tokyo: Hakubunkan, 1907).

[6] A solid body of scholarship examines the various populations under changing levels of Japanese imperial control; see Robert Thomas Tierney, *Tropics of Savagery: The Culture of Japanese Empire in Comparative Frame* (Berkeley: University of California Press, 2010); Paul D. Barclay, *Outcasts of Empire: Japan's Rule on Taiwan's "Savage Border," 1874–1945* (Oakland: University of California Press, 2017); Kirsten Ziomek, *Lost Histories: Recovering the Lives of Japan's Colonial Peoples* (Cambridge, MA: Harvard University Asia Center, 2019); Ambaras, *Japan's Imperial*; and Kate McDonald, *Placing Empire: Travel and the Social Imagination in Imperial Japan* (Oakland: University of California Press, 2017).

22 Building the Nation and Modern Manhood

data via its first census. In this effort, eminent visionaries from a variety of sectors – statesman Ōguma Shigenobu (1838–1922), reform advocate and entrepreneur Fukuzawa Yukichi (1835–1901), statistician Sugi Kōji (1828–1917), surgeon Mori Ōgai (1862–1922), and politician Hara Takashi (1859–1921) – were among the architects of multiple, vast data collections. But the actual measuring, documenting, and recording of the "national body" was literally in the hands of the doctors and nurses in two kinds of locales throughout the empire: military recruitment stations, and elementary and secondary schools.[7] Starting in 1872, a steadily increasing number of twenty-year-old males underwent a physical examination to assess their potential for defending the homeland. Subsequently, in 1876, the first nationwide data were published, documenting 2.9 million conscripts. Almost 18 percent of them were classified as class A or B, the highest levels of fitness for service.[8] After 1902, conscripts throughout the empire and Taiwan were examined and considered for recruitment; gradually, that scope widened to include men in Karafuto, Manchukuo, Taiwan, and Korea as well, resulting in a multiethnic military charged with expanding Japan's imperialist rule.[9] Military physical exams revealed which male bodies were fit – and unfit – for that new kind of service to the nation-state: modern war. They marked and reinforced the soldier as the modern masculine hegemon. But what of those who did not meet that ideal?

For sons of officers, the pressure to meet the expectations of normative masculinity began long before the military physical exam at age twenty. For example, Ōsugi Sakae (1885–1923) failed his first medical exam on account of bad eyesight. But since it was unimaginable for the son of an officer to be classified as "unfit" for military service, the examining doctor "corrected" the result of his eye exam so that he cleared the physical. (As it happens, Ōsugi was an unruly boy. He ended up dropping out of school, and later became a leading anarchist. He was murdered by military police at the age of thirty-nine.)

Severely disabled Shindō Hiroshi did not enjoy such privilege. Remembering the humiliation of being classified as unfit for service, he later wrote a song to capture it. The lyrics include "Even I, the bedridden, was summoned this morning. My mom cooked red rice for me." And, "Might the muscular youths, with rather broad shoulders, come out

---

[7] See Sōmushō Kenkyūkyoku, Statistics Japan, accessed March 22, 2020, www.stat.go.jp/library/meiji150/ijin/ijin05.html.

[8] Kato Yōko, *Chōheisei to kindai Nihon, 1868–1945* (Tokyo: Yoshikawa Kobunkan, 1996), 65.

[9] Kato, *Chōheisei to kindai Nihon.*

of their dressing rooms." Plus the heart-wrenching "Two military physicians approached me and, for a short while, gazed at my knees speechless ... I had spent countless years without lamenting my crippled legs, but being declared exempt and unfit to serve today was devastating."[10]

How can we fathom the feelings of a youth from Gunma who requested a separate examination room because he also "was a cripple." In actuality, he possessed both female and male reproductive organs. Indeed, the pre-exam personnel noted that, though he appeared unambiguously a man when clothed, he looked "just like a woman" when naked. As the youth was on the verge of tears at the humiliation of "being exposed in public with such a strange body," they allowed him to wrap his breasts and conceal his genitalia for his examination – which was brief. A perfunctory assessment deemed him unfit.[11]

Though predicaments such as these were rare, many young men must have felt trepidation about being judged for characteristics that were beyond their control, separate from athletic prowess or muscular form. For a youth to meet the Imperial Army surgeons' definition of a normative, "healthy-bodied [male] individual," he needed a minimum height of 150 cm (4 ft 9 in) and a minimum weight of 50 kg (110 lb). Those who did not meet these norms were classified as "noncitizens."[12]

Over the subsequent decades, the increasingly idealized modern manhood was thus a military manhood, which eventually rose to hegemonic status. But for all efforts to that end, the "hegemonic masculinity" could not maintain a fixed type, and instead remained contestable and, at certain times and places, continued to be nervously guarded, challenged, and manipulated. The military man's hard-won hegemony was a "historically mobile relation"; its "successful claim to authority" held only as long as "collective" "cultural ideal and institutional power" were maintained. In other words, the military man's hegemonic masculinity was reconfirmed by the mechanics of marginalization – of dominance and subordination between groups of men – and the complicity of men who, though without embodying "hegemonic masculinity," nonetheless gained from its patriarchal dividend.[13]

---

[10] Shimizu Kan, "Meijiki ni okeru guntai to shōgaisha mondai: Chōheisei oyobi rikugun chōjitai o chūshin ni," *Shōgaisha Mondai Kenkyū* 36 (1984): 3–20.

[11] Teresa A. Algoso, "Thoughts on Hermaphroditism: Miyatake Gaikotsu and the Convergence of the Sexes in Taishō Japan," *Journal of Asian Studies* 65, no. 3 (2006): 555–73.

[12] *Hikokumin* were distinguished from the "bad soldiers" (*furyō heishi*) who had committed crimes; Shimizu, "Meijiki ni okeru guntai to shōgaisha mondai."

[13] Connell, *Masculinities*, 76–81.

24   Building the Nation and Modern Manhood

But even those who met the minimal physical requirements still needed to meet strict psychological standards, since the intense analytical and disciplinary medical gaze expanded to consider more than just potential soldiers' physiques. Soon the experts' ever-increasing scrutiny highlighted "the problem of weak soldiers" (*jakuhei mondai*), specifying the sorts of "mental conditions" and "mental weaknesses" that were considered responsible for the disciplinary issues of established soldiers.[14] Thus designed to identify the bad apples from the very start, military physical exam reports listed dozens of conditions to watch for; about two dozen of them were grounds for declaring a young man unfit for military service.[15] The standards differed somewhat for the Army and the Navy, but the key criteria were a combination of aspects of a healthy body (free of injuries, disabilities, and serious illnesses) and, ultimately, the ability to function in the military and engage in combat.[16] Military health examiners recorded *ad nauseam* every aspect of the young men they laid eyes on. In thus documenting their subjects' willingness to join the military – as well as their fitness for doing so – recruitment officers and health examiners essentially molded the reputation of the young male population of the day. These officials were on the lookout for conscripts who seemed simple and naïve. They took note of stubbornness and bigotry, and were quick to spot those who seemed "lazy" and "effeminate." And of course they reported anyone who appeared to resent the military or who might be trying to dodge the draft. (I'll return to this topic in the next section.) Altogether, consider the irony: The manuals regarding character and conduct for military cadets and enlisted men alike identified as positive indicators of "wit and intelligence" the ability to write and use logic, the ability to express oneself with reason, and skills in mathematics. However, it was the data from the physical examinations that actually clinched decisions about a young man's fitness for military service.[17] Some of these data were regularly published in local newspapers. As a whole, these assessments informed population norms and policies for decades thereafter, making deep impressions in the populace far beyond the men who were conscripted.

Yet it would take more than just a military exam to forge the hegemonic masculinity that the bureaucrats and ideologues desired, since these tactics only worked on those young men and their families who

---

[14] Shimizu, "Meijiki ni okeru guntai to shōgaisha mondai," 5.

[15] The exact names of categories and the number of categories changed somewhat over time, but, according to one such report, twenty-three conditions were listed by 1902; see Shōheisha, *Chōhei kensa* (Tokyo: Tosho Shuppan Kyōkai, 1902), 41–42.

[16] Shimizu, "Meijiki ni okeru guntai to shōgaisha mondai," 7.

[17] Tomoda Yoshitaka, *Seikō Jiten* (Tokyo: Buyōdō, 1932), 47.

Measuring Hegemonic Masculinity

25

took pride in their eligibility for military service. Many others questioned the value of being found worthy of the emperor's armed forces and were even more ambivalent about going to war. Indeed, key obstacles for manning the Imperial Armed Forces could be found in the numerous strategies young men employed to dodge the draft – such as self-injury or starving themselves to avoid being the minimum weight. Add to these the long list of exemptions to the draft. During the first two decades of conscription, only about one in thirty twenty-year-old men was drafted; the other twenty-nine were exempt, eldest sons being most important among them.

A longer-term process over the next seven decades involved both the reformulation of military ideals and the conscious crafting of a positive conscript identity. For the former, the task of reformulating military ideals called for the appropriation of some notion of a "samurai spirit." Though the samurai of the Tokugawa era had previously enjoyed prominent class status and the respect that was attached to it, by the late nineteenth century they had become militarily and politically irrelevant, and were dismissed as "arrogant layabouts who wear two swords and call themselves warriors." But carefully crafted references to the samurai warrior *tradition* served to ideologically reappropriate their former glory – a classic move in inventing a tradition.[18] This renewed image was later exploited in the service of wartime campaigns to encourage and maintain support for the war at Japan's home front, a necessary measure given that soldiers lived ever further from Japan's shores for ever longer stretches of time.[19]

As for the modern take on the reappropriated warrior image, military visionaries realized they needed to craft a "positive identity for servicemen." The new conscripts of the late nineteenth century needed reasons to feel good about being soldiers, whether this was achieved via a reputation of superior masculinity or from the benefits of being identified with loyalty, virtue, good conduct, and honesty.[20] And so the visionaries

---

[18] D. Colin Jaundrill, *Samurai to Soldier: Remaking Military Service in Nineteenth-Century Japan* (Ithaca, NY: Cornell University Press, 2016), 173.

[19] Mass culture that celebrated Japan's growing empire had been produced long before the formal beginning of the Asia-Pacific War, and a number of tropes centering on the soldier were ubiquitous in a range of publications and other material objects, including for women and children; see Sabine Frühstück, *Playing War: Children and the Culture of Militarism in Modern Japan* (Oakland: University of California Press, 2017); Barak Kushner, *The Thought War: Japanese Imperial Propaganda* (Honolulu: University of Hawai'i Press, 2007); Sharalyn Orbaugh, *Propaganda Performed: Kamishibai in Japan's Fifteen-Year War* (Leiden: Brill, 2014); John Dower, *War without Mercy: Race and Power in the Pacific War* (New York: Pantheon, 2012).

[20] Jaundrill, *Samurai to Soldier*, 172.

26 Building the Nation and Modern Manhood

concocted various scenarios that provided opportunities for veneration. At railway stations soldiers were sent off, cheered by women and children; in field hospitals soldiers were allowed to be vulnerable, weak, and immature; and back home, carefully choreographed burial ceremonies honored the dead while also containing the mourning – lest the patriotic fire of honorable service be smothered by the ashes of the departed.

The visual culture of the time further established the notion of the military man's body as standing for the nation. References to the Japanese nation-state and expanding empire were often made in the guise of adult male figures that appeared as older brother or father figures, signaling superior maturity – maturity of both the Japanese man's physique and Japan's civilization. Additional visuals produced a matrix that featured models for the public to emulate: soldiers as ideal-type men engaged in the work of war, boys aspiring to become them, girls cheering them on, and women fulfilling their three-part designation: nurturing sons to healthy and strong adulthood, nursing them when they returned wounded from battle, and mourning them when they breathed their last.[21] Such visuals included tall men in uniform departing from train stations, with girls, boys, and women waving them off and cheering them; women always in aprons, no matter whether preparing a meal or attending to a child or wounded adult family member; and children pictured in a range of activities designed to signal how they too played their part. In this way, recruitment rhetoric shifted from coercive discipline to appeals to the nobler aspects of servicemen's spirit.[22]

In 1872 the state introduced compulsory elementary education for boys and girls – an arrangement that also involved scrupulous data collection. So while the military physical examination system began to name the markers of valorized masculinity in new medical and social-scientific terms, a school health examination system – which quickly spread to every prefecture and town in Japan proper, and later to the colonies as well – aimed to accomplish the same for children. In a continuous flood of detailed data, the hygiene offices within municipalities meticulously assessed children's height, weight, strength, lung capacity, and (the absence) of a host of diseases and other health conditions assumed to be hereditary, as well as such "conditions" as literacy and poverty. Thick reports were produced, from which key data was

---

[21] Frühstück, *Playing War.*
[22] The conscription system was changed in 1889, and again in 1927, to eliminate exemptions for first sons and other circumstances that slowed the production of the modern military that the political elite envisioned, laying the groundwork for total mobilization after 1937; see Jaundrill, *Samurai to Soldier,* 172.

published in local and national newspapers – data that attested to children having become ever taller and heavier, both signs of increasing health and strength. (The city of Nara, for instance, proudly recorded for the year 1919 that, in comparison to ten years earlier, the height of the fastest-growing boys had increased by 4.21 cm for seven-year-olds, 4.13 cm for eight-year-olds, 4.32 cm for nine-year-olds, 4.47 cm for ten-year-olds, 4.70 cm for eleven-year-olds, 4.78 cm for twelve-year-olds, 4.62 cm for thirteen-year-olds, and 4.57 cm for fourteen-year-olds.)[23] The colonial administration of Taiwan published similar data, highlighting that the growth of boys (from the "inner territory" or "*naichi*") between the ages of seven and fourteen (almost 19 cm) was greater than that of Taiwanese boys (10 cm) in the same age group.[24] Thus, bodies, particularly male bodies, remained the target for meticulous measurement.

Of course, this compulsory education was part of the overall nation-building strategy. Among their fellow visionaries, Mori Arinori and Itō Hirobumi in particular saw in schools an important site for addressing what they felt was lacking in the Japanese people – thoroughly disciplined minds and bodies. With the implementation of the School Ordinance (Gakkōrei) in 1887, Mori, a pioneer of modern education, introduced the core goals of the new education system: namely, the creation and cultivation of the spirit to defend the nation – which of course further fed into the hegemonization of military masculinity. This idea spread through multiple channels from urban centers into the regions, first via school textbooks and education and, later, through mass culture that targeted an increasingly stratified consumer base including children, youth, and adults alike. By the time of the Sino-Japanese War (1894–1895), even the gender ideology of school textbooks had shifted toward a new tolerance for and encouragement of dangerous play for boys – simply in the hope that such games would further familiarity with and admiration of soldiers and soldiering.[25] For four decades thereafter,

---

[23] Nara Shiyakusho, *Nara-shi shōgakkō jidō shintai kensa tōkeihyō* (Nara: Shiyakusho, 2019).

[24] Taiwan Sōtokufu Naimukyoku Gakumuka, *Taishō rokunendo Taiwan sōtokufu gakkō seito oyobi jidō shintai kensa tōkeisho* (Taipei: Taiwan Sōtokufu Naimukyoku, 1919), 5; see also Taiwan Sōtokufu Bunkyōkyoku Gakumuka, *Shōwa ninendo Taiwan sōtokufu gakkō seito jidō shintai kensa tōkeisho* (Taipei: Taiwan Sōtokufu Bunkyōkyoku, 1929). Kate McDonald discusses the fragility of place names signifying geographical and political boundaries in *Placing Empire*.

[25] Yamasaki Hiroshi, "Kindai dansei no tanjō," in *Nihon no otoko wa doko kara kite, doko e iku no ka?*, ed. Asai Haruo, Itō Satoru, and Murase Yukihiro (Tokyo: Jūgatsusha, 2001), 38.

28   Building the Nation and Modern Manhood

schools collaborated in staged recreations of recent battles, war games that in time would engage thousands of children's bodies and minds.[26]

Crafting the "military gods" of the late 1930s and early 1940s was a feat that took enormous effort and faced frequent challenges. For instance, the thousands of unruly young men engaged in large-scale maneuvers often disrupted the normal flow of life in rural areas, thus losing favor with some in those communities. When injured soldiers returned home to heal, they often felt alienated by a society that seemed distant and frivolous to them. In turn, these soldiers forced those civilians to hear about and essentially deal with the darker side of military service and war.[27] In the early twentieth century, the new generation of young adults castigated "rich men's sons" for being "soft and spoiled," and a "New Man's Society" (*Shinjinkai*) attempted to sweep away their elders' "wickedness, vulgarity, and lack of principle."[28]

The idealization of the military man also depended on the promotion of a rigid gender divide that cast men exclusively as combatants, ignoring the range of roles within the military other than in combat, and definitely dismissing the "modern boys" of the 1920s who were believed to seek individual fulfillment in a display of androgyny that horrified government officials and social critics.[29] Establishing that gender divide entailed the crafting of women's roles exclusively as men's willing supporters – or, if not active supporters then at least silent, passive ones. The Women's National Defense Association (Kokubō Fujinkai), formed in 1932, was a key organization working to ensure both the rallying of women and their simultaneous complicity. Its members promoted the efforts of "women on the home front" (*jūgo no josei*), helped nurture and maintain women's virtues, combated "delinquent thought" and pacifism, encouraged the raising children to be of use to the empire, and aimed to obfuscate any doubt or resistance they encountered. For example, members of the Women's National Defense Association visited the homes of dispatched soldiers to offer help to soldiers' wives, act as their counsellors and confidants, and ensure that they remain virtuous.[30]

---

[26] Yamasaki, "Kindai dansei no tanjō," 38; Frühstück, *Playing War*.
[27] For insightful details on transformation of the soldier as masculine hegemon during the final war years see Benjamin Uchiyama, *Japan's Carnival War: Mass Culture on the Home Front, 1937–1945* (Cambridge: Cambridge University Press, 2019), 139–49.
[28] Robert J. Smith and Ella Lury Wiswell, *The Women of Suyemura* (Chicago, IL: University of Chicago Press, 1982), xi, 56.
[29] Donald Roden, "Taishō Culture and the Problem of Gender Ambivalence," in *Culture and Identity: Japanese Intellectuals during the Interwar Years*, ed. J. Thomas Rimer (Princeton, NJ: Princeton University Press, 1990), 37–55.
[30] Kanō Mikiyo, *Onnatachi no "jūgo"* (Tokyo: Inpakuto Shuppankai, 1995).

Regardless, some young women remained unconvinced of their elders' efforts to turn them into good wives and mothers and even resented being excluded from active service. The closest they got to honorably serving as combatants was to volunteer to join a military entertainment troupe or to train as nurses. Some even ignored the resistance of their parents in order to be as close as possible to the frontlines.[31] The producers of mass culture at the height of the Asia-Pacific War exploited such pressures or ambitions on the part of girls and young women. Numerous texts, illustrations, paintings, and photographs representing the sacrifice the war demanded paired the "white-robed hero" cum injured returnee soldier with the "precious [nurse] goddesses," notably also clad in white caps and uniforms.[32] But, as it happens, at the most likely site of injured servicemen encountering nurses – the field hospital and camp at large – both idealizations proved fragile. The soldier could die or remain an invalid; and, since she was in the constant company of brutalized males, the nurse's virtue was also at risk.[33] This was not a minor phenomenon: not counting the Imperial Armed Forces' victims, 2.4 million Imperial servicemen died in the Asia-Pacific War. Of those who survived, many returned home severely injured, disabled, and traumatized, and the number of soldiers discharged on account of mental illness increased from 1.56 percent in 1938 to 22.32 percent in early 1944.[34] The militarized masculine hegemon stumbled long before his metaphorical death in 1945.

Furthermore, the deeply ideological complementary pairing of the white-robed injured soldier with the white-uniformed field nurse projected a rigid heteronormative order that belied the homosocial communities of both soldiers and nurses. Autobiographies and memoirs, however, often reveal more than the propagated official ideology. Life in military school, at least as remembered by Ōsugi Sakae, was laced with "same-sex love" and frequent, harshly punished incidents of "sexual misconduct." Ōsugi's sexual advances toward his fellow trainees at the military academy in part led to his expulsion over "lack of discipline."[35] Famed war writer Hino Ashihei describes at least one homoerotic

---

[31] Sakata Kiyo, *Onna no mita senjo* (Nagoya: Arumu, 2002 [1942]), 6–7; Kameyama Michiko, *Kindai Nihon kangoshi: II sensō to* (Tokyo: Domesu Shuppan, [1984] 1997), 165.

[32] Lee K. Pennington, *Casualties of History: Wounded Japanese Servicemen and the Second World War* (Ithaca, NY: Cornell University Press, 2015), 163–94.

[33] Anzai Sadako, *Yasen kangofu* (Tokyo: Fuji Shobōsha, 1953).

[34] Uchiyama, *Japan's Carnival War*, 135.

[35] Ōsugi Sakae, *The Autobiography of Ōsugi Sakae*, trans. with an introduction by Byron K. Marshall (Berkeley: University of California Press, 1992), 64, 65, 68, 71, 77, 80, 114, 117.

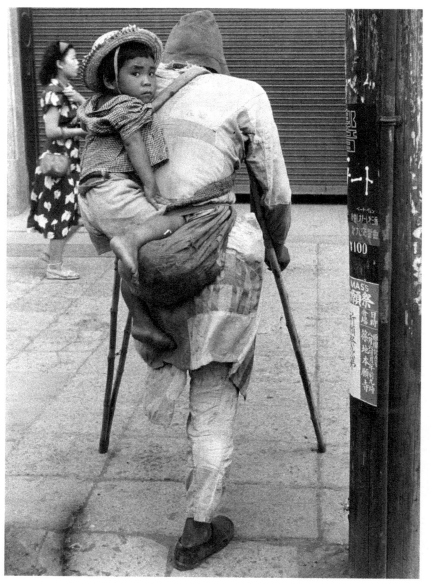

Figure 1.1 War veteran with child; photograph by Domon Ken, 1950. Printed with the kind permission of Domon Ken Archive

Measuring Hegemonic Masculinity

incident between two soldiers on retreat through the jungle of Burma.[36] Similar occurrences can be found in the memoir of otherwise ordinary field nurse Anzai Sadako. Indeed, in the contemporaneously conventional idiom of jealousy and love letters, Anzai recounts a romantic relationship of two female nurses gone awry when one learns her lover has shared affections with a third nurse.[37] I explore same-sex sexuality further in Chapter 6. Here it will suffice to note that hints about same-sex sexual and romantic encounters in wartime historical sources are rare.

In June 1945, the failing Japanese regime implemented the Volunteer Military Service Law, which declared women proper Imperial subjects and thus eligible for the draft – thereafter they could serve alongside male soldiers at the front. Only women who were ill, pregnant, or essential to the survival of the household were exempt. In the case of their death, female combatants were promised a burial at Yasukuni Shrine in Tokyo, just like male soldiers of the Imperial Army and Navy. As a final desperate move, the Women's National Defense Association was dissolved, and its few members – only a small number of young women and girls – redistributed in combat corps intended to assist the military in the event of an Allied invasion of Japan.[38] Not surprisingly, their impact was minimal. Miyagi Kikuko, for instance, was assigned to the Maiden Lily Student Nurse Corps in Okinawa, from where she was sent to the front to a doomed defense intended to slow the US advance. Mere weeks before Japan's surrender, the media proudly reported that girls were fighting at the front, praising the fighting spirit of Okinawan girls in particular.[39] The girls in Miyagi's unit had been trained to do simple tasks to help injured soldiers; they never imagined they would work side-by-side with military doctors. They also likely had not expected to move dead bodies, or offer milk with potassium cyanide to assist severely wounded soldiers in their "suicides."[40] Miyagi's memoir, written many years later, describes the almost complete breakdown of the barrier between men

---

[36] Hino Ashihei, *Seishun to deinei* (1948), cit. in Mark McLelland, *Queer Japan from the Pacific War to the Internet Age* (Lanham, MD: Rowman & Littlefield, 2005), 44.

[37] Anzai, *Yasen kangofu*.

[38] David C. Earhart, *Certain Victory: Images of World War II in the Japanese Media* (Armonk, NY: M. E. Sharpe, 2008), 179; Sasaki Yōko, *Sōryokusen to josei heishi* (Tokyo: Seikyūsha, 2001), 121–47.

[39] Linda Isako Angst, "The Rape of a Schoolgirl: Discourses of Power and Gendered National Identity in Okinawa," in *Islands of Discontent: Okinawan Responses to Japanese and American Power*, ed. Laura Hein and Mark Selden (Lanham, MD: Rowman & Littlefield, 2003), 142; Earhart, *Certain Victory*, 203.

[40] Sabine Frühstück, "'The Spirit to Take Up a Gun': Militarizing Gender in the Imperial Army," in *Gender, Nation and State in Modern Japan*, ed. Andrea Germer, Vera Mackie, and Ulrike Wöhr (London: Routledge, 2014), 163–79; Miyagi Kikuko, *Himeyuri no shōjo: Jūrokusai no senjo* (Tokyo: Kōbunken, [1995] 2002), 62, 85.

32   Building the Nation and Modern Manhood

as combatants at the front and women as supporters at home, which had been carefully crafted over decades. Yet she reconfirms the ideological essence of war as being quintessentially masculine when she identifies the war's end as the moment when her femininity (and her innocence) was reestablished – when she was "finally able to shed the military clothes and *be a girl* again."[41]

Is the Company *Man* a Real Man?

The military man's hegemonic masculine status proved destined for a creeping and, in the end, dramatic fall. Veterans of the Imperial Japanese Army and Navy returned home to a very different society from the one they had fought for (see Figure 1.1). Many were injured or disabled; all were symbolically disgraced by the defeat. The service member almost immediately lost his status as a hegemonic icon of masculinity. Even wounded ex-servicemen who had previously been hailed as white-robed heroes quickly receded from the dominant narratives of postwar Japan; in their stead appeared memories and memoirs filled with the voices of failed kamikaze pilots, bereaved families, and atomic-bombing survivors.[42] From within the newly shrunk boundaries of the archipelago emerged the interrogatory 1960s and 1970s, with their pronounced antiwar sentiments and newly complicated relationship to expressions of patriotism and nationalism. Altogether, formerly "integrative rituals of patriotic fervor had evolved in disintegrative and alienating cultural practices of conspicuous consumption."[43]

The Imperium's August 15, 1945, declaration of surrender and its subsequent collapse had an enormous impact across Asia.[44] The Allied powers repatriated over 6 million Japanese nationals from colonies and battlefields throughout Asia, and deported more than a million colonial subjects from Japan to their countries of origin. In 1946, Japan enacted a constitution that vowed peaceful cooperation with all nations. For a small number of men in the archipelago, the end of the war marked the beginning of an ongoing struggle to define and identify with a new kind of military masculinity – one based on a new concept of heroism, one that, for once and for all, kills off the notion that the only true heroes are dead heroes. The Self-Defense Forces, successor to the Imperial Army

---

[41] Miyagi's eagerness to rescue the gender order as the natural one to "return to" is echoed in much of the historiography of modern Japan, exceptions being made only for some of the extraordinary female individuals whose voices are heard in other chapters of this book. Miyagi, *Himeyuri no shōjo*, 195–97 [my emphasis].
[42] Pennington, *Casualties of History*.   [43] Uchiyama, *Japan's Carnival War*, 139–49.
[44] This moment of collapse is brilliantly analyzed in Uchiyama, *Japan's Carnival War*.

Is the Company *Man* a Real Man?

and Navy, had to ask themselves whether theirs would be a place "for a new style of heroism."[45] Indeed, finding that place was essential, squeezed as they were between a constitution that essentially prohibits their existence and a population that, by and large, blamed their predecessor for both the bloody war and crushing defeat. Today, SDF service members are carefully trained, their conduct closely monitored – both at home and abroad – in frequently articulated acknowledgment of the enormous violence their predecessors inflicted.[46] (See Chapter 4.) From the time of their first international peacekeeping mission to Mozambique in 1992 to 1993, the Self-Defense Forces embraced some version of the "globally sensitive patriotism" that philosopher Martha Nussbaum proposed in her 2008 article of that title.[47] At least two generations of service members embrace the idea that, in contrast to killing and dying for the emperor, applying one's life, and sometimes risking it, for the welfare of the (diffuse) "public" that sometimes signifies the entire world – from disaster-relief missions to peacekeeping operations around the world – offers a reasonably positive avenue toward such a new style of heroism, one of which "they can be proud" in a distinctly understated way.[48]

The promulgation on November 3, 1946, of the postwar constitution also unsettled the long-held understandings of both the state and gender. Regarding the state, Article 9 of the constitution explicitly renounced the state's right of belligerency: war was no longer a sovereign right of the nation, the threat or use of force no longer a means of settling disputes. Instead, a new military establishment, the SDF, would labor under strict

---

[45] The phrase is from Alain Badiou's talk "The Contemporary Figure of the Soldier in Politics" presented at the University of California, Los Angeles, January 2007.

[46] Yet Japan's constitutional pacifism continues to be undermined by a bilateral security agreement with the United States and a strong US military presence in Japan, primarily in Okinawa. Sabine Frühstück, "After Heroism: Must Real Soldiers Die?," in *Recreating Japanese Men*, ed. Sabine Frühstück and Anne Walthall (Berkeley: University of California Press, 2011), 91–111.

[47] Martha Nussbaum, "Toward a Globally Sensitive Patriotism," *Daedalus* 137, issue 3 (2008): 78–93.

[48] Frühstück, *Uneasy Warriors*, 122. The Global Peace Index is calculated by the Institute for Economics & Peace in Sydney, Australia, and lists Japan (for 2019) in 9th place after Iceland, New Zealand, Portugal, Austria, Denmark, Canada, Singapore, and Slovenia, and far ahead of the UK (45th), South Korea (55th), Vietnam (57th), China (110th), and the USA (128th); see Global Peace Index 2019, Institute for Economics & Peace, www.visionofhumanity.org/wp-content/uploads/2020/10/GPI-2019web.pdf (accessed May 31, 2021). As for violent crimes, the World Population Review lists Japan as the country with the lowest homicide rate with 0.2 cases per 100,000 inhabitants, followed by Singapore, China, Hong Kong, Luxembourg, Indonesia, Norway, Oman, Switzerland, United Arab Emirates, and China; see https://worldpopulationreview .com/countries/murder-rate-by-country/ (accessed March 22, 2020).

34   Building the Nation and Modern Manhood

civilian control. Regarding the sexual and gender order of its citizens, Article 24 proclaimed the "equality of the sexes," articulating key areas of concern as choice of domicile, divorce, property rights, inheritance, and "other matters pertaining to marriage and the family."[49] The building of the military man as hegemonic masculine ideal had taken the work of three generations; after roughly another three generations, the transformation of ideal manhood in postwar Japan continues to be a dynamic process.

Many of the young men raised before and during the war proved to be unprepared for the new democratic sex/gender regime the constitution established, a regime that many women readily embraced. Indeed, one critic publicly blamed men for the snail's pace at which gender relations had been changing. In a series of articles first published in *The Japan Times*, a certain Uenoda Setsuo demanded in 1952 that young men be "raised to appreciate modern women" in order for all to live "happy married lives." Uenoda considered it "a great misfortune" that parents failed to realize the necessity of rearing their male offspring so that they would keep up with "the progress made in women's world." To that end, Uenoda cited the 242,339 family court cases of the prior five years: half had been divorces, 70 percent of which had been filed by wives. Uenoda had no doubt why: Chiefly responsible for most divorces was husbands' reluctance to recognize marriage as a "cooperative institution based on the equality of the sexes."[50] (For more, see Chapter 3.)

As for the role of the masculine hegemon, it was taken on by a dramatically different kind of man: the white-collar, middle-class, "company man" or "salaryman." Staying clear of the so-called 3K – "*kitsui, kitanai, kiken*" ("hard, dirty, and dangerous [work]") – a proper salaryman embodied a middle-class lifestyle. He had a solid bank account, funded by his work in a clean office – work that afforded him an income that fully supported his household, which was maintained by a stay-at-home wife who took care of children he rarely saw, let alone helped raise.[51] Of the "soldier" image he retained only the will of self-sacrifice, his diligence and effort invested in a company rather than offered to his

---

[49] For digital versions of the English translations of the Japanese constitutions from 1889 and 1946 see "The Constitution of the Empire of Japan," National Diet Library, www.ndl.go.jp/constitution/e/etc/c02.html (accessed May 31, 2021); and "The Constitution of Japan," Prime Minister of Japan and His Cabinet, https://japan.kantei .go.jp/constitution_and_government_of_japan/constitution_e.html (accessed May 31, 2021).

[50] Uenoda Setsuo, *Japan – Yesterday and Today: Sketches and Essays on Japanese City Life* (Tokyo: Tokyo News Service, [1952] 1956).

[51] More recently, a new generation of salarymen has added a couple of other terms to the desirable job's description, namely: "*kakkowarui*" for work with a "bad reputation,"

Is the Company *Man* a Real Man? 35

country.[52] In exchange, he benefited from two important structural traits of the Japanese employment system from which most women, blue-collar workers, and employees of mid-sized and small companies were excluded – "lifetime employment" and the "seniority principle." Both provided salarymen a high level of security and predictability.[53]

Although less than a third of gainfully employed Japanese men successfully embodied this postwar iconic masculinity, many more aspired to it, and were inspired by its representation in popular culture. Consider three transmedial examples, productions that include some combination of *manga*, animation, television, and film. The hugely popular *Otoko wa tsurai yo!* (*It's Tough Being a Man!*, 1969–1995) is best known as a TV film series that portrayed a comic alternative to the salaryman in a peripatetic peddler. The more recent *Salaryman Kintarō* (*Sararīman Kintarō*, 1994–2002), which catered to a younger audience, follows a former gang member into the white-collar world of high-rise corporate buildings and a masculine environment vastly different from the gangs in which he had first become his own man. He had promised his late wife to become a salaryman and properly raise their child, and he makes good on his promise in rather unconventional and entertaining ways. *Densha Otoko* (*Train Man*, 2005), produced for the same generation, paints a sympathetic picture of an *otaku* who struggles to win a career woman's heart.[54] In these three cases and countless others, the companies at the heart of the stories they tell impose their interests on every minute of salarymen's lives, with even their (strictly hetero)sexual desires permeated by an economy of restoration, healing, and maximum productivity for the benefit of the company.[55] The written word also played a role. Particularly during the 1980s and 1990s, dozens of self-help books

---

"*kaerenai*" for work that is too demanding to allow them to go home at a reasonable time, "*kyūryō sukunai*" for a low salary, "*kyūnichi nai*" for "no vacation," and "*karada o kowasu*" for being damaging to one's body; see Hatenablog, www.shinjin85.net/entry/2017/04/08/002633; or even 7K, accessed 31 May 2021, www.atusi-sora.com/2017/03/28/ (accessed May 10, 2020).

[52] Robin LeBlanc, *The Art of the Gut* (Berkeley: University of California Press, 2010), 148; Ezra F. Vogel, *Japan's New Middle Class: The Salary Man and His Family in a Japanese Suburb* (Berkeley: University of California Press, 1967); David W. Plath, *Long Engagements: Maturity in Modern Japan* (Stanford, CA: Stanford University Press, 1980).

[53] Schad-Seifert, "Dynamics of Masculinities in Japan," 33–34.

[54] Susan Napier, "Where Have All the Salaryman Gone? Masculinity, Masochism, and Technomobility," in *Recreating Japanese Men* (Berkeley: University of California Press, 2011), 154–76.

[55] Anne Allison, *Nightwork: Sexuality, Pleasure, and Corporate Masculinity in a Tokyo Hostess Club* (Chicago, IL: University of Chicago Press, 2009); and the more recent Koch, *Healing Labor*.

36   Building the Nation and Modern Manhood

appropriated masculine caricatures of the past, hailing the salaryman as a "modern samurai," a "company warrior," and a "fiercely fighting company employee" – in short, the epitome of masculine maturity, with workaholic habits and the unambiguous will to sacrifice their individual interests for the company's benefit.[56] Some books offered more straightforward practical advice on how to become or be a successful salaryman. The dominance of the archetype of the company man was also ubiquitous in the marketplace, a bastion supported by time-management tools, energy-enhancing products, and hangover remedies – in addition to a large, easily accessed market of heteronormative sex workers.[57] (see Chapter 5.) Around 1980 several high-ranking business executives who were still in their prime years suddenly died without any previous sign of illness, adding the term "death through overwork" (*karōshi*) to the popular collective vocabulary of Japanese social self-diagnoses.[58]

Despite such scratches on the shiny surface of the masculine ideal, the salaryman's reign lasted until the late twentieth century, when a series of events put the brakes on Japan's impressive postwar rise to becoming one of the largest economies in the world.[59] In early 1990s, the bursting of Japan's asset price bubble resulted in a severe financial crisis and long period of stagnation that became known as the "lost decade(s)." In 2004, Japan's birthrate of 1.26 hit its lowest point in history, marking the beginning of a shrinking population. Then, just when economic recovery seemed likely, the global financial crisis of 2008 impacted another generation. Next, the March 11, 2011, triple disaster – earthquake, tsunami, and nuclear meltdown – in northeastern Japan almost buried the salaryman, literally and figuratively, as the pillar of a stable national and family economy. As for moving beyond 2021, the exact severity of the global economic impact of COVID-19 is still under debate, but a resurrection of the salaryman as masculine figurehead seems increasingly unlikely.

Of course, throughout the decades of his reign, many men did not embody the salaryman's hegemonic mode of masculinity – whether they simply failed to achieve it or else resisted or rejected it entirely. These ranged from men in the creative and cultural industries and blue-collar

---

[56] Schad-Seifert, "Dynamics of Masculinities in Japan," 33–44.
[57] Koch, *Healing Labor*, 3.
[58] The term was coined in 1978. It was not until the mid-to-late 1980s, during the bubble economy, when several high-ranking business executives who were still in their prime years suddenly died without any previous sign of illness, that the term entered Japanese public life; see "Karoshi," Wikimedia Foundation, last modified May 29, 2021, 2:40, https://en.wikipedia.org/wiki/Karoshi.
[59] Ezra F. Vogel, *Japan as Number One: Lessons for America* (Cambridge, MA: Harvard University Press, 1979); Ishihara Shintarō, *The Japan That Can Say No: Why Japan Will Be First among Equals*, trans. Frank Baldwin (New York: Simon & Schuster, 1991).

jobs to day laborers to the most disadvantaged, including the homeless. Among the homeless, a population whose vast majority is male, some men had bad luck, or had "not been given a fair chance" to begin with; others were ruined by drinking or gambling. Yet even among the most unfortunate were some who retained a notion of manliness that is tied to self-reliance and who critiqued the stereotypical salaryman as being far from self-reliant himself and instead "[relied] on his company, his boss, [and] his wife."[60] Most significant in this construct is seeing how the survival strategies available to these nonconforming men carry different implications for masculinity as constructed relative not only to other men and even less to women but in relation to broader mainstream society and the state.

Manning the Changing Tables

At the beginning of this chapter three men were cited who initiated the call for restoring the distinctly militarized masculinity they expressed such heartfelt nostalgia for. But, in fact, none of them had ever actually embodied that ideal. Hashimoto Ryūtarō, who first made the rallying cry, was eight years old at the end of World War II, at which time later torchbearer Ishihara Shintarō was a teenager. Abe Shinzō was not even born until 1954. But all three men spent their formative years under the spell of a strict, idealized military masculinity – only, when their turn came to fill that role, it no longer existed.[61] And though many today scoff at the notion of this hypermilitary vision, even provocative popular art icon Murakami Takashi seems to sympathize somewhat with the sentiment of a more properly masculine past. On the occasion of a book publication, *Little Boy: The Arts of Japan's Exploding Subculture* (2005), designed to celebrate his social, cultural, and art-historical global impact, he mused that the demise of Japanese men lay in the fact that they had never overcome the humiliating infantilization attributed to them by

---

[60] Tom Gill, "Failed Manhood on the Streets of Urban Japan: The Meanings of Self-Reliance for Homeless Men," in *Recreating Japanese Men*, ed. Sabine Frühstück and Anne Walthall (Berkeley: University of California Press, 2011), 177–202; and Tom Gill, *Yokohama Street Life: The Precarious Career of a Japanese Day Laborer* (Lanham, MD: Lexington Books, 2015).

[61] From a yet younger generation's perspective, it seems even less comprehensible that Abe would not recognize the irony in proposing wartime Japan as one of truer masculinity precisely at a moment when the impending "demographic collapse" resulting from the reversal of the population pyramid had been producing ever fewer young men who could be recruited into the SDF.

38   Building the Nation and Modern Manhood

Allied occupation commander General Douglas MacArthur.[62] Speaking in widely publicized Senate hearings on May 5, 1952, MacArthur had reported that his guiding philosophy during the occupation had been to treat the Japanese as twelve-year-olds. What MacArthur did not mention, and apropos Murakami's book's title, Little Boy was also the code name given to the first of two American atomic bombs dropped on Hiroshima on August 6, 1945.

Thus, the intended vision of this military masculinity was not just to distinguish it from femininity – it was sought as a distance from childhood as well. Maturity has remained key in the debate about Japanese masculinity. In the wake of the asset bubble crash, a range of public figures decided that the crash was as good a moment as any for gender relations to require a reset. Organizations were founded and campaigns launched with the mission of changing males' ideals – especially in how they envisioned their roles in society and at home – as well as of reexamining men's relations to women, their families, the economy, and the state. One such group, Men's Lib, emerged in Osaka in 1991; within a few years, as Men's Center Japan, it launched a bimonthly newsletter titled *Men's Network*. In 1996, the sociologist Itō Kimio published an *Introduction to Men's Studies* (*Danseigaku Nyūmon*) that has since, along with numerous subsequent publications, made him the poster child of the newly autonomous (and gender egalitarian) male *par excellence*. He expressed particular concern over the era's distinct "men's problems." These included the large number of men who remained unmarried despite wishing to be and the rising divorce rate among middle-aged and older couples. In addition, he cited a number of role-strain phenomena resulting from the fact that conventional roles were no longer perceived as bringing their customary rewards, such as individual fulfillment, material gain, or social respect. Note that, by and large, these "new men's" organizations took shape not as part of but parallel to the formation of LGBT+ organizations, with limited overlap. So, while Itō might have appeared to be progressive regarding his recognition of gender-specific problems of men, he envisioned the men he wrote about to be heteronormative males in or seeking heteronormative relationships.

Around the time of the asset crash, prime minister Hashimoto was the first government official to speak of an "international gender discourse" and of "gender" as an object of policy at the occasion of the creation of Japan's first Bureau for Gender Equality within the Prime Minister's Office, citing his concern about the future of the populace at large and

---

[62] Murakami Takashi, *Little Boy: The Arts of Japan's Exploding Subculture* (New Haven, CT: Yale University Press, 2005), 152.

Manning the Changing Tables

the sustainability of social structures.[63] Recognizing Japanese men's spiraling lack of interest in having children, in 1992 the Ministry of Health, Labor, and Welfare implemented the first law that included fathers as beneficiaries of parental leave.

A quarter-century on, a study co-conducted by the National Institute of Population and the Social Security Research Institute found that more than 80 percent of Japanese men leave the household and childrearing to their wives, even though 82.8 percent of women wish their husbands would equally share both.[64] Subsequently, in 2010 prime minister Abe promoted the Ikumen Campaign, which was designed to discursively tie childrearing to men. (*"Ikumen"* is a neologism constituting the second character of the Japanese word for "education" [*kyō-iku*] and the English word "men.") The Personnel Bureau of the Cabinet Secretariat issued the Ikumen Passport (*ikupasu*) – a sixty-five-page treasure trove of information designed to help fathers succeed as child caregivers, husbands, and housekeepers – which offers, among other useful information, point-by-point legal guidance (including concerning parental leave), policy-makers' and experts' advice, recommended daily schedules, checklists, and the "real voices" of experienced men.[65] Though some men eschewed the invented term, deeming "fatherhood" sufficient to identify the men who bear an equal share of household and childrearing duties, clearly many believed that a well-publicized new definition was in order.[66]

---

[63] Schad-Seifert, "Dynamics of Masculinities in Japan," 35.

[64] National Institute of Population and Social Security Research Institute (Kokuritsu Shakai Hosho Jinkō Mondai Kenkyūjo), www.ipss.go.jp/ (accessed May 31, 2021). Another study found that even heterosexual men with middle-class incomes who have never been married cannot but envision marriage as an arrangement based on their spouses staying home and taking care of the household and children on their own; see Nemoto Kumiko, Makiko Fuwa, and Kuniko Ishiguro, "Never-Married Employed Men's Gender Beliefs and Ambivalence Toward Matrimony in Japan," *Journal of Family Issues* 34, no. 12 (2012): 1673–95.

[65] "Ikumen Passport," www.ktr.mlit.go.jp/honkyoku/soumu/jinji/wlbalance/content/03_004.pdf (accessed May 31, 2021). The national government also produces "mutual help handbooks" – clearly geared toward unassuming fathers. These provide detailed advice on how to juggle work and family life, with the family being featured, rather unrealistically, as a three-generation formation that includes three small children and a dog; see "Ikuzi Handbook," www.jinji.go.jp/ikuzi/handbook.pdf (accessed May 31, 2021).

[66] At least this is how one blogger, a father of two named Fujio, reports all his daily family tasks, which he shares with his wife; see Fujio Cafe, April 8, 2019, https://fujiocafe.com/kosodate-myhome/word-ikumen/ (accessed May 31, 2021). For representations of fathers in film, see Christie Barber, "Beyond the Absent Father Stereotype: Representations of Parenting Men and Their Families in Contemporary Japanese Film," in *Routledge Handbook of Japanese Media*, ed. Fabienne Darling-Wolf (London: Routledge, 2018), 228–40.

40   Building the Nation and Modern Manhood

In 2016, another creative (and amusing) attempt to promote both work–life balance (referred to as WLB) and, more specifically, paternity leave brought a group of governors together in a campaign video titled "The Governors Are Pregnant" (*Chiji ga Ninpu ni*). It features ten male governors engaged in ordinary, everyday activities – taking public transport, shopping for groceries, climbing stairs, doing laundry and the dishes – while wearing a sort of late-stage pregnancy harness, complete with full belly and swollen breasts, in a show of solidarity for what pregnant women experience. Interspersed with these scenes are factual statements such as "Worldwide, Japanese husbands do the least housework," "Men who have experienced pregnancy take on a positive attitude towards housework and raising children," "96.7% of men who have experienced pregnancy agree with the statement that men must also do housework and raise the children," and "Happiness is when family and work are balanced."[67] The nonprofit organization Fathering Japan could not agree more. Its members share the goal of "becoming smiling dads" – indeed, "dads [worthy of] the era of 'beautiful harmony.'"[68] (It is customary for each emperor's era to be granted a unique name; that of the current emperor, Naruhito, is the era of "beautiful harmony.")

Yet the core mantra of these campaigns, that "the participation of men in childcare is not only important for families but for fathers themselves as well," has remained a hard sell. Though today Japan leads the world in fully paid paternity leave – six months – in 2017 only one man in twenty took that leave. Most young fathers report that their companies do not support paternity leave, or that they did not want (or did not feel encouraged) to take it. Hence, the notion of men in heterosexual relationships equally sharing household and childrearing duties remains somewhat fantastical.[69]

Similar representations of paternal involvement fall short of convincing readerships that the era of shared parenthood has arrived. In 2018, the

---

[67] For the work–life balance campaign video, see Michelle Hughes, "3 Male Governors in Japan Experience What Life Is Like for Pregnant Women," Sora News 24, September 29, 2016, https://soranews24.com/2016/09/29/3-male-governors-in-japan-experience-what-life-is-like-for-pregnant-women/ and at the Kyushu site, www.kyushu-yamaguchi-wlb.com/chiji/ (accessed May 31, 2021). See also "Work–Life Balance Book," www.kyushu-yamaguchi-wlb.com/ (accessed October 1, 2021).

[68] Fathering Japan provides a range of services and events and keeps an active calendar; see their website, https://fathering.jp/index.html (accessed May 31, 2021).

[69] Masako Ishii-Kuntz, "Balancing Fatherhood and Work: Emergence of Diverse Masculinities in Contemporary Japan," in *Men and Masculinities in Contemporary Japan* (London: Routledge, 2003), 198–216; "Japan Offers Most Paid Leave for Fathers in the World but Few Take It," *Kyodo News*, June 13, 2019, https://english.kyodonews.net/news/2019/06/78563c3875f3-japan-offers-most-paid-leave-for-fathers-in-world-but-few-take-it.html (accessed May 12, 2020).

Japanese edition of *Harper's Bazaar* featured Nakamura Shidō – third-generation Kabuki actor superstar and film and video game hero – in its May issue. On the cover, Nakamura cradles his adorably yawning, completely naked baby against his own naked chest – a once in a quarter-century mainstream magazine cover motif (see Figure 1.2 and book cover). Nakamura is partially dressed in kimono (as a Kabuki actor would be) but styled with bleached blonde hair (as a movie actor would be). The caption announces, "Nakamura Shidō, with new life."

The interview is couched in the wonder of new fatherhood, mentioning the uncanny detail that his baby was born on the anniversary of the death of Nakamura's mother. In one of those tired attempts to signal "everyday (rather than 'celebrity') fatherhood," Nakamura makes a point of confessing that he "uploaded his newborn's photograph" (ostensibly on his social media account) even though "he never wanted to be one of those parents."[70] Similarly, when Koizumi Shinjirō – son of former prime minister Koizumi, member of the conservative Liberal Democratic Party and the current minister of the environment – announced that he would take "*two full weeks* of paternity leave" in January 2020, he hastened to add that he would continue to "prioritize [his] official duties and thorough crisis management" and "not skip important public activities." Regardless, mainstream media expressed enthusiasm over his nod to work–life balance, however slight that nod actually was.[71]

In an entirely different angle on new manhood, progressive men's organizations have announced that the true solution for both men's happiness and gender equality lies in men receiving greater "autonomy" from both the corporate world and the state. Indeed, many members of a new generation of working-class men have made peace with earning less money in exchange for working fewer hours and thus having more control over their time while lowering their expectations of upward mobility.[72] Adding to this discussion is the strange sequence of developments that have resulted from the structural reforms initiated by then prime minister Koizumi Junichirō, who aimed to achieve both the short-term objective of economic recovery and the medium-term objective of

---

[70] Erica Sakurazawa, "Nakamura Shidō, atarashii mei to tomo ni/SHIDO NAKAMURA, NEW BORN," *Harper's Bazaar*, May 2018, 277.

[71] Masumi Koizumi, "Environment Minister Shinjiro Koizumi Challenges Japan's Workplace Norms with Decision to Take Paternity Leave," *Japan Times*, January 15, 2020, www.japantimes.co.jp/news/2020/01/15/national/shinjiro-koizumi-paternity-leave/#.Xrtw1sZlC7M (accessed May 12, 2020) [my emphasis].

[72] Annette Schad-Seifert, "J-Unterschicht: Japans junge Generation im Zeitalter der gesellschaftlichen Polarisierung," in *Japan: Lesebuch IV – J-Culture*, ed. Steffi Richter and Jaqueline Berndt (Tübingen: Konkursbuch Verlag, 2008), 86–105.

Figure 1.2 Photograph of Nakamura Shidō with his baby. Printed with the kind permission of *Harper's BAZAAR*, May 2018; photograph by Kurigami Kazumi. See "Contact," Shido Nakamura, accessed May 31, 2021, https://shidou.jp/contact. A Google collection of online images of Nakamura can be found at https://images.app.goo.gl/RHS9pVAKaXw5YUQe7.

fiscal consolidation. These policies have led to dramatically decreased income for the majority of men, as well as a sharp increase in temporary and insecure employment – resulting in the emergence of a surprising trend concerning male maturity. Faced with daunting, even confusing Japanese male-centric work culture and conventional gender role expectations, thousands of younger Japanese have rejected the roles expected of them, responding by withdrawing from conventional social interaction, with various degrees of self-isolation. A vast number of youngsters have become "shut-ins," individuals who refuse to engage with the physical social world around them, essentially opting to bow out of society completely. In 2010, the Japanese government estimated there were as many as 700,000 so-called *hikikomori* – meaning "pulling inward, being confined" – expressing concern that many more will soon join them in what social critics often interpret as a refusal to grow up.[73] Another group, identified by the acronym NEET, are fifteen- to thirty-four-year-olds who are Not engaged in or seeking Education, Employment, or Training – as well as being unmarried and not engaged in housework. Not surprisingly, both groups are entirely financed by their parents. A third, primarily male group is a young generation of "*furītā*" – a neologism that combines the English word "free" with the last syllable of the German word "*Arbeiter*," meaning workers – individuals in temporary employment who increasingly reject the social expectation of becoming the main or sole breadwinner of a family via a dedication to lifetime employment. Instead, many embrace a more flexible lifestyle, ironically at the very moment when their future has become less secure and their socioeconomic status more likely to decline.[74] As for socio-economic inequality across the population, and in comparison to other parts of the world, Organisation for Economic Co-operation and Development (OECD) data from the 1970s showed that Japan was very similar to the most socioeconomically egalitarian countries of northern and some parts of western Europe. Current data, by contrast, show levels of income inequality and poverty that are alarmingly similar to those of the United States, the most unequal economy of the Global North.[75]

One thing is clear: The naturalized and even institutionalized nexus between ideal masculinity and a white-collar lifestyle has broken down

---

[73] Michael Hoffman, "Nonprofits in Japan Help 'Shut-ins' Get Out into the Open," *Japan Times*, October 9, 2011, www.japantimes.co.jp/news/2011/10/09/national/media-national/nonprofits-in-japan-help-shut-ins-get-out-into-the-open/ (accessed March 9, 2021).

[74] Schad-Seifert, "Dynamics of Masculinities in Japan," 42.

[75] Organisation for Economic Co-operation and Development (OECD), "Economic Survey of Japan 2019," www.oecd.org/japan/

44   Building the Nation and Modern Manhood

for a large portion of the younger generation. No day passes without social critics in Japan and elsewhere noting "the making of modern immaturity," namely, the strange phenomenon of boys no longer being eager, able, or willing to grow up.[76] This lament seems unfair, especially given the present diversification of masculine gender roles driven by men's changing life-course expectations amid economic developments that undermine the possibility of achieving once-hegemonic salaryman masculinity. One would expect that the flattening and diversifying male and masculine hierarchy would bring about a higher level of gender equality, but globally comparative gender indices tell a different story.[77] No matter which measure or mode of calculation, no matter the method of analysis, the assessment is the same. We have seen the disappearance of a dominant hegemonic masculinity, the emergence of a new precarity, and the rapid diversification of masculinities and genders more generally, and yet such unprecedented sociocultural and economic changes have not dramatically increased gender equality.[78]

[76] Gary Cross, *Men to Boys: The Making of Modern Immaturity* (New York: Columbia University Press, 2008), 5.

[77] The United Nations Development Programme calculates the Gender Inequality Index based on "human development" indicators. Japan is one of sixty-two countries that the UN classifies as having "very high human development" but ranks only in 19th place on the "Gender Inequality Index," http://hdr.undp.org/en/content/gender-inequality-index-gii (accessed May 31, 2021). The "Global Gender Gap Report 2020," published by the World Economic Forum, ranks Japan in 121st place with regard to the Global Gender Gap Index, which measures economic participation and opportunity, educational attainment, health and survival, and political empowerment; see World Economic Forum, "Global Gender Gap Report 2020," www3.weforum.org/docs/WEF_GGGR_2020.pdf (accessed May 31, 2021).

[78] Liv Coleman, "Will Japan 'Lean In' to Gender Equality?" *U.S.–Japan Women's Journal* 49 (2016): 3–25; Eto Mikiko, "'Gender' Problems in Japanese Politics: A Dispute over a Socio-Cultural Change towards Increasing Equality," *Japanese Journal of Political Science* 17, no. 3 (September 2016): 365–85; Tomomi Yamaguchi, "'Gender Free' Feminism in Japan: A Story of Mainstreaming and Backlash," *Feminist Studies* 40, no. 3 (2014): 541–72. Regarding the fall of the salaryman, see James E. Roberson and Nobue Suzuki, eds., *Men and Masculinities in Contemporary Japan: Dislocating the Salaryman Doxa* (London: Routledge, 2001); J. S. Eades, Tom Gill, and Harumi Befu, eds., *Globalization and Social Change in Contemporary Japan* (Melbourne: TransPacific Books, 2000). Nobody in Anglo-American anthropology has contributed more to our collective knowledge about socioeconomically marginalized men in contemporary Japan than has Tom Gill; see Tom Gill, "When Pillars Evaporate: Structuring Masculinity on the Japanese Margins," in *Men and Masculinities in Contemporary Japan: Dislocating the Salaryman Doxa*, ed. James Roberson and Nobue Suzuki (London: Routledge, 2005); Tom Gill, *Men of Uncertainty: The Social Organization of Day Laborers in Contemporary Japan* (Albany: State University of New York Press, 2001); Tom Gill, "Whose Problem? Japan's Homeless as an Issue of Local and Central Governance," in *The Political Economy of Governance in Japan*, ed. Glenn Hook (London: Routledge, 2005), 192–210.

From the late nineteenth century to the middle of the twentieth, an important component of the vision of what it meant to be a man – for male youths, their families, and their communities – was the prospect of a healthy young man being conscripted and then going to war when called upon. The end of World War II put a thorough, lasting end to that ideal, giving rise to a new dominant mode of masculinity embodied in the salaryman. Young men today do not aspire much to either. Rather, many find themselves liberated from the rigid gender role expectations of their forefathers' generations, self-consciously experimenting with gender norms and transgressing them, all the while struggling to escape the intimate embrace of the "cruel optimism" of late capitalism.[79]

Literature and Visual Culture

The Columbia Anthology of Modern Japanese Literature, Volume 2: From 1945 to the Present[80] offers a range of literary perspectives on the soldier during the first half of the twentieth century; three pieces that stand out are Tayama Katai's "One Soldier," Yosano Akiko's "Beloved, You Must Not Die," and Hino Ashihei's "Earth and Soldiers." For a popular wartime comic on the period – plus a timely critique of its content – see Shimada Keizō, "The Adventures of Dankichi," in *Reading Colonial Japan: Text, Context, and Critique.*[81] And *Confessions of a Mask* (1958) by the iconic Mishima Yukio considers the reflections of an adolescent boy and his attraction to men at the outbreak of war.[82]

The militarized masculinity that was increasingly idealized in modern Japan is addressed in complex fashion in Kobayashi Masaki's film trilogy *Ningen no Jōken* (*The Human Condition*, 1959–1961)[83] and superbly embodied by the figure of Captain Yanoi (Sakamoto Ryūichi) in Ōshima Nagisa's *Senjō no Merī Kurisumasu* (*Merry Christmas,*

---

[79] Lauren Berlant, "Cruel Optimism," in *The Affect Theory Reader*, ed. Melissa Gregg and Gregory J. Seigworth (Durham, NC: Duke University Press, 2010), 93–117.

[80] J. Thomas Rimer and Van C. Gessel, eds., *The Columbia Anthology of Modern Japanese Literature, Volume 2: From 1945 to the Present* (New York: Columbia University Press, 2005).

[81] Shimada Keizō, "The Adventures of Dankichi," in *Reading Colonial Japan: Text, Context, and Critique*, ed. Michele M. Mason and Helen J. S. Lee (Stanford, CA: Stanford University Press, 2012), 245–70.

[82] Mishima Yukio, *Confessions of a Mask*, trans. Meredith Weatherby (New York: New Directions, 1958).

[83] Kobayashi Masaki, Matsuyama Zenzō, and Inagaki Koichi, from the six-volume novel by Junpei Gomikawa, *Ningen no Jōken* (*The Human Condition*), directed by Kobayashi Masaki (Tokyo: Shōchiku, 1959–1961).

46   Building the Nation and Modern Manhood

Mr. Lawrence, 1983).[84] Representing a new, civilian masculinity of the postwar decades, the kind-hearted vagabond Tora-san (Atsumi Kiyoshi) stole many a heart in representing hapless manhood in Yamada Yōji's film series *Otoko wa tsurai yo!* (*It's Tough Being a Man!*, 1969–1995).[85] The salaryman cum father figure is a man of ordinary talents and aspirations in Morita Yoshimitsu's *Kazoku Gēmu* (*Family Game*, 1983),[86] which captures the dysfunctional middle-class nuclear family. And the trials and tribulations of current-day manhood are featured in two very different films: Murakami Shōsuke's *Densha Otoko* (*Train Man*, 2005)[87] focuses on the inability of a paradigmatic *otaku* to court a young woman without the constant help of his virtual social network,[88] while the father figure in Koreeda Hirokazu's *Manbiki Kazoku* (*Shoplifters*, 2018)[89] personifies a precarious manhood and a failing fatherhood.

[84] Ōshima Nagisa and Paul Mayersberg, from memoirs by Sir Laurens van der Post, *Senjō no Merī Kurisumasu* (*Merry Christmas, Mr. Lawrence*), directed by Ōshima Nagisa (Tokyo: Shochiku, 1983).

[85] Yamada Yoji, Asama Yoshitaka et al., *Otoko wa tsurai yo!* (*It's Tough Being a Man!*), directed by Yamada Yōji (Tokyo: Shōchiku, 1969–1995).

[86] Kobayashi Yoshinori and Morita Yoshimitsu, from the novel by Honma Yōhei, *Kazoku Gēmu* (*Family Game*), directed by Morita Yoshimitsu (Circle Films, 1983).

[87] Arisa Kaneko, from the novel by Hitori Nakano, *Densha Otoko* (*Train Man*) directed by Murakami Shōsuke (San Francisco, CA: VIZ Media, 2005).

[88] For an excellent analysis of the changing modes of masculinity as represented by *Densha Otoko*, see Napier, "Where Have All the Salarymen Gone?," 154–75; Annette Schad-Seifert, "Japans Single-Gesellschaft – Der Trend zu Partnerlosigkeit in Umfragen des National Institutes of Population and Social Security Research," in *Japan in der Krise*, ed. Annette Schad-Seifert and Nora Kottmann (Wiesbaden: Springer Fachmedien, 2019), 75–97; Annette Schad-Seifert, "Womenomics: A Model for a New Family Policy in Japan?," in *Family Life in Japan and Germany: Challenges for a Gender-sensitive Family Policy*, ed. Uta Meier-Gräwe, Miyoko Motozawa, and Annette Schad-Seifert (Wiesbaden: Springer, 2019), 157–76.

[89] Koreeda Hirokazu, *Manbiki Kazoku* (*Shoplifters*), directed by Koreeda Hirokazu (Tokyo: GAGA, 2018).

2   Controlling Reproduction and Motherhood

One day in 1935, a young woman who had migrated to Tokyo to find gainful employment wrote a letter to her parents back in Suye Mura, a village in Kyūshū. She included a packet of condoms – which were expensive then – noting: "Use these! You have too many children."[1] As it happens, national population policy at the time sought to aggressively increase the number of births *while* simultaneously accommodating the sexual desires of soldiers on their imperialist advance in Asia (see Chapter 4). To this end, national health campaigns emphasized condoms' potential for preventing a range of sexually transmitted diseases. Condoms for civilians were available from pharmacies or by mail order under the label "hygiene sacks" (*eisei sakku*). While the record doesn't reveal details of provenance, the most likely brand was Okamoto, which was the main producer of condoms designated for the military, with names such as Attack Number One (Kōgeki Ichiban), Attack Champion (Totsugeki Ichiban), and Iron Cap (Tetsu Kaputo).[2]

Today, the circumstances for promoting the diligent use of condoms, along with the quality of condoms themselves, have dramatically changed. For example, in a nod to both the film *Godzilla* and the global commercial reach of the popular culture around it, a 2016 commercial for Okamoto Zero One condoms features two copulating dinosaurs ostensibly from 70 million years ago, when "the world had no love." After some thrusting the female pulls away and ferociously growls at the male. The male turns away in shame. Next comes the slogan "Mankind has Okamoto," followed by "Let's wear 'love.'" Thus, love and condoms are equated with conscientious copulation. In fact, the aesthetic and

---

[1] Smith and Wiswell, *The Women of Suyemura*, 89.
[2] Ōta Tenrei, *Nihon sanji chōsetsu hyakunenshi* (Tokyo: Shuppan Kagaku Sōgō Kenkyūsho, 1976), 266. Okamoto Industries Inc. was established in 1934. Its headquarters are situated in Tokyo, with its research and development center and manufacturing plants located in three major cities in Japan and subsidiaries in Hong Kong, China, the United States, Thailand, and Vietnam. Today, Okamoto is the largest latex and rubber manufacturer in Japan.

rhetoric across many different condom ads are endlessly creative and innovative. They heavily employ a popular cultural emphasis on cuteness, and they have largely succeeded in thoroughly commercializing and normalizing the product itself. Indeed, condoms have triumphed over other contraceptives. In modern and contemporary history, condoms and condom ads have become just one sign of how thoroughly sex, love, reproduction, and health have been radically rearranged.

This chapter relates the stormy history of the control and management of reproduction and family planning. This history ranges from the extremes of infanticide, a common intervention practiced for centuries and far into the modern period, to abortion, the most common means of ending unwanted pregnancy in the twenty-first century. In between the two lie a great many struggles: including the everyday qualms of women, couples, families, and households lacking the means, technology, and power to prevent conception, survive abortion, or commit infanticide; a series of radical transformations regarding how women's bodies were known, managed, and viewed and by whom – and how women took control of reproduction and redefined motherhood; and the various battles of those striving to have their own biological children.

Today, the public debate about reproduction in Japan is almost uniformly driven by concerns about young women's (much less about young men's) desire to have babies and the demographic crisis that has resulted from the lack of that desire. This status quo stands in stark contrast to dominant views in previous generations. When some of Japan's leading intellectuals and modernizers, such as Fukuzawa Yukichi and Ueki Emori, discussed human rights in the 1870s and 1880s they were demanding women's rights as well as men's. They also aimed at overcoming class distinctions and promoting an egalitarian society. At the same time, they reintroduced a binary difference between male and female, and declared motherhood the core principle of women's nature. But these were men talking about the state of women; it was not until the early twentieth century that women began to noticeably enter and drive the debate.

Angles of this debate included questions such as who should have control over reproductive technologies and rights, especially in relation to the status of women in society. This discussion was intertwined with the "woman question" more generally. It also intersected with the "population problem," which provided a platform for redefining women's roles, status, and rights in society – while also involving a whole other set of actors, namely the proponents of Japanese imperialism and colonialism forcefully competing with the birth-control movement, each seeking grand-scale solutions for their agenda. As for birth control, while a range of reproductive technologies and methods were researched, developed, and utilized, the debate remained tied to interest in legalizing abortion. The quest to legalize abortion was increasingly at odds with Japan's imperialist ideology, which sought rapid population growth. Amidst this debate women realized the political capital of their wombs – the expansive potential of their bodies that would, if fully functional, improve their status as imperial subjects for the price (and prize) of the expansion of the empire. Rhetorically, at least, women came to embody and occupy that interface by virtue of their potential to be mothers.

Revolutionizing Birth

The historical record worldwide suggests that women rarely kill. When they have committed murder, the vast majority of their victims have been unbearable husbands and unwanted newborns. For the most part, these women's reasons were pragmatic and predictable: abuse for the former, economic hardship for the latter. As for the latter, since at least 1646 the premodern Shogunate forbade paid-for abortions, and yet only lightly punished them – by banning the offender from the environs. Indeed, far into the twentieth century, the killing of a newborn, by any culprit, was considered less of an offense than the murder of an older victim would be. Judgments of infanticide were somewhat flexible, often resulting in wildly varying sentences that appeared to be motivated more by concern for regulating sexuality, morality, and patterns of familial authority than for pronatalism.[3]

The notion of the "transmigration of souls" governed much of the acceptance of abortion and infanticide in premodern Japan. According to this belief, children up to the age of seven were not fully fledged humans and could, thus, be sent back to the "other world" with no particular harm caused. As it happens, historically there was significant variation in whether a household needing to limit its size chose abortion or infanticide as its means. Considerations during "the long retreat of infanticide" included the safety and health of the pregnant woman, the ability to raise an additional child, and the preference for male children.[4] In general, the decision was made by the head of household, who often aimed for a balance of two boys for each girl.

---

[3] Susan L. Burns, "Introduction," in *Gender and Law in the Japanese Imperium*, ed. Susan L. Burns and Barbara J. Brooks, 1–17 (Honolulu: University of Hawai'i Press, 2013).
[4] Fabian Drixler, *Mabiki: Infanticide and Population Growth in Eastern Japan, 1660–1950* (Berkeley: University of California Press, 2013).

50   Controlling Reproduction and Motherhood

Such life-and-death questions were the stuff of legends. Yanagita Kunio (1875–1962) – who founded the field of Japanese folklore studies (*minzokugaku*) and compiled and published the *Legends of Tōno* in 1910 – has shared how matters of pregnancy, birth, infanticide, and other methods of family planning were retold countless times in rich, anxious, and wondrous folk stories. "Certain children" who were deemed "grotesque" were indeed "hacked to pieces, put into small wine casks, and buried in the ground."[5] Another chronicler of small-town life, Saga Junichi, recorded that, fortunately, some managed to avoid such butchery; Suzuki Fumi, born in 1898, survived a botched attempt to be killed at birth – just how we do not know – on account of her "terrible ugliness," phrasing that most likely speaks of a disfiguring disability.[6]

And when, decades later, the former geisha Masuda Sayo learned of a baby boy being abandoned in 1956, she wanted to shout out loud, "Never give birth to children thoughtlessly!" Remembering her own sad childhood as an essentially abandoned girl who was sent to work as a nursemaid at the age of six in 1931, she felt no pity. Instead, she recalls, "I was assailed by a sudden desire to grab hold of that child and wring his neck. I wanted him to vanish from this world while he still knew nothing, and the effort of restraining myself made me sweat. I told people that if the child were mine, that's what I'd do." So certain was she that there had never "been an abandoned child who's ever gone on to be as happy as other people" and "that most go through life lurking in the shadows, living in fear and trembling, embittered because the world has treated them unfairly."[7] People around Masuda laughed at her rant but this is not to say that the business of child abandonment and assisting with birth, abortion, or infanticide was viewed without prejudice. For centuries the traditions of Shinto and other popular beliefs had associated childbirth with impurity. Birth was seen as a "white impurity," menstruation was a "red impurity," and death a "black impurity." And so those engaged in the business of assisting with birth were identified with those impurities and marginalized as such. Regarding the thus disreputable labor of midwifery, a sixteen-year-old girl's story is a case in point. In 1922, this girl was preparing for the entrance exam to a teachers' college

---

[5] Yanagita Kunio, *The Legends of Tōno*, trans. Ronald A. Morse (Tokyo: Japan Foundation, [1910] 1975), 41–42.
[6] Saga Junichi, *Memories of Silk and Straw: A Self-Portrait of Small-Town Japan*, trans. Garry O. Evans (Tokyo: Kōdansha International, 1987), 203–205.
[7] Masuda Sayo, *Autobiography of a Geisha*, trans. G. G. Rowley (New York: Columbia University Press, [1957] 2003), 160. For a current-day perspective on apprentice geisha and their cultural capital, see Jan Bardsley, *Maiko Masquerade: Crafting Geisha Girlhood in Japan* (Oakland: University of California Press, 2021).

when the village policeman suggested she instead attend the newly founded school for midwives and nurses. Intrigued, as well as inspired by photographs she had seen of nurses in white uniforms, she ended up taking the exam – without informing her parents. When her family received notice that she had been admitted, her father was furious at the notion that she wanted to become a midwife. Much like contemporaries of his generation, he saw midwifery as the work of *those other people* (the lowest outcasts, *burakumin*). "We are poor," he fumed, "but this is an honorable house. I won't have you sullying the family name." Despite her father's scorn, the girl had no patience for his old-fashioned views, and attended the school anyway.[8]

This particular family thus straddled two different eras in and attitudes toward family planning. The father still retained the view of centuries past that cast the business of birth as unclean, whereas the daughter looked to the future of its increasing professionalization and in line with the direction in which Japan was consciously headed. At the end of the nineteenth century, and in the wake of increasing hostility toward China, the Japanese elite had turned away from Chinese models of governance – including the governance of knowledge – and looked instead to Europe, adopting the Prussian medical system in the process. The Meiji government (1868–1912) recognized the medical system as a pillar of the new nation-state in the making, and in 1868 decreed the first nationwide Law Regulating the Sale of Drugs and the Practice of Abortion Techniques by Midwives (Sanba no baiyaku sewa oyobi dataitō no torishimarihō). In 1880, the "crime of abortion" (*datai no tsumi*) was included in new criminal laws, and was later carried over unchanged as Articles 212 through 216 in the new Criminal Code of 1907. Additional legislation was implemented during the 1930s, together with a host of laws regulating women's bodies, reproduction, and the body politic at large.[9] The significance of this "revolution of birth" was enormous, complex, and dramatically uneven for all it affected – individuals, families, and whole communities – for decades to come.[10] Another tale speaks to this period of transition, this one a Kyūshū fisherwoman's recollection of how, in her grandmother's days (at the end of the

---

[8] Brigitte Steger, "Geburtshilfe – vom unreinen Gewerbe zum Karriereberuf oder: Die Dissemination staatlicher Kontrolle ins Private," in *Getrennte Welten, gemeinsame Moderne? Geschlechterverhältnisse in Japan*, ed. Ilse Lenz and Michiko Mae (Opladen: Leske und Budrich, 1997), 150–78.

[9] Sabine Frühstück, *Colonizing Sex: Sexology and Social Control in Modern Japan* (Berkeley: University of California Press, 2003), 120–21.

[10] Fujita Shinichi, *Osan kakumei* (Tokyo: Asahi Bunko, 1988); for further discussion, see Steger, "Geburtshilfe," 150–78.

52   Controlling Reproduction and Motherhood

nineteenth century), there had been fewer children per family because that generation had performed abortions and infanticide. Her mother, by contrast, had heard of a woman who after killing her newborn had subsequently been interrogated by the police. Worried about such a frightening prospect, her mother had decided not to kill her last born, the little sister of the fisherwoman.[11]

Following the 1880 "crime of abortion" law, the rate of infanticide dropped significantly. And yet saving infant lives was not the objective; it was the integration of medicine and police control that appealed to the builders of the Meiji state. This system forcefully drove the transformation of the concept of childbirth. In the Meiji state, as the police became the guardians of both public order and public health, pregnancy, birth, and the maternal body became an object of hygiene and surveillance policy. Indeed, pregnant women beyond their first trimester were subject to police surveillance. In the multigenerational households of rural communities and premodern times, childcare and the raising of children had been a communal task. By contrast, the distinctly modern designation of mothers as primary caretakers transformed both the issues of unwanted offspring and the needs of children more generally into "women's problems" – be they physical, economic, or political. Previously, practical knowledge of family planning, birthing, and child-rearing had been passed on from (mostly) women of one generation to the next. Very few women were assisted by a midwife. With the introduction of a centralized medical system – and the establishment of gynecology and obstetrics, pedagogy and pediatrics, and the general professionalization of the maintenance and management of population health – expertise shifted into the hands of mostly male doctors, who thereafter trained nurses and midwives.[12]

It took until the third decade of the twentieth century for medical innovation to catch up with the "modern-day" sophistication of policing pregnancy and birth. Two medical doctors working separately, Hermann Knaus (1892–1970) in Austria and Ogino Kyūsaku (1882–1975) in Japan, unlocked the mysteries of the menstrual cycle in terms of "fertile days" – normally occurring between nineteen and twelve days prior to a female's next menstrual period. In 1930 they combined their research as the Knaus–Ogino Method of "natural birth control," also known as Ogino Periodical Abstinence Method (*Ogino-shiki shūki kinryoku*

---

[11] Gail Lee Bernstein, "Women in Rural Japan," in *Women in Changing Japan*, ed. Joyce Lebra et al. (Boulder, CO: Westview Press, 1976), 29–31.

[12] Brigitte Steger describes this transition in "From Impurity to Hygiene: The Role of Midwives in the Modernisation of Japan," *Japan Forum* 6, no. 2 (1994): 175–87.

hininhō) or Safe Period Method (*anzenkihō*).[13] Almost immediately, the revolutionary information made its way into mainstream women's magazines and supplements. For instance, in 1933 the subscribers of the women's magazine *The Housewife's Companion* (*Shufu no Tomo*) received with their February issue a hefty supplement: *Methods for Pregnancy, Safe Birth, and Child Rearing* (*Ninshin to Ansan to Ikujihō*). The book includes a description of a method for avoiding pregnancies, an illustration of a Simplified Chart of Fertile and Infertile Days, and a range of statistics and information of varying scientific value (see Figure 2.1). Beginning with the less scientific, these included suggestions for the most likely season to become pregnant, speculations about how to know the sex of a fetus – even the intriguing question of the chances of influencing having a boy or a girl. Note that, though the entire 500-page book brimmed with advice on pregnancy and for new mothers – adorned by lots of images of lovely babies – half of the last page was an advertisement for a pessary, another "easy-to-use contraceptive device."[14] Then, with the June issue of 1933, subscribers received *The Women's Hygiene Dictionary* (*Fujin Eisei Jiten*), a 400-plus-page book containing a wide range of health information, including articles and statistical tables on the presumed connections between menstruation, conception, and the baby's sex; and a "Simplified Table of Pregnancy Days." (This latter table was an obvious reference to the Knaus–Ogino Method, though neither doctor was named.)[15]

The Housewife's Companion was founded in 1917. By the 1930s, it had more than 600,000 subscribers and targeted a mass market of both young and middle-aged married women who, aspiring to a middle-class, nuclear family life, educated themselves in matters of birth control, housekeeping, home management, and finances. And yet, despite intense propaganda designed to encourage large families – "procreate and multiply" (*umeyo, fuyaseyo*) – information about birth control was

---

[13] Knaus presented his revolutionary findings at the twenty-first meeting of the German Society for Gynecology (Deutsche Gesellschaft für Gynäkologie) on May 23, 1929: "First, egg cells are only fertile for a few hours; semen have to get to an egg cell within the female reproductive apparatus within two days; and, fertilization is only possible within a very short window around the moment of ovulation." In 1930, Ogino achieved similar research results, which is why this "natural birth control method" was named the Knaus–Ogino Method. Their research was first discussed in English by Leo J. Katz, *The Rhythm of Sterility and Fertility in Women: A Discussion of the Physiological, Practical, and Ethical Aspects of the Discoveries of Drs. K. Ogino (Japan) and H. Knaus (Austria) Regarding the Periods When Conception is Impossible and When Possible* (Chicago, IL: Latz Foundation, 1934).

[14] Shufu no tomo-sha, ed., *Shufu no Tomo nigaku-gō furoku: Ninshin to Ansan to Ikujihō* (Tokyo: Shufu no Tomo-sha, 1937), 475.

[15] Shufu no tomo-sha, ed., *Fujin Eisei Jiten* (Tokyo: Shufu no Tomo-sha, 1933), 143, 230.

54 Controlling Reproduction and Motherhood

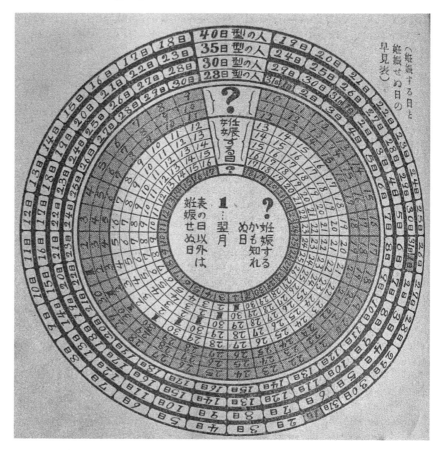

Figure 2.1 Fertility graph from a supplement to *The Housewife's Companion* (*Shufu no Tomo*), titled *Ninshin to Ansan to Ikujihō*, February 1933. Private collection.

ubiquitous, readily found in magazines and newspapers, via word of mouth, or even in the post, whether purchased via mail order or proffered by one woman to another. And those women with access to ever-better birth control were able to become much more independent – and also, of course, contraception became a lucrative market.

These advances in modern knowledge and practices went hand in hand with, one, an unprecedented medicalization and quantification of women's bodies and, two, the "commercialization" of both mothers' and

Revolutionizing Birth 55

babies' health (see Figure 2.2).[16] This twin fact contrasts with the medical attention to male bodies discussed in Chapters 1 and 4, which took place almost entirely within the military and was largely limited to preserving men's fighting ability by controlling the spread of infectious disease.

But in civilian society, the protection of "innocent wives and children" was big business. For instance, an advertisement in the April 1935 issue of the household magazine *Popular Medicine* (*Tsūzoku Igaku*, p. 175) illustrates this claim: A half-page advertisement promoted thirty-six different products for contraception, the prevention of venereal disease, or both. Among them were "sacks for men and women [providing] limitation and protection" (essentially condoms and pessaries), silk sponges, and disinfectant creams variously advertised as "tools of birth control," unspecified "specialized articles and medicines for men and women," and "friends of familial harmony." The illustration adorning the ad features a man in a business suit (marking him as white-collar and middle class), who appears to be either putting on or taking off his shoes, and a woman in a kimono, who appears to be offering him one of the "specialized articles." But which product is she offering? Is she his wife or his lover? While leaving many questions unanswered, the image establishes that it is women who are responsible for such hygiene and health matters – and that men needed to be prompted and coaxed into using them. (Adding to the hygiene burden was the fact that condoms were usually used more than once, with thorough cleansing advised in between uses.)

The prices for these products varied widely. In the 1930s, an urban middle-class household income in Japan proper was about ¥75. As for how far that salary would stretch, the entrance fee to a public bath cost about ¥0.07, a 1.8-liter bottle of medium-quality sake cost approximately ¥1.48, and a train ticket could cost from ¥0.55 to ¥2.65. In the *Popular Medicine* ad, a pack of three condoms cost from ¥1 to ¥3; a pessary cost ¥1.50. One of each, plus ¥0.10 for shipping, would have been a substantial expense for many – more than twice the cost of the average bottle of

---

[16] Interestingly, like condoms, modern sanitary napkins had a rubber component and were, along with a range of other cosmetic products, named with western female names. For instance, in September 1926 (and in subsequent issues), the household magazine *Popular Medicine* (*Tsūzoku Igaku*) advertised Daiwa's "industrially produced" Victoria sanitary napkin (*gekkeitai*), whereas the July 1927 issue of *Fujin Kōron* promoted a similar product, emphasizing that "no matter whether western or eastern dress was worn, it [would] fit perfectly and safely." At the same time, the market for baby products took off, with even mainstream magazines running full-page advertisements for "mother's milk substitutes," promoting dry milk and condensed milk as "top-of-the-line substitutes (of mother's milk)."

Figure 2.2 Morinaga Dry Milk advertisement, supplement to *The Housewife's Companion* (*Shufu no Tomo*), vol. 16, no. 9, September 1, 1932. Private collection.

sake. And that was within the Japanese mainland; customers throughout Japan's expanding empire could pay four times those prices.[17]

Another medical doctor by the name of Ōta Tenrei (1900–1985), a graduate of the Kyūshū Imperial University's Medical School, also studied the menstrual cycle. Since Ōta ran a gynecological practice in one of Kyōto's poorest neighborhoods, and was associated with the Socialist Party and the Labor-Farmer Party (Rōdō Nōmintō), he was reputed to be a "socialist" doctor. In 1932, he introduced an intra-uterine device (IUD) called the Ōta-type Contraceptive Ring (*Ōta-shiki hinin ringu*) or Ōta Ring.[18] It was only hesitantly welcomed by metropolitan birth-control activists. Obstacles to its swift adoption included the fact that it could only be fitted by a doctor, as well as its initial hefty price of ¥10. In addition, soon after its introduction the Ordinance Regulating Harmful Contraceptive Devices of 1930 was amended, and prohibited the IUD, citing it as dangerous to women's health. (This turn of events was most likely in part due to the procreationist ideology at the time. As such, the Ōta Ring did not really take off until the 1950s.)[19]

Despite these revolutionary innovations, the primary means by which households limited their family size remained (illegal) abortions. And so (mostly male) medical researchers and practitioners joined forces with labor activists, feminists, and anti-imperialists in the fight to both legalize abortion and develop and market safe, affordable options for contraception (*ninshin chōsetsu*) or, more ambiguously, "birth control" (*sanji seigen*).

Contracepting Imperialism

The imperialist regime, however, bemoaned Japan's "lack of space" and, instead of investing in contraceptive technologies, aggressively pursued mass migration to Japan's colonies as core solution to the country's "overpopulation." Given that these cries echoed statements by Nazi Germany, the cause was taken on by one Dr. Martin Schwind (1906–1991), a high-school teacher and member of the German East

---

[17] For the illustration, see Frühstück, *Colonizing Sex*, 116–17. Prices were taken from *Shūkan Asahi*, ed. *Nedan no Meiji Taishō Shōwa Fūzoku-shi* (Tokyo: Asahi Shinbunsha, 1981).

[18] Both his contraceptive innovation and his engagement as obstetrician and gynecologist – notwithstanding his leftist political work on behalf of women's health and contraception and the disadvantaged classes – Ōta was also an avid proponent of euthanasia; see Astghik Hovhannisyan, "Ōta Tenrei's Defense of Birth Control, Eugenics and Euthanasia," *Contemporary Japan* 30, no. 1 (2018): 28–42.

[19] Frühstück, *Colonizing Sex*, 146–47; see also Shiozaki Toshio, "Shikyūnai ninshin kagu ni kansuru kenkyū: Toku ni Ōta ringu to rūpu to no hikaku kenkyū," *Nihon Sanka Fujin Kagakkai Zasshi* 25, no. 1 (1973): 1–9.

58 Controlling Reproduction and Motherhood

Asiatic Society (Deutsche Gesellschaft für Natur- und Völkerkunde Ostasiens) in Tokyo.[20] In a public talk, Schwind mocked US concerns about Japan's population growth (from 33.5 million in 1870 to over 70 million in 1940 – just in Japan proper). His talk was published in the Society's periodical in 1940 – two and a half months after the German invasion of Poland, which marked the beginning of World War II in Europe. (A bit more than a year later, the Imperial Japanese Navy Air Service would attack Pearl Harbor, marking the entry of the United States into the war in Asia.) Schwind wrote that, surely, his Führer's claim was applicable to any populace, including Nazi Germany's ally Japan:

The words that the Führer imparts on our souls, are applicable to any Volk whose situation compares to ours: "Never forget that the holiest right in this world is the right to soil that one wants to cultivate; and the holiest sacrifice is the blood that one spills on its behalf. Only large-enough space secures a Volk's freedom of existence."

Clearly, he felt that the same "logic" ought to apply to Japan at the expense of its colonies.[21]

The Japanese imperialist regime hardly needed encouragement. Its criminalization of abortion and infanticide, and even restrictions on condom use were to undergird the aggressive expansion of the empire as part of the remedy to the "lack of space." Japanese birth control activists thus pursued their goals within an increasingly militarist and imperialist environment. For the more radical women's groups already engaged in debates – about the roles and status of women, the significance of motherhood, and political, economic, and social inequality – "the population problem" provided a new platform for the redefinition of all these concerns. Some early feminists had vigorously campaigned for a woman's right to choose her partner in matrimony based on "love" rather than having the choice made for her for strictly family and household considerations.

An additional forum for such deliberations emerged in new women-only magazines such as *Bluestockings* (*Seitō*), wherein women debated not just the meaning and significance of motherhood but also the right to

---

[20] The Gesellschaft für Natur- und Völkerkunde Ostasiens was founded in Tokyo in 1873 as an independent entity by German merchants, scholars, and diplomats with the objective of fostering research on Japan and other East Asian countries and increasing public understanding of East Asia. For more see Ostasiengesellschaft at https://oag.jp/ (accessed June 7, 2021).

[21] Martin Schwind, "Japanische Raumnot und Kolonisation," in *Mitteilungen der Deutschen Gesellschaft für Natur- und Völkerkunde Ostasiens* XXXII, part C (1940): 2–17. In the quotation, Schwind is paraphrasing Hitler's *Mein Kampf* (Munich: Franz Eher Verlag, 1925–1926).

Contracepting Imperialism

postpone or even decline motherhood altogether, in favor of instead pursuing talents and aspirations. From these discussions emerged a contentious proposal introduced in 1917 by one of the founders of *Bluestockings*, the leading feminist Hiratsuka Raichō. One of many threats to a healthy pregnancy, and to a child's prospect for maturing to adulthood, was both hereditary and venereal diseases, particularly syphilis. To help contain those risks, Raichō proposed legislation that would require men to be tested for venereal diseases prior to marriage – and then prohibit them from marrying if found infected. (It was widely assumed that venereal diseases were transmitted by prostitutes.) Her attempt failed. Notably, at the time national and state governments around the world either already had or were contemplating legislation that sought compulsory sterilization of certain individuals. What is more, two decades later the Japanese government did implement a National Eugenics Law (1941), though they had turned Raichō's intention upside down. Instead of forbidding infected men from marrying, the law prescribed – on the basis of certain medical conditions – the forced sterilization of women likely to produce severely ill offspring.

But as for the debate in 1917, socialists and other progressives among the educated, political, and medical communities took a complementary but different route to population control. Emphasizing the ignorance of farmers and laborers, as well as the inevitable hardships of their lives, progressives demanded not only the legalization of abortive and contraceptive means of birth control but also facilities for birth-control consultation and education – all to grant citizens control over their own reproductive destinies. Some advocates cited this as the only strategy for lifting farmers and workers out of poverty, and identified multiple births as the largest obstacle to that lofty goal. Others warned how overpopulation – and the subsequent need to expand territory – could readily lead to war. Some looked beyond the boundary of the empire. For instance, when a certain Iijima Ginjirō proudly tallied, by prefecture, the total number of inquiries about birth-control methods made to the Kyōto-based Society for Birth Control – 6,674 for just 1924 – he listed Taiwan, Chōsen, Manshū, Karafuto, and Nanyō among them, signaling the normalization of Japan's imperialism even for many progressive medical experts and social reformers who otherwise railed against an increasingly militaristic state.[22]

A range of activists provided assistance. Beginning in the 1920s and continuing throughout the 1930s, midwife and activist Shibahara Urako

---

[22] Iijima Ginjirō, "Nihon no jutai chōsetsu undō – Sangā-joshi torai no ato," *Sanji Chōsetsu Hyōron*, no. 4 (May 1925): 39–41.

60   Controlling Reproduction and Motherhood

(1887–1955) regularly traveled from her Osaka home to fishing villages along the coast of the Japanese sea – far from the epicenter of political activism and class struggle – teaching hygiene and assisting in family planning. Shibahara also earned her license against the will of her father, although he was not worried about the family name but believed that women did not need formal education. Deeply invested in justice for women and welfare for the powerless, even repeated arrests did not stop her from performing abortions for women in need.[23] Doctor Majima Yutaka, having learned the latest abortion techniques while visiting Switzerland and England, in the mid-1920s founded a Sex Education and Counseling Facility (*seikyōiku sōdansho*) where he examined mostly working-class women, provided condoms or pessaries for one-third the market price, and instructed on natural birth-control methods.[24] While he did offer those services, he grew frustrated at how often the first time a patient came to him was when she sought not advice but a (still illegal) abortion as her only way out of a dire situation. In such instances, Majima and doctors like him frequently documented fake diagnoses so that they could legally end such pregnancies, and they often did so free of charge. Like Shibahara, Majima was arrested at least once; he was also accused of belonging to an "abortion club" (*datai kurabu*) of doctors "willing to perform illegal abortions for the bourgeois class."

Activists without medical expertise tended to promote education over abortion, and so favored enabling women and families to actively practice family planning on their own. In addition, their activities were influenced by their class distinctions, which affected the level of radicalism they were willing to engage in. For instance, Yamamoto Senji (1889–1929), a biologist who taught at Dōshisha University, conducted the first quantitative surveys about sexual behavior among his all-male students. He was also a representative of the Labor-Farmer Party's left wing (Rōdō Nōmintō), and an outspoken anti-imperialist. Since he strongly opposed abortion, he instead favored broadcasting knowledge about the Knaus–Ogino Method as well as what he and others referred to as "constructive birth control methods" or "cultured methods" (for *coitus interruptus*, which was named "Onan method" or *Ōnanfū*, after Genesis 38:9–10, which in traditional Christian usage designated both masturbation and "unnatural forms of intercourse" between a man and woman). Unno

---

[23] Fujime Yuki, "Aru sanba no kiseki: Shibahara Urako to sanji chōsetsu," *Nihon-shi Kenkyū* 366 (1993): 93.

[24] Yet counseling centers for birth control sold condoms for ¥0.20 or ¥0.30 and pessaries for ¥0.30 or ¥0.40; Mikiso Hane, *Reflections on the Way to the Gallows: Rebel Women in Prewar Japan* (Berkeley: University of California Press, 1988), 152.

Yukinori (1879–1955) was a social theorist and author of one of the first works on eugenics in Japan, *On the Improvement of the Japanese Race* (*Nihon Jinshu Kaizōron*, 1910). At his various public talks he discussed how sexual desire impacts all aspects of social life – happiness, health, marriage, the future of children; indeed, all of cultural life. As such, he emphasized how contraception is the mechanism by which individual women and families could take control of all these aspects of their lives.[25]

These figures promoted not sexual freedom per se – that would come with the use of contraceptive methods – but rather the benefits to family health and prosperity. And yet there were still many who were not in a position to benefit from this guidance. It was this segment of the population that activist-baroness Ishimoto Shizue (1897–2001) worked to help. Ishimoto's influence ranged from the birth-control instruction she offered for a time to women who worked the coal mines in rural Japan to the friends in both Japan and the United States that she knew as a member of the aristocracy. She shared much of Margaret Sanger's philosophy about the necessity of ensuring family planning guidance is available to everyone, especially the poor.[26] But her sympathies for the "have-nots" did not extend across the empire. Indeed, as late as 1939 – two years after the Japanese Imperial Army committed the massacre in Nanking – she refused to condemn Japanese imperialism, claiming that "the time [had] not yet come for us Japanese intellectuals to discuss China." These views ran counter to the anti-imperialism of Yamamoto Senji, the Dōshisha University biologist noted earlier, who publicly spoke out against Japan's expansionist politics from early in the twentieth century.

It should be noted that when birth-control activists spoke publicly, they were careful to promote birth-control methods and devices exclusively for families with children who could not economically or medically afford to have more.[27] As an additional safeguard against censorship, activists insinuated that their publications were only suited for select readers, labeling them "scientific" or "for experts only."

---

[25] Frühstück, *Colonizing Sex*, 141–44.

[26] Ishimoto Shizue remained an avid activist for much of the first half of the twentieth century and became one of very few women Diet members in the second. Blessed with a long life, she was extensively eulogized when she died in 2001 at the age of 104. Situating Ishimoto's life and work within a dynamic transnational context, Aiko Takeuchi-Demirci focuses on her close relationship with Margaret Sanger: sister-in-arms, doyenne of birth control in the United States, and founder of the American Birth Control League – which was later renamed Planned Parenthood; *Contraceptive Diplomacy: Reproductive Politics and Imperial Ambitions in the United States and Japan* (Stanford, CA: Stanford University Press, 2018).

[27] Frühstück, *Colonizing Sex*, 145–51.

62 Controlling Reproduction and Motherhood

In 1929, Yamamoto prepared a petition to the Lower House that proposed the legalization of abortion based on a number of criteria, mostly concerning pregnant women's health. Unfortunately, Yamamoto was stabbed to death by a right-wing radical on March 5 of that year and was thus stopped short in his efforts. But several comrades in the fight – including *Bluestockings* founder Hiratsuka Raichō, "abortion club" doctor Majima Yutaka, baroness Ishimoto Shizue, and Christian socialist, parliamentarian, and pacifist Abe Isoo – took up the banner on his behalf. Under the name Japanese Birth Control Federation (Nihon Sanji Chōsetsu Renmei), they drafted a petition to legalize a doctor's prescription of contraceptives or performing an abortion provided one of three indicators – medical, eugenic, or socioeconomic – were met. They brought forth their efforts in August 1932 (soon after Ōta Tenrei introduced his Ōta Ring IUD). In yet another blow, their timing was overshadowed by the Japanese Imperial Army invading Manchuria, and the Home Department rejected the petition. The movement thus lost its momentum.

Less than a decade later, a very different law went into effect: the National Eugenics Law (Kokumin Yūseihō) of 1941. This was prompted entirely by the state's interest in suppressing the procreation of people with hereditary diseases or conditions believed to be hereditary, including alcoholics, criminals, lepers, the mentally ill, and the physically disabled. According to official data, in the ensuing four years 454 people, a majority of them women, were forcibly sterilized on eugenic grounds.[28] For decades to come, the premise of eugenics remained tacitly in play concerning the reproductive decision-making of (or "on behalf of") people with particular illnesses and disabilities. And yet, despite its draconian intentions, the practice of forced abortions nonetheless opened the door to legalizing the practice of elective abortion and contraceptive technologies. In 1948, the National Eugenics Law was renamed the Eugenic Protection Law (*Yūsei Hogohō*), and was reshaped in no small part by Ishimoto and Ōta. Thereafter, women could qualify for a legal abortion based on several medical, economic, and social indicators: if the pregnant woman, the father, or one of their relatives had a hereditary physical or mental illness; if either parent-to-be had leprosy or a nonhereditary mental illness; or if "the continuation of the

---

[28] Matsubara Yōko, "The Eugenic Border Control: Organized Abortions on Repatriated Women, 1945–1948," *Japan Forum* 32, no. 1 (2020): 1–20; Kōseishō Imukyoku, *Isei Hachijūnen-shi* (Tokyo: Insatsukyoku Chōyōkai, 1955), 828. For global abortion laws, see Guttmacher Institute, "An Overview of Abortion Laws," last modified June 1, 2021, www.guttmacher.org/state-policy/explore/overview-abortion-laws.

Contracepting Imperialism 63

pregnancy or subsequent childbirth were likely to seriously harm the mother's physical or economic well-being," such as in cases of rape. As such, in the wake of World War II, the Japanese legislature thus embraced one of the world's most liberal abortion laws to date.[29] Japanese women immediately availed themselves of the practice; Japan's annual birth rate has, for the most part, retained a downward trajectory ever since.

In 1996, the Eugenic Protection Law was replaced by the Maternal Protection Law, and all eugenic provisions were deleted. In so doing, Japan seemingly extricated itself from the global history of eugenics of the first half of the twentieth century, which had devastating consequences for thousands of individuals under Japanese militarist rule, and many more elsewhere around the world, including in the United States, but nowhere near as massively and horrifically as in Nazi Germany. And yet today, eugenics technologies and logics have been informing reproductive laws and practices around the world, normalizing, systematizing, and individualizing decisions about the termination of a pregnancy based on tests that allow the sex and health of a fetus to be determined with varying degrees of accuracy, along with a long list of potential medical conditions that might hamper its desirability and normativity.[30] In Japan, prenatal scanning is less routine than in some countries. Pregnancy is less governed by the politics regarding the rights of the mother as opposed to the personhood of the fetus. Rather, the focus is on the social life of the child, the welfare of the family, and the question of the wider social good.[31]

---

[29] The intricacies of the law's formation and its underlying problems are best analyzed in Tiana Norgren *Abortion before Birth Control: The Politics of Reproduction in Postwar Japan* (Princeton, NJ: Princeton University Press, 2001) and Matsubara Yōko, "Sōten toshite no seimei," *Gendai Shisō*, November 2003. Sterilization laws have disproportionally affected people with leprosy and people with disabilities; see Susan Burns, *Kingdom of the Sick: A History of Leprosy and Japan* (Honolulu: University of Hawai'i Press, 2019). For a global comparison today, see Guttmacher Institute, "An Overview of Abortion Laws."

[30] A growing literature in bioethics and biopolitics confirms the reach of eugenics in things reproductive in large parts of the world, including posthumous reproduction, IVF treatments, and surrogacy; see Tsipy Ivry, *Embodying Culture: Pregnancy in Japan and Israel* (New Brunswick, NJ: Rutgers University Press, 2010); Rene Almeling, *Sex Cells: The Medical Market for Eggs and Sperm* (Berkeley: University of California Press, 2011); Jennifer Robertson, *Robo sapiens japanicus: Robots, Gender, Family, and the Japanese Nation* (Oakland: University of California Press, 2017).

[31] Amy Borovoy, "Beyond Choice: A New Framework for Abortion?," *Dissent* (Fall 2011), accessed April 9, 2020, www.dissentmagazine.org/article/beyond-choice-a-new-framework-for-abortion.

64   Controlling Reproduction and Motherhood

Why Have Babies?

The next development in family planning would not come until 1960, but once it did, it offered much greater promise than any previous method other than the condom: the contraceptive pill. Austrian-born chemist Carl Djerassi (1923–2015) was one of the first to synthesize the hormone norethindrone, which led to the development of the first birth-control pill, earning Djerassi the moniker "Father of the Pill." (Note, though, that the origin story of the first viable oral contraceptive was significantly more transnational and complicated.[32]) The pill was first approved for contraceptive use in the United States in 1960, but its severe side effects prompted the Federal Drug Administration (FDA) to take it off the market in 1988. Subsequently, lighter-dose pills were developed and have been successfully marketed worldwide.

In Japan, the introduction of the contraceptive pill followed a thorny path, largely because of low public trust in both the pharmaceutical industry and governmental regulation bodies for most of the immediate postwar period. One of the most publicized reasons for this resulted from the government's irresponsible handling of what was called Minamata Disease. This severe neurological disease, which affected thousands, was eventually identified as being mercury poisoning, caused by the Chisso Corporation's chemical factory having released its industrial wastewater into Minamata Bay from 1932 to 1969.[33] Other circumstances contributed to the delay in the low-dose pill that was developed later. In the 1970s, many worried that it might trigger widespread female promiscuity. In the mid-1980s, the discovery of the human immunodeficiency virus brought concerns that young people in particular might

---

[32] Gabriela Soto-Laveaga, *Jungle Laboratories: Mexican Peasants, National Projects, and the Making of the Pill* (Durham, NC: Duke University Press, 2009).

[33] The disease caused severely debilitating symptoms in humans and animals and killed thousands. Infants born with its congenital form suffered from a range of infantile disorders, including cerebral palsy. Historian Timothy S. George describes the long struggle toward justice for survivors of the Minamata scandal in *Minamata: Pollution and the Struggle for Democracy in Postwar Japan* (Cambridge, MA: Harvard University Asia Center, 2002). The gravity and long-term impact of Minamata Disease triggered a wave of publications across a range of disciplines, including law, photography, and environmental studies: Kawamura Hiroki, "The Relation between Law and Technology in Japan: Liability for Technology-related Mass Damage in the Cases of Minamata Disease, Asbestos, and the Fukushima Daiichi Nuclear Disaster," *Contemporary Japan* 30, no. 1 (2018): 3–27; Luke Nottage, *Product Safety and Liability Law in Japan: From Minamata to Mad Cows* (London: Routledge, 2004); Kuwabara Shisei, *Kuwabara Shisei Shashinshū: Minamata Jiken* (Tokyo: Fujiwara Shoten, 2013); Sean Michael Wilson and Akiko Shimojima, *The Minamata Story: An Eco Tragedy* (Berkeley, CA: Stone Bridge Press, 2020).

Why Have Babies? 65

assume the pill prevents HIV/AIDS. In addition, the commonality of condom use made the legalization of the pill less urgent, and, as it happens, Japan's reproductive remuneration system made abortion a profitable business for Japanese doctors. Adding to this history is the fact that Viagra had been approved for the Japanese market after less than a year of testing – which drew protests from proponents of the low-dose pill, who accused the state of yet again being more interested in facilitating and enhancing male sexual desire and satisfaction than in enabling women to take control of contraception. Despite all these hurdles, the light-dose pill was finally legalized in 1999.

Today, fewer women in Japan (along with East and Southeast Asia) than in most post-industrialized societies are users of the contraceptive pill, with condoms and IUDs being the most common contraceptive devices, and abortion being comparatively more easily accessible. In most industrialized democracies, abortion is legal within the first trimester or twelve weeks; the limit in Japan is twenty-two weeks; in most industrialized democracies, legal abortions are performed "for cause"; Japan's allowance for cause include rape and physical, mental and/or economic maternal health – which is more lenient than in many other countries.[34]

Japan, along with large swaths of East Asia and Northern and Western Europe were among the first populations, however, to experience the metamorphosis of the issue of reproduction into a demographic crisis. In these regions, the birth rate is below replacement – meaning that, on average, not every adult produces a child for the next generation. In light of overpopulation in some parts of the world and environmental destruction in all, one might think lowering the world's population would be ideal. The more immediate effect on national economies, however, includes both dramatic economic decline and an uneven balance of elders needing more care than can be provided for them. The public debate about the increasingly rapid aging of society began in the 1980s.[35]

[34] United Nations Department of Economic and Social Affairs, *World Family Planning 2020*, accessed March 15, 2021, www.un.org/development/desa/pd/sites/www.un.org .development.desa.pd/files/files/documents/2020/Sep/unpd_2020_worldfamilyplannin g_highlights.pdf, 7. Tiana Norgren's *Abortion before Birth Control* remains a key work on the politics of reproduction. For a different perspective, see Borovoy, "Beyond Choice: A New Framework for Abortion?" For the role of some religions in reproductive decisions, see Helen Hardacre, *Marketing the Menacing Fetus in Japan* (Berkeley: University of California Press, 1997).
[35] Sabine Frühstück, "Rhetorics of Reform: On the Institutionalization and De-institutionalization of Old Age," in *Aging and Social Policy: A German–Japanese Comparison*, ed. Harald Conrad and Ralph Lützeler (Munich: Iudicium, 2002), 299–351; Robertson, *Robo sapiens japanicus*; Johan Rochel, "Protecting Japan from

66   Controlling Reproduction and Motherhood

Initially, the central concerns were the challenges to the welfare and institutional care for the elderly. These prompted the political elite to rhetorically revive the "traditional Japanese family values" that had once ensured that elders would receive care at home. This "revival" brought two main effects. First, the multiplication of for-profit care facilities – in lieu of underfunded public ones – led to a stratification of care facilities and support systems overall; the well-off enjoyed much better care than the underprivileged. And, second, shifting the responsibility for elder care back to "families" in actuality meant into the hands of middle-aged daughters and daughters-in-law, many of whom prefer gainful employment outside the home. And while other countries have sizable populations of immigrants, who can be more willing to take on low-paid work or might not have other opportunities, Japan's long-standing resistance to immigration has limited its solutions to the problem. More recently, the promotion of robots has been hailed as an answer to labor shortages, but it is only partial. In the meantime, as ever-fewer people wish to have children, and Japanese society remains comparatively resistant to other means of rejuvenating the population, elected leaders have grown increasingly desperate.

One of the more unusual regional governmental responses is the scare-and-blame tactics of Fukui prefecture. In 2005, at a time when the country was experiencing historic lows of 1.26 children per woman, Fukui's unexpected rise to 1.5 suggested it had miraculously bucked the national trends of spiraling negative fertility rates.[36] The prefectural government capitalized on Fukui's new status as a fertility stronghold. Within a year, public relations materials featured Fukui's fertility rate alongside glossy photos of tourist sites and popular local foods. Fertility became commoditized – suddenly advertised in Japanese and foreign-language brochures alike. One pamphlet in particular stated: "[d]eclining birthrates are progressing due to a drop in the number of married couples with children" because "the younger generation is delaying and even forgoing marriage." In one swoop, the prefectural government's casual conservatism nonchalantly assumes that a heteronormative married

---

Immigrants? An Ethical Challenge to Security-based Justification in Immigration Policy," *Contemporary Japan* 30, no. 1 (2018): 164–88; Takeda Hiroko, *The Political Economy of Reproduction in Japan: Between Nation-State and Everyday Life* (New York: RoutledgeCurzon, 2005); Merry Isaacs White, *Perfectly Japanese: Making Families in an Era of Upheaval* (Berkeley: University of California Press, 2002).

[36] *Fukui Josei Netto Report*, vol. 10, LadyGo Fukui, 2010, accessed June 1, 2021, www.pref .fukui.lg.jp/doc/joseikatuyaku/ladygo/f-netreport_d/fil/010.pdf; for the most current data see *Fukui Josei Netto Report*, vol. 50, LadyGo Fukui, accessed April 9, 2020, www.pref .fukui.lg.jp/doc/joseikatuyaku/ladygo/f-netreport_d/fil/050.pdf.

Why Have Babies? 67

couple is the only possible base for having children, while also blaming the young generation for not marrying at the right time – if at all.[37] Though the next example also comes from Fukui prefecture, it serves to tie together this chapter with Chapter 1. The 2010 campaign titled "From Love and Marriage to Birth and Childrearing: Supporting the Stages of Life!" distinctly reinforces the normalization of marriage and childbirth. One pamphlet portrays this ideal family as a three-generational unit in which grandparents help raise their grandchildren. (Note that, in this happy place, those same elders will *not* simultaneously require their own caretaking.) In the cover illustration, "Father" is seated in the forefront with an infant on his lap; "Mother" is in the background, slightly out of focus. Clearly, Fukui's Child and Family Health Division has decided that, from now on, fathers and grandparents will readily assume much larger roles in the domestic sphere – no doubt as the result of state-sanctioned obligatory paternity leave, bosses drastically cutting workloads, and coworkers wholeheartedly supporting male employees' yearning to take up an equal share of the household burden and "live for their families."[38] Indeed, there is paternity leave. There is even the Gender Equality Bureau Cabinet Office (Naikaku-fu Danjo Kyōdōsanka-kyoku); it advertises the "Sankyū Papa Purojekuto," which can be read both as "Thank You, Papa, Project" and as "Paternity Leave Papa Project."[39] In addition, the improvement of parental leave benefits and the expansion of childcare centers are at the top of what the Equality

---

[37] At the very time that a growing number of people embrace non-heteronormative identities, political institutions – including the national government – cling to a vision of marriage, family, and household that is obsolete for a large portion of the population. Former prime minister Abe Shinzō's *Innovation 25*, for example, envisions for Japan's future both nostalgic recreations and ethnonationalist policies. See Robertson, *Robo sapiens japanicus*.

[38] In reality, nationwide, only 11.3 percent of elderly persons live in a three-generation household – although Fukui boasts a rate of 20.2 percent, as noted in Fukui Prefecture, *Omoshirodēta*, www.pref.fukui.lg.jp/kids/statics_kiji.php?eid=00017

[39] The Japanese pronunciation of "thank you" is similar to the pronunciation of the Japanese word for "sankyū" (literally "birth leave," or also "paternity leave"); Office of Gender Equality, *The Present Status of Women and Measures: Fifth Report on the Implementation of the New National Plan of Action toward the Year 2000* (Tokyo: Office of Gender Equality, 1996); Frances McCall Rosenbluth, "The Political Economy of Low Fertility," in *The Political Economy of Japan's Low Fertility*, ed. Frances McCall Rosenbluth (Stanford, CA: Stanford University Press, 2008), 4; Gordon Mathews, "Finding and Keeping a Purpose in Life: Well-Being and *Ikigai* in Japan and Elsewhere," in *Pursuits of Happiness: Well-being in Anthropological Perspective*, ed. Gordon Mathews and Carolina Izquierdo (New York: Berghahn Books, 2009); Masahiro Yamada, "The Growing Crop of Spoiled Singles," *Japan Echo* (June 2000): 49–53; James M. Raymo, "Later Marriages or Fewer? Changes in the Marital Behavior of Japanese Women Author(s)," *Journal of Marriage and Family* 60, no. 4 (1998): 1023–34. For a regional perspective on the topic, see Emiko Ochiai and Barbara

68   Controlling Reproduction and Motherhood

Office refers to as its Plan for Raising Children in a Peaceful Environment.[40] However, though these pieces of the puzzle are important, they do not complete the picture. The fact that many women delay (or avoid completely) marriage and childbearing appears to result from three significant realities: the difficulty of balancing a career with having a family, the desire to maintain some measure of independence rather than being relegated to the home, and the reluctance of men to help with the household and childcare.[41]

Changes to the customs, norms, and rules that governed reproduction since the late nineteenth century constitute a series of revolutions: from the unclean business of midwifery to the professionalization, medicalization, policing, and institutionalization of pregnancy and birth. This chapter began with a young woman recognizing a core obstacle to her family's well-being and modest prosperity in a remote village of southern rural Japan. Her considerations governed much of modern history from the late nineteenth century to the mid-twentieth and beyond: namely, the question of how to have fewer children given the lack of effective birth-control technologies. Less than 100 years on, the opposite problem produces increasingly desperate strategies in Japan and the region at large, as well as in the Global North more broadly: how to encourage and facilitate childbirth and childrearing. Thus far, Japanese answers to this question remain fairly ineffectual.[42]

Literature and Visual Culture

Any of Higuchi Ichiyo's stories will provide insights into womanhood and motherhood around 1900; of particular note is "The Thirteenth Night" (1894).[43] Equally enthralling is Hirabayashi Taiko's "Self-Mockery"

Molony, eds., *Asia's New Mothers: Crafting Gender Roles and Childcare Networks in East and Southeast Asian Societies* (Folkestone: Global Oriental, 2008).

[40] Gender Equality Bureau Cabinet Office, 2016, accessed June 1, 2021, www.gender.go.jp/research/yoron/index.html.

[41] Iwata Masami and Ōsawa Machiko, eds., *Naze josei wa shigoto o yameru no ka* (Tokyo: Seikyūsha, 2015); Ekaterina Hertog, "'The Worst Abuse against a Child Is the Absence of the Parent': How Japanese Unwed Mothers Evaluate Their Decision to Have a Child outside Wedlock," *Japan Forum* 20, no. 2 (2008): 193–217; James M. Raymo and Akihisa Shibata, "Unemployment, Nonstandard Employment, and Fertility: Insights from Japan's 'Lost 20 Years,'" *Demography* 54, issue 6 (December 2017): 2301–29.

[42] For a critical global analysis, see Matthew Connelly, *Fatal Misconception: The Struggle to Control World Population* (Cambridge, MA: Belknap Press, 2008).

[43] Higuchi Ichiyo, *In the Shade of Spring Leaves: The Life of Higuchi Ichiyo with Nine of Her Best Stories*, trans. Robert Lyons Danly (New York: W. W. Norton, 1981), 241–52.

(1927).[44] In Enchi Fumiko's *The Waiting Years*[45] (1957), the heroine Tomo struggles with her marriage to an unfaithful husband – her powerlessness reaffirmed with each new woman who enters the picture. Kawakami Mieko's brilliant *Breasts and Eggs* (2019),[46] opens with: "If you want to know how poor somebody was growing up, ask them how many windows they had." Thus begins an often harrowing portrayal of a middle-aged single woman's quest to adopt a child.[47]

The film *The Sisters of Gion* (Mizoguchi Kenji, 1936) provides a fascinating portrayal of two sisters' efforts to stay afloat as geisha with very different approaches to life, love, and money. Togashi Shin's *Oshin* (1983) is a serialized morning television drama that follows the life of Tanokura Shin from the Meiji period to the 1980s. The series was one of Japan's most-watched series of all time and has aired in sixty-eight other countries.

---

[44] Hirabayashi Taiko, "Self-Mockery," in *To Live and To Write: Selections by Japanese Women Writers, 1913–1938*, ed. Yukiko Tanaka (Seattle, WA: Seal Press, 1987)

[45] Enchi Fumiko, *The Waiting Years*, trans. John Bester (Tokyo: Kōdansha, [1957] 1980).

[46] Mieko Kawakami, *Breasts and Eggs*, trans. Sam Bett and David Boyd (New York: Europa Editions, 2020).

[47] Amanda C. Seaman's *Writing Pregnancy in Low-Fertility Japan* (Honolulu: University of Hawai'i Press, 2017) analyzes some of the most riveting contemporary works that fictionalize the wonders, horrors, and practicalities of pregnancy and birth. The book makes an excellent read by itself, and is a superb guide to literary examples.

3 Redefining Womanhoods

Consider two texts written by a twenty-five-year-old Japanese woman by the name of Hiratsuka Raichō in September 1911. The first concerned daily life: "Because it is such an unsuitable environment for spiritual focus and the realization of dormant Genius, I loathe all the irritations that go with housework." With the second, Raichō announced the publication of *Seitō* (*Bluestockings*), Japan's first feminist, all-female-authored magazine with the lines: "In the beginning, Woman was truly the Sun. An authentic person. Now, Woman is the Moon. Living off another, reflecting another's brilliance, she is the moon whose face is sickly." For Raichō, the sun represented "overflowing brightness and warmth illuminating the entire world and nurturing all things."[1] While cantatorially powerful, identifying woman's origin with the sun must have seemed ambiguous to at least some of Raichō's educated readers. They might have associated the sun with the Shinto sun goddess Amaterasu and the fact that, according to Japanese mythology, the emperors are direct descendants of Amaterasu. Perhaps they even sensed irony in the launch of a radical feminist magazine by symbolically mobilizing the deity that was mythologized to be at the very origin of the patriarchy the author of the announcement would set out to challenge her entire life. Regardless, *Seitō* was integral to what would later be known as first-wave feminism, and Raichō (1886–1971) was one of its leaders.

This chapter examines various notions of womanhood along with self-determination and equality, and the roles women carved out for themselves since the end of the nineteenth century. This was a radical project that met with adamant resistance from men and, at certain times, from many women as well. After all, women used to be taught submission and obedience within a rigidly patriarchal order. The urtext of sexual

---

[1] Hiratsuka Raichō in *Seitō*, September 1911; see Jan Bardsley, *The Bluestockings of Japan: New Woman Essays and Fiction from Seitō, 1911–16* (Ann Arbor: Center for Japanese Studies, University of Michigan, 2007), 94–103. Hiratsuka was born Hiratsuka Haru but adopted the pen name Raichō (Thunderbird).

difference, *Greater Learning for Women* (*Onna Daigaku*, the oldest still existing version is from 1729) was authored by Kaibara Ekken (1630–1714). It justified women's subordinate status with their innate tendencies toward indocility, discontent, slander, jealousy, and silliness and trickled down into various primers written for women throughout the Tokugawa period (1603–1868). *Greater Learning for Women* was most widely read by the aristocratic and warrior classes and their modern descendants, and it was reprinted many times far into the modern period. It was not challenged much until Fukuzawa Yukichi denounced it and published his own, *New Women's Higher Learning* (*Shin Onna Daigaku*, 1899), demanding that women be given rights to develop into independent individuals in order to contribute to the advancement of Japan based on reforms in education, responsibilities and freedoms, and marriage.

The self-conscious embrace and selective adaptation of various facets of western modernity, culture, and technology at that time was followed, during the first two decades of the twentieth century, by increasingly critical attitudes toward the West and a reconsideration of "Japan," as the country had embarked on an anti-colonial colonialism. This shift, though in part fueled by World War I, was also shaped by the numerous domestic social, economic, and political issues that emerged from the processes of industrialization and urbanization. In addition, new professions such as train conductor, telephone operator, or typist shaped new classes of people, including the urban middle class. Altogether, the populace sought to cope with and address various problems that were increasingly impacted also by the changes the growth of an overseas multiethnic empire brought to society. The postwar reshuffling of the relationship between state and citizenry was again impetus to the politicization and diversification of styles of womanhood, a process that has continued ever since.

Roles and Rights

Reviewing the last 150 years reveals much courage and determination – in addition to some wrong paths taken and some reactionary moments embraced. How far have women in Japan come? Women and the roles of women were at the center of public concern from the start. The more radical ones among the progressive activists for freedom and people's rights in the 1880s demanded equal rights for men, women, and children. Talented nation and empire builders attached great value to women. They did so not in pursuit of some kind of democracy and primarily because of women's capacity to become mothers. Today, this move might strike us as "traditional." Then, it was everything but.

72 Redefining Womanhoods

In actuality, it was a radical step away from older, neo-Confucian conceptions of women as inherently untrustworthy and thus incapable of taking care of children. Womanhood, then, would be an inherently contradictory concept. And, for a long time, the very capacity to become a mother remained both the basis for as much as the main hurdle to equality. For the next century and a half changing governments and state agencies continued to negotiate women's value and rights with motherhood remaining at the center of the debate, no matter whether education, suffrage, love, marriage, or equality in the workplace were at stake. "Motherhood" would variably become a badge of honor or a hindrance to the honor of full citizenship, a matter of nature or of choice; it would lurk at every turn to further or corrupt, gild or harm the women who challenged the status quo of a rigidly gendered social order that appeared to be forever stacked against them.

The vagaries of this variability that women were subjected to was a secret to no one. In 1876, statesman Mori Arinori (1847–1889) lamented how "[throughout] Asia, women are looked down on." Striving to counter this reality, he wrote: "The position ordained for woman to occupy is one of the highest and most sacred ever created by the will of the Supreme Being ... Women are the mothers of human beings; they are the mothers of the country and nation."[2] In other speeches, he suggested that girls' education was even more important than that of boys, because young women would have to take over a household as soon as they got married, after which they would be the "natural teachers" of their future children. In short, education was to make them "good wives [and] wise mothers" (*ryōsai kenbo*).[3] Following the Sino-Japanese War of 1894–1895, Mori became Japan's first education minister, and the Japanese state adopted a *de facto* woman policy, prescribing his concept of the "good wife, wise mother" as ideal womanhood, establishing girls' high schools, and incorporating lessons on sex roles into its moral-education textbooks. Then, in around 1900, some prominent thinkers revived neo-Confucian views on women that had governed the upper echelons of feudal society and rearticulated them for the masses in the language of modern science: the "maternal instinct" – Elisabeth Badinter's great "motherhood myth" – was what justified investment in girls' formal education and what made women

---

[2] Ivan P. Hall, *Mori Arinori* (Cambridge, MA: Harvard University Press, 1973).
[3] Kathleen Uno, "Womanood, War, and Empire: Transmutations of 'Good Wife, Wise Mother' before 1931," in *Gendering Modern Japanese History*, ed. Barbara Molony and Kathleen Uno (Cambridge, MA: Harvard University Asia Center, 2005), 498.

Roles and Rights

inherently suitable as experts of raising and educating the next generation.[4]

By contrast, ethics classes in girls' high schools were unambiguous regarding the gendered values of modern visionaries. "Life as a woman" was described in three rubrics: marriage, housewife, motherhood. One representative textbook, *Girls Ethics Instructions* (*Joshi Shūshinkun*, 1935) noted that, according to the law, marriage was the "promise of one man and one woman to live together for their entire lives." Each individual had their place in this country, that "is besotted with love and drenched with sweat." In this environment, the "true and earnest Japanese woman" ought to recognize and abide by the "way of marriage," "the ethics of being a housewife," and the "sanctity of motherhood."[5] It goes without saying that girls' education was also deeply nationalistic. For instance, one-time president of Kyōto University Konishi Shigenao's pedagogical treatise, *New Basic Shōwa Pedagogy for Girls* (*Shinsei Junkyo Shōwa Joshi Kyōikugaku*, 1937), noted that "the core of our country's education is loyalty and filial piety ... no matter whether [the subject is] geography, history, drawing, or gymnastics, it is not Japanese education if divorced from loyalty."[6] These views on "life as a woman" echoed far into the twentieth century.

Some of the new women's magazines were among its vehicles, contributing to grooming girls according to the new state-sponsored ideal. Other magazines offered a wide range of perspectives for their readers to embody, adapt, and make their own. *The Woman's Magazine* (*Jogaku Zasshi*) was the first such women's magazine. Founded in 1885, it favored Christianity and promoted monogamy, equal rights for women, and marriages based on love; so as to appeal to a large readership, it offered a variety of texts written by prominent educators and promising women writers.[7] For instance, the April 11, 1891, issue offered an editorial addressed to girls' schools' principals and parents that included the curriculum. An ad for the five-year course of study at the private Meiji Girls' School highlighted how it augmented standard Japanese curriculum with daily two-hour English classes and four professional

---

[4] I am borrowing the notion from Elisabeth Badinter's *The Myth of Motherhood: An Historical View of the Maternal Instinct* (London: Souvenir Press, 1982).

[5] Shiohara Tamiji, *Joshi shūshinkun* (Kyōto: Shiohara Gakuen Kenkyūjo, 1935), 55–57.

[6] These were strong and unambiguous words from a prominent pedagogue who had been fired from his position as president of Kyōto University only five years prior because of his uncompromising stance on academic freedom in the so-called Takigawa Incident. Konishi Shigenao, *Shōwa joshi shin kyōikugaku* (Kyōto: Nagasawa Kinkōdō, 1937), 7.

[7] The magazine was founded by Iwamoto Yoshiharu and Kondō Kenzō. Iwamoto was also a cofounder of the girls' school Meiji Jogakkō and the Tokyo Women's Christian Temperance Association.

74   Redefining Womanhoods

qualifications: embroidery, sewing, stenography, and drawing.[8] Several informative articles described the then-current status of women in Germany, revealed the secrets of longevity, explained the relationship between religion and learning, appraised a prominent female pioneer of women's education, and provided the transcript of an interview with the head of an asylum, and offered a selection of poems by Leo Tolstoy. There was also a children's column, several longer pieces of literature, and more poetry. Another full page was devoted to advertisements for books. Other ads echoed a wide range of concerns, promoting books on health and home remedies for the entire family as well as the merits of owning a piano.

The Woman's Magazine was pitched to the wives and mothers of the growing urban middle class. Such designated "states[wo]men of the home" were instructed on all aspects of managing a household and raising children. One article even outlined how to allocate husbands' salaries to maintain a reasonable monthly household budget, recommending that all expenses be documented and that the nest egg be augmented. Indeed, if frugal housewives could set aside ¥2.50 every month for two years, they could afford to send their sons to prestigious private universities. This goal was compared with how less-thrifty women might spend money. With the same ¥2.50, they would buy two records, three or four train trips, ten movie tickets, or twenty-five bars of really nice soap. Anticipating readers' irritation at such frugality, the article promised that household economics would become more fun as one became better at it.[9]

Most important, *The Woman's Magazine* was one of a handful of magazines that discussed not just the big-picture goals of women's rights advocates – and the means by which to reach those goals – but also the meaning of their demands in the context of turn-of-the-century state and society formation. Advocates sought marital equality and economic independence for women. For that, it was imperative to overcome the historic denigration of women that informed norms such as "respect the male, despise the female," stress control of male sexuality through the banning of polygamy, support women's dignity and subjectivity, and further rights of social and state participation. These early women's rights advocates did not gain the political voice they wanted, but they did spread their message into the public realm of civil society.

---

[8] "Shiritsu Meiji jogakkō shinnyū seito boshū," *Jogaku Zasshi*, no. 260 (April 11, 1891): inside cover.
[9] Yamashita Iwao, "Kasei," *Jogaku Zasshi*, no. 260 (April 11, 1891): 20–21.

Early women's rights advocates such as Shimizu Toyoko (1868–1933), Kishida Toshiko (1863?–1901), and Wakamatsu Shizu (1864–1896) adopted a wise approach toward their goal. They promoted the idea that women needed to be citizens – to have the right to participate in political discourse and activities – not just as an essential human right, but also because it benefited society as a whole. Citizen wives and mothers were best equipped to educate their children to become wise citizens and to support their husbands, a large majority of whom were also excluded from political participation.[10] Ultimately, they knew that it was women's education that would lead to women's rights of personhood. Editors, publishers, and advertisers thus cultivated young women's desires and anxieties regarding marriage, entry into the workplace, social status, and life satisfaction.[11] A survey conducted by the city of Tokyo in 1924 showed that 80 percent of the females in what would soon be referred to as "white-collar" positions – nurses, office clerks, sales clerks, teachers, telephone operators, and typists – regularly bought newspapers and magazines, as did more than 40 percent of female factory workers as well.[12] Most readers of mass women's magazines shared the middle-class socioeconomic strata. But middle-class *identity* had less to do with income and family status than with educational background. In 1927, more than 300,000 girls attended a four-year women's "higher" school or "normal" school.[13] Graduating from such a school earned a young woman entry into middle-class society.

The fact that women's magazines covered employment options, training required for jobs, monthly salaries, and the prospects for employment and advancement indicate that it was assumed that these issues were increasingly relevant to women. These topics encouraged a new spin on the established concept of women's "self-cultivation" that had previously spoken to and for the patriarchal nation-state.[14] The girls' and young women's magazine *The World of Women's Learning* (*Jogaku Sekai*, 1901–1925), a top seller at 70,000–80,000 copies per issue, recognized the new burdens that modern women were taking on. In one of its caricatures, a visibly sweating woman on a bicycle is asked (in English): "Are you fond of society?" The bicycle itself was a symbol of

[10] Barbara Molony, "The Quest for Women's Rights in Turn-of-the-Century Japan," in *Gendering Modern Japanese History*, ed. Barbara Molony and Kathleen Uno (Cambridge, MA: Harvard University Asia Center, 2005), 463–92.
[11] Elyssa Faison, *Managing Women: Disciplining Labor in Modern Japan* (Berkeley: University of California Press, 2007), 107–08, 137.
[12] Maeda, *Kindai dokusha no seiritsu*, 222.
[13] *Teikoku tōkei nenpan*, cit. Maeda, *Kindai dokusha no seiritsu*, 219.
[14] Faison, *Managing Women*, 107–08, 137.

76   Redefining Womanhoods

modern, independent womanhood. And knowledge of English reflected a modern secondary education. The woman is transporting what looks like 1,000 things, including an enormous box from which dangle a pen and an ink container, a painting palette and brushes, tennis and badminton rackets, kitchen items, food containers, and a tea pot. The caption suggests that she learns household management, studies English, learns to cook and to sew, and studies music, science, and natural history. The caption notes: "her baggage is heavy and the road exceedingly long"[15] (see Figure 3.1).

In fact, many young women embraced the notion of self-cultivation so as to enhance their cultural capital, and the means by which women pursued this self-cultivation serve as an archive for how a middle class is formed.[16] That said, class distinctions strongly influenced women's capacity for emulating this new ideal since the majority of women struggled to support their families, to the extent that their children needed to work as well. Ultimately, the shiny images of middle-class nuclear families rarely reflected reality; many marriages were arranged, and many were unhappy.[17]

A 1924 poll noted that 40 percent of female factory workers also delighted in reading mass-market women's magazines.[18] And that same message of cultivating romance and marriage was pitched to such workers as well. No matter their pitiful living and working conditions, young female migrant workers in cotton mills, for instance, also dreamt about a better life, even though one amateur ethnographer documented their attitudes toward love as pragmatic, their morals as questionable, and noted that many lost their virginity through male factory workers' or supervisors' violations rather than via the kinds of romances they read about in magazines (see Figure 3.2).[19]

Indeed, Japanese female factory workers received some measure of gender management in which company programs and cultivation group

---

[15] An issue of *The World of Women's Learning* cost 20 Sen (a fifth of ¥1). "Kanojo wa kasei o manaberi," *Jogaku Sekai* 4, no. 23 (October 5, 1914), 38.

[16] Barbara Sato, "Commodifying and Engendering Morality: Self-Cultivation and the Construction of the 'Ideal Woman' in 1920s Mass Women's Magazines," in *Gendering Modern Japanese History*, ed. Barbara Molony and Kathleen Uno (Cambridge, MA: Harvard University Asia Center, 2005), 99–130.

[17] Tokuda Shūsei, *Arakure (Rough Living*, 1915), trans. Richard Torrance (Honolulu: University of Hawai'i Press, 2001), 60.

[18] Maeda, *Kindai dokusha no seiritsu*, 222.

[19] In contrast to early folklorists and ethnographers Gonda Yasunosuke, Kon Wajirō, and Yanagita Kunio, Hosoi Wakizō (1897–1925) was a trade union activist who died young, at the age of twenty-nine, during the same year his book was first published; see *Jokō aishi* (Tokyo: Kaizōsha, [1925] 1996), 329–42, available via the National Diet Library at https://dl.ndl.go.jp/info:ndljp/pid/1021433.

Roles and Rights

Figure 3.1 A caricature of a new woman's woes *The World of Women's Learning* (*Jogaku Sekai*, 1901–1925), titled "Are you fond of society?" Private collection.

78 Redefining Womanhoods

Figure 3.2 At the beginning of the twentieth century, the majority of women in Japan proper and throughout the empire had no choice but to carry on working as farmers or fishers, often with babies on their backs and children in tow. Photograph of two women with their children fishing (1919). Printed with the kind permission of the Library of Congress.

activities taught them the proper modes of feminine virtue. Many elements of paternalist policies adopted to this end emphasized women's role as future wives and mothers; offered educational opportunities in the domestic arts, home economics, and etiquette; and promised to protect young women's chastity through careful monitoring of their whereabouts and behavior as if they were eligible for social mobility into a middle-class household where they would be exclusively charged with being a good wife and wise mother.[20]

New Women, Modern Girls

This was the world that *Bluestockings* cofounder Hiratsuka Raichō would mold. She and other feminists sought control of their own sense of selves as women and strove to embody and breathe life into a new concept of womanhood, that of "new women" (*atarashii onna*). Such new women would be characterized by autonomous personhood, a belief in the freedom of love, and the pursuit of a distinctive women's culture. Some of the young new women became fierce political activists, like Fukuda Hideko (1865–1927) and Itō Noe (1895–1923). Others were well-known writers and poets, like Yosano Akiko (1878–1942) and Raichō. Some in their circle had even lived miniature revolutions of their own, such as Yamada Waka (1879–1957), who escaped rural poverty and trafficking as a sex slave to later write a consultation column for women in the *Tōkyō Asahi Shinbun* newspaper and serve on a semigovernmental committee during the Asia-Pacific War (see Figure 3.3). These feminists and others heatedly debated women's roles in Japanese society within the pages of *Bluestockings*. In so doing, they made the "woman question" a controversial, much-discussed topic beginning in the 1910s far beyond its pages.[21]

In contrast to similar discussions at the end of the nineteenth century, these debates were mainly carried by women who shared an interest in a diverse set of problems, including questions of love, motherhood, sexual freedom, birth control, and women's suffrage. Their views ranged from those of conservative feminists like Yamada Waka, who promoted the valorization of motherhood so as to improve the status of women; to

---

[20] Faison, *Managing Women*, 107–08, 137.

[21] Indeed, by the time *Seitō* folded in February 1916, it had been banned three times, excluded from girls' schools across the nation, and denounced by prominent educators and other public figures. Jan Bardsley, "*Seitō* and the Resurgence of Writing by Women," in *The Columbia Companion to Modern East Asian Literature*, ed. Joshua S. Mostow, Kirk A. Denton, Bruce Fulton, and Sharalyn Orbaugh (New York: Columbia University Press, 2003), 93–98.

Figure 3.3 On December 7, 1937, Yamada Waka was received by Eleanor Roosevelt to deliver a message of peace from the women of Japan. Apparently, Waka told the first lady that the women of Japan and China did not hate each other but, instead, wanted to work together to end the ongoing conflict. Printed with the kind permission of the Library of Congress.

New Women, Modern Girls   81

more radical feminists like Yamakawa Kikue (1890–1980), Yosano
Akiko, and Harada Satsuki, who insisted on women's right to manage
their own family planning without any intrusion by the state. For all their
differences, however, they knew that, for many women, sexuality was
more a domain of restriction, repression, and danger than a domain of
exploration, pleasure, and agency.

When these feminists proudly adopted the label "new women" they
embodied introspective, rigorously honest women who defined their own
ethical code. They wrote strongly worded articles that demanded political rights, questioned the importance of chastity, explored the meaning
of abortion and motherhood, and debated the politics of prostitution.
They took themselves seriously as intellectuals and writers and as women
with desires and aspirations. They also became known for their unconventional love lives, including divorces, multiple marriages, children with
different fathers, and affairs with married men and other women.[22] They
fought in myriad ways to redefine the roles that had been designed for
them by two generations of modern men, their efforts frequently frustrated by significant economic obstacles.

In the public sphere of early-twentieth-century Japan, the "new woman"
competed with the "modern girl" or "*moga*," who was associated not with
rights and equality but with the rise of mass consumer culture. Yet a rigid
distinction between one and the other defies sociocultural realities at the time
when a "new woman" was just as easily accused of being a "modern girl."

Globally, *moga* were inspired by gendered consumer culture and conspicuous consumption, but young women also embraced the new woman
habitus for their defiance against patriarchal control over women's bodies
and sexuality, their cosmopolitical urban taste, and the new sense of
femininity they represented.[23] In Tokyo and other large cities, western
fashions informed young women's choices of both apparel and pastimes,
including clothing, short hair, social dancing, and strolling and window
shopping in the streets of urban Japan. Tokyo's modern girls brokered
styles for young women in the periphery – be it remote, poor, and agrarian
Okinawa, the long-term colonies of Taiwan and Korea, or other cities
elsewhere in the Japanese empire and Asia at large – "Japanization" was *de
rigueur*. Take, for instance, the ambivalent mélange characteristic of colonial modernity in Okinawa. Upper-class families in particular saw value for

---

[22] Bardsley, *The Bluestockings of Japan*, 1–21.
[23] Ruri Ito, "The 'Modern Girl' Question in the Periphery of Empire: Colonial Modernity
and Mobility among Okinawan Women in the 1920s and 1930s," in *The Modern Girl
around the World: Consumption, Modernity, and Globalization*, ed. Alys Eve Weinbaum
et al. (Durham, NC: Duke University Press, 2008), 240–62.

82   Redefining Womanhoods

their daughters in the "moral cultivation" that trained them for their roles as desirably comfortable future housewives – such as flower arranging, Japanese traditional music, and sewing. Prior to 1885, most girls had been illiterate; even upper-class girls had been trained to work as artisans (or to otherwise practice commerce) so as to contribute to the household economy. At the same time, educated wives became desirable for men with aspirations of social mobility. Girls themselves recognized that secondary schooling, particularly when done in the mainland, could be a "means of self-fulfillment, an escape from the shackles of patriarchal authority, and an adventure in the 'outer world.'" They also saw in *moga* styles and hobbies – cinema, social dances, or tennis – expressions of defiance against patriarchal control over their bodies.[24]

In theory, promoters of the new woman spoke for those of their sex throughout mainland Japan and its colonies. But, of course, women in a position to contemplate redefining themselves and pursuing individual agency were in the minority. Women outside the metropolitan sphere did not often encounter the more daring of their gender. Far more women worked, in factories and agriculture for example, and had little room for modern thinking. After years of war, intimidation, and political machinations, Japan annexed Korea in 1910. Thereafter, various theories about common ancestry and the presumed sameness of Japanese and Koreans took root. But Koreans living and working in the Japanese inner lands rarely experienced sameness, whether in their relations with fellow workers, their treatment by companies and labor unions, or the cultural, social, and economic support available to them. This was also true for women from Okinawa, which had been annexed by Japan in 1872 after having been a semi-independent kingdom of the Ryūkyūs under the influence of both China and Japan. Regarding both Koreans and Okinawans, differences in language and custom proved much more salient to employers and co-workers than did the various discourses of assimilation and inclusion, some universal ideal of womanhood or even the ever-intensifying rhetoric about everybody being the Japanese emperors' children. Workers organized based on ethnic difference. Korean and Okinawan ethnicity in the factory context erased gender altogether.[25] Half of Japan's textile factory workers were women, including individuals from the colonies. A much larger number was employed in agriculture, namely 6.3 million or 45 percent in 1920, and 7.1 million or 53 percent in 1940.[26]

By and large, prominent feminists had few words for or about colonized fellow females. Whether this is because they became actively or passively

---

[24] Ito, "The 'Modern Girl' Question in the Periphery of Empire," 257.
[25] Faison, *Managing Women*, 107–08, 137.   [26] Faison, *Managing Women*, 140, 142.

New Women, Modern Girls   83

aligned with imperialist ideology by virtue of their class affiliation, or shared a provincialism characteristic of many intellectuals in the metropole, is not entirely clear. Despite Raichō's extensive authorship, including two auto-biographies written at different times in her life, she did not speak out against Japan's imperialism or the war until after it had ended. Though she had adamantly opposed the emperor-centered, patriarchal nation-state early in her life, she spent the war years in the countryside growing vege-tables and working on a novel. One sympathetic biographer saw in that "an act of passive noncooperation."[27] Indeed, many Japanese intellectuals had done the same. On several occasions, however, Raichō's words reveal an even more ambiguous perspective on the emperor and Japan's aggression. In 1936, for instance, she wrote in an article in the national newspaper *Yomiuri Shinbun*, at the time of a failed military coup: "I feel more strongly than ever my good fortune in having been born in a nation presided over by an emperor who is a living god and with whom his myriad subjects can immediately be at one ... In submission to the Imperial Will ... women, too, fervently hope to do their best."[28]

Yosano Akiko is another case in point. In the September 1904 issue of the literary magazine *Myōjō*, she published the forty-line poem, "Brother, Do Not Give Your Life" (*Kimi shinitamō koto nakare*) after she had sent it with a letter as an impassioned plea to her younger brother Chūzaburō, then serving with the Imperial Army in the Russo-Japanese War at Port Arthur. Courageously critical of the Russo-Japanese War, the poem still moves many readers to tears. The first few lines read as follows:

> Oh, my brother, I weep for you.
> Do not give your life.
> Last-born among us,
> You are the most beloved of our parents.
> Did they make you grasp the sword?
> And teach you to kill?
> Did they raise you to the age of twenty-four?
> Telling you to kill and die?[29]

Two and a half decades later, in 1928, the South Manchurian Railway Company had become the Japanese empire's chief instrument for the economic exploitation of Manchuria. When the company funded an

---

[27] Teruko Craig, "Translator's Afterword," in Hiratsuka Raichō, *In the Beginning Woman Was the Sun: The Autobiography of a Japanese Feminist*, trans. with an introduction and notes Teruko Craig (New York: Columbia University Press, 1992), 311.

[28] Craig, "Translator's Afterword," 330.

[29] For the complete poem and a critical reading, see Steve Rabson, "Yosano Akiko on War: To Give One's Life or Not – A Question of Which War," *Journal of the Association of Teachers of Japanese* 25, no. 1 (April 1991): 45–74.

84   Redefining Womanhoods

extensive trip for Yosano and her husband to China, Manchuria, and Mongolia, she voiced no objections to the Japanese imperialism that had secured for them both the setting and the conveyance. Indeed, even her unpublished notes from that trip indicate no discomfort. Much like for other prominent female (and male) contemporaries, in Yosano's account "Japan appears to remain the only reality that has meaning for her and enables her to gain peace and serenity or overcome loneliness." China, Manchuria, Mongolia are only there in her account "to be seen, but only rarely interacted with [...] the object of an outside gaze."[30]

Equally astonishing is Ishimoto Shizue's lifelong silence on her war-time perspective on Japanese imperialism (see Chapter 2). Ishimoto (1897–2001) is rightly remembered for her persistent trans-war efforts on behalf of the legalization of safe and legal birth control methods. Like Yosano, she traveled to Korea and China – albeit in 1922. In her travel-ogue, she acknowledges the sacrifice of her own countrymen's lives on behalf of expanding the empire. She also sympathizes with the poor working women of Korea in particular, who "were put under more fetters and lived a more depressing life of wasteful patience." But otherwise, her notes about Koreans and Chinese mention only their lack of vitality and hygiene.[31] She translated into English Hino Ashihei's *Wheat and Soldiers* (*Mugi to Heitai*) and *Soil and Soldiers* (*Tsuchi to Heitai*), two short books about ordinary Japanese soldiers' everyday experiences at the front. When she sent copies of her translations, published by Farrar and Rinehart in New York, to her friends in America, her accompanying note included "a prayer for the new civilization that is coming to the Orient" – an obvious reference to the Japanese imperialist regime taking hold of Asia.[32] Sadly, the freedoms these heroines of radical political change envisioned for some did not extend to the various peoples of the multi-ethnic empire they inhabited.

Suffrage and Pacifism

On August 15, 1945, Emperor Hirohito announced Japan's World War II defeat in a four-and-a-half-minute radio speech. On November 3, 1946, he announced Japan's new constitution, which forbade Japan to

[30] Yosano Akiko, *Travels in Manchuria and Mongolia*, trans. Joshua Fogel (New York: Columbia University Press, 2001).

[31] Baroness Ishimoto Shidzué, *Facing Two Ways: The Story of My Life*, with an introduction and afterword by Barbara Molony (Stanford, CA: Stanford University Press, [1935] 1984), 213–19.

[32] Ishimoto Shidzue, "Translator's Foreword," in *Wheat and Soldiers*, trans. Ishimoto Shidzue (New York: Farrar & Rinehart, 1939), ix–xii.

wage war and introduced women's right to vote. The significance of both cannot be overestimated. Raichō was ambivalent about the latter. She admitted that, thinking "back to the twenty-odd-year efforts of feminists that underlay this turn of events," she "could not bring [herself] to accept the gift with good grace and unmitigated joy" when, suddenly, "along with the *humiliation of defeat* [my emphasis] the right to vote was to be handed to women on a platter, through no efforts of their own. How ironic!"[33] The Conscription Decree of 1872 had tied three generations of men to the nation-state and its pursuit of mass violence and empire (see Chapter 1). The constitution of 1946 was the platform on which the realization of women's suffrage coincided with the constitutional commitment to state pacifism. For generations to come, political women embraced both.

Among the many momentous freedoms this constitution guaranteed, Article 24 secured equality with regard to marriage and property, providing respite from the wartime view equating womanhood with multiple motherhood and self-sacrifice (see Chapter 2).[34] The previous focus on marrying young to start large families thus gave way to preoccupations on how to choose the right spouse and build a happy marriage – concerns that a new wave of publications were all too glad to promote. A particularly notable trend in mass magazines concerned women's bodies and sexual desires, as could be seen from the literature-laden *Romance* (*Romansu*) to the more explicit *Married Sex Life* (*Fūfu no Seiseikatsu*). Readers of a 1954 issue of *Married Life* (*Fūfu Seikatsu*) learned, for instance, that "99 percent of husbands [knew] nothing about their wives' sensual spot," about which they were offered extensive insights on the "clitoris technique."[35] Along with such revelations came "teaching guides" on "newly married couples' sexual intercourse" or "healthy married love."[36] The message was clear: women's new freedom from arranged marriages meant men needed to demonstrate *particular* skills as being among their assets. Indeed, they ventured to suggest that

---

[33] Hiratsuka Raichō, *Watakushi no aruita michi* (Tokyo: Shinhyōron-sha, 1955), 268–69; see also Craig, "Translator's Afterword," 330.

[34] Article 24 can be found on the government webpage "The Constitution of Japan," Prime Minister of Japan and His Cabinet, accessed March 16, 2021, https://japan.kantei.go.jp/constitution_and_government_of_japan/constitution_e.html.

[35] Such was advertised on the cover of *Fūfu Seikatsu* 12 (1954) and occupied more than twenty pages of the magazine. Importantly, a note on the cover announced that the magazine was not to be sold to minors.

[36] Like numerous other such magazines, the August 5, 1949, issue of *Fūfu no Seiseikatsu* contained a "Teaching Manual on Couples' Healthy Sexual Love" that was mixed in with erotic stories from around the world, advice on and ads for contraceptives, and a range of other texts and illustrations that were designed to both educate and entice.

86   Redefining Womanhoods

the stability of marriage no longer rested on wives' subservience; it now depended on their (sexual) happiness.

Science and fiction from around the world rose to the challenge. Consider just two of many examples: a 1953 supplement of the magazine *Style (Sutairu)* – its cover a pastiche of enticing stills from the 1942 film *Arabian Nights* – offered multiple "ways of recognizing one's partner in matrimony," including the Chinese Zodiac, references to Scheherazade, handline reading and handwriting, and guides on assessing body and body-part shapes and types.[37] But note that, though exoticizing references to far-away places were in part remnants of romanticized empire-building, these magazines' fantasy-building led their readership to anywhere but the former empire.[38] The pages of the April 1949 issue of *Sunflower (Himawari)* were graced with flowers of the Alps and Paris but particularly India. In general, South Asia, mostly uncompromised as it was by Japanese imperialism, conveniently lent itself to Orientalism and was often featured in postwar Japanese mass and popular culture.

This is not to say that serious topics weren't covered as well. That same issue of *Himawari* also reported on the September 21, 1948, UN meeting in Paris, where Eleanor Roosevelt in a speech at the Sorbonne posited that worldwide human rights would be the basis for peace. One article celebrated the accomplishments of Tsuda Umeko (1864–1929), prominent educator and founder of Tsuda College. Another piece, curiously titled "The Beautiful Words of a Working Girl" even though written by a man, offered reflections on young women and gainful employment, ultimately suggesting that boredom due to tedious work tasks gives way to perseverance and patience.[39] Such sentiments were aimed at the numerous young women now holding positions as post office clerks, telephone operators, secretaries, and street-car conductors.

Returning to the topic of new beginnings, more politically engaged women set out to purge motherhood of its wartime militarist stains by tying their capacity to become mothers to pacifism. Hiratsuka Raichō, as vice president of the Women's International Democratic Federation founded in Paris in 1945, was instrumental in forming the World Congress of Mothers that eventually brought together women from more

---

[37] "Unsei handan: Zenkyūhyaku gojūsan-nen no kekkon no aite o shiru hō," *Sutairu* 1953.

[38] Published and (mostly) illustrated by graphic artist and fashion designer Nakahara Junichi (1913–1988), *Himawari* was a monthly magazine that ran for only five years, from 1947 to 1952, with a total of sixty-seven issues. It was devoted to fashion, beauty, and dreams – such as making a doll's dress from a pattern, or following the recipes for elegant treats to be served at a beginning of school party – at a time when dreaming was possible again.

[39] Kotani Tsunao, "Shigoto ni mukau taido," *Himawari* 30 (March 1949): 28–29.

than sixty countries. Initially, the Japanese arm of this organization, the Japan Mothers' Congress (Nihon Hahaoya Taikai), included a diverse set of women from middle-class housewives to childless, unemployed, and impoverished women – even survivors of the atomic bombs.[40] Within private settings, they discussed the many ways war had brought on childhood poverty, malnutrition, unemployment, child suicide, and the prostitution of young girls. In public discourse, they reclaimed and defined their own identities while also recasting motherhood into a pacifist political force – deployed not by the state but by women themselves – with the aim to build and maintain the peace that the whole world needed.[41] In April 1953, Raichō founded the Japan Federation of Women's Organizations (Nihon Fujin Dantai Rengōkai or FUDANREN). From its inception, the Federation called for the removal of American military bases in Japan and opposed the manufacture and use of nuclear weapons. It has since continued to promote feminist causes always in conjunction with pacifism and antimilitarism. When Raichō gathered with friends to celebrate the fiftieth anniversary of *Seitō* and commemorate deceased members in October 1961, *Seitō* had become synonymous with the early women's movement, and Raichō a feminist icon well before her death in 1971.[42]

Women's Liberation: *Ūman Ribu*

The next generation ushered in dramatically more radical times while recognizing the continued centrality of the twin governance of sexuality (particularly the liberation of women's sexuality) and state mass violence (particularly regaining control of the means of warmaking) to Japan's democracy. The 1960 renewal of the US–Japan Mutual Cooperation and Security Treaty was first signed as a precondition to formally end the occupation of Japan in 1952. The renewal included a status-of-forces agreement in Article 6 that would allow the stationing of US military on Japanese territory. To this, millions of Japanese demonstrated their collective protest. The radical right saw the treaty as continued

---

[40] Vera C. Mackie, "From Hiroshima to Lausanne: The World Congress of Mothers and the Hahaoya Taikai in the 1950s," *Women's History Review* 25, no. 4 (2016): 671–95.

[41] Hillary Maxson, "From 'Motherhood in the Interest of the State' to Motherhood in the Interest of Mothers: Rethinking the First Mothers' Congress," in *Rethinking Japanese Feminism*, Julia C. Bullock, Ayako Kano, and James Welker (Honolulu: University of Hawai'i Press, 2018), 39–40.

[42] Until the end of her life, Raichō continued pacifist activities, marching against nuclear weapons, the US–Japan Security Treaty, US military installations in Japan, and the Vietnam War; Craig, "Translator's Afterword," 315.

88   Redefining Womanhoods

subservience to US security interests, while the radical left saw a resurgence of Japanese imperialism.[43] Indeed, a focus on state violence and anti-imperialism characterized the protest movement throughout the 1960s. A range of new left groups emerged from it – among them the women's liberation movement (*ūman ribu*).

Deliberately decentralized and anti-hierarchical, the women's liberation movement rejected established forms of authority. Of primary concern: the state and anti-state violence that had ultimately ended many women's lives, not improved them. The movement also broke from the sexism and the internal sexist division of labor favored by the masculinist definition of revolution. Instead, these women chose to reconceive and rearticulate legitimate sites of politics, beginning with the concepts of everydayness, localism, and authentic encounters with others.[44] The women's liberation movement's first public rally took place on October 21, 1970, International Anti-War Day. The movement's most widely circulating journal, *Women's Eros* (*Onna Erosu*), ran from 1973 until 1982. Within the atmosphere of liberation many women embraced new professional opportunities. In Japan's metropole and urban centers, during the high-growth period of the 1970s, state agencies and corporations primarily saw the public relations potential – particularly when targeting an international audience – of showcasing women who served in previously male-dominated professions. For instance, the English-language periodical *Japan* showcased Japanese advancements in technology, industry, and culture. Published by the Ministry of Foreign Affairs in collaboration with the *Mainichi Newspaper*, the glossy magazine featured women in stylish ads for kimonos, sewing machines, and food items. Female professionals also began to appear in photographs of the Tokyo Money Market, electronic data-processing centers, and other sites of 1970s market capitalism. One issue from 1973 includes a full-page photograph of the Tokyo policewomen drum corps; the associated article was titled "Lady Police: Popular Asset to the Metropolitan Force" (see Figure 3.4).

The article's message is – characteristically for mainstream media at the time – wrapped in the breezy tone of innovation that, at the same time, sexualizes and infantilizes the women it describes. The article praises the "feminine touch" that the "lady cops" lend to the police boxes previously populated by only police*men*. It highlights the attention to

---

[43] Nick Kapur, *Japan at the Crossroads: Conflict and Compromise after Anpo* (Cambridge, MA: Harvard University Press, 2018).

[44] Setsu Shigematsu, *Scream from the Shadows: The Women's Liberation Movement in Japan* (Minneapolis: University of Minnesota Press, 2012), 45, 61–62.

Women's Liberation: *Ūman Ribu*

Figure 3.4 The November 1973 cover of *Japan*, a glossy photo magazine published in Tokyo, featured the police women's drum corps. Printed with the kind permission of the Mainichi Shimbun

90   Redefining Womanhoods

detail these "girls" offer on emergency calls, while also noting that, despite original doubts about whether "female officers' voices would instill confidence in citizen callers," they in fact "carry better" on the phone. One can almost hear the relief with which the article's tone suggests that, under normal circumstances, women were not a force to be reckoned with, by fellow male policemen or by criminals. This was in part because about half of them, "being women after all," left the force "due to marriage or childbirth after serving five or six years." When not rendered endearing, however, female professionals were apparently experienced as threat to male dominance. An exceptional Tajima Kazuko is described as someone with "seventeen years of service" and as "most feared by pickpockets on trains."[45]

While some blue-collar women participated in the women's liberation movement, many more were too busy struggling in the rapidly transforming labor market. Consider the longshore workers of Kanmonkō Port near Fukuoka in Kyūshū. By the 1970s, four generations of women had worked there, loading and unloading cargo alongside men. But with increased mechanization and the energy crisis of 1973, the women were the first to lose their jobs.[46] These women were proud of their abilities of doing physically demanding labor while also taking care of their families. They found it difficult to be pregnant while doing their work, and considered themselves lucky that nightwork was already prohibited then because otherwise they could not have kept working while pregnant. In winter, they worked through freezing temperatures and with frostbite on their feet, often thinking about quitting but unable to afford to do so.[47] To them, the middle-class housewife and stay-at-home mother notion of womanhood that the women's liberation movement so forcefully aimed to overcome and that conservative parties continued to promote, remained a distant ideal (see Figure 3.5).

Mainstreaming Feminism and Backlash

Operating within a heterogeneous terrain, the women's liberation movement quietened down in the mid-1970s. Even speech itself quietened, as

---

[45] "Lady Police: Popular Asset to the Metropolitan Force," *Japan* 11, no. 2 (1973): 9.

[46] Hayashi Eidai (1933–2017) was a journalist and local historian who conducted oral histories of forced labor during Japan's empire. The current volume compiled photographs taken between 1975 and 1983 of the longshore(wo)men who worked alongside men loading and unloading cargo in Fukuoka prefecture, Northern Kyūshū.

[47] Hayashi Eidai, *Shashin kiroku: Kanmonkō no onnaokinakashi-tachi* (Tokyo: Shinhyōron-sha, 2018), 73. See also Kaori Shoji, "Historical Truths Can Take Decades to Unearth," *Japan Times*, February 15, 2017, accessed June 1, 2021, www.japantimes.co.jp/culture/2017/02/15/films/historical-truths-can-take-decades-unearth/ and the Aragai website, accessed June 1, 2021, http://aragai-info.net/.

Figure 3.5 In 1968, the conservative Liberal Democratic Party (Jiyū Minken-tō) paired its generic campaign slogan, "Your vote will improve Japan," with a photograph of a cheerful mother and a toddler-aged boy. Printed with the kind permission of the Library of Congress

92   Redefining Womanhoods

oppositional consciousness gave way to a new politically neutral tone of public discourse. From this a new academic feminism, which largely adopted Eurocentric paradigms of feminist knowledge production, emerged in dozens of women's groups working with the government to implement various education and labor reforms. Determined to solidify reforms on a grander scale, the United Nations named 1975 International Women's Year; indeed, the next ten years were considered the UN Decade for Women, during which time the UN "focused on the policies and issues that impact women, such as pay equity, gendered violence, land holding, and other human rights." As for the distinctly academic side of this evolution, universities established women's studies programs and courses.[48] Altogether, this new generation dissociated itself from the earlier movement, instead promoting a politically neutral, objective, inclusive scholarly project. Representatives of this academic feminism – ranging from sociologist Ueno Chizuko (1948–) to economist Osawa Mari (1953–) and their protégés – have dominated public debates ever since. Subsequently, the step-by-step mainstreaming of feminism has furthered, though not finalized, gender equality. The meanings and exact manifestations of such remain contested on the national, regional, and local levels, and, admittedly, these reforms were conceptualized within a mostly heteronormative binary framework. Nonetheless, in Japan, the next decades would witness passage of the Convention on the Elimination of All Forms of Discrimination against Women in 1985, the Equal Employment Opportunity Law in 1986, and the Basic Law for a Gender Equal Society in 1999.[49] In 1994, Ōsawa Mari – until a few years prior the only female sociologist at the Institute of Social Science of the University of Tokyo – called for a "gender revolution" in Japan's social sciences. In 1996, the government-sponsored Council for Gender Equality announced that this century was "significant in that equality between men and women has become accepted as a universal value" and claimed that "in Japan the construction of the social framework has taken place to materialize that concept for the first time in human history."[50]

The normative expectation that Japanese women will quit their jobs once they enter the reproduction phase of their lives still strongly influences women's life choices. (See also Chapter 2.) New media-generated

---

[48] Shigematsu, *Scream from the Shadows*, 172–75.
[49] Yamaguchi, "'Gender Free' Feminism in Japan."
[50] See "Council for Gender Equality," Prime Minister of Japan and His Cabinet, November 11, 2020, accessed March 17, 2021, https://japan.kantei.go.jp/99_suga/actions/202011/_00019.html.

Mainstreaming Feminism and Backlash · 93

buzzwords capriciously promote or disparage women for how they approach professional aspirations, marriage, and children. In many ways, it would seem that women will (continue to) be derided no matter which route they take. In the wake of the 1986 Equal Employment Opportunity Law, the "flying woman" (*tonderu onna*) or "career woman" was first hailed as the antithesis of the "full-time housewife" (*sengyō shufu*) and as a sign of a newly achieved equality in the workplace. But all too soon this life path was dismissed as being egocentric and selfish, nothing but the prioritization of career at the expense of marriage and childrearing. Similarly, for most of the postwar era, the "education mother" (*kyōiku mama*) signified a woman whose every breathing moment was diligently invested in her children. But in the 1980s, mass media decided to scold these women for imposing their own "frustrated ambitions" on their children, and in extreme cases for even "managing" their blossoming sexuality.[51] The expression "parasite singles" (*parasaito shinguru*), coined in 1999 and reminiscent of the early-twentieth-century "modern girl," specifically criticized young women who not only remained unmarried but also continued to live with their parents, despite having incomes. In 2003, the term "loser dogs" (*makeinu*) mocked unmarried, childless women without means. And behind the 2004 term "demon hags" (*onibaba*) stood its creator's call to prevent the existence of such women in the first place. This could only be accomplished by women "confronting the reality of their own bodies," by which one author means to suggest that female bodies were fundamentally designed for heterosexual intercourse and childbirth without which they "cannot release [their] energy and thus will become hysterical demon hags."[52]

Perhaps such recurring misogynist rhetoric was in part informed by increasing anxiety in conservative quarters of Japanese media and society over the fact that ever larger numbers of Japanese women had stopped listening to them. The trajectories of marriage rates, birth rates, and employment rates suggest as much. With regard to marriage rates alone: in 1970, of Japanese men and women between the ages of thirty-four and thirty-nine, about 90 percent were married; by 2015, that figure had

---

[51] Anne Allison, *Permitted and Prohibited Desires: Mothers, Comics, and Censorship in Japan* (Berkeley: University of California Press, 2000).

[52] Tomomi Yamaguchi, "'Loser Dogs' and 'Demon Hags': Single Women in Japan and the Declining Birth Rate," *Social Science Japan Journal* 9, no. 1 (2006): 109–14; see also Annette Schad-Seifert, "Makeinu und arafō – Die discursive Production von weiblichen Verlierer- und Gewinner-Images im aktuellen japanischen Fernsehdrama," in *Frauenbilder – Frauenkörper: Inszenierungen des Weiblichen in den Gesellschaften Süd- und Ostasiens*, ed. Stephan Köhn and Heike Moser (Wiesbaden: Otto Harrassowitz, 2013), 417–36; Yamaguchi, "'Gender Free' Feminism in Japan."

94   Redefining Womanhoods

fallen to 64 percent for men and 71 percent for women.[53] Oddly, though it still takes two to form a marriage, responsibility for the reduced marriage trend is usually placed at the feet of women. And though it is true that it is typically male *journalists* who coin misogynist language, much of the negative rhetoric aligns with the conservative sector's concerns about the low birth rate and the associated threat to "family values." Neither accusations nor threats solve key issues, such as the lack of childcare facilities, extended maternity leave, tax rules that suppress women's earnings, and a pension system that discourages earning.[54]

Flash forward to the triple disaster of March 11, 2011, when northern Japan was hit by a devastating earthquake, tsunami, and nuclear accident. The subsequent "disaster nationalism" was paired with the partial revival of the cultural hegemony of the mother and housewife that had been, as Ofra Goldstein-Gidoni phrases it, "practically synonymous with womanhood."[55] It was as though only the nurturing female could comfort stricken Japan, and so she was beckoned from every corner.

Eventually, popular culture found a way to recast women's standard feminine roles as if they were new. Consider images of homebound women cast as happy, cute, and romantic "charisma housewives." Such imagery suggested that marriage, far from being a gateway to a life of constraint, can actually be a means for continued self-actualization and fun. Says Kurihara Harumi, a "celebrity homemaker" who has made it her lucrative business to market the charisma housewife: "When I tighten an apron, I feel that I am ready to work. I would like to enjoy cooking and housework, dressed fashionably. A nice apron does something to create an opportunity to enjoy daily life.[56] And, while Kurihara's success is mostly domestic in both senses of the word, the younger Marie Kondo has projected the same cheerfully suffocating spirit to the rest of the globe with books and, most recently, a Netflix show.[57]

---

[53] "World Marriage Data 2019," United Nations, Department of Economic and Social Affairs, accessed June 1, 2921, https://population.un.org/MarriageData/index.html#/maritalStatusData. (Note, the chart will likely load data for Afghanistan; close the "Afghanistan" button to select "Japan" for its data.)

[54] Yamaguchi, "'Loser Dogs' and 'Demon Hags,'" 113; Tomomi Yamaguchi, "Japanese Women and Work: Holding Back Half the Nation," *The Economist* 29 (March 2014).

[55] Ofra Goldstein-Gidoni, "Consuming Domesticity in Post-Bubble Japan," in *Consuming Life in Post-Bubble Japan: A Transdisciplinary Perspective*, ed. Katarzyna J. Cwiertka and Ewa Machotka (Amsterdam: Amsterdam University Press, 2018), 107–27.

[56] Kurihara Harumi, "Consuming Domesticity in Post-Bubble Japan," in *Consuming Life in Post-Bubble Japan: A Transdisciplinary Perspective*, ed. Katarzyna J. Cwiertka and Ewa Machotka (Amsterdam: Amsterdam University Press, 2018), 121.

[57] Marie Kondo's website is called KonMari; accessed May 27, 2021, https://konmari.com.

But though cute and sweet appeals to some, many young women continue to associate the normative role of housewife and mother with a loss of autonomy, individuality, and self-realization – especially given how many other kinds of enticing opportunities are within reach.[58] Today, Japanese women's labor force participation rate – 74 percent among those aged twenty-five to sixty-four – equates with figures in most other postindustrial economies of the Global North. While of course these findings represent significant improvement and promise for Japan's women of the twenty-first century, the facts are not all optimistic. A much larger share of women than men work in temporary employment, constituting 65.5 percent of part-time employment, which is often insecure, non-career, and low-paid.[59] In this respect, women in Japan are much more like women from the Republic of Korea (63 percent), Norway (66 percent), and Israel (68 percent) than women in France (73 percent), Spain and the United Kingdom (74 percent), and Germany, Switzerland and Austria (77 percent, 78 percent, and 79 percent).[60]

In May 2018, the Japanese Diet passed a nonbinding act initiated by a female citizen's group that urges political parties to field equal numbers of female and male candidates. At the time, Japan ranked 165th out of the 193 countries in the *Women in Parliament* report, published annually by the Inter-Parliamentary Union in time for International Women's Day on March 8. Whereas the proportion of female members in national parliaments around the globe has increased from 11.3 percent in 1995 to 24.3 percent in January 2019, Japan still remains below the 1995 level – only 10.2 percent of Japanese House of Representatives lawmakers are female.[61] In many ways, the corporate world mirrors the gender order in politics. In Japan, only 5.2 percent of board seats are held

---

[58] Schad-Seifert, "Makeinu und arafō," 418–19; Yamaguchi, "'Loser Dogs' and 'Demon Hags.'"

[59] Government of Japan, "Women's Empowerment," Cabinet Public Relations Office, Cabinet Secretariat, JapanGov, accessed March 17, 2021, www.japan.go.jp/diversity/women/index.html.

[60] OECD iLibrary, "OECD Labour Force Statistics," Organisation for Economic Co-operation and Development, accessed March 17, 2021, https://doi.org/10.1787/23083387. See also Our World in Data, "Representation of Women in Low-Paying Jobs," Global Change Data Lab, accessed March 17, 2021, https://ourworldindata.org/economic-inequality-by-gender#representation-of-women-in-low-paying-jobs; Glenda S. Roberts, "Leaning Out for the Long Span: What Holds Women Back from Promotion in Japan." *Japan Forum* 32, no. 4 (2020): 555–76.

[61] "Gender Imbalance: Japan's Political Representation by Women Lowest in G20," *Nippon.com*, March 8, 2019, Nippon Communications Foundation, accessed September 28, 2020, www.nippon.com/en/japan-data/h00409/gender-imbalance-japan%E2%80%99s-political-representation-by-women-lowest-in-g20.html.

96   Redefining Womanhoods

by women, compared to 41 percent in Norway, 37.2 percent in France, 26.2 percent in Germany, 19.7 percent in Austria, and 17.6 percent in the United States.[62] Indeed, one of the great ironies of Japan's gender order is this: much of the rigid gender ideology of the modern period was rationalized by the division of labor that highly valued and assigned war-making to men and baby-making to women. From 1946 onward, despite the instantaneous and complete dismantling of both the male soldier's prestige and the state's constitutional commitment to militarism, gender inequality persists to a puzzling degree. Moreover, despite the fact that women's legal status has vastly changed since late-nineteenth-century progressives demanded such changes, Japan is a prime example for how large swaths of the late capitalist, democratic Global North continue to be far from a region of gender equality.[63]

Literature and Visual Culture

Japanese literature is rich with stories of female lead characters. Among the most captivating are Uno Chiyo's *The Story of a Single Woman* (2003),[64] Kirino Natsuo's *Grotesque: A Novel* (2007),[65] and *The Modern Murasaki: Writing by Women of Meiji Japan* (2006).[66] Tanizaki Junichirō delivers a masterfully uncomfortable variation on the modern new woman in *Naomi* (2001).[67] *Yellow Rose* (1923)[68] by Japan's first openly lesbian writer Yoshiya Nobuko is a must-read. Murakami Haruki's novel *Norwegian Wood* (1987)[69] is a love story set in the 1960s. Regarding present-day precarity, Murata Sayaka describes the almost completely ordinary life of a young woman without talents in *Convenience Store Woman* (2019).[70]

---

[62] I cite from page 11 of Deloitte Global Center for Corporate Governance, *Women in the Boardroom: A Global Perspective – Sixth Edition*, 2019, accessed September 28, 2020; you can download the report, "gx-risk-women-in-the-boardroom-sixth-edition.pdf," at www2.deloitte.com/global/en/pages/risk/articles/women-in-the-boardroom-global-perspective .html#.

[63] The gender order within the Self-Defense Forces is described in Frühstück, *Uneasy Warriors*.

[64] Uno Chiyo, *The Story of a Single Woman*, trans. Rebecca Copeland (Doncaster: Bailgate Books, 2003).

[65] Kirino Natsuo, *Grotesque: A Novel*, trans. Rebecca Copeland (New York: Knopf, 2007).

[66] Rebecca Copeland and Melek Ortabasi, eds., *The Modern Murasaki: Writing by Women of Meiji Japan* (New York: Columbia University Press, 2006).

[67] Tanizaki Junichirō, *Naomi* (New York: Vintage, 2001).

[68] Yoshiya Nobuko, *Yellow Rose*, trans. Sarah Frederick (Los Angeles: Expanded Editions, 2016).

[69] Murakami Haruki, *Norwegian Wood*, trans. Jay Rubin (New York: Vintage, 2000).

[70] Murata Sayaka, *Convenience Store Woman*, trans. Ginny Tapley Takemore (New York: Grove Press, 2019).

Shane O'Sullivan's *Children of the Revolution* (2010)[71] is a documentary that focuses on Shigenobu Fusako and Ulrike Meinhof, prominent leaders of the Japanese Red Army and the German Red Army Faction, respectively. In Ozu Yasujirō's *Late Spring* (1949),[72] based on the book *Father and Daughter* by Hirotsu Kazuo, dutiful daughter Noriko forgoes marriage to take care of her father. Ozu Yasujirō's *Tōkyō Monogatari* (*Tokyo Story*, 1953)[73] is a riveting family portrait of a multigenerational family in the 1950s. And Linda Hoaglund's *ANPO: Art X War* (2010)[74] addresses anti-militarist political, feminist, cultural and artistic expressions.

[71] *Children of the Revolution*, directed by Shane O'Sullivan (London: E2 Films, 2010).
[72] Noda Kōgo and Ozu Yasujirō, based on Hirotsu Kazuo's novel, *Late Spring* (directed by Ozu Yasujirō (Tokyo: Shōchiku, 1949).
[73] Noda Kōgo and Ozu Yasujirō, *Tōkyō Monogatari* (*Tokyo Story*), directed by Ozu Yasujirō (Tokyo: Shochiku, 1953).
[74] Linda Hoaglund, *ANPO: Art X War* (2010).

4 Sex at War

In 1899, eighteen-year-old Japanese pharmacist Nakano Chūzō was collecting samples of medicinal plants when he stumbled unwittingly into the settlement of Dakekan – Aboriginal territory in Taiwan that was resistant to Japanese colonizers. He was captured and sentenced to execution. Luckily, Yayutz, the sixteen-year-old daughter of the Dakekan chief, was smitten with the young man, and intervened to save his life. Though she succeeded, Taiwan and Japan were nonetheless at war, and Nakano was an enemy. Rather than giving in and letting go of him, Yayutz broke with her family and fled with him to Taipei. The couple later married and lived happily ever after.[1]

In her study of colonial peoples, historian Kirsten Ziomek recovered Yayutz' and Chūzō's story of love across enemy lines in a number of different versions. The actual story must have been quite different, she cautions, since it reproduces a romantic trope of the time: native girl falls for Japanese man, transforms into an almost-but-not-quite Japanese girl, and behold – Japanese imperialism is legitimized.[2] Of course, no setting of empire-building or war-making, in Asia or elsewhere, will be devoid of romantic and sexual liaisons.[3] When young people fell in love with those their elders failed to accept, many lovers sought freedoms elsewhere; as for the story of this book in particular, that "elsewhere" was often in colonies of the Japanese empire, and the women involved were often nurses, entertainers, or prostitutes. But stories like that of Yayutz and Chūzō were multiplied and amplified *ad nauseam* in contemporaneous and immediate postwar literature and films – variously deployed to celebrate Japanese imperialism, atone for the mass violence in the name of the emperor, recover individual soldiers' humanity, and reiterate the threat of killing and dying in terms of overwhelming affection and

---

[1] Ziomek, *Lost Histories*, 200–01.   [2] Ziomek, *Lost Histories*, 200–01.
[3] Paul D. Barclay, "Cultural Brokerage and Interethnic Marriage in Colonial Taiwan: Japanese Subalterns and Their Aborigine Wives, 1895–1930," *Journal of Asian Studies* 64, no. 2 (2005): 323–60.

eroticism.[4] Such hyper-romanticizations of war have worked to conceal the vast web of military sexual mass violence – much of which was organized and systematic, and most of which victimized women and girls. This chapter describes how, throughout the empire and along the frontlines, sexual violence occurred as a result of insufficient interest and/ or ability in controlling the behavior of members of the Japanese Imperial Army from the Russo-Japanese War in 1904–1905 to the end of the Asia-Pacific War in 1945.[5] It also examines the continuing legacy of organized military sexual violence, an issue that still burdens Japan's relations with its former colonies today and puts Japan at odds with international law.

Systemic Military Sexual Violence

I have described in Chapter 1 how, historically, sex – at least for men – had been seen as one of the joys of life: a form of entertainment and comfort with the potential to extend a healthy lifespan.[6] Chiefly informed by Sigmund Freud, early-twentieth-century notions of men having a sexual instinct only deepened the assumption of the inevitability of male sexual desire – as well as the impossibility, of individual men or the state, to completely control it. In wartime, both the prevalence of sex for payment (the subject of Chapter 5) and these modern assumptions about male sexual desire governed military policies that provided for, tolerated, and organized sexual violence – only to conceal and deny much of it after Japan's defeat in 1945. And this military sexual mass violence was widespread – from organized mass rape behind the frontlines to disorganized violence committed by advancing or retreating troops, all in the pursuit of imperialism.

The medical experts of the Japanese Imperial Army were central to acknowledging what they assumed to be the nature of male sexual desire. As military recruitment staff had begun to document the rates of illnesses among conscripts and troops in the 1870s, they made an interesting discovery: many young men – often sexually inexperienced – who had been found fit for service at the conscription exam had become infected

---

[4] Dower, *War without Mercy.*

[5] The similarities with attitudes and wartime policies in Nazi Germany are striking; see Sabine Frühstück, "Sexuality and Sexual Violence," in *The Cambridge History of the Second World War*, ed. Michael Geyer and Adam Tooze (Cambridge: Cambridge University Press, 2015), 781–83.

[6] Janet R. Goodwin, *Selling Songs and Smiles: The Sex Trade in Heian and Kamakura Japan* (Honolulu: University of Hawai'i Press, 2007); Amy Stanley, *Selling Women: Prostitution, Markets, and the Household in Early Modern Japan* (Berkeley: University of California Press, 2012); Sabine Frühstück, "Sex zwischen Wissenschaft und Politik," in *Nachrichten der Gesellschaft für Natur- und Völkerkunde Ostasiens* 155–56 (1996): 11–41.

100   Sex at War

with a sexually transmitted disease before entering the barracks for mandatory military training – a time period of two to three years. Many of these conscripts marked their rite of passage with a visit to a prostitute. From these developments the military command considered it essential to manage and exploit soldiers' sexual needs as much as possible – while also accepting that those needs could never be completely controlled.

A group portrait taken at the end of World War I represents this perspective in near-perfect form. The image centers on a teenaged Imperial Army captain in uniform surrounded by a more-senior military entourage and a handful of civilian officials. Sharing a smirk with his uniformed companions, the captain sits astride a canon, his eyes and the canon pointed straight at the viewer – suggesting that militarism and masculinity, if not one and the same, are at least complementary. Either way, the tableaux unmistakably ties male virility to mass violence, mirroring both actual male behavior in war and military policy regarding service members' sexual needs. (This confident captain, by the name of Michinomiya Hirohito, would later become a lieutenant in the Imperial Navy – and then crown prince, Shōwa-era emperor, and wartime commander in chief.)

As early as during the Russo-Japanese War in 1904–1905, the Imperial Army attempted to control the sexual activities of soldiers by both authorizing certain existing brothels for military-only use and building new brothels exclusively for Japanese soldiers. Initially, only Japanese women – prostitutes as well as other desperately poor and undereducated women – were recruited into these establishments. Though, for many, "recruited" was not the applicable term; thousands upon thousands of Japanese women who sought work overseas – women referred to as "*karayuki*" or those "who go to China" or those "who go abroad" – were lured through coercion, deception, or abduction into years of sex slavery somewhere in Japan's expanding empire. Many of these women had been sold to brothels by their own families to ease economic hardship. Others had been recruited from the poorest locales of rural Japan under the pretense of finding work as maids or textile factory workers. Government statistics show that by 1910 there were close to 20,000 Japanese women registered as overseas prostitutes; another 40,000 women were registered in public brothels within Japan proper.[7]

---

[7] Though the Emancipation Act of 1872 both freed those in bondage and prohibited the buying and selling of persons for any type of service, the law did not bring about significant social change; the only change for the women who had no alternative options was to be issued a prostitution license by the government. See Yamazaki Tomoko, *Sandakan Brothel No. 8: Journey into the History of Lower-Class Japanese Women*, trans. Karen Colligan-Taylor (London: Routledge, 1998), xvii–xviii. Regarding the legal situation, see Daniel V. Botsman, "Freedom without Slavery? 'Coolies,'

Systemic Military Sexual Violence

The development of these brothels, whose use was often restricted to or primarily designated for soldiers of the Imperial Army, provided a ready-made model for the large-scale enslavement of women from Korea, China, Indonesia, and other locales across the Japanese empire – enslavement that became increasingly systematic after the Japanese Imperial Army marched into Manchuria in 1931.

Japanese activists seeking to criminalize prostitution mostly concerned themselves with the sale of women in Japan's urban centers (see Chapter 5); indeed, there were twice as many women working in the sex trade in Japan as in the rest of the Japanese empire. But some reformists also opposed supplying women for Japan's colonizers. One woman, for instance, the wife of a parliamentarian, wrote to the abolitionist movement's journal *Purity* (*Kakusei*) that she would "rather help her son dodge the draft than expose him to prostitution while serving in the military."[8] Since the military administrators did not share this mother's concern for her son's morals, they strove to suppress criticism of the behavior of imperial troops, wherever they were stationed. But they did share her concern about his physical health. Convinced as they were of the inevitability of servicemen indulging their sexual needs, the military medical elite saw military-use brothels as the best means by which military physicians could tend to troops and prostitutes alike. One such brothel prostitute, a woman from Kyūshū lured overseas under false pretenses, described the prescriptive requirements of her daily life:

We never forgot to disinfect ourselves when the man was done. Near the bed in the corner of the room was a basin filled with a red disinfectant solution. Each time we finished we would carefully wash both the man's and the woman's private parts and wipe them with tissue paper. Because this solution chilled us inside, we prostitutes hardly ever got pregnant. [E]very seven days, without fail, we had to go to the hospital for an examination. Syphilis – if you had that, you know, your body would rot. Your whole body would be covered with pustules and you would die a terrible death, or else you would go mad. We never missed an examination, because we didn't want that to happen to us.[9]

To be sure, the control of soldiers' access to sex was guided predominantly by concerns about the *men's* health. Though the basic policy was to treat the women who became infected, in some places the women were abandoned or even killed.[10]

Prostitutes, and Outcastes in Meiji Japan's 'Emancipation Moment,'" *American Historical Review* 116, no. 5 (December 2011): 1323–47.

[8] Hinata Daigishi Fujin, "Fujin shakai to geishōgi mondai," *Kakusei* 1, no. 3 (1911): 40–43.

[9] Yamazaki, *Sandakan Brothel No. 8*, 69.

[10] George Hicks, *Comfort Women: Japan's Imperial Regime of Enforced Prostitution in the Second World War* (New York: W. W. Norton, 1997), 95.

102   Sex at War

Health examinations carried out by military hospitals and academies confirmed that one in ten recruits – several tens of thousands of men – suffered from at least one venereal disease. The most common were gonorrhea, cancroid, and syphilis, as found in all fighting armies at the time. And, as elsewhere, until effective medication was developed, the diseases were treated with various baths, painful injections, and special grasses and tinctures.[11] The authors of hygiene manuals for the Japanese Imperial Army and the Navy claimed that a combination of condoms and creams applied to the genitals before and after sexual intercourse was the most effective means of preventing sexually transmitted diseases. More often, however, venereal diseases such as syphilis remained untreated – which led to repeated skin eruptions and ulcers, hair loss, and the deterioration of the nose and, later, the brain – the "going mad" that the woman from Kyūshū mentioned above. As field nurse Anzai Sadako recalled in her memoir *Field Nurse* (*Yasen Kangofu*, 1953), patients inevitably suffered from the loss of motor nerve control, spinal cord phthisis, progressive paralysis, and mental illness.

Accordingly, it was in military hospitals that venereal diseases were first systematically researched, and where antibiotics such as Salvarsan – jointly developed by Paul Ehrlich and Hata Sahachirō in 1909 – were first introduced for treatment.[12] Since long-term documentation of cases revealed that venereal diseases increased during times of war, the army ordered weekly medical examinations of thousands of men and severely punished those who were diseased – rules that would remain in place for decades to come.[13] It was only between the implementation of the General Mobilization Law (Kokka Sōdōinhō) in 1938 and the Law for the Strengthening of the National Body (Kokumin Tairyokuhō) in 1941 that the legislation for the prevention of venereal diseases shifted significantly toward covering the entire population.

The military health education and the punishment of infected soldiers, often by degradation or beating, was only partly effective however. So authorities introduced more practical measures, beginning with the distribution of condoms,[14] which came into widespread use at the beginning of Japan's aggression against China in 1931. Soldiers who left their

---

[11] Kariya Haruo, *Edo no seibyō* (Tokyo: Sanichi Shobō, 1993), 22–23.
[12] Japan's policies with regards to Jewish refugees are examined in Martin Kaneko, *Die Judenpolitik der japanischen Kriegsregierung* (Berlin: Metropol, 2008).
[13] Kaigunshō Imukoku, *Nisshin senyaku kaigun eiseishi* (Tokyo: Kaigunshō imukyoku, 1900).
[14] Jūgun ianfu 110-ban henshū iinkai, ed., *Jūgun ianfu 110-ban: Denwa no mukō kara rekishi no koe ga* (Tokyo: Akashi Shoten, 1992), 104.

bases were instructed to carry "hygiene matches": small boxes containing two condoms. From 1938 until the end of World War II, rubber factories were put under the jurisdiction of the military, and condoms were formally classified as "war munitions." The Imperial Army Ministry's Bureau of Supplies provided condoms creatively named Iron Cap for the Imperial Japanese Navy and Attack Number One and Attack Champion for the Imperial Japanese Army.[15] But though the condoms were available at the military brothels – the so-called comfort stations, the first of which was established in Shanghai in 1931 – the means of enforcing their use remained limited. Even for the service members who embraced this protection, production was insufficient. For example, the 32 million condoms distributed in 1942 to the Japanese military amounted to roughly twenty condoms per man for the year, and left condoms entirely unavailable in some locations for long stretches of time. That said, some "comfort station" managers sold condoms locally, and some soldiers took the effort to wash and reuse their rationed condoms.[16]

But the true insufficiency of these efforts could be seen in the fact that venereal diseases were rampant. And so, as Japanese colonial rule expanded, and the Japanese women working in the brothels were increasingly infected, Chinese, Korean, Dutch, and other girls and women under Japanese colonial rule were lured or forced into military-controlled sexual slavery – ostensibly to protect the soldiers themselves from venereal disease and local women from sexual assault. This operation was euphemistically referred to as the "[military] comfort women system" (*ianfu seido*). (Though the "comfort stations" were established for soldiers and other employees of the military, they were also made available to civilian traders – as long as their activities did not deplete the intended "recreation for military personnel."[17]) The system of sexual abuse established for Japanese troops throughout the vast Asia-Pacific region exploited between 80,000 and 200,000 women of various ethnic and

---

[15] Jūgun ianfu 110-ban henshū iinkai, ed., *Jūgun ianfu 110-ban*, 74; Chin Sung Chung, "The Origin and Development of the Military Sexual Slavery Problem in Imperial Japan," *positions: east asian cultures critique* 5, no. 1 (1997), 229, accessed June 2, 2021, https://doi.org/10.1215/10679847-5-1-219.

[16] Jūgun ianfu 110-ban henshū iinkai, ed., *Jūgun ianfu 110-ban*, 74; Hayashi Hiroshi, "Rikugun no ianjo kanri no ichisokumen: 'Eisei sakku' kōfu shiryō o tegakari ni," *Kikan: Sensō Sekinin Kenkyū Sōkangō* 1 (Fall 1993): 12–19.

[17] Hayashi Hirofumi, "Die Verwicklung der japanischen kaiserlichen Regierung in das System der Militärbordelle ('Troststationen')," in *Erzwungene Prostitution in Kriegs- und Friedenszeiten: Sexuelle Gewalt gegen Frauen und Mädchen*, ed. Barbara Drinck and Chung-Noh Gross (Bielefeld: Kleine Verlag, 2006), 120; Han Won-Sang, "Das japanische Militär im Krieg und sein System der Sexsklaverei," in *Erzwungene Prostitution in Kriegs- und Friedenszeiten: Sexuelle Gewalt gegen Frauen und Mädchen*, ed. Barbara Drinck and Chung-Noh Gross (Bielefeld: Kleine Verlag, 2006), 170.

104 Sex at War

national backgrounds and social circumstances – including women of occupied territories such as Burma, Indonesia, the Pacific Islands, the Philippines, and Taiwan.

A great majority of these women, as much as 80 percent, were Korean. One Korean woman named Mun described how she was abducted into this servitude at the age of sixteen:

> One day, I went over to Haruko's house to visit. As the sun was going down, I left her house and headed home. Before I'd walked very far, a Japanese man in a military uniform approached me. Suddenly, he grabbed my arm and pulled me, saying something to me in Japanese. That was a time when even hearing the word "policeman" was a scary thing, so I was led off without saying a word ... I thought I was being taken to the military police.[18]

Instead, Mun was taken to a sexual slavery station in northeastern China. Another Korean woman named Kim Hak-sun described her first night at the "comfort station" to which she was taken at the age of seventeen:

> An officer came into the room and led me into the room next door, separated from the first by a cloth curtain ... I struggled against him, but he dragged me into the neighboring room by force. The officer tried to undress me while he was hugging me. I resisted, but my clothes were eventually all torn off. In the end, he took my virginity. That night I was violated twice by the officer.[19]

More ambiguous cases of recruitment reflect on the gender order in various parts of the empire. For instance, eighteen-year-old Mun P'il-gi had always longed for a proper school education, but her father denied her that simply because she was a girl. So when a local Korean man she knew to be an agent for the Japanese offered her that education, she went with him without even telling her parents about it. But the truck the man put her on took her to Manchuria, where she spent years as a "comfort woman" for the Imperial Army.[20]

These were only three among thousands of girls and women enslaved and abused throughout the empire. Held under what amounted to a regime of systematic mass rape, these girls and women were forced to work as nurses, cooks, waitresses, and seamstresses during the day. At night they were regularly raped and often also beaten.

The recruitment of these women was in the hands not only of the military leadership in Tokyo but also of other agencies of the state,

---

[18] Yoshimi Yoshiaki, *Comfort Women: Sexual Slavery in the Japanese Military during World War II*, trans. Suzanne O'Brien (New York: Columbia University Press, [1995] 2000), 107.

[19] Yoshimi, *Comfort Women*, 139.

[20] C. Sarah Soh, *The Comfort Women: Sexual Violence and Postcolonial Memory in Korea and Japan* (Chicago, IL: Chicago University Press, 2009), 85.

particularly the police, the Ministry of Foreign Affairs, the government of Taiwan, and semigovernmental bodies. The Police Bureau ordered the prefectural governments and colonial administrators throughout the empire to identify and support suitable recruiters,[21] who in turn would use methods modeled on the techniques of recruiting civilians into military service. After 1940, as large parts of the Pacific came under Japanese rule, sexual slavery stations were established across the Japanese empire, including in Burma, the Andaman-Nikobar Islands, the Indian territories in the West, Indonesia, and the Solomon and Marshall Islands. When Japan began to prepare for the offensive of the Allied Forces, such stations were also established in Okinawa and other, mostly urban, parts of Japan.[22]

Military men's views on the system were mixed. One young man under Hirohito's command matter-of-factly claimed in 1937 Nanjing that "the men's fleshly desires, exacerbated by tedium, needed to be relieved,"[23] an opinion likely shared far beyond the military, and even by women. Such, at least, was the perspective of a Japanese field nurse by the name of Anzai Sadako, who had been employed first by the Japanese Imperial Army on the Chinese front and later by the Allied occupation forces. Anzai's memoir, *Yasen Kangofu*, is one of the few day-to-day accounts of a female nurse who had marched with the advancing Japanese Imperial Army. Without a hint of concern for the women and girls involved, or the circumstances that got them there, Anzai recalled finding it "hard to think poorly of soldiers who frequented the military brothels."[24] And yet, some men neither thought nor acted in line with this view; to some the arrangement even seemed aberrant. When one Japanese soldier was asked about his visit to a brothel, he described it as "dull." When asked why, he responded, "There is just no passion" – to which the other exclaimed, "Idiot! What the hell did you expect!?"[25]

One Japanese officer recalled his experience in Nha-trang, Vietnam, in the following terms:

The none-too-simple reality of it was that, rather than being stimulated, I felt I had been exposed to some grotesque world. Standing in line in broad daylight, doing it right under the nose of the people waiting for their turn, and the vivid image of men coming out one after another with their pants still half open. This ritual proceeded in conveyer-belt fashion in an atmosphere of a particular sort of

---

[21] Hayashi, "Die Verwicklung der japanischen kaiserlichen Regierung," 112.

[22] Hayashi, "Die Verwicklung der japanischen kaiserlichen Regierung," 108.

[23] Ishikawa Tatsuzō, *Soldiers Alive*, trans. Zeljko Cipris (Honolulu: University of Hawai'i Press, 2003).

[24] Anzai, *Yasen kangofu*, 158–59.   [25] Ishikawa, *Soldiers Alive*, 173–74.

106   Sex at War

tension, and rather than raising my spirits, made me, who knew nothing of the forbidden fruit of the tree of knowledge, flinch.[26]

Historian Yoshimi Yoshiaki readily attests to the system as having a "factory" mentality wherein soldiers and officers alike considered women "only as things or sex objects," affirming to themselves that "comfort stations" were necessary. One officer in the 11th Army Signal Corps, for instance, described this deeply gendered state of affairs as follows:

During the battle, which lasted about fifty days, I did not see any women at all. I knew that as a result [of being without access to women] men's mental condition ends up declining, and that's when I realized once again the necessity of special comfort stations. This desire is the same as hunger or the need to urinate, and soldiers merely thought of comfort stations as practically the same as latrines ... Women were regarded only as tools of the sexual desires of military personnel.[27]

In July 1937, Japan began a full-scale invasion of China, bringing in more than one million Japanese troops. Beginning on December 13, 1937, over the course of six weeks these troops committed mass rape and murder of civilians in Nanking.[28] In part as a response to what one author has termed "the forgotten Holocaust of World War II," the "military comfort women system" was expanded exponentially.[29] By September 1942, an additional 400 "comfort stations" had been established: 100 in North China, 140 in Central China, 40 in South China, 100 in South East Asia, 10 in the Southern Seas, and 10 in Sakhalin. The young women who were lured or forced into these South East Asian stations were of many nationalities and ethnicities, including Chinese, Taiwanese, overseas Chinese, Malay, Thai, Filipina, Indonesian, Burmese, Vietnamese, Indian, Eurasian, Dutch, Timorese, Japanese, Korean, and Pacific Islanders – and possibly Laotians and Cambodians as well.[30]

Amnesia and Legacies

After Japan's surrender in 1945, the vast majority of Japanese military personnel and civilians living abroad returned to Japan aboard

---

[26] Yoshimi, *Comfort Women*, 140.   [27] Yoshimi, *Comfort Women*, 199.

[28] Joshua A. Fogel, ed., *The Nanjing Massacre in History and Historiography* (Berkeley: University of California Press, 2000), 4.

[29] Iris Chang, *The Rape of Nanjing: The Forgotten Holocaust of World War II* (New York: Basic Books, 2012).

[30] Hayashi Hirofumi, "Government, the Military and Business in Japan's Wartime Comfort Woman System," *Asia-Pacific Journal: Japan Focus* 5, no. 1 (January 2, 2007), accessed May 20, 2020, www.japanfocus.org/-Hayashi-Hirofumi/2332#sthash .W7DHcUVk.dp.

Amnesia and Legacies 107

evacuation ships. And though a considerable number of sex slaves were sent home as well, a great number were denied that option.[31] Many of the women forced into mass rape stations were abandoned, killed, or subjected to the Allied Forces as prisoners of war – where they were dubbed "Japanese girls" even when recognized as being both sex slaves and nationalities other than Japanese. When repatriation was initiated a year or two later, only a fraction of the women returned to their homelands; many more feared the stigmatization of their now "impure bodies," and so wandered with no country to call their own. Those who did return home concealed their wartime experiences; reflecting their limited professional experience and skills, many took jobs as factory laborers and nurses.[32]

In the meantime, during the Allied occupation of Japan sexual and sometimes romantic relations sprang up between the victorious male occupiers and Japanese women. Following the wartime logic applied to the Japanese Imperial Army and Navy – namely, that military-controlled sex stations would prevent uncontrolled rape – the Japanese government established official brothels while occupation forces service members also committed thousands of rapes. These brothels segregated black service members from the white so as to please occupation authorities. Though the brothels ran a brisk business, employing from 60,000 to 70,000 women over the course of eight months, they were abruptly closed again in response to widespread venereal disease. It was at this juncture that the commercial sex market proliferated, and more – and more diverse – women entered and transformed the industry – an object of commentary by journalists, social critics, children, and producers of mass and popular culture alike.[33] For example, beginning in 1954 the Vermont-based Charles E. Tuttle published a cartoon titled *Babysan's World: The Hume'n Slant on Japan*. The work's illustrator Bill Hume, writer John

---

[31] Yoshimi, *Comfort Women*, 192.

[32] Kang Sung Hyun, "The 'Seen Side' and 'Blind Side' of U.S. Army Photography: The Still Pictures and Motion Pictures of the Korean 'Comfort Girls' in Myitkyina, Sungshan, and Tengchung," talk presented on February 19, 2018, Department of East Asian Studies, University of Chicago, trans. Sandra H. Park. See also Kang Sung Hyun and Jung Keun-Sik, "The Organization and Activities of the US Army Signal Corps Photo Unit: Perspectives of War Photography in the Early Stages of the Korean War," *Seoul Journal of Korean Studies* 27, no. 2 (2014): 269–306.

[33] Tanaka Yuki, *Japan's Comfort Women: Sexual Slavery and Prostitution During World War II and the US Occupation* (London: Routledge, 2002); Sarah Kovner, *Occupying Power: Sex Workers and Service Members in Postwar Japan* (Stanford, CA: Stanford University Press, 2012). The number is from Vera Mackie, *Feminism in Modern Japan* (Cambridge: Cambridge University Press, 2003), 136. For the history of sexual mass violence during World War II in Africa, see Judith Byfield and Carolyn Brown, eds., *Africa and World War II* (Cambridge: Cambridge University Press, 2015).

108   Sex at War

Annarino, and Tuttle himself had all been members of the Allied forces. While in Japan with the US Army, Tuttle had worked with the Japanese newspaper industry and had married a Japanese woman from Hokkaido. In establishing his publishing company he remained deeply invested in furthering the understanding between the English- and Japanese-speaking worlds. *Babysan's World* features US sailors of varying levels of wit interacting with a pin-up style Japanese woman named Babysan – her name being a composite of "baby" and the Japanese word for "Ms." Babysan speaks broken English, loves American clothes and shoes, and is constantly in the company of soldiers. It is also assumed that she enjoys casual and compensated sex, though none is ever featured. The cartoon, which was also published in US military magazines, is light and meant to harmlessly entertain. It delights in the possibilities of encounters between scandalously available young women of Japan and Allied forces men from the American hinterlands, many of whom had never been outside of their home towns until they were drafted. At the same time, it is also utterly ignorant of how it symbolically perpetuates the brutal wartime interconnection between sex and deeply gendered violence – or at least the threat thereof. In its drawings and its words, the cartoon's suggestive humor largely relies on sexual innuendo and cultural misunderstandings, a formula that has persisted to this day, particularly in cartoons and other popular cultural products that feature the US armed forces with the aim of dampening local resistance.[34] Only one of several comics on the US soldiers' experience during the occupation that Tuttle published, *Babysan's World* was very popular at the time, in both Japan and the United States (see Figure 4.1).

The prolonged presence of US armed forces in Japan has remained contentious to this day, particularly with regard to prostitution around bases and sexual violence perpetrated by US service members. Inspired by this contention, the collaborative video-projection "Made in Occupied Japan," by feminist artists Shimada Yoshiko and Bubu De la Madeleine, captures the sexualized moment of postwar occupation that Bubu experienced as a prostitute in current-day Japan (see Figure 4.2).[35]

---

[34] I am adopting Carl Gabrielson's argument in "Welcome to Japan! How U.S. Marine Corps Orientation Materials Erase, Coopt, and Dismiss Local Resistance," *Journal of American–East Asian Relations* 26, no. 4 (2019): 397–425.

[35] For an extensive description of their collaborations, see Ayala Klemperer-Markman, "Art, Politics and Prostitution in Occupied/Contemporary Japan: The Voice of a Sex Worker," in *Postgender: Gender, Sexuality and Performativity in Japanese Culture*, ed. Ayelet Zohar (Newcastle upon Tyne: Cambridge Scholars Publishing, 2009), 229–49; and BuBu de la Madeleine and Yoshiko Shimada, "Made in Occupied Japan," in *Consuming Bodies: Sex and Contemporary Japanese Art* (Chicago, IL: University of Chicago Press, 2004).

Figure 4.1 Cover of David Hume's *Babysan's World: The Hume'n Slant on Japan* (1954).

Figure 4.2 "Made in Occupied Japan" is a collage by Shimada Yoshiko (left), impersonating an occupation soldier, with Baby De la Madeleine (right), embodying a sex worker. Printed with the kind permission of Shimada Yoshiko.

Amnesia and Legacies

It joins many other works that critique the continued US military's presence in Japan, along with collaborations that address Japanese wartime sexual violence against women, as well as the attempts of former prime minister Abe Shinzō's administration to suppress the acknowledgment and commemoration of former "comfort women."

The politically meaningful parallels Shimada and Bubu draw between military prostitution and wartime sexual slavery are deeply troubling. Chapter 5 provides a critical history of sex work; here it is important to highlight the politicization of the slippage between sexual slavery and prostitution or sex work. Japanese government officials have repeatedly acknowledged the war and, in many different ways, Japan's role as an aggressor. Yet the issue of military sexual slavery only came to the fore in December 1991, when the Korean survivor Kim Hak-sun filed a widely publicized lawsuit against Japan, marking one beginning of what its participants call the Movement to Resolve the "Comfort Women" Issue ("Ianfu" Mondai Kaiketsu Undō). In January 1992, historian Yoshimi Yoshiaki published evidence that "proved conclusively that the military had played a role in the establishment and control of 'comfort stations.'" That same month, then-prime minister Miyazawa Kiichi explicitly used the term "comfort women," announcing publicly: "I apologize from the bottom of my heart and feel remorse for those people who suffered indescribable hardships." Miyazawa was the first prime minister to do so. During a meeting with then-president of the Republic of Korea, Roh Tae Woo, Miyazawa told his host:

We Japanese should first and foremost recall the truth of that tragic period when Japanese actions inflicted suffering and sorrow upon your people. We should never forget our feelings of remorse over this. As Prime Minister of Japan, I would like to declare anew my remorse at these deeds and tender my apology to the people of the Republic of Korea.[36]

He apologized again the following day in a speech before South Korea's National Assembly. Eventually – following multiple testimonies of women who had been subjected to sexual violence by the Japanese wartime military, and at the conclusion of a government study – on August 4, 1993 then-chief cabinet secretary Kono Yōhei issued what is called the Kono Statement. This important document reads as follows:

---

[36] "Japanese Premier Begins Seoul Visit," *New York Times*, January 17, 1992, accessed June 2, 2021, www.nytimes.com/1992/01/17/world/japanese-premier-begins-seoul-visit .html.

The government of Japan has been conducting a study on the issue of wartime "comfort women" since December 1991. I wish to announce the findings as a result of that study.

As a result of the study, which indicates that comfort stations were operated in extensive areas for long periods, it is apparent that there existed a great number of comfort women. Comfort stations were operated in response to the request of the military authorities of the day. The then Japanese military was, directly or indirectly, involved in the establishment and management of the comfort stations and the transfer of comfort women. The recruitment of the comfort women was conducted mainly by private recruiters who acted in response to the request of the military. The government study has revealed that in many cases they were recruited against their own will, through coaxing, coercion, etc., and that, at times, administrative/military personnel directly took part in the recruitments. They lived in misery at comfort stations under a coercive atmosphere.

As to the origin of those comfort women who were transferred to the war areas, excluding those from Japan, those from the Korean Peninsula accounted for a large part. The Korean Peninsula was under Japanese rule in those days, and their recruitment, transfer, control, etc., were conducted generally against their will, through coaxing, coercion, etc.

Undeniably, this was an act, with the involvement of the military authorities of the day, that severely injured the honor and dignity of many women. The government of Japan would like to take this opportunity once again to extend its sincere apologies and remorse to all those, irrespective of place of origin, who suffered immeasurable pain and incurable physical and psychological wounds as comfort women.

It is incumbent upon us, the government of Japan, to continue to consider seriously, while listening to the views of learned circles, how best we can express this sentiment.

We shall face squarely the historical facts as described above instead of evading them, and take them to heart as lessons of history. We hereby reiterate our firm determination never to repeat the same mistake by forever engraving such issues in our memories through the study and teaching of history.

As actions have been brought to court in Japan and interests have been shown in this issue outside Japan, the government of Japan shall continue to pay full attention to this matter, including private research related thereto.[37]

The statement unequivocally acknowledged that the Japanese Imperial Army had been involved, directly and indirectly, in the establishment of so-called comfort facilities, and that coercion had been used in the

---

[37] The Kōno Statement is published in English on the website of the Ministry of Foreign Affairs; "Statement by the Chief Cabinet Secretary," Ministry of Foreign Affairs of Japan, accessed June 2, 2021, www.mofa.go.jp/a_o/rp/page25e_000343.html.

Amnesia and Legacies

recruitment and retention of the women subjected to systematic sexual mass violence. Kōno's was a call for historical research and education. It demanded that the subject of sex forced upon girls and women by the Japanese state be included in history textbooks. In the global arena, in part as a result of the Nuremberg and Tokyo trials, among other events, sexual violence against combatants and civilians no longer passes as an unfortunate but inevitable component of war, but is firmly understood as a war crime.[38] As of the 1949 Geneva Conventions and the 1977 Protocols, wartime rape, including forced prostitution, had become illegal under international law. But only since the 1990s has sexual violence drawn international attention as "particularly gruesome, atrocious, widespread, and systematic in many conflicts," from the governments of Guatemala, Haiti, Liberia, Peru, Rwanda, Sierra Leone, and the former Yugoslavia – and, more recently, the Central African Republic, the Democratic Republic of Congo, and Uganda.[39] In 1998, the International Criminal Court in Rome signed a statute that named rape, sexual slavery, and enforced prostitution both as war crimes (Article 8) and as crimes against humanity (Article 7), and thus put gender violence in the same category as torture and genocide. In 2001, the redefinition of rape as "violation of innate human rights" – instead of the original phrasing of the violation of "honor" and "dignity" – resulted in the indictment, and conviction, for rape as a crime against humanity in the Yugoslav Tribunal in The Hague.[40]

That said, in Japan, right-wing conservatives have taken issue with the demonization of wartime military sexual violence, leading to calls to revise the Kōno Statement, debates about its representation in history textbooks, and contesting the establishment of "comfort women" statues around the world.[41] In turn, the Kōno Statement has also invigorated the formation of a movement and transnational organized efforts of disparate

---

[38] Yoneyama, *Cold War Ruins*.

[39] Rhonda Copelon, "Toward Accountability for Violence against Women in War: Progress and Challenges," in *Sexual Violence in Conflict Zones: From the Ancient World to the Era of Human Rights*, ed. Elizabeth D. Heineman (Philadelphia: University of Pennsylvania Press, 2011), 232.

[40] Maria Höhn and Seungsook Moon, eds., *Over There: Living with the U.S. Military Empire from World War Two to the Present* (Durham, NC: Duke University Press, 2010), 402; Carol Gluck, "Operations of Memory: 'Comfort Women' and the World," in *Ruptured Histories: War, Memory, and the Post-Cold War in Asia*, ed. Sheila Miyoshi Jager and Rana Mitter (Cambridge, MA: Harvard University Press, 2007), 74–75; Soh, *Comfort Women*.

[41] Yamaguchi Tomomi, Nogawa Motokazu, Tessa Morris-Suzuki, and Koyama Emi, *Umi o wataru "ianfu" mondai: Uha no "rekishisen" o tou* (Tokyo: Iwanami Shoten, 2016); Maki Kimura, *Unfolding the "Comfort Women" Debates: Modernity, Violence, Women's Voices* (New York: Palgrave Macmillan, 2016); Gluck, "Operations of Memory," 47–77; Iwasaki Minoru and Steffi Richter, "The Topology of Post-1990s Historical

114   Sex at War

women's groups, including the Violence Against Women in War-Network Japan (VAWW-NET), to expand their agenda from "comfort women" specifically to violence against women at US military bases, as well as to violence against women in armed conflicts around the world. As these groups' efforts intensified and increasingly aligned with the findings in 1998 of the UN Sub-Commission on Prevention of Discrimination and Protection of Minorities: that the Tokyo War Crimes Trial "[had failed] to prosecute sexual enslavement," in December 2000 the groups organized a Women's International War Crimes Tribunal on Japan's Military Sexual Slavery. With sixty-four survivors participating from nine countries, the team of international jurists "found the Japanese state and emperor Hirohito guilty of war crimes and a crime against humanity."[42] The official verdict, issued a year later at The Hague, included the following in the final judgment:

> The Crimes committed against these survivors remain one of the greatest unacknowledged and unremedied injustices of the Second World War. There are no museums, no graves for the unknown "comfort woman," no education of future generations, and there have been no judgement days for the victims of Japan's military sexual slavery and the rampant sexual violence and brutality that characterized its aggressive war.[43]

Despite this judgment, the Kōno Statement has been repeatedly criticized by conservatives, including former prime minister Abe. Abe's recent calls for revision of the statement, as well as his refusal to acknowledge the validity of research findings and survivor testimonies that led to the judgment, have prompted severe criticism by some of his political elders, including former prime minister Miyazawa, progressives in Japan, and governments and civic organizations like those involved in the establishment of commemorative statues around the world – far beyond those of countries formerly under Japanese colonial rule.[44] Notwithstanding many

---

Revisionism," trans. Richard Calichman, *positions: east asia critique* 16, no. 3 (2008): 507–38; Tessa Morris-Suzuki, "You Don't Want to Know about the Girls? The 'Comfort Women,' the Japanese Military and Allied Forces in the Asia-Pacific War," *Asia-Pacific Journal* 13, issue 31, no. 1 (2015), accessed June 2, 2021, http://apjjf.org/2015/13/31/Tessa-Morris-Suzuki/4352.html; Yoneyama, *Cold War Ruins*.

[42] Eika Tai, *Comfort Women Activism* (Hong Kong: Hong Kong University Press, 2020), 28–29.

[43] See also Women's International War Crimes Tribunal Archives, *Breaking the History of Silence – The Women's International War Crimes Tribunal for the Trial of Japanese Military Sexual Slavery*, directed by Video Juku (Tokyo: VAWW-NET Japan, International Organizing Committee for the Women's International War Crimes Tribunal, 2001), accessed January 21, 2021, https://archives.wam-peace.org/wt/en/video.

[44] Official Japan's frequently ambiguous stance toward acknowledging imperial Japan's past aggression and the military's – and thus the state's – role in the sexual slavery system is reflected in a long series of carefully phrased apologies; for an incomplete list,

Global Commemorations   115

public formal acknowledgments of and apologies for Japan's imperialist role in the Asia-Pacific War – by Miyazawa and Emperor Akihito (1989–2019), among a long list of other public figures – some Japanese political and other public figures have repeatedly reignited the debate about the military sexual slavery system.[45] Indeed, to this day, representatives of the ultraconservative political and educational elite worry anew that truthful history education about the Japanese empire – including the sexual slavery system in particular – might hamper the patriotism of younger generations.[46] Their attempts to suppress the public acknowledgment and commemoration of former military sex slaves have spread into expatriate communities around the world. From Seoul to Berlin, small portions of Japanese expatriate communities along with representatives of the Japanese government resist the erection of statues and memorials, variously insisting that they misrepresent history and injure Japan's reputation along with their own standing in their respective communities in the present.[47]

Global Commemorations

Over the last thirty years, a flood of publications in several languages has examined the sexual slavery system. This reexamination is in large part nurtured by a new feminist movement "characterized by postcolonial historical consciousness, transnational solidarity, intersectionality, feminist ethics, and mutual transformation." Its most recent body of works situates the Japanese system within a comparative context and with an eye on its increasingly global legacies.[48] During times of war, and during

---

see "List of war apology statements issued by Japan," Wikimedia Foundation, last modified May 31, 2021, 07:02, https://en.wikipedia.org/wiki/List_of_war_apology_statements_issued_by_Japan; J. Berkshire Miller, "The Abe Statement of Japan's War Guilt: Regional and Historical Implications," *EastWest.ngo*, June 25, 2015, accessed May 20, 2020, www.eastwest.ngo/idea/abe-statement-japan%E2%80%99s-war-guilt-regional-and-historical-implications.

[45] Tessa Morris-Suzuki, "Ever-Shifting Sands of Japanese Apologies," *East Asia Forum*, February 22, 2016. For many years, the *Asia-Pacific Journal: Japan Focus* has made it its business to closely follow the trajectory of the debate about Japan's wartime sexual slavery system. For how the debate migrated to the US and elsewhere, see Yoneyama, *Cold War Ruins*. For a current state of what has become a transpacific debate, see Tomomi Yamaguchi, "The 'History Wars' and the 'Comfort Woman' Issue: Revisionism and the Right-Wing in Contemporary Japan and the U.S.," *Asia-Pacific Journal: Japan Focus* 18, issue 6, no. 3 (March 15, 2020), accessed June 2, 2021, https://apjjf.org/2020/6/Yamaguchi.html.

[46] Frühstück, *Uneasy Warriors*.

[47] Yukiko Koga, *Inheritance of Loss: China, Japan, and the Political Economy of Redemption after Empire* (Chicago, IL: University of Chicago Press, 2016).

[48] Ueno Chizuko, Araragi Shinzō, and Hirai Kazuko, eds., *Sensō to seibōryoku no hikakushi e mukete* (Tokyo: Iwanami Shoten, 2018); Tai, *Comfort Women Activism*, 5.

116   Sex at War

the Asia-Pacific War in particular, the boundaries between different kinds of sexual and gender violence have not always been clear-cut; this predicament has left some former "comfort women" conflicted – not only about the former colonialist Japanese state and the military establishment that severely exploited and violated them, but also about the home communities they had been taken from. Indeed, even many of their parents had adhered to a gender ideology that at best suppressed girls' dreams and ambitions and at worst supported the very mindset that had led to their enslavement.[49]

Artists Kim Seo-Kyung and Kim Eun-Sung designed the first Statue of Peace. Since December 14, 2011, it has stood in front of the Japanese embassy in Seoul, put there at the behest of the Korean Council for Justice and Remembrance for the Issues of Military Sexual Slavery by Japan in order to mark the thousandth Wednesday demonstration in support of former "comfort women" and inspiring the erection of many other statues and monuments commemorating them around the world, including in several locales in Japan, South Korea, China, Vietnam, the Philippines, Australia, the United States, and, most recently, Germany. On September 28, 2020, the Working Group on Comfort Women (Arbeitsgruppe Trostfrauen) within the Korea Communication & Research Center (Korea Verband) erected a bronze Statue of Peace in Berlin-Moabit (see Figure 4.3). Gifted by the Korean Council for Justice and Remembrance, the declared purpose of the statue was to "alert people to the topic of sexualized violence" and to "commemorate the more than 200,000 girls and women from 14 countries that the Japanese military had enslaved during the Asia-Pacific War." Thirty civic organizations in Germany had united to support the statue's installment. Signaling the event's and the statue's significance as local (Berlin, both current capital and former operational center of the Nazi regime), regional (large parts of Asia formerly victimized by Japanese imperialism), and global (with numerous instances of mass sexual violence during war), the ceremony featured three female speakers who addressed an overwhelmingly female audience: a representative of the local city district office; a representative of the Korea Verband, a politically independent, German-speaking information and cooperation platform for people "interested in the history and culture of Korea"; and a former

---

[49] "Japan May Delay Sending New Ambassador to South Korea amid Renewed Tensions," *Japan Times*, January 15, 2021, accessed January 21, 2021, www.japantimes.co.jp/news/2021/01/15/national/south-korea-ambassador/.

Figure 4.3 Bronze Statue of Peace in Berlin-Moabit, Germany.

118   Sex at War

director of the Ravensbrück National Memorial, which was built at the site of a Nazi concentration camp.[50]

Like dozens of its namesakes around the world, the Statue of Peace in Berlin is a stark reminder that the Asia-Pacific War constituted an unprecedented, vast web of both overt and concealed sexual incitement and mass violence. And, like all its namesakes, this statue prompted swift condemnation by the Japanese government, which pressed for its removal.[51] This almost folklorically predictable sequence highlights the conservative Japanese state's repeatedly reoccurring reluctance to acknowledge its wartime past. The support for such memorials, especially in that they stand far from the original locale of the crimes they illuminate, demonstrates how one wartime state's gendered sexualized mass violence resonates across national and generational boundaries to reach well beyond the individuals upon whom the crimes were inflicted. Significantly, the citizen activists behind the Berlin statue also see it as a memorial and cenotaph of ongoing wars, the plight of refugees, the suffering of marginalized populations, and the violence against girls and women up to the present day.

As the story of Yayutz and Chūzō at the beginning of this chapter suggests, war could be a time of excitement, romantic freedom, and sexual transgression. In fact, for some, the constant threat of death fueled apocalyptic hedonism, romance between unlikely partners, and artistic and literary inspiration. Yet, with the occasional exception, it is in part the longstanding practice by political leaders in Japan and elsewhere to relegate *sexual* mass violence to the role of a mere glitch in military discipline or an uncontrollable *effect* of military mass violence that has prevented us from recognizing what this chapter shows: Japan's imperialist war and empire-building more generally also constituted unprecedented systematic sexual mass violence. The system of sexual slavery, established by the government under the pretext of preventing uncontrolled rape, was hidden from subsequent generations for decades after the collapse of the Japanese empire at the end of the war. That this system can periodically reignite contentious debates, and harm in particular

---

[50] "About Us," Korea Verband, accessed June 2, 2021, www.koreaverband.de/en/.

[51] "Für den Frieden! Gegen Sexualisierte Gewalt! Die Friedensstatue in Berlin," AG Trostfrauen, accessed January 21, 2021, http://trostfrauen.de/friedensstatue-berlin/; "Trostfrauen-Statue darf vorerst doch bleiben," *Berliner Morgenpost*, October 13, 2020, accessed January 21, 2021, www.morgenpost.de/bezirke/mitte/article230658630/Trostfrauen-Statue-soll-weg-Mitte-beugt-sich-Tokios-Druck.html; Julian Ryall, "Korean 'Comfort Women' Statue in Berlin Angers Japan," *Deutsche Welle*, October 1, 2020; Mitch Shin, "South Koreans Welcome Decision to Maintain 'Comfort Women' Statue in Berlin," *Diplomat*, December 7, 2020.

Global Commemorations 119

Japan's relations with South Korea, is both dismissive of the women who had been enslaved and dishonest about Japanese wartime policies and conduct. In addition, such attempts at rearticulation suggest the desire on the part of the Japanese government that the war itself – minus the sexual slavery system – had been legitimate and just.

Literature and Visual Culture

Edogawa Ranpō's story "Caterpillar" (*Kyatapirā*)[52] features the return of a grotesquely injured soldier. Nora Okja Keller's *Comfort Woman: A Novel*[53] is a fictional take on the experiences at the core of this chapter.

A number of documentary films feature the wartime sexual slavery system through survivors' testimonies and historians' assessments, along with the stances of Japanese right-wing organizations. Dai Sil Kim-Gibson's documentary *Silence Broken: Korean Comfort Women* (1999)[54] and Tiffany Hsiung's *The Apology* (2016)[55] both focus on Korean survivors, whereas Ke Guo's *Twenty-Two* (2015)[56] features twenty-two former Chinese "comfort women." And Hara Kazuo's controversial documentary *The Emperor's Naked Army Marches On* (*Yuki Yukite Shingun*, 1987)[57] approaches war memories from the perspective of former soldiers (and perpetrators of horrible crimes).

Film directors have also grappled with the interconnections between military mass violence and sexual violence, including Suzuki Seijun, whose *The Story of a Prostitute* (*Shunpu Den*, 1965),[58] based on the novel of the same name by Tamura Taijiro, tells the story of Harumi, a "comfort woman" on the Manchurian front. In Wakamatsu Kōji's *The Caterpillar* (*Kyatapirā*, 2010)[59] – based on Edogawa Ranpō's story (noted above), has Lieutenant Kurokawa return to his home town – a "military god" turned "soldier freak"[60] – where he is tormented by his flashbacks

[52] Edogawa Ranpō, "Caterpillar," in *Japanese Tales of Mystery and Imagination*, ed. and trans. James B. Harris (North Clarendon, VT: Tuttle, 2012).
[53] Nora Okja Keller, *Comfort Woman: A Novel* (New York: Penguin, 1998).
[54] Dai Sil Kim-Gibson, *Silence Broken: Korean Comfort Women* (San Francisco: Center for Asian American Media, 1999).
[55] Tiffany Hsiung, *The Apology* (Ottawa: National Film Board of Canada, 2016), accessed June 6, 2021, www.nfb.ca/film/apology/.
[56] Ke Guo, *Twenty-Two* (Los Angeles: China Lion, 2015).
[57] Hara Kazuo, *The Emperor's Naked Army Marches On* (*Yuki Yukite Shingun*) (Imamura Productions, Shisso Production, and Zanzou-sha, 1987).
[58] Hajime Takaiwa, based on the novel by Taijiro Tamura, *The Story of a Prostitute* (*Shunpu Den*), directed by Suzuki Seijun (Tokyo: Nikkatsu, 1965).
[59] Hisako Kurosawa and Masao Adachi, *The Caterpillar* (*Kyatapirā*) directed by Wakamatsu Kōji (Tokyo: Skhole Co./Wakamatsu Productions, 2010).
[60] The "soldier freak" is analyzed by Uchiyama, *Japan's Carnival War*, 144.

of the sexual (and other) violence he imparted on women during the war, as well as on his wife prior to being deployed. Acknowledging the global dimension of World War II and the creative attempts at *Vergangenheitsbewältigung* ("overcoming the past") that followed from the 1960s onward, Wakamatsu's disturbing film is a worthy match to European classics of this genre, including Pier Paolo Pasolini's *Salò, or the 120 Days of Sodom* (*Salò o le giornate di Sodoma*, 1975) – based on *The 120 Days of Sodom* by Marquis de Sade – and Liliana Cavani's *The Night Porter* (*Il portiere di notte*, 1974).

5 The Politics of Sexual Labor

Hatakeno Tomato began the process of transitioning at the age of twenty-six, and came out as a transgender woman at the age of twenty-nine. In 1996, she opened Japan's first transgender café and began to speak out about transgender issues. For ten years, Hatakeno engaged in sex work as a "new half bride" (*nyū hāfu yome*). Today, she is a writer and human rights activist invested in depathologizing trans people. In a slim book on sex work, she reflected on her role in Japan's most recent history of trans sex work. Hatakeno notes the transformation of the sex industry in the wake of the AIDS/HIV panic in the 1980s. Then, so-called "fashion health clubs" began to offer an ever-greater variety of sexual services. At the same time, trans establishments diversified along with the mainstream.[1] While Hatakeno recalls that trans sex workers continued to be routinely addressed as Mr. Lady, the term "new half" was adopted for trans people more generally, both as an identitarian label and as one that became more broadly used in media and public discourse. The "half" of "new half" was borrowed from the (old) "half" (*hāfu*) that used to signify biracial people but which has more recently been widely reevaluated and found derogatory. "New" signals the trans aspect of a person in distinction from (old) biraciality. As we shall see in Chapter 6, the 1990s experienced a "trans boom" – and a time of high visibility for sexual minorities in general – which saw a number of trans personalities appearing on television and the establishment of "new half" BDSM (bondage and discipline, dominance and submission, sadism and masochism) clubs, sexual massage parlors, and the like.[2] According to Hatakeno's recollections of the boom, the sexual services on offer were

---

[1] The New Marylin Club is the main site of the film *Shinjuku Boys* by Kim Longinotto and is listed under film recommendations in Chapter 6.

[2] I adopt the Anglo-American acronym here even though, in Japanese, the abbreviation "SM" or "S & M" is most commonly used; in the context of sex commerce, "SM" or "S & M" usually signify not only sadism and masochism but also bondage and discipline (hence "BDSM" in English), together referring to a range of erotic behavior between consenting adults and encompassing various subcultures.

122   The Politics of Sexual Labor

overall not much different from the so-called fashion health establishments that employed cisgender female sex workers. This was with the exception of what was referred to as "reverse anal" (*gyaku anaru*) – trans sex workers performing anal sex on a male customer and vice versa; indeed, "reverse anal" became the key feature of trans fashion health joints. Of course, depending on the extent of their hormone treatment, not all trans sex workers who had kept their penises could necessarily perform that act, and ciswomen sex workers have long used dildos for the same purpose.[3]

Indeed much of the debate about sex work, historically or currently, envisions the sex worker as heterosexual female. For the large majority of sex workers that has been accurate, whether the female had been sold to a brothel by her family, as was common in the past, or she had chosen the sex industry (temporarily) as a means for otherwise unskilled women to earn money. But of course male prostitution has existed all along as well; indeed, it flourished in the Tokugawa period (1603–1868), catering even to a small extent to women. The male sex trade tended to be closely associated with and dependent on the theater world and had substantially declined by the late nineteenth century. (Male prostitutes were far less visible in rural areas.) In contrast, the female trade was dominated by brothel prostitution, which by the middle of the nineteenth century had grown into a huge, independent, and well-integrated industry spanning the archipelago. As for the legality of these practices over the course of centuries leading up to the modern era, in general, "unsanctioned forms of male–female sexuality provoked greater anxiety among shogunal officials than [did] male–male sexuality." This is an enduring fact of Japanese life that plays an intriguing role in Chapter 7 regarding perceptions and suppressions of obscenity. Here it shall suffice to recall that women and men occupied dramatically different roles in households: only women could be alienated as property, used as currency, or held as collateral – in brief, whatever served the domain's interest in either enabling men to raise capital or collecting taxes.[4] Though today's sex-and-entertainment industry no longer legally deems women property, and though the industry also includes male, transgender, and foreign-national sex workers, women – mostly young Japanese women, but also

---

[3] Hatakeno Tomato, "Toransu jendā to sekkusu wāku," in *Sekkusu wāku sutadīsu: Tōjisha shiten de kangaeru sei to rōdō*, ed. SWASH (Tokyo: Nihon Hyōronsha, 2019), 112–15.
[4] Stanley, *Selling Women*, 15–16.

Chinese, Korean, and women of other nationalities – still make up the majority of the trade.[5]

Liberating Prostitutes

This chapter describes the various manifestations of and shifting attitudes toward sex for payment in Japan, from the era of the "pleasure quarters" that "sold" women – plus, at times, men – to the movement to "liberate" prostitutes around 1900 to today's vast sex and entertainment industries. Given the expanse of terrain, a word on nomenclature is in order. During the Tokugawa era (1603–1867) dozens of terms were in use for women who sold sex as an occupation. Some were distinguished by whether they labored legally or illegally or were of higher or lower rank among the prostitutes in the red-light districts. Some terms varied by locality. Other terms, distinguished sex workers from "ordinary" women. Some terms named "ordinary" activities – either as a euphemism for sexual services or in addition to sexual services, such as "tea-steeping girls," "drink-pouring girls," and "meal-serving girls," as well as "laundry girls," and "leg rubbers" who ostensibly rubbed just the customers' two legs while being fully submerged in public baths.

Whatever the name, they all signified one commonality: the exchange of erotic services for payment, usually for currency.[6] As for the most common English-language terms, "prostitute" and "sex worker," these are limiting in different ways. The Japanese term for "prostitution," *baishun*, was only mainstreamed after the Asia-Pacific War. It can mean either "selling spring" or "buying" it, depending on the choice of characters for *bai*, with *shun* ("spring") signifying sex. *Sekkusu wāka*, adapted from "sex worker," is mostly used by activists and lawmakers. As for today's *sekkusu wākas*, those who exchange sex for payment tend to prefer a range of euphemistic terms and references that fudge the line between ordinary kinds of labor and the place at which they practice

---

[5] See Rhacel Salazar Parreñas, *Illicit Flirtations: Labor, Migration and Sex Trafficking in Tokyo* (Stanford, CA: Stanford University Press, 2011); Setoguchi Torao, Masako Izumo Marou, Ranko, Otoki, and a reporter for Ōkē magazine, "Confessions of a Problem: A Roundtable Discussion with Male Prostitutes," in *Queer Voices from Japan: First-Person Narratives from Japan's Sexual Minorities*, ed. Mark McLelland, Katsuhiko Suganuma, and James Welker (Lanham, MD: Lexington Books, 2007), 69–80; Akiko Takeyama, "Intimacy for Sale: Masculinity, Entrepreneurship, and Commodity Self in Japan's Neoliberal Situation," *Japanese Studies* 30, no. 2 (2010): 231–46; and Akiko Takeyama, *Staged Seduction: Selling Dreams in a Tokyo Hostess Club* (Stanford, CA: Stanford University Press, 2016).
[6] Stanley, *Selling Women*, 15; Hans Peter Duerr, *Der Mythos vom Zivilisationsprozess 1: Nacktheit und Scham* (Frankfurt: Suhrkamp Verlag, 1988), 119.

124   The Politics of Sexual Labor

theirs or refer to the sexual and/or gender identities of their staff. They include the already noted fashion health clubs, a term that has replaced the older "soaplands," which offer a range of services that stop short of penetrative vaginal sexual intercourse; *okama* bars that are typically staffed with crossdressing gay men; a small number of host clubs where the staff are mostly heterosexual males who cater to typically heterosexual women; the *onabe* clubs that feature female-to-male transgender staff, like the New Marilyn Club in Tokyo, which makes an appearance in Chapter 6, along with a long list of variations of any of these establishments.

Keen to leave behind, in appearance at least, centuries of thriving "red light districts" – whose most prominent courtesans and geisha were the object of countless works by leading and minor artists and writers alike – modernizers increasingly attempted to control the trade.[7] The earliest modern activists for the prohibition of prostitution were almost exclusively female. One group of middle-class women, inspired by the American Women's Christian Temperance Union, founded a group in Tokyo in 1886; renaming themselves the Japanese Society of Christian Women (Nihon Kirisuto Fujin Kyōkai) in 1893, they merged in 1895 with the newly founded Salvation Army. At the end of the nineteenth century, the Japanese Society of Christian Women had 155 sister organizations across the archipelago and more than 8,000 members, making it one of the most influential women's organizations at the time. Another group, the more radical Alliance for Women's Suffrage (Fusen Kakutoku Dōmei), had more than 1,500 members, most of whom lived in Tokyo.

By the turn of the century, the urban public debate had recast occasional and licensed female sex workers as the source of disease that threatened men's health and – through hereditary sexually transmitted diseases such as syphilis – potentially affected the physical and mental well-being of their offspring, which in turn shattered their families' happiness.[8] And so, when in 1911 a fire almost completely destroyed Yoshiwara, Tokyo's fabled sex trade quarters, a handful of progressive thinkers used the occasion to push to criminalize prostitution via its quest to "liberate" prostitutes (*geishōgi kaihō*). Most prominent among them were Abe Isoo (1865–1949), later a professor of economics at Waseda

---

[7] A dictionary of Japanese sex terms published in 1928 does not list either term; see Matsui Eiichi and Watanabe Tomosuke, *Nihon seigo daijiten: Ingo jiten shūsei 21* (Tokyo: Ōsorasha, [1928] 1997).

[8] Susan Burns, "Bodies and Borders: Syphilis, Prostitution, and the Nation in Japan, 1860–1890," *U.S.–Japan Women's Journal: English Supplement*, no. 15 (1998), 3–30, accessed June 2, 2021, www.jstor.org/stable/42772131.

University and founder of Japan's first social democratic party; Katayama Tetsu (1887–1978), who would become Japan's first socialist prime minister (1947–1948); and Shimada Saburō (1852–1923), a liberal politician and journalist. Calling themselves the Purity Society, the organization published the monthly magazine *Purity* (*Kakusei*) and initiated a prostitution abolition movement (*haishō undō* or *kōgi haishō undō*). Their efforts appeared to bear fruit when, in 1925, they collaborated with the Society of Christian Women, augmenting their ranks – as well as their political influence – with members of parliament, medical doctors, university professors, and well-known Christians and social reformers. They defined "the sexual question" (*seimondai*) as central to a range of issues, including women's suffrage, girls' education, the relations between love and marriage, the family and household system, virginity and monogamy, and the maintenance of the "race." They saw the "liberation of prostitutes" as being key to addressing not just disease but also issues of gender relations and the contract between the individual and the state.[9]

Other abolitionists had yet grander ideas about the connections between prostitution and Japan's status in the world. In 1926, a petition was presented to the government that demanded the immediate end to public prostitution for the sake of the Japanese "empire's international status" and "human rights," because the signatories – all prominent men of industry, politics, and the medical world – viewed prostitution as "damaging to humanity, honor, and public morals." One particularly striking angle of this effort was how one issue brought together men whose politics were otherwise quite far apart. The group included Shibusawa Eiichi and Soeda Jūichi, both influential industrialists and bankers; Suzuki Bunji, a leading anti-war labor activist involved in both the foundation of the Social Democratic Party and the campaigns for the legalization of birth control; Inoue Tetsujirō, a prominent philosopher and proponent of international education who also embraced Japan's imperialism; Kanasugi Eigorō, head of the Tokyo Saiseikai Central Hospital; and Nakahara Ichigorō, head of the Japan Dental University.[10] In short, the question of how to govern prostitution appeared to enthrall everyone.

Yet most officials did not see prohibition as the solution for prostitution; instead, these "regulationists" promoted maintaining the established segregationist system by enforcing ever-tighter control of who

---

[9] Sugita Naogeki, "Seibyō to seishinbyō no kankei," *Kakusei* 14, no. 8 (1924): 17–19.

[10] A copy of the original petition is included in Kawasaki Masako, *Kōshō seido teppai no zehi* (Tokyo: Fujin Shinpō-sha, 1926), 1.

126   The Politics of Sexual Labor

could engage in sex work and with whom. In fact, by the early 1940s, even those who had previously crusaded for the prohibition of prostitution suggested that, for the health and moral benefit of the innocent majority, it was justifiable to sacrifice a small number of women to the trade. A formidable mainstream of regulationists developed, including police, medical doctors, and members of the Ministry of the Interior, all of whom defended the existing system on two counts. One, regulationists insisted that the established system whereby prostitutes received regular health checks effectively – or at least sufficiently – limited the risk of infection of the ordinary population. And two, the red-light districts served as a kind of segregated "public latrine" that contained the rotten morals of the trade, kept at bay the threat to public hygiene and health, and ultimately protected "good" girls and women from unwanted solicitation. Regarding the latter, the mass migration of young men (and women) to urban centers had led to a large concentration of men who postponed marriage due to lacking the means to found a household. In the minds of regulationists, the availability of reasonably priced, reasonably sanitary women offering sex helped secure the socioeconomic order and maintain social peace. Prohibition, by contrast, would prompt an increase in sex crimes.

Critics of this particular logic conceded that, indeed, prostitution was an economic necessity for the women in question but the solution did not lie in controlling prostitution in one way or another but in addressing the economic issues from which such desperate women emerged. Feminist historian and anarchist Takamure Itsue (1894–1964) put this position most succinctly. In an anarchist journal she noted that, historically, prostitution had always been a system sustained by men with means, time, and desire – a point she supported with evidence. Citing a 1915–1918 study carried out in Wakayama prefecture on the clientele of prostitutes, she noted that, of 166,000 customers, the largest group were men between the age of twenty-six and forty-five – suggesting that most of the men who frequented the prostitutes' quarters were of considerable means.[11] Along with many other men, Yamamura Gunpei – founder of the Japanese Salvation Army and a sharp critic of the prostitution system – partially agreed with Takamure. He proposed that men who frequented prostitutes were rich enough to pay, as Takamure suggested. But he also mentioned all those other men who were too poor to marry and for whom the only affordable way of satisfying their sexual urges was paying for sex, even though, surely, they would prefer a love

[11] Takamure Itsue in *Wagakuni*, cit. Andrew E. Barshay, *State and Intellectual in Imperial Japan: The Public Man in Crisis* (Berkeley: University of California Press, 1988), 184–85.

marriage over a fleeting commercial transaction.[12] In actuality, according to a number of other studies, the sex market was enormous, and had a wide range of offerings for men from a variety of professions and classes.[13]

Renewing the Oldest Profession

But what was known about the actual women who sold sex? Apparently very little beyond numbers – numbers that were counted and estimated by a broadening range of local administrative entities throughout the empire, especially tabulating legal and illegal prostitutes along with cases of venereal disease. In order to remedy this situation, in 1919, a small magazine titled *Sex Research* (*Sei no Kenkyū*) printed the following call:

A request to our readers! It is important to collect more data, detailed information, and all kinds of impressions about the social problem of prostitution. We cannot do this research on our own and, thus, request that our readers send us the following information: about the situation of prostitutes in various locales, the ratio of total population and number of prostitutes, registered and unregistered prostitutes, the connections of customs in various regions with prostitutions, and about the emergence of prostitution.[14]

Interestingly, some of the data requested was already documented by local authorities. For example, there were more than 54,000 registered prostitutes in Japan in 1916 (a figure that had increased by 100 percent from an 1884 assessment). This meant that, in a large city like Ōsaka, for instance, there was a 1:101 ratio of prostitutes to adult men; that figure was 1:153 in Kyoto and 1:269 in Tokyo. But even these numbers do not even tell the whole quantitative story, since they exclude 79,000 geisha and 48,000 "bar girls" who either occasionally or regularly sold sex – in addition to other illegal prostitutes. A later survey, documented and published by the Ōsaka City survey office in 1923, indicated that about one in thirty women between the ages of eighteen and twenty-nine at least occasionally took payment for sex. And as for that payment, the price for a brothel visit had increased from ¥2.55 in 1913 to twice as much in 1923. The brothels of Ōsaka alone were visited 3.7 million times

---

[12] Yamamuro Gunpei 1924, cit. Okamoto Kazuhiko, "Taishū no gaku toshite no seikagaku no tenkai," *Gendai Seikyōiku Kenkyū*, no. 14 (1983): 110.

[13] Peter Ackermann, "Respite from Everyday Life: Kōtō-ku (Tokyo) in Recollections," in *The Culture of Japan as Seen through Its Leisure*, ed. Sepp Linhart and Sabine Frühstück (Albany: State University of New York Press, 1998), 27–40.

[14] Kitano Hiromi, "Dokusha e no onegai!," *Sei no Kenkyū: Tokubetsugō–Baiin kenkyū*, January 1, 1919, 54.

128   The Politics of Sexual Labor

a year, amounting to between 2.5 and 20 customers per day and per prostitute.[15]

Without doubt, the vast majority of prostitutes came from Japan's poorest regions, and were daughters of farmers, fishermen, and laborers. In 1924, 28 percent of prostitutes had had just six years of elementary school; 13 percent had never received any formal education. In that same year, a survey published by a representative of the Salvation Army documented that each respondent named "material hardship" as the motivation for entering the sex trade; in fact, the police responsible for registering women as prostitutes made "material hardship" a precondition of that registration.[16] Many women cited the necessity of caring for their children or repaying debts. But the majority wished to support their impoverished families, sometimes to afford medical care for a family member or to pay for the education of (typically) a brother. Some were sold into prostitution by their families for similar reasons.

In such cases, the woman in question was not necessarily stigmatized. For instance, in 1935 Ella Wiswell described in her field journal a young pregnant woman who had returned to her home village in order to give birth before going back to the brothel to which her father had sold her. The women back home warmly welcomed her – perhaps in no small part because she had sent money to her family despite having been sold against her will. In general, about 60 percent of migrant girls and young women, regardless of the type of work, sent money home to support their families, yet only 30 percent of boys and young men did.[17] In another point against the stigma of prostitution, the young women who stayed on the farm often had rosy visions of the city life they imagined the migrant women enjoyed; to them, any city work – whether in a café, a factory, or a brothel – did not seem as hard to them as farm work. Indeed, the boundaries between one kind of workplace and another were porous. Small-scale surveys from the early twentieth century confirm that large numbers of female migrant workers moved from prostitution to factory work and the service industry within a few years. One male author noted in 1925 that an estimated 30 percent of textile workers in the factory that

---

[15] These numbers varied greatly depending on location and price; see Sheldon M. Garon, "The World's Oldest Debate? Prostitution and the State in Imperial Japan, 1900–1945," *American Historical Review* 98, no. 3 (1993): 715, accessed June 2, 2021, https://doi.org/10.2307/2167547.

[16] Garon, "The World's Oldest Debate?," 716.

[17] These numbers are based on a small pool of data available; see Ieda Sakichi, "Seinenkō no seibyō to risonjō mondai," *Kakusei* 29, no. 3 (1939): 17–19.

Renewing the Oldest Profession

employed him had previously worked as prostitutes, in large part because they had been recruited under false pretenses.[18]

Despite a range of more nuanced perspectives, there was a distinct stigma about which almost everyone agreed: prostitutes were a source of venereal disease.[19] The editor of the household magazine *Household Health* (*Katei Eisei*), for instance, warned in distinctly unsympathetic terms, in 1940: "They have beautiful bodies, wear silk and white make-up that makes the skin look beautiful. A layer beneath that beauty, however, lies a rotting body. Very soon their terrible disease will reveal itself, and skin and body will be destroyed from the brain. Those are the horrible venereal diseases: gonorrhea, syphilis, and others."[20] Western visitors echoed such observations. Solicitor and prolific legal translator of Japanese legislation J. E. De Becker wrote:

Thus women who were full of disease were painted and made up to look like young girls, and old hags had their eyebrows blackened with charcoal and their hair fashionably dressed in order to add to their attractions. Many of these prostitutes had their noses eaten away by syphilis, so they had the damage repaired by colored candle drippings. Among them were deaf, dumb, lame persons suffering from amaurosis and other maladies owning to syphilis, which prevented them from practicing in a regular brothel. These whitened their dirty complexions with powder, and the syphilitic sores and wounds in their faces were filled up and concealed by cosmetics, while the handkerchiefs which they bound round their heads did the rest, and guarded against too close an inspection.[21]

The more progressive abolitionists saw more than just a danger for public health; they also saw in the prostitution system an expression of unequal gender relations. Hence, many echoed the demands made by the women's movement under the leadership of Hiratsuka Raichō

---

[18] Hosoi Wakizō, *Jokō aishi* (Tokyo: Iwanami Shoten, [1925] 1974), 282; Smith and Wiswell, *The Women of Suyemura*, 139.

[19] The German dermatologists Erich Hoffmann and F. Schaudinn discovered the syphilis pathogen in 1905, but effective treatment to this centuries-old disease was only available after 1909, when Paul Ehrlich and his laboratory assistant Hata Sahachirō developed the antibiotic medication Salvarsan 606. The next breakthrough was the discovery of penicillin (1929); in the following years, that and other antibiotics provided effective treatment for several venereal diseases. Thereafter, at least in military hospitals, Salvarsan injections became routine treatment.

[20] Yoshii Kaneoka, "Eiseijō kara mitaru kōshō mondai" [The Prostitution Problem Viewed from the Perspective of Hygiene], *Kakusei* 30, no. 1 (1940): 39.

[21] For Becker's translations of Japanese legal texts, see John Mark Ockerbloom, ed., "Online Books by J. E. De Becker," Online Books Page Library, accessed June 2, 2021, http://onlinebooks.library.upenn.edu/webbin/book/lookupname?key=De%20Becker%2c%20J.%20E.%20%28Joseph%20Ernest%29%2c%201863-1929; George Riley Scott, *Far Eastern Sex Life: An Anthropological, Ethnological, and Sociological Study of the Love Relations, Marriage Rites, and Home Life of the Oriental People* (London: Gerald G. Swan, 1943), 188.

130   The Politics of Sexual Labor

(1886–1971). In an effort to protect innocent women and unborn children, she promoted what would have been Japan's first eugenics law designed to require men who wanted to marry to be examined for venereal disease. If a man could not – or would not – produce a negative test result, permission to marry would have been denied. The legislation also proposed that wives of infected husbands should be able to divorce based on that diagnosis. It also specified that people with venereal diseases should be prohibited from sexual relations – or pay a fine of up to the exorbitant sum of ¥300 if they violated that regulation. Writing in 1918, Raichō stated that providing women for the sexual satisfaction of men deemed Japan not worthy of a modern nation from the standpoint of "human rights and individual morals, social mores, and national hygiene."[22] (Ultimately, Raichō's campaign was not successful.)

By the beginning of the 1930s, the movement to prohibit prostitution had faltered. Instead, its members turned their sights on a new threat to social order and sexual morals: in modern, urban dance halls and cafés. They thought of brothel districts as the "old Japan" to be overcome, as marketplaces that catered almost exclusively to men's heterosexual desires. Dance halls, beer halls, and cafés, by contrast, were widely associated with the young generation that had migrated to the cities – a generation swayed by modernism, individualism, and romantic gender relations modeled on western ideals. And at the new dance halls and cafés there were waitresses who sold sex (quietly negotiated, for after hours) as well as food and beverages. These young women chose their workplaces themselves, negotiated terms directly with their employers, and styled themselves as "modern girls" (the object of analysis in Chapter 2). Contemporary cultural critics spoke of this as a time of "erotic grotesque nonsense" when they described, for instance, the Casino Fōrī, where on Fridays dancers shed their clothes – that is, until police stepped in and ordered them to wear, and keep on, skin-colored underwear under those clothes. The grotesquerie idea, introduced by the magazine *Bungei Shunjū* in 1929, reflected what the cultural establishment perceived to be a *zeitgeist* marked by high joblessness, a depressed economy, and a general sense of crisis that found its release in frantic entertainment and sexual perversions. Tokyo alone was home to more than 7,500 cafés and bars, an increasing number of which established

---

[22] Hiratsuka Raichō, *In the Beginning Woman Was the Sun: The Autobiography of a Japanese Feminist*, trans. with an introduction and notes Teruko Craig (New York: Columbia University Press, 1992), 341.

Renewing the Oldest Profession 131

ever more tantalizing sexual attractions and services provided by young female employees often misleadingly referred to as "maids" (*jokyū*).[23] Since members of the anti-prostitution movement were increasingly uncomfortable with these new sites of sexual exaltation and entertainment, they applauded police raids of these establishments and called for additional restrictions. Striving to address the opposite side of that coin, the members of the Society of Christian Women later campaigned against visiting dance halls and cafés – and drinking and smoking to boot.

In 1935, the Purity Society joined forces with and dissolved into the National League for Pure Blood (Kokumin Junketsu Dōmei), one of a range of fascistic-eugenic organizations aiming for the production of healthy recruits and mothers.[24] When the Japanese empire entered a full-blown war with China in 1937, the issue of prostitution became embroiled in wartime politics. Ichikawa Fusae – whose life's work up until then had been both the abolition of prostitution and female suffrage – welcomed the war as a platform to strengthen women's status. In 1941, Raichō joined other prominent members of the women's movement and abolitionists in supporting the implementation of the National Eugenics Law (*Kokumin Yūseihō*), which aimed to sterilize people "of inferior constitution caused by inherited diseases," including syphilis. When during that same year Japan declared war on the United States and Great Britain, Abe Isoo, founder of the Purity Society and then-chairman of the Social Democratic Party, welcomed the development as a "good opportunity to clean up the lack of morals."[25] Through all this, the trajectory of the cause highlighted the shape-shifting character of the sex trade. It also revealed a generational rift that seemed to take both abolitionists and reformers by surprise. Altogether, it laid bare the enormous impact of imperialism and war on sexual culture, wherein power, politics, and morals were interwoven (the central subject of Chapter 4).

Shortly after Japan's defeat in 1945, what remained of the Japanese government helped establish the Recreation and Amusement Association (RAA), which was essentially a system of brothels for the use of occupation forces. Even though prostitution was illegal in most of the United States at the time, the Allied General Headquarters did not concern themselves with the RAA brothels until the incidents of sexually transmitted diseases contracted therein began to threaten the fighting

---

[23] Sabine Frühstück, *Die Politik der Sexualwissenschaft: Zur Produktion und Popularisierung sexologischen Wissens in Japan 1908–1941*, Beiträge zur Japanologie, vol. 34 (Vienna: Institute of Japanese Studies, 1997), 153–54.
[24] Garon, "The World's Oldest Debate?," 727.
[25] Abe Isoo, "Jinkō mondai to danjo mondai," *Kakusei* 32, no. 3 (1942): 3–5.

132   The Politics of Sexual Labor

readiness of the American forces. And so, in 1946, commander in chief Douglas MacArthur issued a decree "to abrogate all laws that permitted licensed prostitution and nullified all contracts that committed any woman to the practice" – though the decree specifically did not criminalize acts of prostitution where "individuals acted 'of their own will and accord.'"[26] As such, the decree's actual consequence did not include the closure of sites for sexual services; it merely negated the laws whereby a brothel could be *licensed* as a brothel. Brothels remained open. Nor did the decree liberate women from debt bondage; they still owed debt – they just could not be *forced* to repay it with sexual services. Such were the circumstances that led to Yoshida Sumiko sending a letter to the Allied occupation authorities (received in October 1946) that read: "Please make it possible for hundreds of women to go home freely to their fathers and mothers as soon as possible. We can do nothing because the employer holds the notes for our debt." All that had taken place was the deregulation of the market referred to as *seifūzoku* – where (primarily) women who provide sex for payment are imagined to be tied to some kind of "sex establishment" (in legal terms: *seifūzoku kanren tokushu eigyō*).[27] Yoshida's plea went nowhere.

The Allied occupation ended in 1952. In 1956, after roughly three and a half centuries of organized, state-sanctioned prostitution and several abortive attempts, spearheaded by congresswomen, the Japanese government passed the Prostitution Prevention Law (*Baishun bōshi-hō*), which remains in place today. Defining prostitution narrowly, in terms of payment for the act of penile–vaginal coitus, it stipulates punishment for the following offenses: public solicitation of prostitution, procurement of prostitution, forced or an attempt to force prostitution, offering or receiving compensation for another's prostitution, and the provision or management of a place for prostitution. As such, rather than attempting to eradicate sexual commerce, the law simply established the conditions under which sex industry businesses could operate.[28] Also, by this specific heteronormative definition of "sex," same-sex commercial sexual services are excluded from the law, and are not acknowledged by the state.[29]

The law's impact on the sex industry has remained debatable. Some of its critics were sex workers themselves. Consider the account of a young

---

[26] Kovner, *Occupying Power*, 30.
[27] Sarah Kovner, "Base Cultures: Sex Workers and Servicemen in Occupied Japan," *Journal of Asian Studies* 68, no. 3 (2009): 777.
[28] Nagai Yoshikazu, *Fūzoku eigyō torishimari* (Tokyo: Kōdansha, 2002).
[29] Natori Toshiya, "Baishun bōshi-hō ihan," in *Fūzoku seihanzai*, ed. Fujinaga Yukiharu (Tokyo: Hōrei Shuppan, [1996] 2005), 127.

woman by the name of Masuda Sayo, who related in her autobiography a tale far too many women had also lived. Having been sent to work as a nursemaid at the age of six, she was later sold to a geisha house at the age of twelve. There, she first worked as a servant while training in the arts of dance, song, shamisen, and drum. At the age of sixteen, she made her debut as a geisha in a hot spring resort house – after which she was subsequently expected to routinely engage in sex for payment. Later, she referred to her life as "half a lifetime of pain and struggle." Aged thirty-two when the law was passed, she was skeptical about both its benefits and efficacy. She wrote the following:

> Prostitution isn't something that will simply disappear just because you've passed a law against it. Probably this stems from a well-meaning attempt to rescue these women from exploitation and profiteering at the hands of rapacious entrepreneurs; but among those making the laws, were there any women like us, who couldn't have survived if they hadn't prostituted themselves? I went to see a newsreel. Those women legislators, all done up in their finery, mincing about so proudly on their tour of the red-light district – they were just having fun, I was forced to conclude. If they thought all that goggle-eyed gawking was going to help them understand what goes on in the whorehouses, they were very badly mistaken.[30]

Pointing out the law's flaws, Masuda asked, "if a geisha or a maid sleeps with a customer and gets paid, isn't that prostitution? ... But if they are accused, they'll just say they're in love with each other."[31] Many women with experience of taking payment for sex agreed, echoing the position made by Takamura Itsue (1894–1964) almost three decades prior: namely, that prostitution was sustained by poverty and the limited possibilities for women to independently make a decent living. Masuda had raised her younger brother on her own. When he contracted tuberculosis, which at the time was essentially a death sentence, he committed suicide so she would not have to sell sex in order to pay for his medical care. Like her, many women at the time supported families and parents whom the war had left incapable of earning a living. Some came from districts where coal mines or factories had closed down, and so had no other opportunities for work. And yet other women tried to escape the chronically low wages of female occupations, such as those in the textile industry.

Indeed, many female prostitutes wanted prostitution to remain a legal option. Prostitutes were far from mute. They had formed a union, published a newspaper, held meetings, and collected signatures for prostitution to remain a legal option for women. Many prostitutes' concerns

---

[30] Masuda, *Autobiography of a Geisha*, 158.   [31] Masuda, *Autobiography of a Geisha*, 158.

134   The Politics of Sexual Labor

came down to the question of how else to make a living.[32] (From the little we know about male prostitutes at the time, their lot was rather similarly governed by the lack of other options.)[33] As Masuda had suspected, rather than eradicating the trade, the Prostitution Prevention Law triggered or at least facilitated three things. First, almost 80 percent of prostitutes surveyed in 1957 reported that "they intended to continue working as prostitutes outside the law." A year later, "more than 60 percent of former proprietors of prostitution businesses had provided for such women by 'changing' to inns, restaurants, bars, rental venues, cabarets, cafés, and so on." Second, the sex industry was gradually taken over by organized crime.[34] And, third, as fewer Japanese women were forced into prostitution by poverty, and with the normalization of relations between Japan and Korea in 1965, Japanese men began to travel abroad on organized sex tours. In turn, Japanese prostitutes were joined by large numbers of non-Japanese sex workers.[35]

The longstanding sentiment that men simply had sexual desires that needed to be catered to has continued to stifle much enthusiasm for stricter or even just unambiguous legislation.[36] From the moment the Prostitution Prevention Law was implemented, the narrow definition of what constitutes illegal sex work led to a diversification of establishments and erotic services that, nominally and legally at least, offer every imaginable sexual service other than penal–vaginal intercourse.

The Work of Sex Today

Today, Japan is home to one of the world's largest sex industries within an even larger market for eroticized intimacy. Despite the Prostitution

---

[32] With few exceptions, historians have had more interest in the abolitionists, including privileged middle-class women, who held that "prostitution is a practice that infringes women's rights as human beings, so that the abolition of licensed prostitution and the criminalization of the sex industry constitute liberation and progress." For insights on prostitutes' opinions, see G. G. Rowley, "Prostitutes against the Prostitution Prevention Act of 1956," *U.S.–Japan Women's Journal: English Supplement*, no. 23 (2002): 48–50, accessed June 2, 2021, www.jstor.org/stable/42772190.

[33] The August 1949 issue of *Ōkē* magazine included a conversation of a group of male prostitutes; Wim Lunsing, trans., "Confessions of a Problem: A Roundtable Discussion with Male Prostitutes," in *Queer Voices from Japan: First-Person Narratives from Japan's Sexual Minorities*, ed. Mark McLelland, Katsuhiko Suganuma, and James Welker (Lanham, MD: Lexington Books, 2007), 71.

[34] Rowley, "Prostitutes against the Prostitution Prevention Act of 1956," 46; Holly Sanders, "*Panpan*: Streetwalking in Occupied Japan," *Pacific Historical Review* 81, no. 3 (2012): 404–31.

[35] Caroline Norma, "Demand from Abroad: Japanese Involvement in the 1970s' Development of South Korea's Sex Industry," *Journal of Korean Studies* 19, no. 2 (2014): 399–28.

[36] Kovner, *Occupying Power*, 30.

The Work of Sex Today 135

Prevention Law, there are an estimated 222,000 sex workers legally employed in approximately 22,200 legal businesses that offer a variety of sexual services gilded by ever new names, ranging from the oldest soaplands and their variants (bathhouse brothels), *hotetoru* (hotel Turkish bath) and *mantoru* ("mansion" Turkish bath), and strip joints to the newer "fashion health" clubs, love hotels (or "boutique" or "fashion" hotels for trysts), image clubs (styled in fantasy themes such as a classroom, a doctor's office, a train carriage – even a corporate setting), BDSM clubs, pink salons (offering all kinds of massage services), delivery health services (home visits), and escort services.[37] This list does not include illegal businesses, what feminist sociologist Susan Watkins calls the "gangsterized zones of the informal economy."[38]

In an interview conducted by anthropologist Gabriele Koch, a retired sex worker who goes by the name Sachiko captured the normalcy and permanency of the sex industry in present-day Japan. Koch asked Sachiko about one of the effects of the March 11, 2011 earthquake, tsunami, and nuclear disaster: the short-term moratorium to a wide range of entertainment and celebratory activities out of a sense of solidarity with the victims – and how that had affected Tokyo's sex industry. Koch reports that Sachiko "could not keep herself from laughing," and assured her interviewer that, given the permanency of "the male search for intimacy and gratification – and for the feminized care of sex workers," commercial sex would outlive every other industry.[39]

The three laws governing the industry specify what is legal and what is not. The 1956 Prostitution Prevention Law defines what can be deemed a prescribed site of sexual pleasure. First implemented in 1948, the Law Regulating Entertainment Businesses (Fūzoku eigyōtō no kisei oyobi gyōmu no tekiseikatō ni kan suru hōritsu) has undergone several changes and is currently designed to recognize and oversee businesses in which women offer male clients a range of explicitly sexual services. And the 1947 Child Welfare Act, amended in 2017, bans minors from working in the sex and entertainment industries to protect them from both "obscene acts" and alcohol consumption, although background checks are

---

[37] Gabriele Koch found that, according to Police Agency data for 2018, 31,925 businesses are known under the legal category of "sex industry"; *Healing Labor*, 175, n. 9.

[38] Watkins, "Which Feminisms?," 7. For a detailed timeline and map of Japan's sex and entertainment industry, see SWASH (Sex Work and Health), ed., *Sekkusu wāku sutadīsu: Tōjisha shiten de kangaeru sei to rōdō* (Tokyo: Nihon Hyōronsha, 2019), 238–47.

[39] Koch, *Healing Labor*, 3.

136   The Politics of Sexual Labor

nonexistent.[40] Neither of the latter two laws explicitly address male customers. Being charged with controlling the sex industry, the police consider it low priority. They are careful to not appear to endorse the sex industry while, at the same time, they avoid standing in the way of the industry so long as it does not violate the law.[41]

Many sex workers are attracted by the high pay – especially for those in their twenties and thirties – and the autonomy of their work. Some engage in sex work just as a temporary, stop-gap measure, and transition through different segments of the wide-ranging industry. And in many ways sex work is representative of the gendering of labor and the economy at large.[42] For example, many female sex workers articulate their engagement in distinctly female heteronormative terms, namely as healing labor, "a carefully constructed performance of intimacy that commingles maternal care with sexual gratification. They invest considerable effort in making their care emotionally authentic, but the value of this labor rests on their successful enactment of the very assumption of naturalized femininity commonly used to justify women's exclusion from the professional economy." This is in spite of the fact that "the art of seduction" – which anthropologist Akiko Takeyama describes as being key mechanics of host clubs – also magnifies a dynamic of the affect economy. In contrast to female heteronormative sex workers, then, heteronormative male hosts present their working lives in narratives of entrepreneurship that echo Japan's male corporate structure.[43]

The sex industry's customers are even less studied than the sex workers themselves. Shinobu, a "queen" (or dominatrix) in a BDSM club, describes a commonality regarding male customers:

Everybody who comes here wants to be entering another world. That goes for me and the other queens, too. Some of us go home to husbands and children who don't know anything about this. Some are strait-laced office workers. Some are just pulling the wool over their parents' eyes. ... Men come here and bare their true selves. And then *we* go home and bare our true selves in our own man's arms. Or maybe those aren't our true selves. ... All people are actors to some extent, except when they are completely alone. That's why, in my heart, I don't believe anything about anybody.[44]

---

[40] For an English translation of the law, see "Child Protection Law and Policy: Japan," Library of Congress Law Library, last modified December 30, 2020, accessed March 19, 2021, www.loc.gov/law/help/child-protection-law/japan.php.

[41] Koch, *Healing Labor*, 31, 45.

[42] For a detailed timeline and map of Japan's sex and entertainment industry, see SWASH, ed., *Sekkusu wāku sutadīsu*, 238–47.

[43] Takeyama, *Staged Seduction*, 174.

[44] Amy Yamada, "Kneel Down and Lick My Feet," trans. Terry Gallagher, in *Monkey Brain Sushi: New Tastes in Japanese Fiction*, ed. Alfred Birnbaum (Tokyo: Kodansha International, 1991), 187–203.

The Work of Sex Today 137

A BDSM club might not mirror customers' mindsets and motivations across the whole range of services in the sex industry. At least in a collection of interviews with men of all ages, *Men Who Buy and Men Who Don't Buy* (*Kau Otoko, Kawanai Otoko*), male customers describe their motivations and diverse experiences. They claim to have been dragged into a club by work colleagues, sought it out in a moment of frustration over a failed love affair, or were simply curious – along with many other casual or pragmatic explanations.[45] In many ways, they reflect the police's relatively laissez-faire attitude and approach to their charge of controlling the sex industry.

As for the understanding of sex work as labor and of sex workers as workers, no other event has been quite as impactful as HIV/AIDS, which brought sex workers' own perspectives to the foreground, pushed the rearticulation of prostitution as "sex *work*," and the reconfiguration of prostitutes as "sex *workers*" with labor rights and human rights, some-what destigmatizing the source of income and making sex workers' working conditions healthier and safer.[46] Bubu de la Madeleine (who we already encountered in Chapter 4) has been an important figure in this shift. Inspired in part by Carol Leigh's 1987 book, *Sex Work: Writings by Women in the Industry* (published in Japanese in 1993), Bubu adopted the book's key argument: that sex workers are workers and thus had the right to be protected from violence and crime. A range of activist organizations came into being around this time, beginning with EMPOWER in 1985 and the Global Network of Sex Work Projects (NSWP) in 1990. Bubu's own involvement is deeply personal. Her activism on behalf of sex workers started when a friend came out as a gay HIV-positive man; she started working in a "pink salon" in Kyoto in order to fund perform-ances that she staged with that friend, when there was no treatment or therapy for HIV/AIDS. Sadly, Bubu's friend died of AIDS-related com-plications in 1995.

Bubu's activism has ranged from HIV/AIDS poster-making projects for high schools and teachers to her own "pro sex corner," where she performs how to teach sex-industry customers safer sex practices. She has also given sex work health and safety presentations at the Tenth

---

[45] Pandora, ed., *Kau otoko, kawanai otoko* (Tokyo: Gendai Shokan, 1995).

[46] In a book that aims to describe "sex work" from the perspective of its practitioners, the editorial group SWASH (Sex Work and Sexual Health) emphasizes the labor aspect of sex work. SWASH also supports another group, RC-NET, that is devoted to survivors of sexual violence. The book aims to both reposition sex work that is associated with "night work" within academic discourse and refocus research on the practitioners themselves. SWASH, ed., *Sekkusu wāku sutadīsu*, 1–4. "RC-NET" is short for Rēpu Kuraishisu Nettowāku; accessed December 17, 2020, https://rapecrisis-net.org/.

138   The Politics of Sexual Labor

International AIDS Conference in Yokohama in 1994, which focused on Asia and Asians, women, and persons with hemophilia. At the conference, it was also confirmed that transmission predominantly occurred via intravenous drug use and heterosexual relations – as opposed to same-sex relations as presumed early on in the debate about the disease.[47] In 1995 she cofounded the Japanese branch of SWEETLY – Sex Workers! Encourage, Empower, Trust and Love Yourselves! – with activists on behalf of Tokyo's sex industry workers, lesbian rights, and survivors of sexual violence.[48] And in 1999 the director of the National Institute of Infectious Diseases within the Ministry of Health and Welfare engaged Bubu in a study to determine the best policy for HIV prevention. This connection culminated in the foundation of SWASH (Sex Work and Sexual Health), with which the organization Pureisu Tokyo promotes the union of sex work and sexual health as both a right and a mutual commitment to be made between workers and customers.

Bubu is careful to acknowledge that her experience as a sex worker and activist is unlikely to be representative of sex workers overall. She is aware that most sex workers do not engage with rights rhetoric or participate in advocacy campaigns – even though many sex workers are keenly aware of their risky, insecure labor conditions.[49] As for why that is, Rhacel Salazar Parreñas found that at least some Filipina hostesses "may not want rescue," per se, since for many that would mean being out of a job; but they do want "job improvement and labor market flexibility."[50] Echoing Masuda Sayo's doubts about the 1956 Prostitution Prevention Law, Parreñas also notes that the rhetoric of rescue privileges a narrative of law and order over the subjective needs and experiences of communities

---

[47] G. J. Haas, "'Yakugai' AIDS and the Yokohama Xth International AIDS Conference," *Common Factor* 10 (April 1995): 1–22.

[48] SWASH, ed., *Sekkusu wāku sutadīsu*, 25–27. Pureisu Tokyo is a community-based organization devoted to informing about and supporting HIV/AIDS patients and their families; Place Tokyo, June 2, 2021, https://ptokyo.org/. Bubu's artwork has been analyzed in light of her sex work by Klemperer-Markman, "Art, Politics and Prostitution in Occupied/Contemporary Japan."

[49] Meryll Dean, "Sold in Japan: Human Trafficking for Sexual Exploitation," *Japanese Studies* 28, no. 2 (2008): 165–78. The situation is grimmer for internationally trafficked sex workers and others working in the sex and entertainment industries. The International Labour Organization Report on Human Trafficking for Sexual Exploitation in Japan (2005) states that "most trafficking victims who managed to escape complain of labor-related violations, which include complaints of the work being completely different from that in their contract, low wages or non-payment of wages, excessively long working hours, mandatory night work, unsafe or hazardous work environment, and poor accommodation provided by establishments." See Darrell Moen, "Sex Slaves in Japan Today," *Hitotsubashi Journal of Social Studies* 44, no. 2 (2012): 35–53.

[50] Parreñas, *Illicit Flirtations*, 175.

The Work of Sex Today 139

and women, reinforces the notion that sex work is inherently degrading and demeaning to women, and ultimately denies women agency, flattening the experience of women and homogenizing and thereby ignoring their needs.[51] Besides, advocacy and activism require time and energy to spare, which most sex workers lack – along with many other hardworking people, whatever their profession.

Much of what has governed sex for money since the late nineteenth century – places, conditions, labor relations, and plenty of other circumstances – has massively changed. Yet, despite the complex transformation of what sex work was a century and a half ago, many of this history's sex workers have one thing in common: their sense that they lack other viable options. As important as sex work activism is, anthropologist Gabriele Koch's research also brings to light the limitations of that activism: sex workers' understanding of how much their *work* augments male productivity is closely intertwined with their own insecure and unstable labor conditions. Consider too the way that sex work being conceived of as "restorative" (*iyashi*), affective, and "intimate" also fulfills – cruelly, and perhaps more literally than any other gainful activity – the promise of "emotional capitalism" that Eva Illouz has diagnosed for late capitalism. Emotional capitalism, she writes, "has imbued economic transactions – in fact most social relationships – with an unprecedented cultural attention to the linguistic management of emotions, making them the focus of strategies of dialogue, recognition, intimacy, and self-emancipation." It should come as no surprise, then, that "emotional capitalism" is thoroughly sexualized and gendered, possibly more so in Japan than elsewhere.[52]

Literature and Visual Culture

Kawabata Yasunari's *Yukiguni* (*Snow Country*, 1948)[53] tells the story of a wealthy married man who falls in love with a geisha at a remote hot spring. In Amy Yamada's story "Kneel Down and Lick My Feet" (1991),[54] a dominatrix shares her thoughts on her business, her clients, and the world more generally.

---

[51] Parreñas, *Illicit Flirtations*, 6.
[52] Eva Illouz, *Cold Intimacies: The Making of Emotional Capitalism* (Cambridge: Polity Press, 2007), 109.
[53] Kawabata Yasunari, *Yukiguni* (*Snow Country*), trans. Edward Seidensticker (Tokyo: Tuttle, [1956] 2017).
[54] Yamada, "Kneel Down and Lick My Feet."

140   The Politics of Sexual Labor

Street of Shame[55] is a 1956 black-and-white film directed by Mizoguchi Kenji that tells the stories of several Japanese women of different backgrounds who work together in a brothel. In 2018, the film was selected to be screened in the Venice Classics section at the seventy-fifth Venice International Film Festival. *Girls of Dark* (*Onna Bakari no Yoru*, 1961),[56] directed by Tanaka Kinuyo, features a prostitute who is put into a reformatory as a result of a police raid; once released, she tries to build a new life for herself. The somewhat self-explanatory film *History of Postwar Japan as Told by a Bar Hostess* (1970)[57] by Imamura Shōhei is not to be missed. And the documentary *The Great Happiness Space: Tale of an Osaka Love Thief* (2006)[58] by Jake Clennell describes the daily (and nightly) routines of an Osaka host club's hosts and clients.

[55] Narusawa Masashige, based on the novel by Shibaki Yoshiko, *Street of Shame*, directed by Mizoguchi Kenji (Tokyo: Daiei, 1956).
[56] Tanaka Sumie, *Girls of Dark* (*Onna bakari no yoru*), directed by Tanaka Kinuyo (Tokyo: Toho, 1961).
[57] Imamura Shōhei, *History of Postwar Japan as Told by a Bar Hostess* (*Nippon sengoshi: madamu onboro no seikatsu*) (Tokyo: Toho, 1970).
[58] *The Great Happiness Space: Tale of an Osaka Love Thief*, directed by Jake Clennell (UK, 2006).

6   Queer Identities and Activisms

In Chapter 1, I referenced how some late-nineteenth-century conscripts felt anxiety, agony, and shame regarding what were then collectively classified as their "strange bodies." Yet just a few decades later, the sexology of the early twentieth century introduced a dramatically different tone. In 1922, a collection of stories titled *Thoughts on Hermaphroditism* (*Hannannyokō*) provocatively proposed: "Won't the hermaphrodites that are today called abnormalities someday come to call single-sex men and women abnormalities?" At this time, low- and mid-brow cultural circles and sexologists alike were fascinated, not just with sexuality in most general terms, but also with "hermaphrodites," grotesque bodily deformations, and bizarre crimes. Commentators described their subjects in the languages of fantasy and fiction and of medical or psychiatric diagnoses, collectively reflecting an awareness of sexual and gender ambivalence and ambiguity.[1] "Hermaphroditism" then signified much more than today's clinical definition of "intersex" would suggest. "Intersex" refers to individuals born with sex characteristics such as genitals or chromosomes that do not fit the typical definitions of male or female.[2] Depending on the author, "hermaphroditism," by contrast, could refer to a physical, psychological, or emotional state, which could be tied to a practice or condition, thus signifying several of the possibilities captured in today's acronym "LGBTQIA+" (lesbian, gay, bisexual, transgender, queer and/or questioning, intersex, asexual/ agender – with "plus" encompassing any preference not named).

Roughly another four decades later, in the film *Funeral of Roses* (*Bara no Sōretsu*, 1969), the camera focuses closely on an individual in Kimono with a traditional female hairdo framing a face made up appropriately for

---

[1] Algoso, "Thoughts on Hermaphroditism."

[2] The Intersex Initiative Japan is an international collaborative effort. Intersex activism in Japan goes back at least to 1995 when Hashimoto Hideo, a.k.a. Hasshi, founded the organization that is known today as PESFIS, or Peer Support For Intersexuals, which provides support and information for intersex people and their families in Japan; Intersex Initiative Japan, accessed June 22, 2020, www.intersexinitiative.org/japan/.

142   Queer Identities and Activisms

a bar hostess. The hostess identifies as a "gay boy," in the parlance of the day: she is a transgender male to female, or "new half" (*nyū hafu*).[3] In a documentary-style interview, an off-camera voice queries her thoughts on getting married. Marriage, she responds, would be impossible now that she "could not *become* a man again."[4] At the time, it would have been conventional to inquire of a young woman of marriageable age her plans for marriage. But within the realm of this documentary, the question represents a rigid concept of marriage, the then-fixed marker of gender conformity and heteronormativity, leaving unanswered whether this impossibility is identitarian, physical, psychological, legal – or all or none of those.

Fast-forward another five decades, to an era when the very multitude of this question is readily addressed by performance artist Saebōgu/Saeborg. Simultaneously and self-consciously pushing the boundaries of a series of trans-culture meanings, she claimed: "If I undid my body, I could be the person I wanted. I could transcend humanity. Neither male nor female."[5] In much of her work, Saebōgu/Saeborg uses rubber to create a second skin, and describes herself as "imperfect cyborg, half human, half plaything."[6]

Culture and Knowledge

This chapter traces the various iterations of non-heterosexual bodies and relations in modern and contemporary Japanese culture that ultimately lead to today's LGBTQIA+ community. At its most united, this community refuses a number of the analytical opposites that are addressed by anecdotal articulations of sexual and gendered selves: male/female, sex/gender, human/cyborg, body/mind. To one degree or another, in one way or another, each member of today's LGBTQIA+ community lives "the composite character of gender" that makes it "fundamentally ambivalent and ambiguous, capable of fluctuating between or being assigned to more than one referent or category – and thus capable of

---

[3] The older term "half" (*hāfu*) referred to bi-racial individuals—half one race, half the other – although the term is now acknowledged to be derogatory. "New half" (*nyū hāfu*) for transgendered individuals follows the same concept, signifying "half man, half woman" (rather than both male and female, or something altogether non-binary).

[4] Unnamed individual interviewed on camera in the film *Funeral of Roses* (*Bara no Sōretsu*), written and directed by Toshio Matsumoto (Tokyo: Art Theatre Guild, 1969) [emphasis added].

[5] See the documentary *Queer Japan*, written by Graham Kolbein and Anne Ishii, directed by Graham Kolbein (Los Angeles: Altered Innocence, 2019).

[6] The short performance/installation *Saeborg Land* was part of the 2019 program of the Tasmanian midwinter festival Dark Mofo; accessed June 3, 2021, https://saeborg.com/.

Culture and Knowledge 143

being read or understood in more than one way."[7] At their most politically ambitious, LGBTQIA+ bodies and lifestyles would not only achieve
full citizenship and equality in all areas of life, including marriage, but
would also transform social (sexual and gender) constraints and
norms altogether.

Similarly – and this also serves as a vital backdrop for this book as a
whole – the Japanese word and character for "*sei*" or "*seibetsu*," which is
typically interpreted as "biological/physiological sex," does not neatly
translate into Anglo-American conceptions of either "sex" or "gender";
indeed, common Japanese parlance does not differentiate among "*seibetsu*, sex, and gender." Instead, "*seibetsu*" has an ambiguity capable of
both – to conflate them or to enliven the fluidity and flexibility of sex and
gender. (And it did so long before Judith Butler's book *Gender Trouble*
powerfully conceptualized "gender" as a kind of improvised performance.[8]) Meanings and word use in the present have remained fluid and in
flux. This also goes for acronyms. "LGBT" and "LGBTQIA+" are
widely circulated and have been readily adopted. As more and more
institutions have established diversity centers, and even the most conservative political parties in Japan maintain working groups to advocate for
and address issues related to sexual minorities, "LGBT" has often been
the preferred label to capture all non-cis/heteronormative individuals.
Activism-oriented individuals and organizations that see themselves as
part of the community have retired the older term "gay" (that has always
captured more than the Anglo-American equivalent) in favor of the term
"queer." "Queer" resists the pigeon-holing of identities – and thus represents more than just L, G, B, T, Q, I, or A – and instead posits an anti-
essentialist ontology in reimagining sexual identities as always already
fluid, performative, and flexible in the spectrum. "Queer" defies heteronormativity, and as such performs much-needed cultural and theoretical
work. That said, I also acknowledge the way imprecise terminology can
bludgeon identity, and I wish to honor the struggles over words in the
same way that I honor the identity struggles themselves. So I will vary the
vocabulary in order to be both historically correct and to highlight the
malleability of nomenclature.

---

[7] Robertson, *Takarazuka*, 140.
[8] Adrienne Renee Johnson, "*Josō* or 'Gender Free'? Playfully Queer 'Lives' in Visual *Kei*,"
Asian Anthropology 19, no. 2 (June 8, 2020): 119–42, accessed June 3, 2021, https://doi
.org/10.1080/1683478X.2020.1756076; S. P. F. Dale, "An Introduction to X-Jendā:
Examining a New Gender Identity in Japan" *Intersections: Gender and Sexuality in Asia
and the Pacific* 31, accessed June 3, 2021, http://intersections.anu.edu.au/issue31/dale
.htm; Butler, *Gender Trouble*.

144   Queer Identities and Activisms

The history of those who adopt the LGBTQIA+ realm is more than just a story that begins with culture, moves to knowledge, transforms sex acts into identities, and dissolves a rigidly binary sex and gender order in trans fluidity – though it is all that too. In addition, key historical moments have been shaped by reconfigurations of what the concepts of sex, gender, and sexuality mean. What is the significance these concepts have adopted? Sometimes, struggles over them explicitly borrowed the authority of history and tradition. At other times, they aggressively dismissed such. The complexity of these rhetorical and political moves becomes clear when considering earlier same-sex cultures.

From the Middle Ages (1185–1603) to the end of the Edo period (1603–1867), an elaborate, long-standing male–male sexual culture could be found among the warrior class, Buddhist monks, and in the theater and entertainment world. Warriors typically married and had children, but they also thought nothing of demanding complete devotion from their underlings, often including sexual favors and even romance. These underlings were idealized as "beautiful boys," and theirs was praised as beauty that could only be attained by boys and men of the samurai class, not by women. A variant of such relations in samurai castles could also be found in Buddhist monasteries, just couched in spiritual terms.[9] This male–male sexuality did not amount to an identity; it was simply a facet of the loyalty expected – the boys loved by their masters but having little agency of their own, and the masters characterized as "men who love youths," albeit not exclusively.

Most famously, Ihara Saikaku's *Great Mirror of Male Love* (*Nanshoku Okagami*, 1642–1693) is a collection of forty stories that vividly describe such relations, which made this work an everlasting point of reference for several generations of men: those who maintained these practices, those who strove to curtail the mainstreaming of such practices, and the scholars keen on studying both. In his day, Ihara's collection enjoyed broad appeal, since such affairs were quite ordinary in the archipelago's bustling cities. Later on, however, the book was frequently censored.

From the moment of its inception in 1868, the Meiji government introduced a flood of new laws that redrew the line between the public and private spheres, including new styles of policing bodies, life, and death – most effectively via the apparatuses of the police that registered pregnancies, births, and prostitutes along with other individuals and events, as well as the

---

[9] Or Porath, "Nasty Boys or Obedient Children? Childhood and Relative Autonomy in Medieval Japanese Monasteries," in *Child's Play: Multi-sensory Histories of Children and Childhood in Japan*, ed. Sabine Frühstück and Anne Walthall (Oakland: University of California Press, 2017), 17–39.

Culture and Knowledge

military and schools that measured bodies and diagnosed physical and mental aberrations and diseases. And yet only one law strove to prohibit or exclusively regulate same-sex relations. Under the label *"keikan"* for "sodomy," it was briefly designated a criminal practice in 1872 under the guidance of the French legal expert Gustave Emile Boissonade. But since Japanese authorities were disinclined to enforce a law that disregarded the spiritual aspects of male–male sex in Japanese culture, the law was dropped in 1880. As for female–female sex, beyond women being the designated bearers of children (see Chapter 2) and the rare subjects of violent crimes (which then cast them as "poison women"[10]), prior to the modern era, their sexual desires were of little interest to authorities.

That said, hand in hand with the rise of new academic disciplines around 1900 emerged ever-more new approaches to "the discovery and appropriation of desire." Similar to individuals, institutions, and the agencies of modern nation states elsewhere and in close conversations with them, a range of new experts turned to studies and ruminations about sexuality. Social reformers and political radicals, biologists, pedagogues, and sexologists assumed or proposed truths to be found and instrumentality to be dismantled or exploited. As often as they played into the hands of policy- and lawmakers, they fought them in efforts to rescue truth, liberate desire or improve people's lives. Those attracted to their own sex, gender-benders, hermaphrodites, and a range of nonheterosexual and gender-variant individuals, identities, practices, and communities were central to their concerns.[11] In the early 1900s, same-sex sexuality in Japan was no longer a matter proscribed within the context of Buddhist monasteries and historic warrior culture of the past or the entertainment world of the present. Under significant influence of European thought on the state of humanity, same-sex sexuality had become a matter of knowledge – specifically in medicine, sexology, psychology, and pedagogy – as well as a matter of literary self-reflection à la Ōgai Mori's autobiographical story "Vita Sexualis" (*Wita Sekusuarisu*).[12] Ōgai (1862–1922) was only one of many writers at the time to encounter the wrath of the authorities. When "Vita Sexualis"

---

[10] For such "poison women," see Christine L. Marran, *Poison Woman: Figuring Female Transgression in Modern Japanese Culture* (Minneapolis: University of Minnesota Press, 2007).

[11] Historically, gender-bending and cross-dressing have been century-old practices on and off the various stages of Japanese theater – from Kabuki to Takarazuka; see Robertson, *Takarazuka*.

[12] Frühstück, *Colonizing Sex*; see also James Reichert, *In the Company of Men: Representations of Male–Male Sexuality in Modern Japan* (Stanford, CA: Stanford University Press, 2006), 202–03.

146   Queer Identities and Activisms

(*Wita Sekusuarisu*) was published in 1909, the magazine issue in which it appeared was banned. His tale described a range of sexual conversations and experiences he played a part in or witnessed. The witnessed episodes include the extramarital affair of a schoolmate's mother, the sorrow of a mother over her son's affair with a prostitute, and the constant banter among male students about which of them preferred boys. As for the autobiographical episodes, though he barely escapes the violent advances of a few older students, he endures a same-sex assault when he is twelve. When he reports the incident to his father, the father reacts with the utmost imperturbability, signaling this was just one of the many essentially unavoidable dangers of boyhood – and simply cautions him to be careful. When the scandal around "Vita Sexualis" erupted, Ōgai was already a prominent public figure whose authority rested in being both a medical doctor and a literary giant. Having risen to the rank of surgeon general and head of the Bureau of Medical Affairs in the Ministry of War, he was esteemed for his accomplishments as a physician, scientist, military officer, and government official. He was also admired for his ability as author, critic, and public intellectual.

The censorship of "Vita Sexualis" represents a watershed moment in the understanding of same-sex sexuality, one that highlights a shift already in motion to modern notions of homosexuality.[13] The concepts captured in the terms for the love of beautiful boys were replaced with the new term "*hentai seiyoku*," meaning "perverse sexual desire" or perhaps "queer sexual desire," which emphasized the physicality over the spiritual aspects of male–male sexuality. A different term was coined for female–female sexuality, which was believed to be centered on the emotional and spiritual: "*dōseiai*," or "same-sex love" – thus, love as opposed to (just) desire. Indeed, a certain Croatian-Austrian ethnologist, folklorist, sexologist, and Slavist by the name of Dr. Friedrich Solomon Krauss (1859–1938) was one of several foreign commentators who found in 1907 that "homosexual love in Japan is almost as widespread as in other countries although it is less visible and only presents itself to observers with a sharpened gaze."[14] What Krauss did not reveal was whether it was

---

[13] At the time, "hentai" was a neologism for the then medically inflected label "perverse," but I agree with Wim Lunsing, who translates it as "queer," given the proliferation of its use in middle- and low-brow media in the 1920s and 1930s – as well as in relevant media and popular culture since at least the 1990s; Lunsing, "Japan: Finding Its Way?," 309. Regarding the mentioning of a self-described hermaphrodite, see Gregory M. Pflugfelder, *Cartographies of Desire: Male–Male Sexuality in Japanese Discourse, 1600–1950* (Berkeley: University of California Press, 2007), 300.

[14] Friedrich S. Krauss and Tamio Satow, *Japanisches Geschlechtsleben: Abhandlungen und Erhebungen über das Geschlechtsleben des japanischen Volkes* (Hanau am Main: Folkloristische Studien, [1907] 1911), 160.

Culture and Knowledge 147

male–male or also female–female love that revealed itself to his sharp eye. His Japanese contemporaries at least also found it difficult to detect instances of female–female love, although some cultural critics assembled lists of typical behavioral habits, such as unusually frequent letter writing; writing the friend's name over and over again; holding each other's hands when meeting; having long, "dreaming" conversations; singing the friend's praises; not envying the friend's good points; or, conversely, being highly envious; eschewing anything that keeps the two apart; showing off their relationship; a self-conscious disregard of taboo; and taking pleasure in getting their own way.

Enter Yoshiya Nobuko. The first openly lesbian public figure of twentieth-century Japan, Yoshiya (1896–1973) was born into a well-off household in Niigata as the only girl among four siblings. After moving on her own to Tokyo at the age of nineteen, she quickly made her name within an increasingly vocal urban culture of female and feminist expression (see Chapter 3). She was first published at the age of twelve. A series of short stories, *Flower Tales* (*Hana Monogatari*, 1916–1924), made her famous in her early twenties. Her novel *Women's Friendship* (*Onna no Yūjō*), serialized in *Fujin Kurabu* (1933–1935), solidified her status both as a celebrity and as one of the most prolific, well-known, and best-paid writers of the day.[15]

Yoshiya shared a lifelong relationship with a woman she loved at first sight. Determined and radical, and operating within a society in flux and at war, she pursued the legitimization of their relationship using what was then the primary (and possibly only) strategy for "non-traditional" couples: she adopted her. (To this day, adoption – by which one becomes a member of the other's household register – is the only way to achieve the legitimacy of a marriage certificate, which is a bone of contention for queer individuals who pursue marriage equality.) Yoshiya explained the decision to adopt her partner in a letter as follows:

Chiyo-chan. After reading your letter I resolved to build a small house for the two of us. ... Once it is constructed, I will declare it to be a branch household (*bunke*), initiate a household register [listing, by law, all family members], and become a totally independent household head. I will then adopt you so that you can become a legal member of my household (adoption being a formality since the law will not recognize you as a wife. In the meantime, I aim to get the law reformed). We will have our own house and our own household register. That's what I've

---

[15] Jennifer Robertson, "Yoshiya Nobuko: Out and Outspoken in Practice and Prose," in *Same-Sex Cultures and Sexualities: An Anthropological Reader*, ed. Jennifer Robertson (London: Blackwell, 2005), 196–211.

148   Queer Identities and Activisms

decided. ... We'll celebrate your adoption with a party just like a typical marriage reception – it will be our wedding ceremony.[16]

Though she wrote this in 1925, the adoption did not take place until 1957. Her partner's parents had resisted the decision, and Yoshiya had hoped, as noted, to instead reform the law to allow a traditional marriage. Though she strived for that reform, her lifelong prominence did not build into a movement until much later – one that remains only partially successful to this day.[17]

Before his 1922 pronouncement about "hermaphrodites," Miyatake Gaikotsu had speculated more generally about the future of sexual and gender identities. By then, same-sex love had become one of a series of "perversions" – in the parlance of the time – and same-sex sexuality had become an object of medical diagnosis and treatment, but not a subject for law. Indeed, anxious early twentieth-century commentators in Japan and worldwide declared "same-sex love" to be a "disease of civilization" much like alcoholism and tuberculosis are.[18] During the 1920s, homosexuality became ever more finely segmented in binary opposites modeled after "ideal" heterosexual relations: male versus female, active versus passive, congenital versus acquired, true versus "pseudo," permanent versus temporary, complete versus particle, simpler versus compound, and so forth. And yet even in this new paradigm, male–male sexuality remained at the core of the debate. It was no longer simply articulated as older and younger men and/or boys, but as indefinite variations on husbands and wives, or at least masculine-feminine couplings.[19]

From within this milieu, Gaikotsu envisioned the dissolution of the sexual and gender binaries that the notion of a "perverse sexual desire" had solidified.[20] Indeed, such radical pondering was to be expected from someone like him – humorist, activist, author, and publisher of an astonishingly wide range of works. Much like the editors of *Le Charivari* in Paris, *Punch* in London, and *Die Fackel* in Vienna, with his *Humor Newspaper* (*Kokkei Shinbun*) Gaikotsu frequently provoked censorship – only to then mock the censors for aiming to suppress social and

---

[16] Robertson, "Yoshiya Nobuko."
[17] Robertson, "Yoshiya Nobuko," 164; Jennifer Robertson, "Introduction: Sexualizing Anthropology's Fields," in *Same-Sex Cultures and Sexualities: An Anthropological Reader*, ed. Jennifer Robertson (London: Blackwell, 2005), 1–11; Robertson, "Yoshiya Nobuko."
[18] Pflugfelder, *Cartographies of Desire*, 285.
[19] Pflugfelder, *Cartographies of Desire*, 261–62, 301.
[20] Miyatake Gaikotsu, *Hannannyokō* (*Thoughts on Hermaphroditism*, 1922), in *Miyatake Gaikotsu Chosakushū*, vol. 5, ed. Tanizawa Eiichi and Yoshino Takao (Tokyo: Kawade Shobō Shinsha, 1986), 325–29. I follow Teresa A. Algoso's critical analysis of the text, "'Thoughts on Hermaphroditism.'"

Queer Spaces 149

political disorder or supposedly upholding national moral health. In many of his writings, Gaikotsu calibrated routine attempts at placating both the hypocrisy of the Japanese ruling class and the increasing authoritarianism of the regime. *Thoughts on Hermaphroditism* was no different.

Reading Gaikotsu, one can hear him laugh out loud. Covering a wide range of legends, hearsay, and rumors about sexually and gender nonnormative individuals, the story collection of *Thoughts on Hermaphroditism* was intended as much to entertain and scandalize as to lay out "an utopian vision of a future in which the human race would evolve to complete cultural and physiological hermaphroditism."[21] The collection was printed and distributed "under the table" with the note "not for sale" next to the copyright information so as to evade censorship. Highlighting the transnational nature of sexology, the more factual portions of *Thoughts on Hermaphroditism* echoed the influential and (mostly) contemporaneous writings of German physician and sexologist Magnus Hirschfeld, including the educational brochure "What Must the Population Know about the Third Sex?" ("Was muss das Volk vom dritten Geschlecht wissen!" Eine Aufklärungsschrift, 1901), the book *Berlin's Third Sex* (*Berlins drittes Geschlecht*, 1905), and the numerous publications of his thoughts and findings on "psychological [or emotional] transsexuality" in his periodical *Yearbook of Sexual Intermediate Types* (*Jahrbuch für sexuelle Zwischenstufen*, 1899–1923), a quarterly publication devoted to scientific, literary, and political topics related to sexual and gender minorities.[22] From Gaikotsu's Tokyo to Hirschfeld's Berlin, at the beginning of the twentieth century an ever-broader range of medical doctors, intellectuals, scientists, and social reformers considered questions about and the revolutionary potential of recognizing "intermediate types" beyond the binary gender order and sexual heteronormativity.

Queer Spaces

The ground shifted again during the 1950s and 1960s when new alliances took shape in the public sphere. Then, those living "ordinary"

---

[21] For a close reading of Gaikotsu's *Thoughts on Hermaphroditism*, see Algoso, "Thoughts on Hermaphroditism," 558.

[22] Magnus Hirschfeld, "Was muss das Volk vom dritten Geschlecht wissen! Eine Aufklärungsschrift," ed. Wissenschaftlich-humanitäres Comitee (Leipzig: Verlag von Max Spohr, 1901); Magnus Hirschfeld, *Berlins drittes Geschlecht* (Berlin: Verlag von Hermann Seemann Nachfolger, 1904); Magnus Hirschfeld, *Jahrbuch für sexuelle Zwischenstufen mit besonderer Berücksichtigung der Homosexualität* (*Yearbook of Sexual Intermediate Types with Special Consideration of Homosexuality*) (Leipzig: Max Spohr, 1899–1933).

150   Queer Identities and Activisms

homosexual lives were mostly private, and viewed in tandem with and in regard to their proximity to a number of other sexual and gender non-heteronormative individuals: unmarried adults, single mothers, and cohabiting, unmarried, heterosexual couples.[23] Eventually, gays and lesbians became the subject and object of what Japanese media referred to as a "gay boom," one marked by a new style of same-sex identity. During this era, "gay boys" similar to the kimono-wearing hostess described at the beginning of this chapter had founded their own meeting places, "gay bars," which they could regularly and safely frequent. Sexual diversity was also celebrated in a magazine, *Adonis* (*Adonisu*), which also served as a means for homosexual men to meet and exchange views and experiences.[24]

In the 1970s, effeminate male homosexuality again became associated with the entertainment world and was increasingly seen as being quite separate – from not just mainstream society but also ordinary gay and lesbian individuals. It was from this larger population that sprang Tōgō Ken's (1932–2012) Miscellaneous People's Association (*Zatsumin no Kai* also *Zatsumintō*), which sponsored the Miscellaneous People Party that devoted itself to radical gay politics. The association attracted a range of people whose sexual and lifestyle choices placed them outside the mainstream: sexual minorities, including transgender, lesbians, gay men, and sex workers; along with divorced individuals, single parents, and people living in unconventional family arrangements. Altogether, the association constituted one beginning of a sexual rights movement most broadly conceived.

Tōgō – a bar owner, pornographer, gay magazine editor, political candidate, social activist, and occasional singer and actor – had left his bank job, wife, and children behind to come out and be one of the first gay men to politicize his sexual identity. On public television and elsewhere, he dismissed the notion of "obscenity" (*waisetsu*) being associated with same-sex sexuality and pornography, and criticized the discrimination of sexual minorities. He publicly cross-dressed, wore make-up, spoke in a soft sing-song more typical of female voices, and reclaimed the previously derogatory term *okama* ("fag") for people like himself: "What's wrong with being a fag?" he asked. "What's shameful about being a fag? Why is it wrong for a man to love a man? Why is it wrong for a woman to love a woman? What is shameful is living a lie.

---

[23] Lunsing, "Japan: Finding Its Way?," 308.
[24] Mark McLelland, "Introduction," in *Edges of the Rainbow: LGBTQ Japan*, by Michel Delsol and Haruku Shinozaki (New York: New Press, 2017), 6–9.

Queer Spaces   151

What is shameful is not loving others."[25] Controversial among the LGBT+ community was his uncompromising perspective on sex-change surgery: he adamantly opposed it. For Tōgō, the tension between a male anatomy and a female appearance was the productive site of personal transformation and social confrontation *par excellence*. Sex-change surgery, by contrast, signaled the will to conform to a binary heteronormativity and was thus devoid of political potential.[26] While a radical in his own right, Tōgō's flamboyant and effeminate persona eventually failed to appeal to a younger generation of equally inclusive but more assimilationist queer activists. They recognized as their challenge the necessity to distinguish themselves from the scandalized and sensationalized gay men of the entertainment world and thus from the close association of homosexuality with the entertainment industry. At the same time, many among that younger generation were also keen to distinguish themselves from transgender individuals with whom homosexuality, particularly in the media and entertainment world, had commonly been conflated.

Meanwhile, lesbians continued to be largely invisible and inaudible. They neither knew about nor found much encouragement in the stories of pioneers such as Yoshiya. Nor did they experience the feminist activism of the 1970s and 1980s as being particularly welcoming to lesbians. Nonetheless, at least one early lesbian feminist activist, Sawabe Hitomi, remembers the 1970s as "the seeds," the 1980s as "the sprouts," the 1990s as "the flowering," and the time since as "the fruit" of lesbian activism.[27] From her perspective, that "flowering" coincided with and reinforced a second "gay boom." It too was in part triggered and furthered by a series of new publications that reached a large market. Then Kakefuda Hiroko's critique of "compulsory heterosexuality" and the difficulties it creates for the subjectivization of lesbians in her book, *Being Lesbian* (*"Rezubian" de aru to iu koto*, 1992), went a long way toward alleviating feelings of isolation for its readers. It also catalyzed

---

[25] Mark McLelland, "Death of the 'Legendary Okama' Tōgō Ken: Challenging Commonsense Lifestyles in Postwar Japan," *Asia-Pacific Journal: Japan Focus* 10, issue 25, no. 5 (June 17, 2012), accessed June 3, 2021, https://apjjf.org/2012/10/25/Mark-McLelland/3775/article.html; see also Oikawa Kenji, "Tōgō Ken, the Legendary *Okama*: Burning with Sexual Desire and Revolt," in *Queer Voices from Japan: First-Person Narratives from Japan's Sexual Minorities*, ed. Mark McLelland, Katsuhiko Suganuma, and James Welker (Lanham, MD: Lexington Books, 2007), 263–69.

[26] Tōgō wrote an autobiography titled *Jōshiki o koete: Okama no michi* (Tokyo: Potto Shuppan, 2002); some of his television appearances are available on YouTube.

[27] Sawabe Hitomi, "'Wakakusa no Kai': The First Fifteen Years of Japan's Original Lesbian Organization," in *Queer Voices from Japan: First-Person Narratives from Japan's Sexual Minorities*, ed. Mark McLelland, Katsuhiko Suganuma, and James Welker (Lanham, MD: Lexington Books, 2007), 167–80.

152   Queer Identities and Activisms

the expansion of media specifically geared toward sexual minorities, such as Fushimi Noriaki's *Private Gay Life* (*Puraibēto Gei Raifu Posuto Renairon*, 1991) and the magazine *Queer Japan* (*Kuia Japan*, 1999–2005). An issue of the mainstream women's magazine *Crea* (*Kurea*, 1991) included a special feature on gay men's popularity with young women. Each of these publications helped trigger a wave of coming-out narratives that detailed otherwise ordinary individual experiences on lesbians' and gays' own terms, and increased the recognition and visibility of sexual minorities of all walks of life – all of which fostered a new level of normalization.[28]

Then came HIV/AIDS, the discovery and initial panic of which refocused public mainstream attention on gay *men*. At the same time, since the epidemic provided a clearly defined crisis, it facilitated collaborations among dozens of heretofore disconnected lesbian and gay groups. It also provided the platform to reframe the debate about LGBT+ identities as a much broader subject, namely one of human rights.[29] The first two reported cases of HIV/AIDS in Japan instigated major strides toward equality and recognition, including the founding of two organizations that addressed gays' and lesbians' rights: the citizens group Association for the Lesbian and Gay Movement (OCCUR) and the International Lesbian and Gay Association Japan (ILGA).[30] In 1997, OCCUR won its first high-profile human rights court case, resulting in the elimination of restrictions on gay individuals' presence at a youth hostel, Fuchū Seinen no Ie, which was under the jurisdiction of the Tokyo metropolitan government.[31] In the wake of that landmark case, OCCUR successfully prompted the Japanese Society of Psychiatry and Neurology to drop "homosexuality" from its diagnostic manual and

---

[28] Some of these experiential accounts were translated into English, including Satoru Ito and Ryuta Yanase, *Coming Out in Japan* (Melbourne: Transpacific Press, 2001); Barbara Summerhawk, Cheiron McMahill, and Darren McDonald, eds., *Queer Japan: Personal Stories of Japanese Lesbians, Gays, Bisexuals and Transsexuals* (Norwich, VT: New Victoria, 1998); and Fran Martin et al., *AsiaPacifiQueer: Rethinking Genders and Sexualities* (Urbana: University of Illinois Press, 2008).

[29] Lunsing, "Japan: Finding Its Way?," 308; Mark McLelland, "Introduction," in *Edges of the Rainbow: LGBTQ Japan*, by Michel Delsol and Haruku Shinozaki (New York: New Press, 2017), 6–9.

[30] For current data, see H. Kato et al., "The Importance of Accounting for Testing and Positivity in Surveillance by Time and Place: An Illustration from HIV Surveillance in Japan," *Epidemiology & Infection* 146, no. 16 (December 2018): 2072–78, accessed June 3, 2021, http://dx.doi.org/10.1017/S0950268818002558. One of many NPOs that educate about and promote "living together" with diverse people, including people with HIV/AIDS, is akta in Ni-chome, Tokyo, and sponsored by the Ministry of Health, Labor, and Welfare; accessed June 3, 2021, http://akta.jp/.

[31] Lunsing, "Japan: Finding Its Way?," 302–03.

Prohibitions and Rights 153

instead acknowledge three significant points: that homosexuality is not a perversion, sexual orientation is not a disorder, and homosexuals do not simply "perform the opposite role of one's sex."[32] OCCUR was also the driving force behind the first Tokyo Gay and Lesbian Pride Parade in 1994, which advocated acceptance with slogans such as "Japan with a big heart" (*Kokoro Hiroi Nihon*).

Prohibitions and Rights

During the first two decades of the twenty-first century, LGBT+ individuals found themselves players in a complex interplay between increasingly accepting public opinion, a growing number of progressive local governments and corporations, and a persistently reactionary conservative Liberal Democratic Party (LDP) national government under the leadership of former prime minister Abe Shinzō. For almost a century and a half, no law has stood in the way of either same-sex sexuality or any other nonheterosexualities. A majority of the population agrees that society should be accepting of same-sex sexuality. Close to 80 percent of twenty- to sixty-year-olds support the legalization of same-sex marriage. And finally, on March 17, 2021, a Japanese court ruled for the first time that the government's failure to recognize same-sex marriage is unconstitutional as it violates the right to equality, in a historic verdict hailed by activists as a step toward a change in their lives.[33]

---

[32] OutRight Action International, "Japan: Psychiatrists Remove Homosexuality from List of Disorders," June 1, 1995, accessed June 3, 2021, https://outrightinternational.org/content/japan-psychiatrists-remove-homosexuality-list-disorders. Along with the Society, the World Health Organization adopted and promoted guidelines specifying that, while "the stigmatization and discrimination of gay people can lead to mental-health problems ... homosexuality in itself is not a mental-health problem," and that "clinical literature shows that same-sex sexual and romantic attractions, feelings, and behaviours are sound. They are perfectly acceptable variations of human sexuality." See Sheila Mysorekar, "Homosexuality Is Not a Disease," *Development and Cooperation*, January 8, 2019, accessed June 3, 2021, www.dandc.eu/en/article/world-health-organization-considers-homosexuality-normal-behaviour; plus www.who.int/bulletin/volumes/92/9/14-135541.pdf. It should be noted that, as late as in 1977, the ninth International Classification of Diseases (ICD-9) still listed homosexuality as a disease. It would not be until May 1990 that the forty-third World Health Assembly would endorse the decision to take homosexuality off its list. Therefore, the currently used ICD-10 explicitly states that "sexual orientation by itself is not to be considered a disorder."

[33] According to a large-scale internet survey conducted by Dentsū from January 2019, 8.9 percent of respondents identified as members of sexual minorities (up from 1.3 percent in 2015), and close to 80 percent expressed their support for or acceptance of the legalization of same-sex marriage; Yamashita Chikako, "Dōseikon gōhōka, 8-wari ga kōteiteki Dentsū chōsa no 20–50-dai," *Asahi Shinbun Dejitaru*, January 12, 2019, accessed July 6, 2020, www.asahi.com/articles/ASM1C52Z7M1CUTIL025.html.

154   Queer Identities and Activisms

Representative nationwide public opinion surveys also show that mainstream society has become significantly more sympathetic to trans individuals. For instance, when asked which of a total of eighteen human rights issues needed attention in Japan, 15 percent of respondents felt that more needed to be done to protect the human rights of "people suffering from Gender Identity Disorder" and "people of certain sexual orientations."[34] When asked whether individuals are discriminated against based on their sexual orientation, almost 40 percent responded in the affirmative, noting that discriminatory language was used for nonheteronormative individuals; in addition, more than 20 percent identified other discriminatory behavior, including "staring and marginalizing," "bullying at school or work," and "ignorant behavior at school or work."[35]

Some local governments have energetically tried to address these concerns. And though institutionalized discrimination remains,[36] the politico-legal struggle for an expansion of rights for sexual minorities has achieved a series of successes. In 2003 and 2017, respectively, Japanese municipalities elected the first openly transgender people to public offices: Kamikawa Aya as a Setagaya ward assembly member and Hosoda Tomoya as a councilor for Iruma City (see Figure 6.1). As of June 1, 2020, fifty local governments issue same-sex partnership

According to a global study by the Pew Research Center, acceptance of same-sex sexuality in Japan (54 percent) is significantly higher than in neighboring populations in South Korea (39 percent) and in China (21 percent). These data contrast with societies that are among the most inclusive of sexual minorities, including Czech Republic (74 percent) and Canada, Germany, and Spain (80 to 88 percent). (The United States and Mexico fall in between, with 60 and 61 percent, respectively.) Everywhere women are massively more accepting than are men; generally, the younger generations are also more accepting, but they are dramatically more accepting in Japan, South Korea, and China, where the generational shift is most substantial. For the court ruling, see "Japan Non-Recognition of Same-Sex Marriage Unconstitutional: Court," *NikkeiAsia*, March 17, 2021, accessed June 3, 2021, https://asia.nikkei.com/Spotlight/Society/Japan-non-recognition-of-same-sex-marriage-unconstitutional-court; see also "#EqualityActJapan," Human Rights Watch, accessed June 3, 2021, www.hrw.org/EqualityActJapan.

[34] Granted, concern is shared more widely about the human rights of other groups, including "people with disabilities" (51 percent), "violations of human rights on the Internet" (43.2 percent), "the elderly" (36.7 percent), "children" (33.7 percent), "women" (30.6 percent), and the "survivors of [the 2011 triple disaster in Northeastern Japan, referred to as] 3/11" (28.8 percent); see Naikakufu, *Zenkoku yoron chōsa no genkyū*, 2017, Cabinet Office, Government of Japan, accessed June 3, 2021, https://survey.gov-online.go.jp/genkyou/h27/h26-genkyou/index.html.

[35] Naikakufu, *Zenkoku yoron chōsa no genkyū*; see also Lunsing, "Japan: Finding Its Way?"

[36] Claire Maree, "Queer Women's Culture and History in Japan," in *Routledge Handbook of Sexuality Studies in East Asia*, ed. Vera Mackie and Mark McLelland (London: Routledge, 2015), 230–43.

Figure 6.1 Kamikawa Aya participating in a Tokyo Pride parade. After graduating from university, Kamikawa worked as a man for five years – after which she worked for four years as a woman without disclosing her past as a man. In 2003, Kamikawa was elected for the Setagaya Ward Assembly as Japan's first openly transgender politician. She has worked ever since to improve the lives of diverse minorities.[37] Printed with the kind permission of Graham Kolbein

[37] For Kamikawa Aya's profile, see "Official Website," Ah! Yeah!!, Rainbow Setagaya, accessed June 3, 2021, https://ah-yeah.com/.

156   Queer Identities and Activisms

certificates; though these do not provide legal protection, they do offer some benefits, including the option of applying for public housing.[38] The public sector has also begun institutionalizing anti-discrimination legislation based on sexual orientation and gender identity at the workplace. For instance, in December 2018, four political parties together with a number of independents introduced to the House of Representatives the Proposed Law on the Promotion of the Elimination of Discrimination based on Sexual Orientation and Gender Identity (Seiteki shikō mata wa seijinin o riyū to suru sabetsu no kaishōtō no suishin ni kan suru hōritsuan) to prohibit discrimination, harassment, and bullying at schools on the basis of sexual orientation. In March 2019, legislation banning discrimination against sexual minorities was passed in Ibaraki prefecture. And as of April 2019, the Tokyo Metropolitan Assembly's law prohibiting all discrimination on the basis of sexual orientation and gender identity commits the metropolitan government to raising awareness of LGBT people and "conduct[ing] measures needed to make sure human rights values are rooted in all corners of the city," as well as "[outlawing the expression of] hateful rhetoric in public." And, on April 17, 2020, ninety-six human rights and LGBT organizations sent a letter to the prime minister calling for the passage of a similar nondiscrimination law to apply nationwide.[39]

Picking up on both public sentiment and evolving policies, an increasing number of corporations have begun to recognize sexual minorities as an important segment of both the labor force and clientele. By 2019, a total of 200 Japanese corporations had established guidelines which prohibit discrimination based on sexual orientation and sexual identity; extend customary benefits for marriage, childbirth, and other life-

---

[38] Dale, "Same-Sex Marriage and the Question of Queerness." Despite national government resistance to legal change, municipalities often take the lead regarding legal rights for sexual minorities; see, for instance, "Japan Court Rejects Notion Same-Sex Couples Are de facto Marriage," *Japan Times*, June 4, 2020, accessed June 3, 2021, www.japantimes.co.jp/news/2020/0/04/national/crime-legal/japan-court-rejects-notion-sex-couples-de-facto-marriages/; Osaki Tomohiro, "LDP Lawmaker Mio Sugita Faces Backlash after Describing LGBT People as 'Unproductive,'" *Japan Times*, July 24, 2018, accessed June 3, 2021, www.japantimes.co.jp/news/2018/07/24/national/politics-diplomacy/ldp-lawmaker-mio-sugita-faces-backlash-describing-lgbt-people-unproductive/; Eric Johnston, "LDP Lawmaker Tom Tanigawa under Fire for Saying LGBT Relationships Are 'Like a Hobby,'" *Japan Times*, August 2, 2018, accessed June 3, 2021, www.japantimes.co.jp/news/2018/08/02/national/ldp-lawmaker-says-lgbt-relations-like-hobby/.

[39] Yoshinaga Michiko, *Sei dōitsusei shōgai: Seitenkan no ashita* (Tokyo: Shūeisha, 2000); Ben Chapell and Sherif A. Elgebeily, "Lessons from Gay and Lesbian Activism in Asia: The Importance of Context, Pivotal Incidents and Connection to a Larger Vision," *Sexuality and Culture* 23, issue 3 (2019): 882–905, accessed June 3, 2021, https://doi.org/10.1007/s12119-019-09597-4.

Prohibitions and Rights

changing events to same-sex couples; and provide training to make these new guidelines widely known.[40] As of 2020, over 10 percent of Japanese companies in Japan have policies aimed at protecting the rights of sexual minorities.[41]

Counseling hotlines and self-help groups have also proliferated. For instance, three friends under the leadership of Mizuno Eita founded the self-help group Label X with the support of crowd funding; they also published a collection of essays titled *What Is X Gender? The Status Quo of Diverse Genders/Sexes/Sexualities in Japan* (*X jendā tte nani? Nihon ni okeru tayō na sei no arikata*, 2016). Their book explains the various meanings and experiences of "intersex" to a lay public that remains somewhat confused about the phenomenon.[42] It is just one of a stream of introductory publications about LGBT+ matters intended for a wide audience, such as *Gender Identity Disorder: The Future of Sex Change* (*Sei Dōitsusei Shōgai: Sei Tenkan no Ashita*, 2000) by award-winning author and journalist Yoshinaga Michiko. And some LGBTQI+ groups in Japan have created designated semipublic spaces that provide a certain level of "being out" while also offering protection from the ignorance and potential scorn of mainstream society.

---

[40] The best overview of such corporations can be gleaned from the annual reports of Work with Pride at workwithpride.jp, an organization that aims to transform Japanese corporations and organizations in order to make them welcoming of sexual minorities; see Pride 2019 (*Pride Shihyō 2019 Repōto*), Work with Pride, accessed June 3, 2021, https://workwithpride.jp/wp/wp-content/uploads/2019/12/a4e8c1029929187b4da17e475e465e97.pdf. For individual corporations' takes on such measures, see "Efforts to Promote the Active Role of Differently Abled Individuals, Senior Citizens, and Sexual Minorities (LGBT)," Kirin Holdings Company, Limited, accessed June 3, 2021, www.kirinholdings.co.jp/english/csv/human_resources/diversity_lgbt.html; "Rakuten's LGBT Network and Championing Inclusivity in the Japanese Workplace," Rakuten.Today, June 23, 2017, accessed June 3, 2021, https://rakuten.today/blog/rakuten-lgbt-network.html; Shu Min Yuen, "Unqueer Queers – Drinking Parties and Negotiations of Cultural Citizenship by Female-to-Male Trans People in Japan," *Asian Anthropology* 19, no. 2 (2020): 86–101, accessed June 3, 2021, http://dx.doi.org/10.1080/1683478X.2020.1756073.

[41] "Only 10% of Firms in Japan Have Addressed LGBT Issues, Survey Finds," *Japan Times*, June 13, 2020.

[42] It should be noted that this statement is based on a small sample of 239 students at Miyazaki International College, Miyazaki City, with an *n* of 153; see Jeniece Lusk, "Japanese Millennials and Intersex Awareness," *Sexuality and Culture* 21, issue 2 (2017). In the Anglo-American sphere, Mark McLelland has most consistently traced the history of queer activism in numerous important monographs and anthologies, including *Queer Japan from the Pacific War to the Internet Age*; *Genders, Transgenders, and Sexualities in Japan*, coedited with Romit Dasgupta (London: Routledge, 2005); *Queer Voices from Japan*, coedited with Katsuhiko Suganuma and James Welker; and *Routledge Handbook of Sexuality Studies in East Asia*, coedited with Vera Mackie (London: Routledge, 2014).

158   Queer Identities and Activisms

For all this progress, in most of the country it has remained impossible for same-sex couples to marry – which has led to the creation of organizations such as EMA Japan (Equal Marriage Alliance), which actively "advocates legal recognition of same-sex marriage in Japan."[43] At the national level, policy inertia regarding the explicit prohibition of discrimination on grounds of sex and gender has been the *modus operandi*. In its focus on increasing the country's dwindling birth rate, the national government neglects or even works against the expansion of rights to nonnormative individuals. At the 2016 House of Councilors election, the LDP included in its manifesto that "same-sex marriage is incompatible with the constitution" – although it also included a goal to "[promote] understanding of sexual diversity," while attempting to undermine the constitution's Article 24 for same-sex marriage's potential to further "the breakdown of the family."[44] Conservatives took aim at the respect for the individual and gender equality in domestic life that Article 24 prescribes.[45] Furthermore, these same conservatives perfidiously maintain that "Japan has been tolerant of diverse gender identifications and sexual orientations since the Middle Ages," which has thus created a society "in which there is no need to 'come out' [since] mutual acceptance comes 'naturally.'"[46] Apropos the experience of Yoshiya Nobuko noted earlier in the chapter, one partner in a queer relationship can still legally adopt the other, regardless of their age difference, as a "son" or "daughter" – thereby establishing a family unit that is recorded in the family registry. As such, traditional reactionary conservatism ironically enables an unintended queering of people's lives and identities.

The legal terrain regarding marriage is even more complex for members of the highly stratified LGBT+ community at large. The postwar constitution, promulgated on November 3, 1946, guarantees "the

[43] The NPO EMA Japan (Equal Marriage Alliance) is one of many activist nodes that bring together LGBT+ individuals and organizations; see "About EMA," EMA Japan, accessed June 3, 2021, http://emajapan.org/aboutemajapan.

[44] Olivier Fabre, "Liberal Democratic Party and Tradition May Stymie Push for Same-Sex Marriage in Japan," *Japan Times*, June 19, 2019, accessed June 3, 2021, www.japantimes .co.jp/news/2019/06/19/national/social-issues/liberal-democratic-party-tradition-may-stymie-push-sex-marriage-japan/. Ironically, this position was fortified by the 1999 Basic Law for a Gender Equal Society, which was itself a result of an ultra-conservative critique of and resistance to "gender-free" education; see Maree, "'LGBT Issues' and the 2020 Games." For an analysis of the law, see Claire Maree, "The Un/State of Lesbian Studies: An Introduction to Lesbian Communities and Contemporary Legislation in Japan," *Journal of Lesbian Studies* 11, nos. 3–4 (2007): 291–301, accessed June 3, 2021, https:// doi.org/10.1300/J155v11n03_11.

[45] For Article 24-related activism, see the Ajia Josei Shiryō Sentā's website, Asia-Japan Women's Resource Center, accessed June 3, 2021, http://jp.ajwrc.org/.

[46] Maree, "'LGBT Issues' and the 2020 Games," 4–5.

Prohibitions and Rights 159

essential equality of the sexes" (Article 24) along with equality of all people under the law (Article 14). Sex change is legal; since 2008, transgender individuals who have undergone sex-reassignment surgery can change their legal gender, after which they can marry someone who is subsequently of the opposite sex. This right derives from the 2003 Gender Identity Disorder Act (Law Concerning Special Rules Regarding the Sex Status of a Person with Gender Identity Disorder). That said, the law pathologizes the freedom it grants: to qualify, individuals must be diagnosed with Gender Identity Disorder, twenty years of age or older, and not currently married; they must lack reproductive function, and "have a part of body which assumes the external genital features of the opposite sex"; and they must demonstrate "the will to make himself or herself physically and socially conform with the opposite sex." Thus, while legalizing sex change, the law reinforces binary and static gender norms by essentially forcing transgender people to undergo full sex-change surgery, specifically to no longer have functioning reproductive glands, before having their gender legally registered in the all-important family registry – a requirement upheld by the Supreme Court in February 2019.[47] The court justified the decision so as "to avoid sudden disruptions in a society that still values gender on the basis of biology." This statement prompted condemnation from activists in Japan as well as from the World Health Organization, the European Human Rights Court, and Human Rights Watch. The latter called the decision "incompatible with international human rights standards, against the times, and deviating from best global practices."[48]

[47] Hiroyuki Taniguchi, "Japan's 2003 Gender Identity Disorder Act: The Sex Reassignment Surgery, No Marriage, and No Child Requirements as Perpetuations of Gender Norms in Japan," *Asia-Pacific Law & Policy Journal* 14, issue 2 (2013): 108–17, accessed June 3, 2021, https://outrightinternational.org/sites/default/files/APLPJ_14.2_Taniguchi.pdf; Onoo Chieko, ed., *Kaisetsu: Seidōitsu seishōgai-sha seibetsu toriatsukai tokureihō* (Tokyo: Nihon Kajo Shuppan, 2004); Yoshinaga Michiko, *Seidō issei shōgai* (Tokyo: Shūeisha, 2000). The United Nations and the World Health Organization condemn the requirement that applicants must "permanently lack functioning gonads" as being a violation of human rights. In 2013, the US Diagnostic and Statistical Manual of Mental Disorders (DSM-5) dropped the condition and replaced it with "gender dysphoria" so the diagnosis could focus "on the gender identity-related distress that some transgender people experience (and for which they may seek psychiatric, medical, and surgical treatments) rather than on transgender individuals or identities themselves." See American Psychiatric Association, "Gender Dysphoria Diagnosis," accessed June 3, 2021, www.psychiatry.org/psychiatrists/cultural-competency/education/transgender-and-gender-nonconforming-patients/gender-dysphoria-diagnosis.

[48] Thisanka Siripala, "Japan's Supreme Court Upholds Surgery as Necessary Step for Official Gender Change," *Diplomat*, February 5, 2019, accessed June 3, 2021, https://thediplomat.com/2019/02/japans-supreme-court-upholds-surgery-as-necessary-step-for-official-gender-change/.

160 Queer Identities and Activisms

Note that some LGBT+ individuals are more interested in changing "common sense" than in changing the law – and are thus more invested in acceptance for *shifting* identities than for an innovative yet nonetheless rigid identity that, for some, smacks of "a lifestyle that denies lust and pleasure."[49] Yet others claim for themselves a kind of "radical ordinariness," which can range from rejecting politicized categories and identities to simply being disinclined to widen the push for acceptance into a larger sociopolitical project. Driven by their will to fit into the current social order, they conform to the expectations of gender-normative men and women, living heteronormative lives aligned with their biological sex across a public space and enjoying – again, in rather heteronormative ways – their being LGBT+ together with fellow LGBT+ individuals as well as other variously gendered and sexed ones in hybridized private/public spaces. Though others might see this bifurcation of experiential space as confining, these acceptance-minded members embrace it.[50]

One of the most consistent agitators against LGBT+ rights is the conservative national government, which has long been fueled by the powerful Japan Conference (Nippon Kaigi), an unincorporated far-right organization closely associated with a long line of prime ministers, including Abe Shinzō and currently Suga Yoshihide (2020–present). In contrast to some western countries including the United States, where religious liberty is increasingly used as a pretext to license discrimination, there are no hyper-visible religious groups poisoning the debate around sexual rights, nor have there been religion-inspired laws prohibiting same-sex sexual acts. Though Christians in Japan are in part responsible for reproducing homophobic discourse – as can be found elsewhere – they make up less than 1 percent of Japanese society, rendering their impact on attitudes and practices miniscule.[51] Historically, Japan's prominent religions of Shinto and Buddhism have offered a complex set of values and perspectives on same-sex acts and desires.[52] Today neither is particularly articulate on the topic of sexual orientation. Some

---

[49] Lunsing, "Japan: Finding Its Way?," 313.

[50] Yuen, "Unqueer Queers"; Michelle H. S. Ho, "Queer and Normal: *Dansō* (Female-to-Male Crossdressing) Lives and Politics in Contemporary Tokyo," *Asian Anthropology* 19, no. 2 (2020): 102–18.

[51] Yuri Horie, "Possibilities and Limitations of 'Lesbian Continuum': The Case of the Protestant Church in Japan," *Journal of Lesbian Studies* 10, nos. 3–4 (2007): 145–59.

[52] Or Porath provides a nuanced reading of Shinto and Buddhist sources with regard to sexuality in "The Flower of Dharma Nature: Sexual Consecration and Amalgamation in Medieval Japanese Buddhism" (PhD diss., University of California at Santa Barbara, 2019), accessed June 3, 2021, https://escholarship.org/content/qt4hs1f3n6/qt4hs1f3n6_noSplash_7555f7931c902914e8643738e6137b09.pdf; McLelland, "Introduction," 6–9.

Prohibitions and Rights 161

temples have even begun to offer "same-sex wedding ceremonies," thus explicitly acknowledging sexual diversity.[53] While Shinto is known to be socially conservative, the Shinto sect Konkokyō officially recognized LGBT in February 2018, the first official statement of support of its kind in the Shinto world.[54]

A mix of perspectives can even be found in the fringe Happiness Realization Party (Kōfuku Jitsugen-tō), which is the political wing of the conservative and anticommunist Happy Science religious movement. In a program called "Let's Change Japan" (*"Nihon o kaeyō"*) broadcast in 2020 on the party's own television channel, a heterosexual married couple contemplate various aspects of "Thinking about LGBT." Soft-spoken and pensive, appearing at once open-minded and ignorant, the couple ambiguously converses in dialogue drawn from mythical and religious texts to more pedestrian worries about the potential unhappiness of LGBT individuals in light of discrimination, and the concern that tolerance for sexual diversity might be creating too many people who would not reproduce.[55] The conversation leaves viewers somewhat confused about whether the takeaway is indeed a plea to "change Japan" or rather to rethink such an aspiration but the latter point has been frequently claimed by conservative pundits. For instance, in an article published in the conservative magazine *Shincho 45*, LDP lawmaker Sugita Mio dismissed justifications for efforts by the state and municipalities to invest taxpayers' money into policies supporting same-sex couples specifically because they would not bear children and, thus, be

---

[53] Temples that offer same-sex or LGBT wedding ceremonies explicitly advertise that option on their websites, emphasizing that they "believe all love is equal" and that they "are open to all types of couples." See "Otera de dōsei kekkonshiki, Bukkyō no oshie, dare shi mo shiawase ni: Saitama Saimyōji," *Mainichi Shinbun*, June 9, 2020, https://mainichi.jp/articles/20200609/ddl/k13/040/003000c; Saimyō-ji in Saitama, https://saimyouji-wedding.com/, and Shunkōin in Myoshinji Temple, Kyōto, https://shunkoin.com/weddings/ (all accessed June 3, 2021). That said, such ceremonies remain controversial; see Isaac Stone Fish, "Does Japan's Conservative Shinto Religion Support Gay Marriage?," *Foreign Policy*, June 29, 2015, accessed June 3, 2021, https://foreignpolicy.com/2015/06/29/what-does-japan-shinto-think-of-gay-marriage/.

[54] A major figure in the *transnational* online Shinto community, Rev. Olivia Bernkastel – a Canadian-Japanese currently at Yokosuka Konkokyō Shrine – identifies as LGBT; read her summary of the current stance of Sect and Shrine Shinto at "Shinto and LGBT+ culture: Connected from the ancient to modern era," December 15, 2018, accessed June 3, 2021, https://medium.com/@livingwithkami/throughout-the-years-and-even-now-i-have-often-been-asked-the-view-shinto-holds-in-regard-to-6d9eb0057997.

[55] See party members Yokuni Masumi and Yokuni Hideyuki, a married heterosexual couple, discussing "Thinking about LGBT" ("LGBT ni tsuite kangaeru"), Fukujitsugen-tō ōen TV, June 12, 2019, accessed June 3, 2021, www.youtube.com/watch?v=2q-sWTQJOxE&feature=youtu.be.

162   Queer Identities and Activisms

"unproductive."[56] That said, her piece did not hold much sway; like the Happiness Realization Party, Sugita is a minor political figure, and her article drew a fierce backlash – not only from members of the LGBT+ community but from members of her own party as well.

Does Trans Transform Society?

Roughly 100 years since Gaikotsu first shared his *Thoughts on Hermaphroditism*, his musings have undoubtedly moved closer to fruition – that is, if LGBT+ normalization and mainstreaming is considered such. I have been interpreting, as Gaikotsu advised, the phrasing "cultural and physiological hermaphroditism" as being many things: a version of the advancing dissolution of a binary gender and sexual order; the diversification and decoupling of sexualities and genders; the increased understanding of sex and gender as fluid and flexible – within a spectrum or along a continuum of modes of being and experiences; and a budding acceptance of sexual and gender identities as being not fixed but fluid and malleable. It appears that, along with Japan, in larger swaths of the world than ever before, the longstanding conventional distinctions among sex, gender, and sexuality no longer hold. That said, the (Japan) story has more local and cultural flavor than the increasingly global sexual rights struggle might suggest.[57]

In sum, despite Japan's rich premodern history of sexual and gender diversity, fluidity, and ambiguity, and despite early-twentieth-century propositions of a sex and gender utopia to come, LGBT+ individuals today variably embrace self-determination, fight for an extension of sexual rights, play with or reject their identities' politicization and performative potential, and insist on an ordinariness that is in some cases sharply distinguished – both from an intellectual feminism and from commonly glamorizing and spectacularizing media representations. The more recent welcoming of transgender individuals previously known only in the entertainment world is expanding into society at large, with Ai Haruna (a transgender television personality, entertainer, and activist), Miwa Akihiro (a singer, actor, drag queen, and reigning transgender

---

[56] Osaki, "LDP Lawmaker Mio Sugita Faces Backlash after Describing LGBT People as 'Unproductive.'"

[57] There is a growing body of scholarship that examines the global dimensions of political activism around LGBTQI+ matters. See for instance, Chapell and Elgebeily, "Lessons from Gay and Lesbian Activism in Asia"; Martin et al., eds., *AsiaPacifiQueer*.

performer known for her bright orange wig), and Nakamura Ataru (one of the first truly popular transgender musicians and actresses) leading the way – with lesser known figures such as self-styled "unarchitect," actress, artist, and drag queen Vivienne Sato following suit (see Figure 6.2). Extensive evidence suggests the normalization of LGBT+ existence advances forward, making commonplace the mockery Japan's first out lesbian writer Yoshiya Nobuko offered her heterosexist critics in 1931 when she wrote: "For 365 days of the year I work from morning to night, from deadline to deadline, ... and in the process, I completely forget about the great defect in my life: the absence of a husband."[58]

Literature and Visual Culture

Yoshiya Nobuko's *Yellow Rose* (1923)[59] (Expanded Editions, 2016) and Mishima Yukio's *Confessions of a Mask* (1958)[60] both of which are also recommended in other chapters, would be productively paired with Yoshimoto Banana's *Kitchen* (1987),[61] which explores issues of androgyny and transsexuality in late-twentieth-century Japan.

Matsumoto Toshio's *Funeral Parade of Roses* (*Bara no Sōretsu*, 1969)[62] features Eddie/Pītā and Reda, two "gay boys" or transgender females who compete over Gonda, a nightclub owner and drug dealer. Part feature film, part documentary, *Funeral Parade of Roses* provides a powerful take on 1960s subculture of sex, drugs, and politics (including sex and gender politics). For a current review of a similar scene, there is Graham Kolbeins' beautifully shot *Queer Japan* (2019),[63] which features two generations of trailblazing artists, activists, and some everyday people from the full spectrum of genders and sexualities in contemporary Tokyo. Equally insightful are two other documentaries on non-cis/heteronormative individuals: Kim Longinotto and Jano Williams's

---

[58] Robertson, "Yoshiya Nobuko."

[59] Yoshiya Nobuko, *Yellow Rose*, trans. Sarah Frederick (Los Angeles: Expanded Editions, 2016).

[60] Mishima Yukio, *Confessions of a Mask*, trans. Meredith Weatherby (New York: New Directions, 1958).

[61] Yoshimoto Banana, *Kitchen*, trans. Megan Backus (New York: Washington Square, 1987).

[62] Matsumoto Toshio, *Funeral Parade of Roses* (*Bara no sōretsu*), directed by Matsumoto Toshio (Tokyo: Art Theatre Guild, 1969).

[63] Graham Kolbein and Anne Ishii, *Queer Japan*, directed by Graham Kolbein (Los Angeles: Altered Innocence, 2019).

Figure 6.2 Self-styled "unarchitect," actress, artist, and drag queen Vivienne Sato in a still from *Queer Japan* (2019).[64] Printed with the kind permission of Graham Kolbein

Shinjuku Boys (1995)[65] introduces three *onnabe*, transgender males who work as hosts at the New Marilyn Club in Tokyo; and Ichikawa Jun's *Osaka Story (Ōsaka Monogatari*, 1999)[66] explores the sexuality/ethnicity nexus as the filmmaker comes out as gay to his parents, and discovers that his father has a second family in Korea.

[65] Kim Longinotto and Jano Williams, *Shinjuku Boys* (UK: Second Run, 1995).
[66] Ichikawa Jun, *Osaka Story (Ōsaka monogatari)* (Tokyo, 1999).

7 Sexing Visual Culture

A popular Kabuki interlude, first performed at the Kawarazaki Theatre at Edo in January 1847, had an even more exciting afterlife. An erotic take on this interlude appeared on an undated woodblock print sometime later in the century.[1] It features a large phallus and an equally large vulva, arranged next to each other in erect position. An accompanying poem pokes fun at the game Rock, Paper, Scissors by comparing the game to a sex act:

When it comes to sex,	Bobo wa samazama
every pussy is different	irogoto wa
The dick thrusts back and forth	Henoko hyokohyoko
Once, twice, thrice	mihyokohyoko
When the pussy gets wet	bobo nuranura
Let's try to penetrate	Kuguri to mawariyasho
With a thump, thump,	janjaka nandaka janjaka na[2]
thump	
What could it be?	

The original Kabuki interlude was devoid of any sexual connotations. Adding a parodic poem on an erotic woodblock print was one of several common techniques to turn into a laughing matter what would otherwise have been a plain, unambiguous work of pornography.[3]

A century and a half later, in 2014, Tokyo police arrested sculptor and manga artist Igarashi Megumi. Known for creating art objects designed

---

[1] For additional information on the original Kabuki interlude, see http://ukiyoe.univie.ac.at/detail.asp?docid=602&lang=j&first=1 (accessed December 11, 2020). I am grateful to Or Porath for pointing out that an additional delight for learned readers must have been to appreciate the fact that "bobo" (菩々 translated here as "pussy") is etymologically related to both "enlightenment" (*bodai* 菩提) and "worldly passions" (*bonnō* 煩悩).

[2] The original poem, was written by Sakurada Jisuke III (1802–1877), inspired a *jaken* boom; see Sepp Linhart, "Interpreting the World as a *Ken* Game," in *Japan at Play: The Ludic and the Logic of Power*, ed. Joy Hendry and Massimo Raveri, Nissan Institute/Routledge Japanese Studies (London: Routledge, 2005), 35–56.

[3] Sepp Linhart, "Warum sind die Holzschnitte Japans zum Lachen?," in *Neue Geschichten der Sexualität: Beispiele aus Ostasien und Zentraleuropa 1700–2000*, ed. Franz X. Eder and Sabine Frühstück (Vienna: Turia+Kant, 1999), 134.

166

to demystify female genitalia, Igarashi had made a full-size, bright yellow kayak modeled on her genitalia that she had paddled down the Tama River at the edge of Tokyo. Instead of joining in her laughter, the authorities brought obscenity charges against her, making her the first woman in Japanese history bestowed with that honor.

This chapter describes the social life of representations of sex and sexuality in visual culture, from erotic woodblock prints to video games. Through this history run many questions. For instance, were erotic woodblock prints – and later material or visual representations of such prints – produced solely for the pleasure of men? Or were they also intended as aids for girls' premarital instruction? Are they best viewed as profit-making projects, as pieces of art, or as windows into historical practices and attitudes toward sex? When the nation-builders of the late nineteenth century began to conceive of these representations as "pornography" – which they also did regarding a number of customs, festivals, and rituals centered on the celebration of fertility, potency, and nudity – what were their objections? Were they concerned about morals, social order, or politics? The liberation debates of the early twentieth century pitched "sexual liberation" (and freedom of sexual expression) against increasingly aggressive reproductive policies and middle-class morality – turning sexual exaltation into a tool of social protest and resistance, and inspiring a wave of suppressive state response. And, as for recent feminist art such as the work of Igarashi Megumi, given the abundance of sexually explicit manga, anime, and video games – why the heavy-handed response? One comparison is clear: whereas the regime at the cusp of modern state-building saw in pornography a threat to the social and political order, twenty-first-century lawmakers and citizen activists zoom in on the possible harm pornography represents to children and youth.

Laughing at Semi-Naked Truths in Erotic Woodblock Prints

In 1854, giving in to pressure from the United States, Japan signed the Treaty of Kanagawa, which was Japan's first treaty with a western nation and marked the end of a period of relative seclusion (1639–1854). Americans and Europeans who visited Japan thereafter wrote hundreds of impressionistic articles and books about a plethora of observations, including about public nudity and sexuality (see also Chapter 8). For instance, a certain Captain James D. Johnston – Kentuckian and executive officer of the steam frigate USS *Powhatan* in 1857–1860 – noted an afternoon walk in the port town Shimoda during which he passed a public bath-house "peculiar to the country." When he stopped to look

168   Sexing Visual Culture

through one of the windows, his "nerves were terribly shocked to see the perfect unconcern with which men, women, and children, of all ages, were mingled together in the Adam and Eve style – minus the fig-leaves – and splashing away in the warm water poured over their heads from small pails, with an energy and a disregard of the lookers-on, which could not have been surpassed, in *nonchalance*, by our first parents."[4]

In contrast, the Russo-German gynecologist and photographer Carl Heinrich Stratz (1858–1924) was rather taken by female nudity in Japanese life and art. Instead of averting his eyes, he wrote lengthy, richly illustrated popular works about the beauty of female bodies, including *The Human Form in Japanese Art and Life* (*Die Körperformen in Kunst und Leben der Japaner*).[5] Japanese men, women, and children did indeed bath naked together, privately and in public baths and hot springs, though western visitors were rather mistaken about any "nonchalance" they believed they witnessed. Instead, young women and girls frequently felt uncomfortable about being looked at, and possibly even touched, by men.[6] And they were looked at. Bathing women were prominent motives for artists across centuries, beginning with woodblock prints (*ukiyo-e*), the most popular visual art genre for the remainder of the nineteenth century, during which time several million works were produced annually.[7] Possibly more than half of these woodblock prints featured bodies in sexual scenes in various stages of undress. They were a largely urban phenomenon, with many of them featuring the surroundings of the Yoshiwara, the famous licensed brothel area in Edo (renamed "Tokyo" in 1868). Most artists' repertoire included erotic woodblock prints that were sold under the table for higher prices. In comparison to Chinese erotic pictures, Japanese ones were distinguished by a pronounced realism in the representation of the human anatomy. While the genitals were typically represented disproportionally large, bodies were never completely naked – rather, they were draped with often beautifully decorated

[4] James D. Johnston, *China and Japan Being a Narrative of the Cruise of the U.S. Steam-Frigate Powhatan in the Years 1857,'58,'59, and'60 Including an Account of the Japanese Embassy to the United States* (Philadelphia, PA: Charles Desilver, 1861), 139.
[5] Stratz was a gynecologist, amateur anthropologist, art afficionado, and author of *Die Körperformen in Kunst und Leben der Japaner* (Erlangen: Ferdinand Enke, 1903) – along with numerous other richly illustrated, widely quoted works about female and child bodies.
[6] Ever since Johnston made his observations, historians have described a rather more complex picture of conventions, concerns, and prohibitions affecting public nude bathing; see Hans-Peter Duerr, *Der Mythos vom Zivilisationsprozess 1: Nacktheit und Scham* (Frankfurt: Suhrkamp Verlag, 1988), 116–29.
[7] Hans-Peter Duerr, *Der Mythos vom Zivilisationsprozess 1: Nacktheit und Scham* (Frankfurt: Suhrkamp Verlag, 1988), 121.

Laughing at Semi-Naked Truths 169

pieces of clothing that created a contrast to both partly conceal and highlight the body parts central to the image.[8] Many erotic woodblock prints feature a voyeur – including bathing women on the lookout for a voyeur.[9] Rich in symbolic meanings, images were often staged in unusual locations – including boats, verandas, even rice paddy fields. Anal sex was rarely represented, and almost always involved a young male; even scarcer are woodblock prints that feature fellatio, cunnilingus, sadism, masochism, or fetishism.

Another rarity is the depiction of humans having sex with animals, of which the 1814 work "The Diver and the Octopus" ("Tako to Ama") by Hokusai Katsushika (1760–1849) is the most famous exception. The print depicts a young shell diver lying on her back, intertwined in a sexual embrace with a pair of octopi, the larger of the two performing cunnilingus on the woman while the smaller one fondles the woman's mouth and left nipple. The text on the print conveys the pleasure that both the woman and the creatures derive from the encounter. The print repeatedly inspired later artists, including contemporary pop artist Aida Makoto, whose take on the theme resulted in a 1993 work titled "The Giant Member Fuji versus King Gidra," simultaneously referencing Hokusai's print and King Ghidorah, who had made his first appearance in the Godzilla film *Ghidorah, the Three-Headed Monster* (1964). I will return to Aida below; here it will suffice to note that, in erotic woodblock prints, enlarged male genitals and unusual locations were intended to comically amuse viewers, who also referred to them as "laughter pictures" (*warai-e*). These parodistic erotica targeted a wide audience of varied education, sophistication, tastes, and monetary means, resulting in an equally wide variety of prints, ranging from the crude to the refined – some embellished with clever poems rife with sexual references, often adapted from classical Japanese poems like the one cited at the beginning of this chapter.[10]

There are a number of theories about the reception and use of such erotic woodblock prints. Some scholars have pondered whether they might have been passed on from generation to generation and used for

---

[8] Krauss cites the curious work of a Japanese doctor who claimed in an early-twentieth-century article that "Grosszumptigkeit" (a bit penis) is a racial characteristic of Japanese men. Krauss himself doubts that claim because it has not been corroborated by others; Friedrich Solomon Krauss, *Das Geschlechtsleben in Glauben, Sitte, Brauch und Gewohnheitsrecht der Japaner* (Leipzig: Ethnologischer Verlag, [1907] 1911), 199. A digitized copy of the original work is available care of the Internet Archive, accessed June 4, 2021, https://archive.org/details/BzA_II_1911_2te/page/n11/mode/2up.

[9] Duerr, *Der Mythos vom Zivilisationsprozess 1*, 121.

[10] Linhart, "Warum sind die Holzschnitte Japans zum Lachen?," 134.

instructing young wives, but more recent research has dismissed that as implausible for a number of reasons: many more pictures were produced than would be necessary for such a purpose; many of the complicated positions and unusual locations were unlikely to be replicated in the everyday lives of ordinary people; and often the female bodies were clearly marked as courtesans – by their elaborate hairdo and luxurious kimonos – not ordinary women, let alone wives. Pioneering expert Timon Screech emphasizes the "uneven nature of the links between pornographic images and human behavior" and proposes that the "licensed brothel areas and extra-legal 'hill places' of entertainment … were brought back into the domestic world of duty via the medium of pictures" and "coloured real sexual aspirations." Screech makes another plausible proposition, namely that these "images were consumed compensatorily and were probably used by those who could not venture into the kinds of places depicted."[11]

Today, most experts agree that these pictures were most likely made by men for men to appreciate and be aroused by. The conditions of their production reveal a lot about how the authorities viewed and aimed to control their social impact. Though the production of erotic woodblock prints was never legal, the Tokugawa regime's (1603–1867) policy was characterized by "broad swings between relative openness and Confucian reform," resulting in a more or less oppressive atmosphere at different historical moments. Episodes of censorship seem to have been directed more at covert political messages and depictions of the mixing of social classes than at the sexual content per se.[12] The main mechanism of suppression was a guild system that employed feudal techniques of group punishment to encourage publishers to police themselves. Under these conditions, a whole network of creative individuals needed to come together and keep quiet about their activities, creating a kind of counterculture to the official Confucian values of the elite. The cultural products of this state of affairs frequently mocked both the samurai class as a whole and the Tokugawa regime in particular.

Indeed, it was the interpretation that such erotic woodblock prints ridiculed the ruling classes that caused them, for centuries, to be deemed obscene and injurious to the social and political order, as well as to public morals. Sexual expression rendered in any medium remained prone to

---

[11] Timon Screech, *Sex and the Floating World: Erotic Images in Japan 1700–1820* (London: Reaktion Books), 10.

[12] See "The Constitution of Japan," Prime Minister of Japan and His Cabinet, accessed March 16, 2021, https://japan.kantei.go.jp/constitution_and_government_of_japan/constitution_e.html; Boyce, "Obscenity and Nationalism," 727.

being variously labeled subversive and harmful to society, or to some portion of it, well into the twentieth century.

That said, during the time of Japan's first modern international conflicts – the Sino-Japanese (1894–1895) and Russo-Japanese Wars (1904–1905) – large numbers of erotic woodblock prints, then called "victory pictures" (*kachi-e*), were produced, apparently even with governmental support. At least some of the "comfort bags" sent to soldiers at the frontlines contained small erotic pictures to help them persevere.[13] And yet, just two years after the Russo-Japanese War, erotica was no longer viewed as useful but again as subversive, leading three Tokyo police stations to carry out a raid during which they confiscated 143,000 erotic woodblock prints and 5,680 printing plates – an event that proved to be a setback from which the erotic woodblock print production never recovered.

Several developments contributed to this end. For one, shortly after its establishment in 1868, the Meiji government prohibited the purchase and sale of such "spring pictures" (*shunga*); it also banned nudity from the public sphere. By this time, the Yoshiwara brothel district had been in decline for decades, and with it the core structure of the most libidinous pictures, resulting in the decline of this particular representation of sex. The second stab came from the rise of pornographic lithographs (and, eventually, photographs).[14] Nude lithographs – again favoring beauties after bathing (*yuagari bijin*) – gained popularity as novelty souvenirs and lucrative commodities, marking a turning point in the mass commodification of pictorial representations of the female body. Attempts at deploying (at least partially) naked bodies of women for national promotion crossed over from fine art to commercial posters to promote Japanese luxury products with Japanese female beauties.[15] The mass-produced representations of some of these beauties became "soldiers' idols" during the Asia-Pacific War (1937–1945), although their appeal more often lay in the glamor of their stage or film personae rather than in their overt sexuality.[16] Ultimately, the dominance of woodblock

---

[13] See Kawamura Kunimitsu, *Seisen no ikonogurafi: Tennō to heishi, senshisha no zusō, hyōshō* (Tokyo: Seikyūsha, 2007).

[14] Linhart, "Warum sind die Holzschnitte Japans zum Lachen?," 140.

[15] Jaqueline Berndt, "Nationally Naked? The Female Nude in Japanese Oil Painting and Posters (1890s–1920s)," in *Performing "Nation": Gender Politics in Literature, Theater, and the Visual Arts of China and Japan, 1880–1940*, ed. Doris Croissant, Catherine Vance Yeh, and Joshua S. Mostow, Sinica Leidensia, vol. 91 (Leiden: Brill, 2008), 337.

[16] Oshida Nobuko, *Heishi no aidoru: Maboroshi no imon zasshi ni miru mō hitotsu no sensō* (Tokyo: Junpōsha, 2016); see also Uchiyama, *Japan's Carnival War*, 181–200; Robertson, *Takarazuka*, 89–137.

172   Sexing Visual Culture

prints decreased in favor of newer media, which in time came to include photography, film, and eventually manga, anime, and video games.

Injurious to Modern Morals

The post–World War II generation of creators of sexual expression were readily dismissed as pornographers rather than as the scholars, artists, and social and political critics and reformers they (also) were. This was because the debate about erotic visual culture and its potential for subverting moral and social norms expanded after the end of the Asia-Pacific War when the new democratic-constitutional context brought new questions to the fore: How should policy-makers address the tension between the constitutional right to freedom of speech and the criminal code's obscenity law? How to balance the intent of the artist and the historical context along with modes of circulation and display against the work's reception? Should policymakers assume or dismiss a relationship between the expression of erotic fantasies and their realization in actual life, particularly in the context of visualizations of sexual violence? How should they address the objectification, commodification, and violation of women in visual culture in light of the experience of the same in flesh-and-blood culture? And, further, what about the pornification of children's bodies?

The term "obscene" (*waisetsu*), as well as delineated punishment for obscene material's "public display or sale," first appeared in Article 259 of the Criminal Code of 1880. It was then carried over into Article 175 of the Criminal Code of 1907, which is in force to this day. Today, the law is to sanction "any person who distributes, sells, or publicly displays (or possesses with intent to sell) an obscene writing, picture, or other materials," acts punishable by "penal servitude for not more than two years" or fines "not more than two million and a half yen." An amendment in 2011 included "recording media containing [obscene] electronic or magnetic records, as well as materials distributed by electronic means." The code does not define, however, what constitutes obscenity.[17] Instead, the definition has evolved through a series of judicial decisions that concerned productions in a range of media.

---

[17] For scholarship on censorship during modern and contemporary Japan, see Jonathan Abel, *Redacted: The Archives of Censorship in Transwar Japan* (Berkeley: University of California Press, 2012); Kirsten Cather, *The Art of Censorship in Postwar Japan* (Honolulu: University of Hawai'i Press, 2012); Jay Rubin, *Injurious to Public Morals: Writers and the Meiji State* (Seattle: University of Washington Press, 1984).

Dangers in the Realm of the Senses 173

In 1908, in one of the first trials (concerning naturalist literature) after the implementation of Article 175 – the presiding Tokyo District Court judge defined the proper standard for obscenity as "that which would naturally seem to arouse a sense of defilement when viewed in the light of the moral concepts of the general populace."[18] By 1927, the volume of publications that applied to this definition made the existing post-publication censorship system untenable. And so publishers embarked on various means of anticipatory obedience. In large part as a cost-saving measure, they submitted potentially problematic materials to the Home Ministry censors for pre-publication vetting; they also began a redacting process whereby offensive lines were blackened out or replaced with X's or O's. Other methods of beating the censors at their game included replacing "offensive" phrasing with German, Latin, or Greek words that were obscure to the vast majority of readers; or labeling publications as "subscribers only" or "experts only" so as to putatively narrow the intended audience to readers with strictly medical, scientific, or peda-gogical interests. Ironically, it was in part the specter of censorship that during this period furthered the proliferation of erotic-grotesque mater-ials, much of which were couched in the rhetoric of new scientific disciplines, including criminology, psychiatry, and sexology. This is not to say that such methods were always effective, since unappeased police still arbitrarily rejected much that would otherwise have been published and possibly censored.[19]

Dangers in the Realm of the Senses

Courts that address constitutional obscenity jurisprudence in Japan (and elsewhere) struggle with a central paradox: obscenity law that crimina-lizes particular speech (and other forms of expression) for being offensive nullifies the concept of the freedom of speech, which must include the freedom to offend. More to the point, constitutional law expert Bret Boyce suggests that "obscenity law evidently does little to protect public morality or prevent harm," but "it can be a dangerous weapon in the hands of groups seeking to enforce political, social, and cultural con-formity."[20] Both the arbitrariness and complexity of the obscenity charge are made evident in specific works of three visual artists – Ōshima Nagisa,

[18] Rubin, *Injurious to Public Morals*, 88.
[19] Mark McLelland, "Sex, Censorship and Media Regulation in Japan: A Historical Overview," in *Routledge Handbook of Sexuality Studies in East Asia*, ed. Mark McLelland and Vera Mackie (London: Routledge, 2014), 402–13.
[20] Boyce, "Obscenity and Nationalism," 686.

174   Sexing Visual Culture

Aida Makoto, and Igarashi Megumi – which I will discuss for the next portion of this chapter before turning to video gaming at the end.

The trials about Ōshima Nagisa's film *In the Realm of the Senses* – *L'Empire des sens* (*Ai no Korrida*, 1976) strike me as being particularly pertinent given the continued and almost unrivaled iconicity of the film beyond its rebellious 1970s moment. *In the Realm of the Senses*, which is set in increasingly militaristic 1930s Japan, is based on the true story of the relationship between geisha and prostitute Abe Sada (1905–1970) and the inn owner Ishida Kichizō. Their mutual sexual obsession escalated into Abe killing Ishida via erotic asphyxiation – a violent culmination mirrored by war-frenzied Japan's mobilization toward invading northeast China. Upon Ishida's death, Abe severed his genitals and fled the scene; when police caught up with her several days later, she was still carrying them with her. Abe ended up serving six years' imprisonment for second-degree murder and mutilation of a corpse. At the time, female sexuality was not acknowledged primarily as a source of a woman's lust, but as an object of male pleasure, or simply as a necessity of reproduction. Given this backdrop, Abe's case inspired a substantial body of creative, scientific, and popular works by scientists, artists, philosophers, novelists, and filmmakers. In her autobiography, Abe sets the record straight:

Just as when men redeem a geisha so that they can keep her all to themselves, there are women who are so enraptured with a man that they think of doing what I did. They just don't act it out. There are all kinds of women. There are women who decide that it just is not possible for love to be the standard by which they measure men, and so they measure them by their material possessions. But there are women who just can't stop loving a man. So people need to understand that when an incident like mine happens, it isn't just because a woman is crazy about sex.[21]

From the time of Ōshima's first releases in 1959, his work included themes of questioning social constraints and deconstructing political doctrines, often set during eras of shifting sexual politics. All of these characteristics are at work in *In the Realm of the Senses*. When Ōshima (1932–2013) turned to Abe's story, he made use of two intertwined European trends. The first: the "liberation" and "decriminalization" of sexual expression in line with the "sexual revolution" of the 1960s and 1970s. The second: a rising new generation of filmmakers producing blistering critiques of Europe's wartime regimes through focusing their stories on extreme sexual violence. For example, Liliana Cavani's *The Night Porter* (1974) depicts the revival, in Vienna, of a sadomasochistic

---

[21] William Johnston, *Geisha, Harlot, Strangler, Star: A Woman, Sex & Morality in Modern Japan* (New York: Columbia University Press, 2004), 208; Marran, *Poison Woman*.

Dangers in the Realm of the Senses

sexual obsession that originated in a Nazi concentration camp. And Pier Paolo Pasolini's equally almost-unwatchable *Salò, or the 120 Days of Sodom* (1975), set in fascist Italy, shows a group of libertines kidnapping and subjecting eighteen teenagers to torture that includes horrific scenes of sexual violence.

Since Ōshima was far from naïve about Japan's obscenity law, in producing *In the Realm of the Senses* he followed a complex strategy that allowed him to circumvent strict domestic censorship regulations by bringing the film to Japan after it had been screened in France to great international critical acclaim. Indeed, the film itself was not challenged in the courts – though literature and film scholar Kirsten Cather leaves no doubt that "the trial was likely a scapegoat for the film."[22] Indeed, issues that would be raised in other trials played no role in this one. The prosecution showed no interest per se in ecstatic female bodies, multiple rape (a marginal scene in the film), or even the final instance of extreme sexual and deadly violence. Nor was the question raised whether the film depicted wartime Japan in an undesirably critical light, or if it under-mined the social order or sexual morals of contemporaneous Japan.[23] The obscenity charge concerned a book that derived from the film. It consisted of twenty-four 7- by 10-inch color still photographs, the ori-ginal screenplay, and several essays of film criticism authored by Ōshima. In the book's trial, the prosecution discerned obscenity in twelve "color photographs taken of the poses of men and women engaged in sexual intercourse and sex play," as well as in nine passages of "prose from the screenplay that plainly describe scenes of male–female sexual inter-course, sex play, etc." The prosecution's core question appeared to have been whether any of these materials "arouse[d] a picture in the minds of readers," and whether the visual unfolding of the sex act suggested the "enfolding or enveloping of the reader by the scene." What was at stake was whether a particular image or story constitutes obscenity via trigger-ing further images in viewers' or readers' minds. In the end, the judges

---

[22] Kirsten Cather, "A Thousand Words: The Powers and Dangers of Text and Image," *Positions: East Asia Cultures Critique* 18, no. 3 (Winter 2010): 697, accessed June 4, 2021, www.academia.edu/9910314/A_Thousand_Words_The_Powers_and_Dangers_of_Text_and_Image.

[23] After World War II, Abe Sada's story received massive treatment in literature, film, and scholarship that has mostly celebrated her as a heroine, as an "eroticized icon of emancipation, ideal for having achieved sincerity of the flesh and for being unencumbered by ideological pressures"; see Marran, *Poison Woman*, 136. In general, however, analyses of erotic and pornographic media that aim to appeal to women are few and far between; for a rare exception, see Katharina Helm, "Women's Pleasure Online? A Contrasting Analysis of One Japanese Mainstream and One Women's Pornographic Film from the Internet," *Vienna Journal of East Asian Studies* 8 (2016): 33–64.

176   Sexing Visual Culture

ruled that the book was not obscene. Unlike a film, the pictures in question were deemed to have considerably less potential to arouse, since viewers would detect traces of artifice that would sufficiently mitigate the obscenity of the pictures. In sum, for *In the Realm of the Senses*, as well as in postwar courts more generally, "an obscenity conviction," Cather writes, "depended more on likening written texts to filmic ones and readers to spectators rather than on the object on trial itself." Indeed, "[d]espite the rhetoric in the trials, the legal judgment of obscenity in Japan depended not on the visual or visible but instead on the invitation to imagine an invisible off-screen space, a 'dazzling personal screen' beyond the reach of any control." Altogether, Ōshima's was a landmark censorship trial that highlighted – in a way few other visual cultural images and objects had – various common assumptions made about the power and danger of "literature, as a textual medium, of photography, as a static visual medium, and of film, as a kinetic visual medium."[24]

Viewing the Pain of Others with Aida Makoto

In her 2003 book *Regarding the Pain of Others*, Susan Sontag cautions that "No 'we' should be taken for granted when the subject is looking at other people's pain."[25] This proposition drives her remarks about some weighty concepts regarding photography: how viewers of war photographs are distracted from understanding and owning responsibility for their act of looking; how war photographs have variously been used; and how viewers perceive, remember, or disregard photographs to a variety of ends that the photographer may have never intended – and is most definitely unable to control. A similar set of complications shapes more recent instances of critical commentary on sexual expression at the intersection of art and society.

At stake is not, as in the Ōshima trials, whether a particular image or story constitutes obscenity via triggering further images in viewers' and readers' minds. It is *assumed* that it does. Based on that assumption, a more complex set of accusations is brought into play: first, that the art piece at hand is a representation of actual pain caused to a flesh-and-blood person; and, second, that the object or image constitutes a condonement of the actual harm done to that person – rather than being an artistic critique of instances of such harm being done to flesh-and-blood people. Furthermore, that the bodies of the people represented in such

[24] Cather, "A Thousand Words."
[25] Susan Sontag, *Regarding the Pain of Others* (New York: Picador, 2004), 7.

art objects or images – for instance, victims of sexual violence – are typically female suggests parallels to actual social conditions and power imbalances, which in turn seems to further contribute to the casual sexualization and commodification of female figures in the mainstream entertainment market. In short, the critiques of such art objects and images often center on the fear that they reinforce the status quo of the sexual and gender order in Japanese society at large, which is variously critiqued as being imbalanced or even inherently violent.

Aida Makoto (1965–) is an artist who creates works of manga, painting, video, photography, sculpture, and installation. A retrospective of his work, held at the Mori Art Museum in Tokyo from November 2012 through March 2013, was titled *Sorry for Being a Genius: Monument for Nothing*. Two series of works in particular sparked a widely publicized controversy: Dog (Inu), which features a sexualized amputee girl figure on a dog leash; and Edible Artificial Girls, Mimi-chan (Shokuyō jinzō shōjo, Mimi-chan), which included the 2001 painting *Blender*, in which thousands of tiny naked female bodies or dolls have just begun being mixed in a blender: though most of the bodies are still intact, the blood from those already crushed is rising up the sides of the blender.

The public response to these works was strong citizen protest against expression felt to be specifically harmful to women and children. Among the critics were some of Japan's most outspoken and high-profile feminist scholars, including Muta Kazue, Okano Yayo, and Ueno Chizuko; plus organizations such as Women against Sexual Violence (Sei bōryoku o yurusanai onna no kai), the Women's Action Network, and People against Pornography and Sexual Violence (Poruno higai to seibōryoku o kangaeru kai), a citizens' network.[26] For decades, these individuals and organizations have fought both for gender equality and against gender and sexual violence. They have authored some of the most pertinent research in that vast field, ranging from Muta's pioneering study on the Fukuoka sexual harassment case of 1989–1992 – Japan's first successful legal action regarding sexual harassment – to Ueno's analyses of systematic mass rape during wartime and its legacy in Japan and globally (see also Chapter 4). All of the activists are widely known public intellectuals working against sexual harassment, sexual violence, and sex trafficking.

---

[26] The People against Pornography and Sexual Violence NPO is primarily devoted to women's and children's sexuality and rights and works toward eliminating child abuse, domestic violence, sexual violence, and sexual and power harassment; https://ebanokainpo.wixsite.com/index (accessed October 25, 2020).

178   Sexing Visual Culture

Regarding Aida's retrospective in particular, People against Pornography and Sexual Violence (PAPS) demanded the removal of the works they felt amounted to "child pornography, [an endorsement of] sexual discrimination and sexual violence, and [the advocation of] contempt for and discrimination against people with disabilities." The organization also evoked Article 175 concerning the possession, display, and sale of obscene materials – even though a 2008 Supreme Court ruling had introduced exemptions for "artistic" and "highbrow" materials.[27] Suggesting that the artworks were the result of the actions they reference – sexual abuse, amputation, subordination of a young female – PAPS wrote:

We imagine that the artist and the Mori Art Museum think this exhibition poses a challenge to social convention and public authority, but in reality the exhibition expresses values that wholly endorse the socially dominant view that women and girls exist mostly for the purpose of sexual servitude. In fact, the exhibition promotes this view. Far from posing a challenge to authority, the exhibition is an example of the open and brazen exercise of social authority.

In response, the museum dismissed PAPS's complaint, claiming its right to exhibit and emphasizing the fact that the works in question were displayed in a separate room designated for adults only. In the end, no works were withdrawn from the installation.

In contrast to the vocal objectors, art critics have almost universally defended Aida, attributing his intention as being to critique – not to reinforce – the misogynism of both mainstream erotic media and the rampant objectification of the female form therein. Siding with the museum leadership, they cite the art gallery as a space that directly appeals to visitors to reflect upon the works, not to thoughtlessly consume them. Some critics also pointed to Aida's deliberate choice of the Nihonga technique, the use of mineral-based pigments, so as to allude to traditional Japanese erotic paintings and their application to grotesque imagery – resulting in layers of conflicted meanings.[28] That said, Aida's statements about his work are ambiguous at best, and sometimes glib,

---

[27] Cather, *The Art of Censorship in Postwar Japan*, 298–99, n. 1; Boyce, "Obscenity and Nationalism," 743.

[28] Gianni Simone, "Building a Monument to Nothing: A Fantastic Interview with Makoto Aida," *SFAQ/NYAQ/AQ: International Art and Culture*, September 29, 2014; accessed October 30, 2020, www.sfaq.us/2014/09/building-a-monument-to-nothing-a-fantastic-interview-with-makoto-aida/. *Blender* (2001) is an acrylic-on-canvas exercise in sadomasochism. Standing at 290cm, a huge blender minces young Japanese girls into a bloody mixture. Their facial expressions are clearly visible: blank, aroused, clueless, and pleasured. The way their naked bodies swirl inside the container and press against the glass animates their individual features.

irreverent, and irritating. On the occasion of the retrospective in question, he made an additionally provocative move: an hour-long video feed, *I-DE-A*, displayed at the exhibition shows the artist masturbating in front of the painted Japanese characters for pretty young girls (*bishōjo*).[29] He sees this work as "an ethnographic perspective on Japanese people." Together with other works of his, the video aims to highlight "fantastic elements," including those he considers both pathological and characteristic of Japanese sexuality. Ultimately, though, he ridicules his own analysis: "I'm a kind of Pierrot. I make people upset. I make them laugh. I annoy them. And that's what I'm good at."[30]

And yet the objections expressed by PAPS and other critics are not groundless. Even if the artist intends to critique, and the art critic diagnoses provocation, what would stop others from simply seeing in such art yet another sexist, exploitative image? The second half of the twentieth century saw an immense proliferation of so-called "sexual media" (*sei media*), ranging from the occupation-era pulp magazines to adult magazines, pink films, backroom videos, adult videos, and, most recently, video games – many of which casually and excessively depict female bodies in sexual or sexualized configurations, many of them very young, and frequently in violent scenarios. More often representations of the female form come in the shape of cute young girls – à la Aida's reference in his video performance – who are not granted personalities of their own, their role being only to serve as the object of presumably male desire. Even the female "persocom" in *Chobits*, a manga adapted as an anime television series broadcast in 2002, only comes "alive" when her flesh-and-blood male owner puts his hand between her legs, apparently turning her on.[31] Particularly when such scenes and figures appear in manga and anime, they easily become a bone of contention for feminists, parents, and educators alike.[32] Such critics suggest that the harm embedded in such visual and narrative depictions is multifold. The criticism crystalizes, however, in one specific fear: that the sheer ubiquity of representations of the violation of female figures or the sexual abuse of

---

[29] Tracy Jones, "Monuments to Misanthropy: A Landmark Exhibition for Controversial Artist Makoto Aida at Mori Art Museum," *Tokyo Art Beat*, December 4, 2004, accessed October 30, 2020, www.tokyoartbeat.com/tablog/entries.en/2012/12/monuments-to-misanthropy.html.

[30] Andrew Maerkle, "All Too Human," *ART iT*, April 12, 2013, accessed October 30, 2020, www.art-it.asia/en/u/admin_ed_itv_e/ysx8xtnygdjws7orl0zc.

[31] Thomas Lamarre, "Platonic Sex: Perversion and Shōjo Anime (Part One)," *animation: an interdisciplinary journal* 1, no. 1 (2006): 50–51.

[32] The December 2, 1995 issue of the periodical *Bessatsu Takarajima*, titled "Sei media no 50-nen," is devoted entirely to the development of a "postwar history of desire"; *Bessatsu Takarajima* 240.

180   Sexing Visual Culture

child figures conditions viewers to normalize the violation, sexualization, and commodification of women (and children) – a situation made even worse by the fact that the vast majority of these viewers are young males.

Historically, what has been deemed obscene and dangerous has remained ambiguous and in flux, depending on local social conditions as well as international or global influences. The current prime concern for potential harm to children and youth in part emerged with the rise in the 1980s of erotic manga and anime, a trend that was significantly accelerated in the late 1980s following the horrific murder of four girls, aged four to seven, by Miyazaki Tsutomu, a socially isolated young man with an extensive collection of adult pornography and "Lolita"-style manga and anime featuring sexualized schoolgirl heroines. In the aftermath, cultural critics and pop psychologists were quick to connect Miyazaki's private fantasy life with his real-life actions, and to generalize from one mentally ill young man to a whole generation of (particularly male) manga and anime consumers.

One might respond to that fear as the Mori Art Museum did: by separating, first, Aida's art; and, second, the critical, didactic, provocative, and guarded space within which it is displayed – from the mechanisms of mass culture that distract viewers from understanding and owning responsibility for looking and flesh-and-blood society. Alternatively, one might point out that even the mass marketplace of manga and anime is not exclusively populated by the kind of "pretty young girls" Aida seems to be evoking. It is also populated by "super (pretty young) girls" (*chōshōjo*): females who transform into powerful demons or mighty warriors when betrayed or threatened, such as goddesses, gynoids, alien women, animal girls, female cyborgs, and many others.[33] From the early *Metropolis* (1949) to *Ranma ½* (1987–1996), *Rose of Versailles* (1972–1973, 2013–2018), *Utena* (1996–1998), and *Chobits* (April–September 2002), manga and anime frequently "bend normative categories of sexuality, inventing and reinventing genre paradigms precisely in order to outpace the imposition of static categories."[34] A favorite is the female figure Makie in *Wicked City*, who can transform into a giant spider that sports a toothed vagina with the bite force of a Bulldog.[35] Comparative literature scholar Christopher Bolton points out that "some of the most interesting anime have an ability to call the

---

[33] Hasegawa Yūko, "In Focus: The Chōshōjo Movement," in *From Postwar to Postmodern: Art in Japan, 1945–1989*, ed. Doryun Chong, Michio Hayashi, Kenji Kajiya, and Fumihiko Sumitomo (New York: Museum of Modern Art, 2012), 372–73; Christopher Bolton, *Interpreting Anime* (Minneapolis: University of Minnesota Press, 2018), 138.

[34] Lamarre, "Platonic Sex."   [35] Lamarre, "Platonic Sex," 50–51.

viewer's attention continually back to the particular qualities of the representation itself, and to the ways that it is rarely transparent." This is a far cry from assuming that passive consumer "victims" have been forced by the ubiquitous media into holding reactionary attitudes and ideas. Indeed, other critics have emphasized manga's and anime's potential for reflecting social attitudes and anxieties about gender roles, crises of masculinity in particular, or even broader social change. At the very least – according to the cultural critic Saitō Tamaki in his canonical book, *Beautiful Fighting Girl (Sentō Bishōjo no Seishin Bunseki, 2000)* – viewers do not confuse social reality with fantastic representation; rather, they view reality as one version of fantasy, and consider themselves capable of moving back and forth between one and the other.[36]

Some experts, including Susan Napier, who has pioneered the scholarly analysis of manga and anime in the United States, concede that many female bodies in anime transform – whether the genre is comedy, horror, or pornography – resulting in strong female figures that signal liberation and empowerment. Some even suggest that when such sexual weaponized creatures overpower weak male figures masculinity is under siege in society at large. But these advances quickly recede when, as is all too often the case, the strong female figures must be rescued, and end up married, and possibly even impregnated – ensuring that patriarchal order is restored and old-fashioned social anxieties about gender and sexuality are appeased.[37] Both perspectives apply; indeed, manga and anime are so numerous and varied that all of the above can apply to some extent within any one product.

Accordingly, it is fair to assume that feminist critics and protective parents and teachers will resist what they see as the commodification and sexualization of the female (and, to some degree, the child) body in the public sphere. The question remains whether an art exhibition in a museum is a productive locale for such resistance.

Demystifying the Vagina with Rokudenashiko

Igarashi Megumi (1972–), best known as Rokudenashiko or Good-for-Nothing-Girl, made a name for herself as a sculptor and manga artist. But in 2013 she began to call herself a *"manko* (pussy) artist," eventually embarking on a series of works designed to demystify the vagina, resignify female sexuality, and empower women to speak about their bodies without shame (see Figure 7.1). Using molds of her vulva,

---

[36] Bolton, *Interpreting Anime*, 142, 152.   [37] Bolton, *Interpreting Anime*, 142.

Figure 7.1 A sample of Rokudenashiko's Ms. Manko-chan figurines. Printed with the kind permission of the artist

Rokudenashiko created dioramas (*diora-manko*), action figures (*transformanko*), *manko* iPhone cases, and *manko-chan* fantasy creatures – all of which were subsequently mass-produced as manga, figurines, and stuffed animals in an explicit effort to influence conventional attitudes toward female sexuality. Feminist critics in particular celebrated the hyper-cute Ms. Manko – the lead character in Rokudenashiko's manga memoir titled *What Is Obscenity? How I Became a So-Called Artist* – noting that she subverted the "deadly symbol of the vagina dentata" in a mischievous play on the fear of castration and as protest against conventional attitudes toward the public representation of female genitalia.[38] Rokudenashiko's appropriation of cute culture as a medium of protest, however, has a paradoxical prehistory.

In the 1970s and 1980s, girls and young women created cute culture as a subversive move against what they saw as grown-up conformity. At first sight, one might think Rokudenashiko simply takes her cue from this style, given that she presents herself with Hello Kitty paraphernalia, hair bows, and other girlish accoutrements that defy her mature age.

---

[38] Sara Sylvester, "Drawing Dangerous Women: The Monstrous Feminine, Taboo and Japanese Feminist Perspectives on the Female Form," *Feminist Encounters: A Journal of Critical Studies in Culture and Politics* 4, no. 1 (2020): 1–16.

(She turned forty-eight in 2020.) However, the original subversive intention of this Japanese cuteness backfired when it became massively commodified, mainstreamed, and eventually pornified. Today, any ordinary object of everyday use for any generation and gender is likely available in cute renditions – be they pens and notepads, phone charms, or PR materials of entities ranging from neighborhood cooperatives to corporations to the police and the military. In a world that subscribes to self-transformation as the key to success within the late capitalist market economy, the personal effort to be "cute" and to "appeal" has also deeply penetrated some segments of male subculture. Anthropologist Sharon Kinsella even writes of some males' "orientation towards girlishness and cuteness" as a result of the recession and labor market deregulation from around 2006 onward.[39]

So, while Rokudenashiko's deployment of cute is not immediately unambiguous, she nonetheless aims to repossess and de-pornify female genitals, articulate "an alternative female voice," and "subvert dominant cultural narratives."[40] As such, she works in line with a few feminist artists who employ new media and create personae for activism based on humor and the customization of mass cultural forms via craft.[41] With her particular crafting of digital cultural forms, Rokudenashiko intentionally challenges the sexual politics of the art world as well as the world beyond. She presents "female genitalia as a fictional cute character to signify the openness and naturalness of the female body," keeping at play both its taboo and its cuteness while rendering it an "embodiment of positivity," a "symbol of feminist resistance."[42]

In 2013, Rokudenashiko took her work to a new level with the help of a 3D printer. For her first piece she created a bright yellow full-sized kayak modeled on her vulva – which she funded via crowdsourcing. To those contributing over ¥3,000 to the project she offered the data of the model so they could create their own 3D-printed Rokudenashiko vulva kayak. Though her political–artistic project had many supporters, the Tokyo police did not share her sense of humor; at the end of 2014, she was jailed and formally charged with distributing obscene materials in violation of Article 175.[43] In her defense, Igarashi declared that in Japan female

---

[39] Sharon Kinsella, "Cuteness, *josō*, and the Need to Appeal: *otoko no ko* in Male Subculture in 2010s Japan," *Japan Forum* 32, no. 3 (2020): 432–58.

[40] Sylvester, "Drawing Dangerous Women," 5.

[41] Hasegawa, "In Focus: The *Chōshōjo* Movement," 372–73; Bolton, *Interpreting Anime*, 138.

[42] Sylvester, "Drawing Dangerous Women," 8.

[43] For critical research on Igarashi Megumi's project see Boyce, "Obscenity and Nationalism," 681, 686, 743; Sylvester, "Drawing Dangerous Women"; Anne

184 Sexing Visual Culture

sexual expression was acknowledged only as something designed for men's pleasure,[44] and that "the judicial courts have this idiosyncratic concept of the vagina as something that will arouse men when they see it no matter what." Whereas in her art she works to "take back" what belongs to women in the first place and make it something fun.[45] In a first session of her Tokyo District Court trial, Igarashi's defense lawyers argued that her artwork was unlikely to "arouse in a person unsolicited sexual excitement" as is stipulated by the obscenity law, penal code 175.[46] In such cases, the court is charged with determining whether an exception to penal code 175 should be made based on the artistic or intellectual value of a creative work.

The court chose not to make an exception and found her guilty. Igarashi's defense team countered by insisting that the court had misinterpreted the constitution and had, thus, failed to uphold Article 21, which guarantees "freedom of expression without exception." The subsequent series of trials progressed to the Supreme Court. The art

McKnight, "At the Source (Code): Obscenity and Modularity in Rokudenashiko's Media Activism," in *Media Theory in Japan*, ed. Marc Steinberg and Alexander Zahlten (Durham, NC: Duke University Press, 2017), 250–84; Joel Gwynne, "Japan, Postfeminism and the Consumption of Sexual(ised) Schoolgirls in Male-Authored Contemporary Manga," *Feminist Theory* 14, no. 3 (2013): 325–43; Alessandro Ludovico, "Eine neue Perspektive auf die Do-it-yourself-Kultur," *springerin* 1 (2015): 38–41; Jeannette Catsoulis, "'#Female Pleasure' Review: Fighting the Patriarchy," *New York Times*, October 18, 2019, accessed June 4, 2021, www.nytimes.com/2019/10/17/movies/female-pleasure-review.html.

[44] Jake Adelstein, "Obscenity Arrest May Be Hiding Dirty Politics," *Japan Times*, December 6, 2014, accessed November 7, 2020, www.japantimes.co.jp/news/2014/12/06/national/media-national/obscenity-arrest-may-hiding-dirty-politics/; Michael Hoffman, "Ah, Vaginas! In Defense of Taboos," *Japan Times*, August 9, 2014, accessed November 7, 2020, www.japantimes.co.jp/news/2014/08/09/national/media-national/ah-vaginas-defense-taboos/; Tomohiro Osaki, "Vagina Artist Pleads Not Guilty to Obscenity Charge," *Japan Times*, April 15, 2015, accessed June 4, 2021, www.japantimes.co.jp/news/2015/04/15/national/crime-legal/vagina-artist-pleads-not-guilty-to-obscenity-charge/; "Tokyo Prosecutors Seek Fine in Trial against 'Vagina Artist' Megumi Igarashi," *Japan Times*, February 1, 2016, accessed November 7, 2020, www.japantimes.co.jp/news/2016/02/01/national/crime-legal/tokyo-prosecutors-seek-fine-in-trial-against-vagina-artist-megumi-igarashi/.

[45] Suzannah Weiss, "Meet Rokudenashiko, the Artist Arrested for Making a Boat Out of Her Vagina," *Glamour*, June 19, 2017, accessed November 26, 2020, www.glamour.com/story/rokudenashiko-japanese-artist-arrested-for-vagina-art.

[46] Osaki, "Vagina Artist Pleads Not Guilty to Obscenity Charge"; Loulla-Mae Eleftheriou-Smith, "Megumi Igarashi Found Guilty of Obscenity over 'Vagina Kayak' Artwork," *Independent*, May 9, 2016, accessed November 23, 2020, www.independent.co.uk/news/world/asia/megumi-igarashi-found-guilty-obscenity-over-vagina-kayak-artwork-a7020516.html. A page on the Chikumashobo Ltd. website includes articles about the law and information about her book *Waisetsu tte nan desu ka: "jishō geijutsuka" to yobareta watakushi*, accessed June 4, 2021, www.chikumashobo.co.jp/special/waisetsu/. Weiss, "Meet Rokudenashiko, the Artist Arrested for Making a Boat Out of Her Vagina."

Demystifying the Vagina 185

historian expert witness at that trial agreed with Rokudenshiko's defense that Article 175 did not clearly define "obscenity" and that such labeling often "ignored the context of production, distribution, and presentation of the object or image in question."[47] In July 2020 the Supreme Court found her not guilty regarding the kayak, arguing that it was easily recognizable as a product of pop art. But it found her guilty on the distribution of digital data based on her vulva and fined her ¥400,000 (the equivalent of ca. $3,800), judging that the data were produced for the sole purpose of distributing something obscene.

The ruling highlighted the absurdity of the current system of obscenity regulation, under which "the transmission of a 3D scan of a vulva is a criminal offense but phalluses are freely paraded through the streets at various seasonal Shinto festivals around Japan."[48] Interestingly, neither side brought into play sexually explicit manga and anime. One constitutional law expert also noted that it appeared that "no one except the police ever used the digital data that Rokudenashiko distributed to create an actual model of genitalia, as 3D printers are expensive and fairly rare. In short, the only people ever placed in danger of being aroused, it seems, were the law enforcement officers who had been keeping Rokudenashiko under surveillance."[49] Another constitutional law expert and activist proposed that the solution lies not in the ever-more accurate definition and understanding of "obscenity" but in a fundamental reform of the penal code. Instead of Article 175, what Japanese society needs are new legislation and a full societal debate about policies and laws that punish discriminatory sexual expression and abusive sexual behavior.[50]

Needless to say, the massive media response to the trial in and outside Japan – and a meeting with world-famous Chinese dissident artist Ai Weiei – led to an exhibition in Hong Kong that aimed to "think feminism" with works from artists in Japan and Hong Kong. It featured contributions by Rokudenashiko, Aida Makoto, and Sputniko!, a Japanese-British artist based in Tokyo. And Rokudenashiko retains her

---

[47] Weiss, "Meet Rokudenashiko."

[48] Rokudenashiko, *What Is Obscenity? The Story of a Good-for-Nothing Artist and Her Pussy*, trans. Anne Ishii (Toronto: Koyama Press, 2016), 48–49, n. 450.

[49] Boyce, "Obscenity and Nationalism," 686 and 743.

[50] Shida Yōko, "Rokudenashiko saiban – saikō saiban-ketsu wa nani o sabaita no ka – keijibatsu wa makoto ni hitsuyō na koto ni shiborubeki," *Yahoo Nyūsu Japan*, July 17, 2020, accessed November 26, 2020, https://news.yahoo.co.jp/byline/shidayoko/20200717-00188461/; Yamamoto Poteto, "'Waisetsu hyōgen' kisei to josei sabetsu kokufuku wa kankei nai? Kenpō gakusha Ishida Yōko-shi intabyū," *Wezzy–Gendai o shian suru seikai no nai WEB magajin*, December 27, 2016, accessed November 26, 2020, https://wezz-y.com/archives/39102/3.

186   Sexing Visual Culture

sense of humor: during the COVID-19 pandemic she wore a face mask reading: "Thank you, police."[51]

Silenced Females in Video Gaming

No matter how cutting-edge, revolutionary, and life-changing a technology is initially touted as being, it sometimes appears as if the same old power structures and untroubled gender order reinscribe themselves in it. To follow are three examples in chronological order. Regarding video games, some western critics have noted how in the gamer world the exclusion of flesh-and-blood female players intimately corresponds to the silencing, exploiting, and violating of female figures within the games. In robotics, male roboticists have invented humanoids whose shapes and features mirror the sort of flesh-and-blood human female faces and bodies that have for generations been idealized, objectified, and sexualized in other creative forms and genres of cultural production. Furthermore, the (inter)net idol market in Japan has emerged as yet another sphere into which the unpaid emotional labor that women have conventionally performed in the domestic sphere and in the office has been expanded. Ebihara Yuri, a leader among such young women who earn their fame by creating their personal websites and featuring their photographs and diaries, says: "If someone doesn't find me cute, I want to know why because then I'll work on it to get better at being cute."[52] For all its democratizing effects, "the digital economy has encouraged young women to invest emotional labor into producing cute by making the possibility of earning an income from affective labor contingent upon it."[53]

Almost from their inception, video games have reiterated the objectification and violation of female figures while, at the same time, policing women's desires – in part through the simulation of emotional labor and in part by configuring them as voiceless, passive figures at the margins of a game's narrative. In one influential critique exemplified on the first playable female character in gaming, *Ms. Pac-Man*, Anita Sarkeesian describes this "virtual sexism" in terms that are astonishingly and frustratingly familiar. One, female characters are one-dimensional

---

[51] For a media theoretical analysis, see McKnight, "At the Source (Code)."

[52] Gabriella Lukacs, "The Labor of Cute: Net Idols, Cute Culture, and the Digital Economy in Contemporary Japan," *positions: east asia cultures critique* 23, no. 3 (2015): 487.

[53] Robertson, *Robo Sapiens Japonicus*; Patrick W. Galbraith, "Adult Computer Games and the Ethics of Imaginary Violence: Responding to Gamergate from Japan," *U.S.–Japan Women's Journal* no. 52 (2017): 67–88; Lukacs, "The Labor of Cute."

and defined primarily by their relationship to their male counterparts via their visual properties, their narrative connection, and promotional materials; and two, female characters are recognizable as such by the same old symbolic markers of gender – including pink and pastel colors; bows, makeup, and jewelry; large eyes with long lashes; hair in pigtails; emphasized breasts and hips; and the wearing of skirts, high heels, and midriff-baring outfits. In short, "games, female characters and women are all presented as objects to play with."[54] Ultimately, objectification in computer/console gaming takes on the forms of instrumentality, commodification, interchangeability, violability, and disposability.[55] In addition, these mechanisms are particularly apparent in non-playable characters that provide "environmental texture"; rather than being controlled by players, they instead exclusively serve as "non-playable sex objects."

So far, so familiar. Yet some scholars argue that the interactivity of games provides an additional mechanism of practicing, exercising, learning, and normalizing sexual violence against girls and women – along with dehumanizing them, which in turn discourages empathy toward them.[56] Others have pointed out that it is precisely the "participatory cultures of gaming" that have "aggressively resisted feminist critiques of games[,] and that these forms of male dominated resistance continue to marginalize women in gaming industries and cultures." Scholars have found that "males who were exposed to the objectified female video game characters were the most tolerant of any of the groups towards sexual harassment" and "the longer that people are exposed to these types of images and attitudes the more they develop rape-supportive attitudes." Avatar representation matter as well. The more sexualized the avatar, the more likely women and men are to objectify women, which can lead to extreme subordination of women, such as in terms of the rape myth – prejudicial, stereotyped, and false beliefs about sexual assaults, rapists, and rape victims.[57]

---

[54] See Galbraith, "Adult Computer Games and the Ethics of Imaginary Violence," 70–71.
[55] Anita Sarkeesian, "Ms. Male Character: Tropes vs Women in Video Games," *Feminist Frequency*, November 18, 2013, accessed November 20, 2020, www.youtube.com/watch?v=eYqYLfm1rWA (1,324,736 views as of June 4, 2021); Anita Sarkeesian, "Women as Background Decoration: Part I – Tropes vs. Women in Video Games," *Feminist Frequency*, June 16, 2014, www.youtube.com/watch?v=4ZPSrwedvsg (1,002,752 views as of June 4, 2021). Sarkeesian's points were summarized by Galbraith, "Adult Computer Games and the Ethics of Imaginary Violence," 70–71.
[56] Sarkeesian, "Women as Background Decoration: Part I."
[57] Jennifer DeWinter and Carly A. Kocurek, "'Aw Fuck, I Got a Bitch on My Team!' Women and the Exclusionary Cultures of the Computer Game Complex," in *Gaming Representation*, ed. Jennifer Malkowski and Treaandrea M. Russworm (Bloomington:

188 Sexing Visual Culture

In an interview held in 2014, Sasakibara Gō contemplated the interconnections between comics for girls (*shōjo manga*) and adult computer games. He felt that the games brought together the sort of poetic love stories characteristic of *shōjo* manga and the sex scenes typical of mainstream pornography for men.[58] As a manga and anime critic and gamer, Sasakibara spoke from the three-point intersection of a powerful lucrative industry, obscenity legislation, and the concerns of Japanese and global anti-pornography and prostitution activism. He alluded to the common and possibly distinctly Japanese amalgamation of the cute with the pornographic in Japanese adult video games within a corporate–creative–legal environment that more strongly relies on industry restraint than censorship. Sasakibara also made an effort to distinguish Japanese adult games from those produced elsewhere. He generalized that, in such games in Japan, the player cannot but become aware of "his own violence" or the desire and power to act, suggesting that adult computer games actually "provide a way to work through relations of power and adopt an ethical position against hurting others." His key point is that "these things coexist in the same adult computer games." More importantly, "rather than normalizing sexual violence, ... Sasakibara [is suggesting] that confronting the ugly parts of desire and relationships can lead to an ethics like his own."[59] While Sasakibara offers no evidence for the latter claim actually manifesting among gamers, it should be noted also that distilling distinctly "Japanese" characteristics is rather questionable given that video games are often the product of international collaborations and are played around the globe.[60]

Video games are, of course, a hugely profitable, diverse market, and many games are related to or originate from other multimedia products, such as manga or anime regarding plots and art styles. Even video games that are designed with female players in mind – for instance, *otome* games

---

Indiana University Press, 2017), 63, accessed June 4, 2021, www.academia.edu/34655779/_AW_FUCK_I_GOT_A_BITCH_ON_MY_TEAM_Women_and_the_Exclusionary_Cultures_of_the_Computer_Game_Complex.

[58] Sasakibara Gō was interviewed by Galbraith, "Adult Computer Games and the Ethics of Imaginary Violence," 68; for a flesh-and-blood male porn star's perspective, see Paige Ferrari, "Meet the Hardest Working Man in Porn," *GQ*, March 3, 2015, accessed November 23, 2020, www.gq.com/story/shimiken-japanese-porn-star-interview.

[59] Galbraith, "Adult Computer Games and the Ethics of Imaginary Violence," 82; Sasakibara Gō, "Kizu tsukeru sei, dankai no sedai kara otaku sedai e: Gyarugē-teki sekushuariti no kigen," in *Shingenjitsu: 2*, ed. Ōtsuka Eiji (Tokyo: Kadokawa Shoten, 2003), 101–28.

[60] Sarah Christina Ganzon, "Investing Time for Your In-Game Boyfriends and BFFs: Time as Commodity and the Simulation of Emotional Labor in *Mystic Messenger*," *Games and Culture* 14, no. 2 (2019): 139–53; McLelland, "Sex, Censorship and Media Regulation in Japan," 411.

and casual games – nonetheless contain often stereotypical assumptions about femininity, as well as about how women spend their time and resources. In many such games, emotional labor is encouraged in female players as a means of directing women's desires toward productive activities. Much as can be seen in games favored by males, female players dominate the player communities around these games and many of these discuss their own gameplay and their identity as players and consumers. While these female-oriented games are innovative in many ways, they too have been the object of the longstanding critique of media representation of girls and women.[61]

In sum, sexual expression in visual culture continues to carry the potential to reflect sexual and gender configurations and relations as they are in society – as well as to envision what could be. As such, sexual expression has the potential to subvert, critique, and change, all while the danger and potential harm they entail is negotiated in the public sphere of museums, the marketplace, and the Internet.

Literature and Visual Culture

Kimi Rito's *The History of Hentai Manga*[62] provides a history and examples of erotic/pornographic manga. The book can be productively read alongside Rokudenashiko's *What Is Obscenity? The Story of a Good for Nothing Artist and Her Pussy* (2016).[63]

Three classics top the list: Imamura Shōhei's *The Pornographers* (*"Erogotoshitachi" yori Jinruigaku Nyūmon*, 1966),[64] based on the novel *Erogotoshitachi* by Nosaka Akiyuki, sparked controversy for its comic treatment of voyeurism and incest. Teshigahara Hiroshi's *Woman in the Dunes* (*Suna no Onna*, 1964)[65] is based on Abe Kōbo's 1962 novella of

---

[61] In 2011, the Youth Health Development Ordinance was established in Tokyo to limit children's access to publications that the lawmaker determines to be harmful. It prohibits the sale to people younger than eighteen of publications containing material that is "sexually stimulating, encourages cruelty, and/or may compel suicide or criminal behavior." The ordinance includes manga and anime that have explicit depictions of children engaging in sexual acts. For the exact language of the law, see "Heisei jūichi-nen hōritsu dai-gojūni-gō: Jidō baishun, jidō poruno ni kakawaru kōi-tō no kisei oyobi shobatsu narabi ni jidō no hogo-tō ni kan suru hōritsu," *e-gov hōrei kensaku* (Ministry of Internal Affairs and Communications), accessed December 9, 2020, https://elaws.e-gov.go.jp/document?lawid=411AC1000000052.

[62] Kimi Rito, *The History of Hentai Manga* (Tokyo: FAKKU, 2021).

[63] Rokudenashiko, *What Is Obscenity?*

[64] Imamura Shohei and Numata Kōji, *The Pornographers* (*"Erogotoshitachi" yori jinruigaku nyūmon*), directed by Imamura Shohei (Tokyo: Nikkatsu, 1966).

[65] Abe Kōbo, *Woman in the Dunes* (*Suna no onna*), directed by Teshigahara Hiroshi (Tokyo: Toho, 1964).

190 Sexing Visual Culture

the same name. And then there is of course Oshima Nagisa's *In the Realm of the Senses (Ai no Korrida,* 1976),[66] described earlier. *Blue* (2002)[67] by Andō Hiroshi is about the friendship of two teenage girls that turns into something more. And Maeda Toshio's classic pornographic *La Blue Girl* (1989–1992)[68] is available as anime and manga series.

[66] Oshima Nagisa, *In the Realm of the Senses – L'Empire des sens (Ai no korrida),* directed by Oshima Nagisa (Neuilly-sur-Seine, France: Argos, 1976).
[67] Honcho Yuka, *Blue,* directed by Hiroshi Ando (Japan, 2002).
[68] For more visit "Toshio Maeda: Official Website – They call me 'tentacle master,'" accessed June 6, 2021, at www.urotsukidoji.jp/.

8 Epilogue

This Epilogue reflects on the major currents, twists, and turns that have governed writing about sex, gender, and sexuality. As I hope has become clear throughout this book, such writing has emerged from and has produced stories about acts of traversing, translating, and transgressing – while also being marked by disconnections and discontinuities. Indeed, the field of gender and sexuality studies in Japan has evolved in major ways since the late nineteenth century – when folklorists and ethnologists first recorded sexual legends and beliefs and when a handful of sexologists first studied actual Japanese people's sexual behavior. Sexual ethnology dominated the first few decades of the twentieth century. An early version of what would later be called women's studies also traces its roots to the early-twentieth-century works of women's history. The subsequently emerging gender studies of the late twentieth century has acknowledged the importance of interrogating, in terms of sex and gender, women and femininities as well as men and masculinities. Today, both women's studies and gender studies are in part informed by and coexist with feminist studies and LGBT+ or queer studies. Throughout these trials and tribulations, the core question of what exactly is at stake when studying sex, gender, and sexuality has been intimately entangled with both power relations and the various attempts at changing them.

At the Beginning: The Penis

Much of what Japanese moderns had to say about sex, gender, and sexuality was informed by proto-sociological, -anthropological, and -folklore studies, even before these fields were properly named and established within academic institutions, beginning circa 1900. Studies of sex, gender, and sexuality in modern Japan have been sensitive to both macro and micro connections in a range of settings – local or far-flung, shared and translated widely, and concerning various modes of producing, gathering, and understanding knowledge. Studying sex, gender, and

192   Epilogue

sexuality in modern and contemporary Japan necessitates that we recognize multiple interconnections and their cross-fertilization across regional, national, geographic, and cultural borders – all while keeping our sight on the boundaries and limitations of bodies of knowledge in the making.

The contours of this complexity were already apparent in 1895 when the University of Chicago Press published a thirty-four-page dissertation by Edmund Buckley called *Phallicism in Japan*. As a later bibliographer noted, Buckley's was the first "serious study of any branch of phallicism to be presented to a university,"[1] even though other authors had also touched upon Japanese manifestations of phallicism in their works. *Phallicism in Japan* appeared at a time when the modernizing Japanese state had begun to prohibit phallus-related rituals, deeming them backward and uncivilized, out of sync with more "advanced" Euro-American societies. Yet the slim dissertation traveled to Japan as it were, where author and translator Deguchi Yonekichi (1871–1937) furthered its reach: after Deguchi published a Japanese translation in the *Journal of Anthropology* (*Jinruigaku Zasshi*), phallicism and sexual ethnology became a field of research in Japan as well. Deguchi continued to translate similar western works and in 1917 completed his own book on phallicism, *An Outline of Phallic Worship in Japan* (*Nihon Seishokki Sūhai Ryakusetsu*), which established him as a native pioneer of sexual ethnology. To be sure, his was not a derivative of Buckley's work; innovative in its own right, Deguchi's book was based on the study of documents and conversations with locals all over Japan, conducted at a time when "fieldwork" had not yet been established as a method of inquiry.[2] *An Outline of Phallic Worship in Japan* also made the study of the symbolic representation of mostly male genitals the core subject of early sexual ethnology – indeed, the origin of the academic study of sexuality in Japan.

The study of sexuality at the time was pursued by an all-male cast of scholars whose inquiries into sexuality constituted a transnational project. Books on the "Japanese sex life" written in English, French, and German were often driven by both a nostalgic sense of a more harmonious and less self-conscious past and – given the pressures of modernization at the time – an impulse to enshrine "tradition" in a scholarly form. When international scholars sketched a picture of the "Japanese sex life" that seemed by comparison open-minded and unprejudiced, they routinely framed their books as critiques of European puritanism and

---

[1] Roger Goodland, *A Bibliography of Sex Rites and Customs* (London: Routledge, 1931), 91.
[2] Kawamura Kunimitsu, *Sekushuariti no kindai* (Tokyo: Kōdansha, 1996), 3–32.

At the Beginning

hypocrisy concerning sexual matters. International scholarly pioneers of the early twentieth century, such as Friedrich Solomon Krauss (1859–1938) or Magnus Hirschfeld (1868–1935), came to Japan in the hope of discovering something other than the conservative Christian sexual order they had found so insufferable back in Europe.

A Croatian-Austrian Jewish sexologist, ethnographer, folklorist, and Slavist, Krauss claimed that evaluating a particular society of people by examining simply their military, economic, or, say, literary successes was insufficient; he believed consideration of a society's sexual ethnology was essential to complete the picture. Krauss declared that, since the development and progress of *men* depended entirely on the flourishing of *women*, the foremost goal of the folklorist was to broadcast knowledge about the status of women in a culture. "Sexual activity," in his view, had to be at the core of any analysis of cultural development and progress. In the preface to the first edition of his book *The Sex Life in Beliefs, Morals, Customs and Common Law of the Japanese* (*Das Geschlechtsleben in Glauben, Sitte, Brauch und Gewohnheitsrecht der Japaner*), Krauss stated that recognizing phenomena "unbeautified and uncorrected, in their undisguised reality" before searching for explanations or for higher causes was the most important, if not the only, guiding principle for a true ethnology – and, really, for any true scientific inquiry. His book included such uncorrected phenomena: full-page photographs of stone phalli, explicit erotic woodblock prints, and a long chapter on attitudes toward "homosexual love," in which he claimed that "the old attitude of the samurai continues to live on in quiet and its main carrier still is the military." Though these details prompted the book being explicitly restricted to a specialist readership in order to avoid censorship, for European students of sexuality in Japan, *The Sex Life in Beliefs, Morals, Customs and Common Law of the Japanese* was an impressive account of a man who embraced "reviewing the expressions of eroticism with cool calmness." It also long remained a singular standard work – that is, until other sexologists traveled to Japan.[3]

Subsequently finding Japanese culture enlightened in sexual matters, some of these sexologist visitors marveled at the absence of the hypocrisy they criticized at home. Krauss wrote in 1907: "The Occidental looks at Japan through Occidental glasses: He sees moral degeneration where there is in naked reality nothing but unmediated joy of life and irrepressible joy for sexual matters combined with a lack of any kind of

---

[3] Krauss, *Das Geschlechtsleben*, 1–3, 161. A complete digitized edition is available at the Internet Archive, accessed July 31, 2020, https://archive.org/details/BzA_II_1911_2te/page/n7/mode/2up.

194   Epilogue

hypocrisy."[4] As for that perceived "moral degeneration": when international visitors exhibited naïveté, ignorance or assumptions of superiority, public figures in Japan did not hold back from noting: "It is a general perception of foreign tourists (many of whom are *learned gentlemen*) that Japanese life lacks morality just as its flowers lack a scent. What a sad confession of the moral and intellectual imagination of these tourists themselves!"[5]

Similarly, the German Jewish physician and sexologist Hirschfeld declared in 1933 that no two countries or peoples in the world had identical sex institutions. Hirschfeld had first described and worked with what he named transvestite and transsexual people, theorized, researched, and written about sexuality, as well as agitated for (homo)sexual rights since 1894, and continues to be hailed as the Einstein of sex 150 years later.[6] In Hirschfeld's view, this dissimilarity across different countries and peoples was not based on differences in sexual tendencies, which he considered absolutely alike in all peoples and races. A true understanding of the morality surrounding sex and love, Hirschfeld thought, could be based only on findings of biological and sociological sex research. Hirschfeld hoped that an objective scientific study of humankind and its sexual practices would prepare the complete realization of human sexual rights. He also hoped to find some clues in Japan, where sex and sexuality seemed to be dealt with so differently and where homosexuality was not prohibited by law.[7]

The sexual ethnologists and other sexologists also translated each other's works. They traversed the globe to study in one another's laboratories and research institutes, and collaborate in a variety of ways. Early ethnologist Satō Tamio, for instance, collaborated with Krauss when the latter visited Tokyo to collect materials for his book. And when Hirschfeld lectured about "sexual pathologies" at the Imperial University Tokyo for his world tour in 1931, hundreds of medical doctors from Japan proper, Taiwan, and Korea were in attendance, anxious to exchange insights and findings with him. Among those photographed on that occasion were some who had visited his Institute for Sexual Science (Institut für Sexualwissenschaft, 1919–1933) in Berlin. One was Hata Sahachirō (1873–1938) – director of the Kitasato Institute, Japan's first private medical research facility – who with Paul

---

[4] Krauss, *Das Geschlechtsleben*, 10.
[5] Nitobe Inazō, cit. in *Das Geschlechtsleben*, 13 [emphasis added].
[6] Ralf Dose, *Magnus Hirschfeld: The Origins of the Gay Liberation Movement*, trans. Edward H. Willis (New York: Monthly Review Press, 2014).
[7] Magnus Hirschfeld, *Weltreise eines Sexualforschers* (Frankfurt: Eichborn Verlag, [1933] 2006), xviii–xix.

At the Beginning   195

Ehrlich jointly discovered Salvarsan 606, considered the first effective treatment for syphilis. Also included were Dōi Keijo, a professor of dermatology; Miyake Koichi, a professor of psychiatry; and Irisawa Tatsukichi, a professor of internal medicine, dean of the Faculty of Medicine, and then-emperor Hirohito's personal physician.[8] Hirschfeld's photograph was taken – again and again – in the midst of stone phalli, some 1,000 years old. Many more group photographs featured Hirschfeld with the eminent men of science, medicine, politics, and commerce Hirschfeld met on his journey to Japan.[9] He also wrote fondly of speaking to the leaders of the women's and birth control movements, including Ishikawa Fusae (1893–1981), Ikuta Hanayo (1888–1970), and Ishimoto Shizue (1897–2001) although no photographs with any of them seem to have survived and Ishimoto did not mention the encounter in her own autobiography.[10]

Even though early-twentieth-century medical and scientific innovations typically were transnational and group projects, the commemoration of important innovations was often compressed to hail just one genius – who was almost always male, white, and European or Northern American. For instance, a Russian brochure, *606 and Syphilis* (1910) (see Figure 8.1), describes the discovery and development of Salvarsan 606, the first effective treatment for syphilis, which was jointly discovered by German scientist Paul Ehrlich and Japanese bacteriologist Hata Sahachirō, as noted earlier. And yet, within its pages only Paul Ehrlich's name is mentioned, and repeatedly at that, suggesting that the endorsers – the crème de la crème of Eastern European medicine and epidemiology – neglected to acknowledge Hata's contribution. Similarly, Krauss did not name collaborator Satō Tamio in the 1907 edition of his book *The Sex Life in Beliefs, Morals, Customs and Common Law of the Japanese*, even though Krauss had undoubtedly benefited from the relationship. (He belatedly acknowledged Satō's assistance in a later edition in 1931.) Nonetheless, international scholarly collaborations and encounters, particularly when documented in image and print, often enhanced Japanese scholars' cachet at home – even when their contributions were minimized on the international stage.[11]

While hampering the *study* of sexualities, Japan's attempts to achieve military, political, cultural, and racial leadership via imperialist means

[8] Irisawa Naika Dōsōkai, ed., *Irisawa sensei no enzetsu to bunsho* (Tokyo: Kokuseido Shoten, 1932).
[9] Hirschfeld, *Weltreise eines Sexualforschers*, 80.
[10] Hirschfeld, *Weltreise eines Sexualforschers*, 37–88.
[11] James R. Bartholomew, "Japanese Nobel Candidates in the First Half of the Twentieth Century," *Osiris* 13 (1998): 238–84.

Figure 8.1 This Russian brochure, *606 and Syphilis* (1910), describes the discovery and development of Salvarsan 606, the first effective treatment for syphilis. Private collection

At the Beginning 197

were undergirded, contradictorily, by both massive incitement campaigns and suppression (see Chapters 2 and 4). From 1931 to 1945 in particular, the Japanese political elite and its propaganda machine explicitly articulated the claim on Asia, continuing from earlier times as broker and translator of new knowledge in the region and increasingly conceiving of Asia as a laboratory of Japanese research. Discoveries and research findings of Japanese colonial-era and wartime doctors, scientists, ethnographers, educators, and other handmaidens of imperialism were often distinctly violent and racialized affairs. When the photo journal *Asahi Gurafu* printed a series of black, white, and yellow drawings under the title "The Dawn of the East Asian Race" in its March 2, 1938 edition, however, the scenes of technological advancement and economic activity and prosperity brimmed with the deeply ideological cheerful view of Asian populations under Japanese colonial command (see Figure 8.2).

Each scene combines an (often) dark-skinned, scarcely dressed native with one or more Japanese soldiers in Imperial Japanese Army uniforms – at once emphasizing racial and gender distinctions (only the military is all-male, depicted as if fair or white-skinned), degrees of civilization (only the colonizer is fully and formally dressed – though not all of them are), and the power differential is clearly that of colonizers and colonized (it is the Japanese overseers who are in control, and the colonized who are hard at work). Importantly, the mass violence that preceded the scenes of pre-industrial activity is invisible. The colonialists' thoughts are expressed in text-bubbled words. And those words merely convey congratulations to the locals for increasing their standards of performance, production, or modernization. In turn, the colonized locals under Japanese imperialist control are robbed of their speech with the exception of offering local fruit, committing to learning Japanese, and to cheer Asia. Needless to say, the illustration makes no apology for its simplistic depiction of a newly fabricated "East Asian race."

Rather, around the time of the magazine issue's publication, the increasing "carnivalization" of Japan's war permeated urban public culture. In more remote regions, where the war felt somewhat distant, early attempts at what would much later be called women's studies blossomed and signaled a departure from or at least complement to the earlier sexual ethnology.[12] Only a couple of years prior, in 1935–1936 – when the Japanese empire stretched across Manchuria and far into the Pacific and a full-blown war with China was imminent – Ella Wiswell

---

[12] Uchiyama, *Japan's Carnival War.*

Figure 8.2 "The Dawn of the East Asian Race," the March 2, 1938 edition of the Japanese photo journal *Asahi Gurafu*. Private collection

recorded her conversations with women about their everyday lives in a small village in Kyūshū, Japan's most southern of the four big islands (see Figure 8.3). Without training as an ethnographer but equipped with enough spoken Japanese to confidently converse with the village women, she found them rather independent and self-possessed regarding matters of sex, marriage, and divorce (see Chapter 2).[13]

And 1943 saw the publication of *Women of the Mito Domain* by prominent socialist and feminist Yamakawa Kikue (1890–1980). In a foreboding of things to come, she recalls in a chapter on "The Village during War" how a bird aficionado had taught her many birds' names and their characteristics, exclaiming one day that "no other women folk anywhere in the world [knew] as little about animals as Japanese women." In this respect, "Chinese and South East Asian women were admirable," for they used birds and pigs as dowry and investment whereas Japanese women only knew kimonos. It would be "difficult to win the war just with the swishing of kimonos."[14] Neither at the time of her writing the book nor later when Japan surrendered did Yamakawa let on whether she too thought that the war could have been won if only Japanese women had known birds' and pigs' names.

At Present: Mapping Sexual and Gendered (J-)Humanity

Modern history shows that sexualities have been shaped and, in turn, have shaped economic, political, legal, and social agreements, contracts, and conventions. Individuals and institutions have traversed, translated and transgressed meanings of sex, gender, and sexuality described in this book. We have also seen how sex, previously thought of as biological and constant, and genders, previously thought of as inseparable from sex, have become fluid. As of the third decade of the twenty-first century, sexes and genders appear to have multiplied, the diffusion and inter-amalgamation of sexual and gender boundaries characterizing ever more communities across the globe.[15] In addition, the ways different generations in different parts of the world think about and practice sexuality is as fluid as genders themselves. For instance, Germany and Canada have

---

[13] Smith and Wiswell, *The Women of Suyemura*, 149–75, 262.

[14] Yamakawa Kikue, *Waga sumu mura* (Tokyo: Sankoku Shobō, 1943), 179–80. At that time, the category of "woman" was no longer the "other" in society, but instead a crucial nexus of politics, the nation-state, technology, and women's (and to a lesser extent, men's) everyday lives.

[15] See Jack Halberstam's observations in *Trans: A Quick and Quirky Account of Gender Variability* (Oakland: University of California Press, 2018) and Judith Halberstam, *Female Masculinity* (Durham, NC: Duke University Press, 1998).

Figure 8.3 Ella Lurie Wiswell with unidentified Japanese girls in the summer of 1919 when she spent her childhood there. Printed with gratitude to Wiswell's former student and archivist, Patricia Polansky, and the kind permission of the Ella Lury Embree Wiswell papers, Box 7, Russian Northeast Asia Collection, Hamilton Library, University of Hawai'i

At Present 201

introduced a third sex for legal documents. Homosexuality has become legal in India. And more countries than ever have legalized same-sex marriage, with Taiwan being the first in Asia.[16] The United States Supreme Court ruled that Title VII of the 1964 Civil Rights Act, which among other things bans employment discrimination on the basis of sex, also applies to sexual orientation and gender identity. The decision extends protection in many states to gay and trans workers who previously could legally be fired if their bosses objected to their gender identities or sex lives.[17] Among his first acts as new president in January 2021, Joe Biden ordered the Pentagon to lift its transgender ban. These developments suggest that an ever-larger percentage of the world population has become more optimistic about the possibilities of overcoming established boundaries of gender and sexual practices and identities.

These progressions have been countered by some significant conservative strongholds and backlashes, however. In Singapore there is no antidiscrimination protection and same-sex activities are illegal – though the law is only rarely enforced. South Africa's 1996 Bill of Rights was the first in the world to ban discrimination on the grounds of "sexual orientation," but that country struggles to align those progressive intentions with social, legal, and political practices.[18] Regardless, the fact that sexual and gender rights are as expansive as they are today offers hope for further justice to come. The United States Supreme Court's decision noted above was made only four days after the US administration had

---

[16] Germany is one of the first countries worldwide that introduced the designation "diverse" as a third option for the birth registry; see "Bundestag stimmt für drittes Geschlecht im Geburtenregister," *Frankfurter Allgemeine*, December 14, 2018, accessed June 4, 2021, www.faz.net/aktuell/politik/inland/kuenftig-drittes-geschlecht-im-geburtenregister-waehlbar-15941127.html. Canada was the first country in the Americas to allow its citizens to use an "X" category, joining those in Australia, Denmark, Germany, Malta, New Zealand, and Ireland. India, Ireland, and Nepal are among the countries that provide various third-options; see Mattha Busby, "Canada Introduces Gender-Neutral 'X' Option on Passports," *Guardian*, August 31, 2017, accessed March 6, 2021, www.theguardian.com/world/2017/aug/31/canada-introduces-gender-neutral-x-option-on-passports.

[17] Center for Reproductive Rights, "U.S. Supreme Court's LGBTQ Anti-Discrimination Ruling Comes Only Days after Federal Rule Strips Protections," press release, June 15, 2020; Moira Donegan, "The US Supreme Court Has Given LGBTQ Americans a Rare Bit of Good News," *Guardian*, June 16, 2020, accessed June 16, 2020, www.theguardian .com/commentisfree/2020/jun/16/us-supreme-court-americans-lgbtq.

[18] For situating Japan's modern sexual history within a *longue durée* and within a global frame, respectively, see Sabine Frühstück, "Genders and Sexualities," In *Companion to the Anthropology of Japan*, ed. Jennifer Robertson (London: Blackwell, 2005), 167–82; Sabine Frühstück, "Sexuality and Nation States," in *Global History of Sexuality*, ed. Robert Marshall Buffington, Eithne Luibheid, and Donna Guy (London: Wiley-Blackwell, 2014), 17–56.

202 Epilogue

taken a step in the opposite direction – issuing a federal rule that restricts the rights of LGBT+ people to access healthcare services – while the same court appeared to be striving to make anti-abortion laws insuperable.[19]

We have arrived at current sexuality studies through several turns and generations of scholars. The previously often implicit assumption or at least prioritization of heterosexuality appears to have been dismantled for once and all. Indeed, gender theorist Jack Halberstam is certain that *The End of Normal* has arrived, that mainstream heteronormativity has been transformed – reconfiguring gender and sex in the process – and that "gendered bodies [already] have changed."[20]

I hope this book has shown that, since the late nineteenth century, changes with regard to sex, gender, and sexuality arrangements and their various configurations have been no less radical in Japan than elsewhere – albeit differently configured and weighed. In tandem with developments on the ground, sexuality studies of Japan continue to be a thriving field of inquiry, particularly regarding LGBT+ communities. A range of scholars in history, anthropology, and sociology have made strides toward under- standing the microcosms within which LGBT+ people fashion their sexual and gendered lives in both public and semipublic spheres, espe- cially those of designated cafés, bars, clubs, and even whole districts within large cities. Along the lines of Halberstam's diagnosis, these scholars suggest a certain measure of LGBT+ cultural and social inte- gration. In Japan and elsewhere, they also constitute manifestations of sexual minority activism and expression expanding "queer spaces" – and possibly permeating and transforming previously heteronormative ones.[21]

An optimistic reading of the expanding multitude of studies, forma- tions, and physical and metaphorical spaces that LGBT+ individuals and designations occupy strikes me as being reminiscent of an observation Jorge Luis Borges made in a short text titled "On Exactitude in Science."

---

[19] Center for Reproductive Rights, "The Supreme Court Might Be about to Make It Nearly Impossible to Stop Anti-Abortion Laws," May 30, 2020, accessed June 16, 2020, https://reproductiverights.org/press-room/supreme-court-might-be-about-make- it-nearly-impossible-stop-anti-abortion-laws.

[20] I am adopting a portion of Jack Halberstam's subtitle in *Gaga Feminism: Sex, Gender, and the End of Normal* (Boston, MA: Beacon Press, 2012). Jack Halberstam speaks of "trans*" in order to signify "the multiple ways in which the gendered body has changed." See Jack Halberstam, "The Difference between Male and Female Does Not Hold Anymore," March 1, 2017, accessed June 26, 2020, www.youtube.com/watch?v= JtYaUQ66sp0.

[21] See the special issue "Queer Lives in Japan," *Asian Anthropology* 19, no. 2 (2020): 77–159.

At Present 203

Concerning the rise of cartography, Borges wrote that, in the effort to be ever more exact, cartographers eventually made a map that was as big as the empire the map represented. Adapting that concept for this book's concerns, then, such a map of sexes, genders, and sexualities would represent gendered and sexual humanity in all its true diversity. An optimistic reading would also confirm that Miyatake Gaikotsu's day of reckoning has come: Gaikotsu predicted in 1922 that, instead of considering hermaphrodites "abnormalities," as was the case during his time, one day single-sex men and women would be the ones classified as abnormal (see Chapter 6). His concept of "hermaphroditism" encompassed a physical, psychological, or emotional state, one variously tied to a practice or a condition, thus signifying limitless possibilities captured (and perhaps "arrested") in today's acronym "LGBT+."

Yet there is also a pessimistic reading of such cheerful proliferation. Borges writes how the generation of cartographers of the empire-sized map was replaced by a generation that declared it useless, triggering the end of cartography altogether. Have the topographers of sexuality built the perfect and complete LGBT+ multitude that Miyatake Gaikotsu in Japan, Zhang Jingsheng in China, Magnus Hirschfeld in Germany, and so many others elsewhere dreamt of – only for its force to evaporate soon after its fruition?[22] Do identity movements tend to self-destruct, as Joshua Gamson suggests, because "identity categories are both the basis for oppression and the basis for political power"?[23] What if the LGBT+ community has passed the moment when the vigorous expression of identity in the face of oppression is "an exercise of heroism," and has turned instead to habitual clinging to boundaries that, Leon Wieseltier finds, "easily degenerates into laziness," into "habit devoid of intellectual rigor," into the question only of "Who are you like?" At the least, identity – of sex, gender, ethnicity, race, and so on – can easily turn into an insulation, a doctrine of aversion, an exaltation of impassability, a euphemism for conformity. Worse yet, precisely because an increasing sense of identity might well be experienced "as a sense of psychosocial well-being," the "thirst for wholeness becomes indistinguishable from the thirst for death"[24] – Gamson's "self-destruction," Borges' "end."

While this latter necrotopia might indeed be on the horizon in some corners of the world, ironically, on the Japanese archipelago,

---

[22] Howard Chiang, *After Eunuchs: Science, Medicine, and the Transformation of Sex in Modern China* (New York: Columbia University Press, 2020), 283.

[23] Joshua Gamson, "Must Identity Movements Self-Destruct? A Queer Dilemma," *Social Problems* 42, no. 3 (August 1, 1995): 390–407.

[24] Leon Wieseltier, *Against Identity* (New York: William Drenttel, 1996), 6–14, 32.

contemporary LGBT+ communities, along with queer studies, are attracting increasing attention and welcome while, simultaneously, backlashes are manifesting in many areas of gender and sexuality policymaking, hardening sexual and gender boundaries in the process. How societies, communities, and individuals within them negotiate subjectivities and identities, including sexed and gendered ones, lies at the heart of their well-being. Major historical events, technological innovations, and exceptional individuals can disrupt such negotiations, either reinforcing the status quo or resulting in paradigm shifts. For instance, since the 1960s, some queer individuals in Japan have argued for and embraced their sexuality as a modality rather than an identity, operating to disrupt the smooth functioning of normative space and undoing the dominant logic of identity that represents sex and gender as fixed and knowable terms. Today, conversely, Japanese legislation explicitly declares sex change legal but grants full rights only to individuals who then embody, down to the last physical detail and intrinsic qualities of representation, the other sex and gender – which undermines the very possibility of transcending preconceived boundaries and identities.

At the beginning of the twenty-first century, robotics promised a revolution that would affect everything, from individual households to care facilities for the elderly and on to war-making. Anthropologist Jennifer Robertson found the humanoid robot prototypes conventionally gendered, trending toward distinctly feminine/female and masculine/ male. Indeed, it appeared that at the precise moment when increasing numbers of people around the world are willing to acknowledge that human bodies are distinguished by a great deal of variability, "humanoid robot bodies are effectively used as platforms for reducing the relationship between bodies and genders from a contingent relationship to a fixed and *necessary* one." Roboticists and, by extension, their robots tend to uncritically reproduce and reinforce dominant stereotypes (or archetypes) attached to female and male bodies.[25] Equally telling instances of the persistence of sex and gender ideal types abound.

Perhaps ours is really a quite ordinary moment in that it provides reasons to both cheer and despair. Even though dichotomies between women and men – and heterosexuality, nonheteronormative, and nonsexual plurality – have been empirically false, in Japan and elsewhere, we cannot afford to dismiss them as irrelevant as long as they continue to structure lives and consciousness. Nor can we expect the risks taken by the individuals who appear in this book to necessarily subside – from

---

[25] Robertson, *Robo Sapiens Japanicus.*

At Present

those with bodies deemed too strange for the emperor's army (see Chapter 1) to the artist who conveys subversive messages through kayak-sized female genitals (see Chapter 7). Rather, the words of one seasoned thinker and novelist ring true far beyond the right to equality they were intended to capture. Elena Ferrante warns: "Even if we're constantly tempted to lower our guard – out of love, weariness, or sympathy or kindness – we women shouldn't do it. We can lose from one moment to the next everything that we have achieved."[26]

Interdisciplinary examinations of the shapeshifting of local sexual cultures in Japan and the Asia-Pacific region continue with investigations of the "complex processes of localization, interregional borrowing, and hybridization that underscore the mutual transformation of gender and sexuality." Accordingly, the frames and points of reference that have historically been loosely associated with Europe and, later, increasingly with North America are newly complemented by studies that privilege intellectual relations among Asian countries.[27] Japan's past imperialism highlights the complexity of such a move, contributing to how vital it is that gender and sexuality studies scholars explore further the important inroads a range of determined feminist activists have already forged.[28]

---

[26] Elena Ferrante in an interview with Rachel Donadio, "Writing Has Always Been a Great Struggle for Me," *New York Times*, December 9, 2014, accessed July 27, 2020, www .nytimes.com/2014/12/10/books/writing-has-always-been-a-great-struggle-for-me.html.

[27] Martin et al., *AsiaPacifiQueer*.

[28] Feminist organizations across Asia have worked, sometimes collaboratively, particularly on the issue of wartime sexual slavery. These include the Korean Council for Justice and Remembrance for the Issues of Military Sexual Slavery by Japan (Korean Council) of South Korea, Lila Pilipina of the Philippines, Taipei Women's Rescue Foundation of Taiwan, Japan's Violence against Women in War Research Action Center (VAWW RAC), and Women's Active Museum on War and Peace (WAM), among others. See Tomomi Yamaguchi, "Japan's Right-Wing Women and the 'Comfort Women' Issue," *Georgetown Journal of Asian Affairs* 6 (2020): 45–54; Tomomi Yamaguchi, "The Mainstreaming of Feminism and the Politics of Backlash in Twenty-First-Century Japan," in *Rethinking Japanese Feminisms*, ed. Julia C. Bullock, Ayako Kano, and Japanese Welker (Honolulu: University of Hawai'i Press, 2017), 68–87.

Bibliography

Abe Isoo. "Jinkō mondai to danjo mondai" [The Population Problem and the Problem of Gender Relations]. *Kakusei* vol. 32, no. 3 (1942), pp. 3–5.

Abel, Jonathan. *Redacted: The Archives of Censorship in Transwar Japan* (Berkeley: University of California Press, 2012).

Ackermann, Peter. "Respite from Everyday Life: Kōtō-ku (Tokyo) in Recollections." In *The Culture of Japan as Seen through Its Leisure*, ed. Sepp Linhart and Sabine Frühstück, pp. 27–40 (Albany: State University of New York Press, 1998).

Adelman, Jeremy. "What Is Global History Now? *AEON*, March 2, 2017, https://aeon.co/essays/is-global-history-still-possible-or-has-it-had-its-moment.

Adelstein, Jake. "Obscenity Arrest May Be Hiding Dirty Politics." *Japan Times*, December 6, 2014, www.japantimes.co.jp/news/2014/12/06/national/media-national/obscenity-arrest-may-hiding-dirty-politics/.

Adeney-Thomas, Julia. "Why Do Only Some Places Have History? Japan, the West, and the Geography of the Past." *Journal of World History* vol. 28, no. 2 (June 2017), pp. 187–218.

Algoso, Teresa A. "Thoughts on Hermaphroditism: Miyatake Gaikotsu and the Convergence of the Sexes in Taishō Japan." *Journal of Asian Studies* vol. 65, no. 3 (2006), pp. 555–73.

Allen, Judith A. "Men Interminably in Crisis? Historians on Masculinity, Sexual Boundaries, and Manhood." *Radical History Review*, no. 82 (2002), pp. 191–207.

Allison, Anne. *Nightwork: Sexuality, Pleasure, and Corporate Masculinity in a Tokyo Hostess Club* (Chicago, IL: University of Chicago Press, 2009).

Permitted and Prohibited Desires: Mothers, Comics, and Censorship in Japan (Berkeley: University of California Press, 2000).

Almeling, Rene. *Sex Cells: The Medical Market for Eggs and Sperm* (Berkeley: University of California Press, 2011).

Ambaras, David R. *Bad Youth: Juvenile Delinquency and the Politics of Everyday Life in Modern Japan* (Berkeley: University of California Press, 2006).

Japan's Imperial Underworlds: Intimate Encounters at the Borders of Empire (Cambridge: University of Cambridge Press, 2018).

American Psychiatric Association. "Gender Dysphoria Diagnosis." www.psychiatry.org/psychiatrists/cultural-competency/education/transgender-and-gendernonconforming-patients/gender-dysphoria-diagnosis

Bibliography

Anderson, Marnie. *A Place in Public: Women's Rights in Meiji Japan* (Cambridge, MA: Harvard Asia Center, 2010).

Angst, Linda Isako. "The Rape of a Schoolgirl: Discourses of Power and Gendered National Identity in Okinawa." In *Islands of Discontent: Okinawan Responses to Japanese and American Power*, ed. Laura Hein and Mark Selden, pp. 135–60 (Lanham, MD: Rowman & Littlefield, 2003).

Anzai Sadako. *Yasen kangofu [Field Nurse]* (Tokyo: Fuji Shobōsha, 1953).

Asahi Shūkan, ed. *Nedan no Meiji Taishō Shōwa Fūzoku-shi [A Cultural History of Prices in Meiji, Taishō and Shōwa]* (Tokyo: Asahi Shinbunsha, 1981).

Badinter, Elisabeth. *The Myth of Motherhood: An Historical View of the Maternal Instinct* (London: Souvenir Press, 1982).

Badiou, Alain. "The Contemporary Figure of the Soldier in Politics." Talk, University of California, Los Angeles, January 2007.

Barber, Christie. "Beyond the Absent Father Stereotype: Representations of Parenting Men and Their Families in Contemporary Japanese Film." In *Routledge Handbook of Japanese Media*, ed. Fabienne Darling-Wolf, pp. 228–40 (London: Routledge, 2018).

Barclay, Paul D. "Cultural Brokerage and Interethnic Marriage in Colonial Taiwan: Japanese Subalterns and Their Aborigine Wives, 1895–1930." *Journal of Asian Studies* vol. 64, no. 2 (2005), pp. 323–60.

Outcasts of Empire: Japan's Rule on Taiwan's "Savage Border," 1874–1945 (Berkeley: University of California Press, 2017).

Bardsley, Jan. *The Bluestockings of Japan: New Woman Essays and Fiction from Seitō, 1911–16* (Ann Arbor: Center for Japanese Studies, University of Michigan, 2007).

Maiko Masquerade: Crafting Geisha Girlhood in Japan (Oakland: University of California Press, 2021).

"*Seitō* and the Resurgence of Writing by Women." In *The Columbia Companion to Modern East Asian Literature*, ed. Joshua S. Mostow, Kirk A. Denton, Bruce Fulton, and Sharalyn Orbaugh, pp. 93–98 (New York: Columbia University Press, 2003).

Barshay, Andrew E. *State and Intellectual in Imperial Japan: The Public Man in Crisis* (Berkeley: University of California Press, 1988).

Bartholomew, James R. "Japanese Nobel Candidates in the First Half of the Twentieth Century." *Osiris* vol. 13, no. 1 (1998), pp. 238–84.

Berlant, Lauren. "Cruel Optimism." In *The Affect Theory Reader*, ed. Melissa Gregg and Gregory J. Seigworth, pp. 93–117 (Durham, NC: Duke University Press, 2010).

Bernstein, Gail Lee. "Women in Rural Japan." In *Women in Changing Japan*, ed. Joyce Lebra, Joy Paulson, and Elizabeth Powers., pp. 25–50 (Boulder, CO: Westview Press, 1976).

Berndt, Jaqueline. "Nationally Naked? The Female Nude in Japanese Oil Painting and Posters (1890s–1920s)." In *Performing "Nation": Gender Politics in Literature, Theater, and the Visual Arts of China and Japan, 1880–1940*, ed. Doris Croissant, Catherine Vance Yeh, Joshua S. Mostow, Barend J. ter Haar, and Maghiel van Crevel, pp. 307–46 (Leiden: Brill, 2008; Sinica Leidensia, vol. 91).

208   Bibliography

Bienek, Tabea. "Von 'Erziehungsvätern (*ikumen*)' zu 'lokal vernetzten Vätern (*ikimen*)': Japanische Väteraktivitäten für eine bessere Work–Life-Balance" [From "Education Fathers" to Locally Connected Fathers]. In *Japan in der Krise* [*Japan in Crisis*], ed. Annette Schad-Seifert and Nora Kottmann, pp. 195–220 (Wiesbaden: Springer, 2019).

Bolton, Christopher. *Interpreting Anime* (Minneapolis: University of Minnesota Press, 2018).

Borovoy, Amy. "Beyond Choice: A New Framework for Abortion?" *Dissent*, Fall 2011, www.dissentmagazine.org/article/beyond-choice-a-new-framework-for-abortion.

Botsman, Daniel V. "Freedom without Slavery? 'Coolies,' Prostitutes, and Outcastes in Meiji Japan's 'Emancipation Moment.'" *American Historical Review* vol. 116, no. 5 (December 2011), pp. 1323–47.

Boyce, Bret. "Obscenity and Nationalism: Constitutional Freedom of Sexual Expression in Comparative Perspective." *Columbia Journal of Transnational Law* vol. 56, no. 4 (2018), pp. 683–749.

BuBu de la Madeleine and Yoshiko Shimada. "Made in Occupied Japan." In *Consuming Bodies: Sex and Contemporary Japanese Art* (Chicago, IL: University of Chicago Press, 2004).

"Bundestag stimmt für drittes Geschlecht im Geburtenregister" [The Federal Diet Votes for a Third Sex/Gender in the Birth Registry]. *Frankfurter Allgemeine*, December 14, 2018, www.faz.net/aktuell/politik/inland/kuenf tig-drittes-geschlecht-im-geburtenregister-waehlbar-15941127.html.

Burns, Susan L. "Bodies and Borders: Syphilis, Prostitution, and the Nation in Japan, 1860–1890." *U.S.–Japan Women's Journal* vol. 15 (1998), pp. 3–30.

"Introduction." In *Gender and Law in the Japanese Imperium*, ed. Susan L. Burns and Barbara J. Brooks, pp. 1–17 (Honolulu: University of Hawai'i Press, 2013).

Kingdom of the Sick: A History of Leprosy and Japan (Honolulu: University of Hawai'i Press, 2019).

Busby, Mattha. "Canada Introduces Gender-Neutral 'X' Option on Passports." *The Guardian*, August 31, 2017, www.theguardian.com/world/2017/aug/31/canada-introduces-gender-neutral-x-option-on-passports.

Butler, Judith. *Gender Trouble: Feminism and the Subversion of Identity* (London: Routledge, 1990).

Byfield, Judith and Carolyn Brown, eds. *Africa and World War II* (Cambridge: Cambridge University Press, 2015).

Cather, Kirsten. *The Art of Censorship in Postwar Japan* (Honolulu: University of Hawai'i Press, 2012).

"A Thousand Words: The Powers and Dangers of Text and Image." *Positions: East Asia Cultures Critique* vol. 18. no. 3 (2010), pp. 695–725.

Catsoulis, Jeannette. "'#Female Pleasure' Review: Fighting the Patriarchy." *New York Times*, October 18, 2019.

Center for Reproductive Rights. "The Supreme Court Might Be About to Make It Nearly Impossible to Stop Anti-Abortion Laws." May 30, 2020, https://reproductiverights.org/press-room/supreme-court-might-be-about-make-it-nearly-impossible-stop-anti-abortion-laws.

Bibliography

"U.S. Supreme Court's LGBTQ Anti-Discrimination Ruling Comes Only Days after Federal Rule Strips Protections." June 15, 2020.

Chang, Iris. *The Rape of Nanjing: The Forgotten Holocaust of World War II* (New York: Basic Books, 2012).

Chapell, Ben and Sherif A. Elgebeily. "Lessons from Gay and Lesbian Activism in Asia: The Importance of Context, Pivotal Incidents and Connection to a Larger Vision." *Sexuality and Culture* vol. 23, no. 3 (2019), pp. 882–905.

Chiang, Howard. *After Eunuchs: Science, Medicine, and the Transformation of Sex in Modern China* (New York: Columbia University Press, 2020).

Cho, Sumi, Kimberlé Williams Crenshaw and Leslie McCall. "Toward a Field of Intersectionality Studies: Theory, Applications, and Praxis." *Signs* vol. 38, no. 4 (Summer 2013), pp. 785–810.

Chung, Chin Sung. "The Origin and Development of the Military Sexual Slavery Problem in Imperial Japan." *positions: east asian cultures critique* vol. 5, no. 1 (1997), pp. 219–45.

Coleman, Liv. "Will Japan 'Lean In' to Gender Equality?" *U.S.–Japan Women's Journal* vol. 49 (2016), pp. 3–25.

Connell, R. W. *Masculinities* (Berkeley: University of California Press, 1995).

Connelly, Matthew. *Fatal Misconception: The Struggle to Control World Population* (Cambridge, MA: Belknap Press, 2008).

Copeland, Rebecca and Melek Ortabasi, eds. *The Modern Murasaki: Writing by Women of Meiji Japan* (New York: Columbia University Press, 2006).

Copelon, Rhonda. "Toward Accountability for Violence against Women in War: Progress and Challenges." In *Sexual Violence in Conflict Zones: From the Ancient World to the Era of Human Rights*, ed. Elizabeth D. Heineman pp. 232–56 (Philadelphia: University of Pennsylvania Press, 2011).

Craig, Teruko. "Introduction." In Hiratsuka Raichō, *In the Beginning Woman Was the Sun: The Autobiography of a Japanese Feminist*, trans. Teruko Craig pp. vii–xiii. (New York: Columbia University Press, 1992).

"Translator's Afterword." In Hiratsuka Raichō, *In the Beginning Woman Was the Sun: The Autobiography of a Japanese Feminist*, trans. Teruko Craig, pp. 287–318 (New York: Columbia University Press, 1992).

Cross, Gary. *Men to Boys: The Making of Modern Immaturity* (New York: Columbia University Press, 2008).

Dale, S. P. F. "An Introduction to X-Jendā: Examining a New Gender Identity in Japan." *Intersections: Gender and Sexuality in Asia and the Pacific* no. 31 (2012).

"Same-Sex Marriage and the Question of Queerness – Institutional Performativity and Marriage in Japan." *Asian Anthropology* vol. 19, no. 2 (2020), pp. 143–59.

Danly, Robert Lyons. *In the Shade of Spring Leaves: The Life of Higuchi Ichiyō with Nine of Her Best Stories* (New Haven, CT: Yale University Press, 1981).

Davis, Kathy. "Intersectionality as Buzzword: A Sociology of Science Perspective on What Makes a Feminist Theory Successful." *Feminist Theory* vol. 9, no. 1 (2008), pp. 67–85.

Dean, Meryll. "Sold in Japan: Human Trafficking for Sexual Exploitation." *Japanese Studies* vol. 28, no. 2 (2008), pp. 165–78.

210   Bibliography

Deloitte Global Center for Corporate Governance. *Deloitte: Women in the Boardroom – A Global Perspective* (2018), www2.deloitte.com/global/en/pages/risk/articles/women-in-the-boardroom-global-perspective.html#

DeWinter, Jennifer and Carly A. Kocurek. "'Aw Fuck, I Got a Bitch on My Team': Women and the Exclusionary Cultures of the Computer Game Complex." In *Gaming Representation*, ed. Jennifer Malkowski and Treaandrea M. Russworm, pp. 57–73 (Indianapolis: Indiana University Press, 2017).

Donadio, Rachel. "Writing Has Always Been a Great Struggle for Me." *New York Times*, December 10, 2014.

Donegan, Moira. "The US Supreme Court Has Given LGBTQ Americans a Rare Bit of Good News." *The Guardian*, June 16, 2020.

Dose, Ralf. *The Origins of the Gay Liberation Movement* (New York: Monthly Review Press, 2014).

Dower, John. *War without Mercy: Race and Power in the Pacific War* (New York: Pantheon, 2012).

Drixler, Fabian. *Mabiki: Infanticide and Population Growth in Eastern Japan, 1660–1950* (Berkeley: University of California Press, 2013).

Duerr, Hans Peter. *Der Mythos vom Zivilisationsprozess 1: Nacktheit und Scham [The Myth of the Civilization Process 1: Nudity and Shame]* (Frankfurt am Main: Suhrkamp Verlag, 1988).

Dusinberre, Martin. "Japan, Global History, and the Great Silence." *History Workshop Journal* vol. 83, no. 1 (Spring 2017), pp. 130–50.

Eades, J. S., Tom Gill, and Harumi Befu, eds. *Globalization and Social Change in Contemporary Japan* (Melbourne: TransPacific Books, 2000).

Earhart, David C. *Certain Victory: Images of World War II in the Japanese Media* (Armonk, NY: M. E. Sharpe, 2008).

Edogawa Ranpō. "Caterpillar." In *Japanese Tales of Mystery and Imagination*, ed. and trans. James B. Harris (North Clarendon, VT: Tuttle, 2012).

Eleftheriou-Smith, Loulla-Mae. "Megumi Igarashi Found Guilty of Obscenity over 'Vagina Kayak' Artwork." *Independent*, May 9, 2016, www.independent.co.uk/news/world/asia/megumi-igarashi-found-guilty-obscenity-over-vagina-kayak-artwork-a7020516.html

Enchi Fumiko. *The Waiting Years*, trans. John Bester (Tokyo: Kōdansha, [1957] 1980).

Eto Mikiko. "'Gender' Problems in Japanese Politics: A Dispute over a Socio-Cultural Change towards Increasing Equality." *Japanese Journal of Political Science* vol. 17, no. 3 (September 2016), pp. 365–85.

Fabre, Olivier. "Liberal Democratic Party and Tradition May Stymie Push for Same-Sex Marriage in Japan." *Japan Times*, June 19, 2019, www.japantimes.co.jp/news/2019/06/19/national/social-issues/liberal-democratic-party-tradition-may-stymie-push-sex-marriage-japan/

Faison, Elyssa. *Managing Women: Disciplining Labor in Modern Japan* (Berkeley: University of California Press, 2007).

Ferrari, Paige. "Meet the Hardest Working Man in Porn." *GQ*, March 3, 2015, www.gq.com/story/shimiken-japanese-porn-star-interview

Fish, Isaac Stone. "Does Japan's Conservative Shinto Religion Support Gay Marriage?" *Foreign Policy*, June 29, 2015, https://foreignpolicy.com/2015/06/29/what-does-japan-shinto-think-of-gay-marriage/

Bibliography 211

Fogel, Joshua A., ed. *The Nanjing Massacre in History and Historiography* (Berkeley: University of California Press, 2000)

Frederick, Sarah. *Turning Pages: Reading and Writing Women's Magazines in Interwar Japan* (Honolulu: University of Hawai'i Press, 2006).

Frühstück, Sabine. "After Heroism: Must Real Soldiers Die?" In *Recreating Japanese Men*, ed. Sabine Frühstück and Anne Walthall, pp. 91–111 (Berkeley: University of California Press, 2011).

Colonizing Sex: Sexology and Social Control in Modern Japan (Berkeley: University of California Press, 2003).

"Genders and Sexualities." In *Companion to the Anthropology of Japan*, ed. Jennifer Robertson, pp. 167–82 (London: Blackwell, 2005).

Playing War: Children and the Culture of Militarism in Modern Japan (Oakland: University of California Press, 2017).

Die Politik der Sexualwissenschaft: Zur Produktion und Popularisierung sexologischen Wissens in Japan 1908–1941 [*The Politics of Sexual Science: On the Production and Popularization of Sexual Knowledge in Japan, 1908–1941*], Beiträge zur Japanologie, vol. 34 (Vienna: Institute of Japanese Studies, 1997).

"Queer Lives in Japan." *Asian Anthropology* vol. 19, no. 2 (2020), pp. 77–159.

"Rhetorics of Reform: On the Institutionalization and De-institutionalization of Old Age." In *Aging and Social Policy: A German–Japanese Comparison*, ed. Harald Conrad and Ralph Lützeler, pp. 299–351 (Munich: Iudicium, 2002).

"Sex zwischen Wissenschaft und Politik" [Sex between Science and Politics], *Nachrichten der Gesellschaft für Natur- und Völkerkunde Ostasiens*, vol. 155–56 (1996), pp. 11–41.

"Sexuality and Nation States." In *Global History of Sexuality*, ed. Robert Marshall Buffington, Eithne Luibheid, and Donna Guy, pp. 17–56 (London: Wiley-Blackwell, 2014).

"Sexuality and Sexual Violence." In *The Cambridge History of the Second World War*, ed. Michael Geyer and Adam Tooze, pp. 422–46 (Cambridge: Cambridge University Press, 2015).

"'The Spirit to Take Up a Gun': Militarizing Gender in the Imperial Army." In *Gender, Nation and State in Modern Japan*, ed. Andrea Germer, Vera Mackie, and Ulrike Wöhr, pp. 163–79 (London: Routledge, 2014).

Uneasy Warriors: Gender, Memory and Popular Culture in the Japanese Army (Berkeley: University of California Press, 2007).

Frühstück, Sabine and Anne Walthall. "Introduction." In *Recreating Japanese Men*, ed. Sabine Frühstück and Anne Walthall, pp. 1–23 (Oakland: University of California Press, 2011).

Fujime Yuki. "Aru sanba no kiseki: Shibahara Urako to sanji chōsetsu" [A Midwife's Life Story: Shibahara Urako and Birth Control]. *Nihon-shi Kenkyū* vol. 366 (1993), pp. 90–112.

Fujino Kakinami, Atsuko. "History of Child *Labor* in Japan." In *The World of Child Labor*, ed. Hugh D. Hindman, pp. 881–88 (Armonk, NY: M. E. Sharpe, 2009).

Fujita Shinichi. *Osan kakumei* [*The Revolution of Birth*] (Tokyo: Asahi Bunko, 1988).

Fukui Prefecture. *Omoshirodēta* [*Interesting Data*], www.pref.fukui.lg.jp/index3 .html

212   Bibliography

Furukawa Makoto. "Renai to seiyoku no daisan teikoku" [The Third Empire of Love and Sexual Desire]. *Gendai Shisō* vol. 21, no. 7 (1993), pp. 110–45.

Gabrielson, Carl. "Welcome to Japan! How U.S. Marine Corps Orientation Materials Erase, Coopt, and Dismiss Local Resistance." *Journal of American-East Asian Relations* vol. 26, no. 4 (2019), pp. 397–425.

Galbraith, Patrick W. "Adult Computer Games and the Ethics of Imaginary Violence: Responding to Gamergate from Japan." *U.S.–Japan Women's Journal* vol. 52 (2017), pp. 67–88.

Gamson, Joshua. "Must Identity Movements Self-Destruct? A Queer Dilemma." *Social Problems* vol. 42, no. 3 (August 1, 1995), pp. 390–407.

Ganzon, Sarah Christina. "Investing Time for Your In-Game Boyfriends and BFFs: Time as Commodity and the Simulation of Emotional Labor in *Mystic Messenger*." *Games and Culture* vol. 14, no. 2 (2019), pp. 139–53.

Garon, Sheldon M. "Transnational History and Japan's 'Comparative Advantage,'" *Journal of Japanese Studies* vol. 43, no. 1 (Winter 2017), pp. 65–92.

"The World's Oldest Debate? Prostitution and the State in Imperial Japan, 1900–1945." *American Historical Review* vol. 98, no. 3 (1993), pp. 710–32.

"Gender Imbalance: Japan's Political Representation by Women Lowest in G20." *Nippon.com*, March 8, 2019, www.nippon.com/en/japan-data/h00409/gender-imbalance-japan%E2%80%99s-political-representation-by-women-lowest-in-g20.html

George, Timothy S. *Minamata: Pollution and the Struggle for Democracy in Postwar Japan* (Cambridge, MA: Harvard Asian Monographs, 2002).

Gill, Tom. "Failed Manhood on the Streets of Urban Japan: The Meanings of Self-Reliance for Homeless Men." In *Recreating Japanese Men*, ed. Sabine Frühstück and Anne Walthall, pp. 177–202 (Berkeley: University of California Press, 2011).

Men of Uncertainty: The Social Organization of Day Laborers in Contemporary Japan (Albany: State University of New York Press, 2001).

"When Pillars Evaporate: Structuring Masculinity on the Japanese Margins." In *Men and Masculinities in Contemporary Japan: Dislocating the Salaryman Doxa*, ed. James Roberson and Nobue Suzuki pp. 144–60 (London: Routledge, 2005).

"Whose Problem? Japan's Homeless as an Issue of Local and Central Governance." In *The Political Economy of Governance in Japan*, ed. Glenn Hook, pp. 192–210 (London: Routledge, 2005).

Yokohama Street Life: The Precarious Career of a Japanese Day Laborer (Lanham, MD: Lexington Books, 2015).

Gluck, Carol. "Operations of Memory: 'Comfort Women' and the World." In *Ruptured Histories: War, Memory, and the Post-Cold War in Asia*, ed. Sheila Miyoshi Jager and Rana Mitter, pp. 47–77 (Cambridge, MA: Harvard University Press, 2007).

Goldstein-Gidoni, Ofra. "Consuming Domesticity in Post-Bubble Japan." In *Consuming Life in Post-Bubble Japan: A Transdisciplinary Perspective*, ed. Katarzyna J. Cwiertka and Ewa Machotka, pp. 107–27 (Amsterdam: Amsterdam University Press, 2018).

Bibliography 213

Goodland, Roger. *A Bibliography of Sex Rites and Customs* (London: Routledge, 1931).

Goodwin, Janet R. *Selling Songs and Smiles: The Sex Trade in Heian and Kamakura Japan* (Honolulu: University of Hawai'i Press, 2007).

Goto-Jones, C. S. and L. P. Hartley. "If the Past Is a Different Country, Are Different Countries in the Past? On the Place of the Non-European in the History of Philosophy." *Philosophy* vol. 80, no. 311 (January 2005), pp. 29–51.

Gwynne, Joel. "Japan, Postfeminism and the Consumption of Sexual(ised) Schoolgirls in Male-Authored Contemporary Manga." *Feminist Theory* vol. 14, no. 3 (2013), pp. 325–43.

Government of Japan. "Women's Empowerment." www.japan.go.jp/diversity/women/index.html

Haas, G. J. "'Yakugai' AIDS and the Yokohama Xth International AIDS Conference." *Common Factor* 10 (April 1995), pp. 1–22.

Halberstam, Jack. "The Difference between Male and Female Does Not Hold Anymore." March 1, 2017, www.youtube.com/watch?v=JtYaUQ66sp0

Gaga Feminism: Sex, Gender, and the End of Normal (Boston, MA: Beacon Press, 2012).

Trans: A Quick and Quirky Account of Gender Variability (Oakland: University of California Press, 2018).

Halberstam, Judith. *Female Masculinity* (Durham, NC: Duke University Press, 1998).

Hall, Ivan P. *Mori Arinori* (Cambridge, MA: Harvard University Press, 1973).

Han Won-Sang. "Das japanische Militär im Krieg und sein System der Sexsklaverei" [The Japanese Military at War and Its System of Sexual Slavery]. In *Erzwungene Prostitution in Kriegs- und Friedenszeiten: Sexuelle Gewalt gegen Frauen und Mädchen* [*Forced Prostitution in War and Peace Times: Sexual Violence against Women and Girls*], ed. Barbara Drinck and Chung-Noh Gross (Bielefeld: Kleine Verlag, 2006).

Hane, Mikiso. *Reflections on the Way to the Gallows: Rebel Women in Prewar Japan* (Berkeley: University of California Press, 1988).

Hardacre, Helen. *Marketing the Menacing Fetus in Japan* (Berkeley: University of California Press, 1997).

Hasegawa Yūko. "In Focus: The chōshōjo Movement." In *From Postwar to Postmodern: Art in Japan, 1945–1989*, ed. Doryun Chong, Michio Hayashi, Kenji Kajiya, and Fumihiko Sumitomo, pp. 372–73 (New York: Museum of Modern Art, 2012).

Hatakeno Tomato. "Toransu jendā to sekkusu wāku" [Transgender and Sex Work]. In *Sekkusu wāku sutadīsu: Tōjisha shiten de kangaeru sei to rōdō*, ed. SWASH (Tokyo: Nihon Hyōronsha, 2019).

Hayashi Eidai. *Shashin kiroku: Kanmonkō no onnaokinakashi-tachi* [*Photographic Records: The Female Longshoremen of Kanmon Port*] (Tokyo: Shinhyōron, 2018).

Hayashi Hirofumi. "Government, the Military and Business in Japan's Wartime Comfort Woman System." *Asia-Pacific Journal: Japan Focus* vol. 5, no. 1 (January 2, 2007), www.japanfocus.org/-Hayashi-Hirofumi/2332#sthash

214   Bibliography

"Die Verwicklung der japanischen kaiserlichen Regierung in das System der Militärbordelle ('Troststationen')" [The Japanese Government's Entanglement in the System of Military Brothels ("Comfort Stations")]. In *Erzwungene Prostitution in Kriegs- und Friedenszeiten: Sexuelle Gewalt gegen Frauen und Mädchen* [*Forced Prostitution in War and Peace: Sexual Violence against Women and Girls*], ed. Barbara Drinck and Chung-Noh Gross, pp. 108–24 (Bielefeld: Kleine Verlag, 2006).

Hayashi Hiroshi. "Rikugun no ianjo kanri no ichisokumen: 'Eisei sakku' kōfu shiryō o tegakari ni" [One Aspect of the Management of Army Comfort Stations: Tracking the Sources about the Issuance of 'Hygiene Sacks']. *Kikan: Sensō Sekinin Kenkyū Sōkan-gō* vol. 1 (Fall 1993), pp. 12–19.

"Heisei jūichi-nen hōritsu dai-gojūni-gō: Jidō baishun, jidō poruno ni kakawaru kōi-tō no kisei oyobi shobatsu narabi ni jidō no hogo-tō ni kan suru hōritsu," *e-gov hōrei kensaku* (Ministry of Internal Affairs and Communications), https://elaws.e-gov.go.jp/document?lawid=411AC1000000052

Helm, Katharina. "Women's Pleasure Online? A Contrasting Analysis of One Japanese Mainstream and One Women's Pornographic Film from the Internet." *Vienna Journal of East Asian Studies* vol. 8 (2016), pp. 33–64.

Hertog, Ekaterina. "'The Worst Abuse against a Child Is the Absence of the Parent': How Japanese Unwed Mothers Evaluate Their Decision to Have a Child outside Wedlock." *Japan Forum* vol. 20, no. 2 (2008), pp. 193–217.

Hicks, George. *Comfort Women: Japan's Imperial Regime of Enforced Prostitution in the Second World War* (New York: W. W. Norton & Company, 1997).

Hinata Daigishi Fujin. "Fujin shakai to geishōgi mondai" [Women, Society and the Prostitution Problem]. *Kakusei* vol. 1, no. 3 (1911), pp. 40–43.

Hiratsuka Raichō. *In the Beginning Woman Was the Sun: The Autobiography of a Japanese Feminist*, trans. with an introduction and notes by Teruko Craig (New York: Columbia University Press, 1992).

Watakushi no aruita michi [*The Path I Took*] (Tokyo: Shinhyōronsha, 1955).

Hirschfeld, Magnus. *Berlins drittes Geschlecht* [*Berlin's Third Sex*] (Berlin: Verlag von Hermann Seemann Nachfolger G. m. b. H., 1904).

Jahrbuch für sexuelle Zwischenstufen mit besonderer Berücksichtigung der Homosexualität [*Yearbook of Sexual Intermediate Types with Special Consideration of Homosexuality*] (Leipzig: Max Spohr, 1899–1933).

"Was muss das Volk vom dritten Geschlecht wissen! Eine Aufklärungsschrift," ed. Wissenschaftlich-humanitäres Comitee [What the People Need to Know about the Third Sex! An Enlightenment Manifesto] (Leipzig: Verlag von Max Spohr, 1901).

Weltreise eines Sexualforschers [*The World Journey of a Sexual Scientist*] (Frankfurt am Main: Eichborn Verlag, [1933] 2006).

Ho, Michelle H. S. "Queer and Normal: *Dansō* (Female-to-Male Crossdressing) Lives and Politics in Contemporary Tokyo." *Asian Anthropology* vol. 19, no. 2 (2020), pp. 102–18.

Hoffman, Michael. "Ah, Vaginas! In Defense of Taboos." *Japan Times*, August 9, 2014, www.japantimes.co.jp/news/2014/08/09/national/media-national/ah-vaginas-defense-taboos/

Bibliography

"Nonprofits in Japan Help 'Shut-ins' Get Out into the Open." *Japan Times*, October 9, 2011, www.japantimes.co.jp/news/2011/10/09/national/medianational/nonprofits-in-japan-help-shut-ins-get-out-into-the-open/

Höhn, Maria and Seungsook Moon, eds. *Over There: Living with the U.S. Military Empire from World War Two to the Present* (Durham, NC: Duke University Press, 2010).

Horie, Yuri. "Possibilities and Limitations of "Lesbian Continuum': The Case of the Protestant Church in Japan." *Journal of Lesbian Studies* vol. 10, no. 3–4 (2007), pp. 145–59.

Hosoi Wakizō. *Jokō aishi* [*The Sad History of Women Factory Workers*] (Tokyo: Iwanami Shoten, [1925] 1974).

Hovhannisyan, Astghik. "Ōta Tenrei's Defense of Birth Control, Eugenics and Euthanasia," *Contemporary Japan* vol. 30, no. 1 (2018), pp. 28–42.

Hughes, Michelle. "3 Male Governors in Japan Experience What Life Is Like for Pregnant Women." *Sora News 24*, September 29, 2016, www.soranews24 .com/2016/09/29/3-male-governors-in-japan-experience-what-life-is-likefor-pregnant-women/

Human Rights Watch. "LGBT Equality for Japan as Well (*Nihon ni mo LGBT byōdō o*)." *Human Rights Watch*, www.hrw.org/EqualityActJapan

Ieda Sakichi. "Seinenkō no seibyō to risonjō mondai [Venereal Diseases of Youth and the Issue of Their Separation from Their Villages]." *Kakusei* vol. 29, no. 3 (1939), pp. 17–19.

Iijima Ginjirō. "Nihon no jutai chōsetsu undo – Sangā-joshi torai no ato" [Japan's Movement for Contraception – After Sanger's Visit]. *Sanji Chōsetsu Hyōron* no. 4 (May 1925), pp. 39–41.

Illouz, Eva. *Cold Intimacies: The Making of Emotional Capitalism* (Cambridge: Polity Press, 2007).

Imahashi, Rurika and Francesca Regalado. "Tokyo Olympics Chief Mori Declines to Resign over Sexist Remarks." *NikkeiAsia*, February 4, 2021, https://asia.nikkei.com/Spotlight/Tokyo-2020-Olympics/Tokyo-Olympics-chief-Mori-declines-to-resign-over-sexist-remarks

Inoue Shōichi, Saitō Hikaru, Shibuya Tomomi, and Hasegawa Kazumi. *Seiteki na kotoba* [*Sexual Words*] (Tokyo: Kōdansha, 2010).

Irisawa Naika Dōsōkai, ed. *Irisawa sensei no enzetsu to bunsho* [*Professor Irisawa's Speeches and Writings*] (Tokyo: Kokuseido Shoten, 1932).

Ishihara Shintarō. *The Japan That Can Say No: Why Japan Will Be First among Equals*, trans. Frank Baldwin (London: Simon & Schuster, 1991).

Ishihara Shintarō and Morita Akio. *Nō to ieru Nihon* [*A Japan That Can Say No*] (Tokyo: Kōbunsha, 1989).

Ishii-Kuntz Masako. "Balancing Fatherhood and Work: Emergence of DiverseMasculinities in Contemporary Japan." In *Men and Masculinities in Contemporary Japan: Dislocating the Salaryman Doxa*, ed. James Roberson and Nobue Suzuki, pp. 198–216 (London: Routledge, 2003).

Ishikawa Tatsuzō. *Soldiers Alive*, trans. Zeljko Cipris (Honolulu: University of Hawai'i Press, 2003).

Ishimoto Shidzué. *Facing Two Ways: The Story of My Life*, intro. and afterword by Barbara Molony (Stanford, CA: Stanford University Press, [1935] 1984).

216 Bibliography

"Translator's Foreword." In *Wheat and Soldiers*, trans. Ishimoto Shidzue, pp. ix–xii (New York: Farrar and Rinehart, 1939).

Ito, Ruri. "The 'Modern Girl' Question in the Periphery of Empire: Colonial Modernity and Mobility among Okinawan Women in the 1920s and 1930s." In *The Modern Girl around the World: Consumption, Modernity, and Globalization*, ed. Alys Eve Weinbaum Lynn M. Thomas, Priti Ramamurthy, Uta G. Poiger, Madeleine Yue Dong, and Tanie Barlow, pp. 240–62 (Durham, NC: Duke University Press, 2008).

Ito Satoru and Yanase Ryuta. *Coming Out in Japan* (Melbourne: Transpacific Press, 2001).

Iwasaki Minoru and Steffi Richter. "The Topology of Post-1990s Historical Revisionism," trans. Richard Calichman. *positions: east asia critique* vol. 16, no. 3 (2008), pp. 507–38.

Iwata Masami and Ōsawa Machiko, eds. *Naze josei wa shigoto o yameru no ka* [*Why Do Women Give Up Their Jobs*] (Tokyo: Seikyūsha, 2015).

Ivry, Tsipy. *Embodying Culture: Pregnancy in Japan and Israel* (New Brunswick, NJ: Rutgers University Press, 2010).

"Japan Court Rejects Notion Same-Sex Couples Are de facto Marriage." *Japan Times*, June 4, 2020, www.japantimes.co.jp/news/2020/06/04/national/crime-legal/japan-court-rejects-notion-sex-couples-de-facto-marriages/#.XvZG-_JlC7M

"Japan May Delay Sending New Ambassador to South Korea Amid Renewed Tensions." *Japan Times*, January 15, 2021, www.japantimes.co.jp/news/2021/01/15/national/south-korea-ambassador/

"Japan Offers Most Paid Leave for Fathers in the World but Few Take It." *Kyodo News*, June 13, 2019, https://english.kyodonews.net/news/2019/06/78563c3875f3-japan-offers-most-paid-leave-for-fathers-in-world-but-few-take-it.html

"Japan Non-Recognition of Same-Sex Marriage Unconstitutional: Court." *NikkeiAsia*, March 17, 2021, https://asia.nikkei.com/Spotlight/Society/Japan-non-recognition-of-same-sex-marriage-unconstitutional-court?utm_campaign=RN%20Free%20newsletter&utm_medium=one%20time%20newsletter%20free&utm_source=NAR%20Newsletter&utm_content=article%20link&del_type=3&pub_date=20210320190000&seq_num=4&si=06104862

"Japanese Premier Begins Seoul Visit." *New York Times*, January 17, 1992.

Jaundrill, D. Colin. *Samurai to Soldier: Remaking Military Service in Nineteenth-Century Japan* (Ithaca, NY: Cornell University Press, 2016).

Johnson, Adrienne Renee. "*Josō* or 'Gender Free'? Playfully Queer 'Lives' in Visual Kei." *Asian Anthropology* vol. 19, no. 2 (2020), pp. 119–42.

Johnston, Eric. "LDP Lawmaker Tom Tanigawa under Fire for Saying LGBT Relationships Are 'Like a Hobby.'" *Japan Times*, August 2, 2018.

Johnston, James D. *China and Japan Being a Narrative of the Cruise of the U.S. Steam-Frigate Powhatan in the Years 1857,'58,'59, and '60 Including an Account of the Japanese Embassy to the United States* (Philadelphia, PA: Charles Desilver, 1861).

Johnston, William. *Geisha, Harlot, Strangler, Star: A Woman, Sex & Morality in Modern Japan* (New York: Columbia University Press, 2004).

Jones, Tracy. "Monuments to Misanthropy: A Landmark Exhibition for Controversial Artist Makoto Aida at Mori Art Museum." *Tokyo Art Beat*,

Bibliography 217

December 4, 2004, www.tokyoartbeat.com/tablog/entries.en/2012/12/monuments-to-misanthropy.html

Jūgun ianfu 110-ban henshū iinkai, ed. *Jūgun ianfu 110-ban: Denwa no mukō kara rekishi no koe ga* [*Army Comfort Woman Number 110: The Historical Voice on the Other End of the Phone Line*] (Tokyo: Akashi Shoten, 1992).

Kaigunshō Imukoku. *Nisshin senyaku kaigun eiseishi* [*A Hygiene History of the Navy during the First Sino-Japanese War*] (Tokyo: Kaigunshō Imukyoku, 1900).

Kaori Shoji. "Historical Truths Can Take Decades to Unearth." *Japan Times,* February 15, 2017, www.japantimes.co.jp/culture/2017/02/15/films/historical-truths-can-take-decades-unearth/

Kameyama Michiko. *Kindai Nihon kangoshi II: Sensō to kango* [*The History of Nursing in Modern Japan II: War and Nursing*] (Tokyo: Domesu Shuppan, 1997[1984]).

Kaneko, Martin. *Die Judenpolitik der japanischen Kriegsregierung* [*The Japanese Wartime Government's Policies Regarding Jews*] (Berlin: Metropol, 2008).

Kang Sung Hyun. "The 'Seen Side' and 'Blind Side' of U.S. Army Photography: The Still Pictures and Motion Pictures of the Korean 'Comfort Girls' in Myitkyina, Sungshan, and Tengchung." Talk (University of Chicago), trans. Sandra H. Park, February 19, 2018.

Kang Sung Hyun and Jung Keun-Sik. "The Organization and Activities of the US Army Signal Corps Photo Unit: Perspectives of War Photography in the Early Stages of the Korean War." *Seoul Journal of Korean Studies* vol. 27, no. 2 (2014), pp. 269–306.

"Kanojo wa kasei o manaberi" [She Is Learning Household Economics]. *Jogaku Sekai* vol. 4, no. 23 (October 5, 1914), p. 38.

Kanō Mikiyo. *Onnatachi no "jūgo"* [*Women's "Battlefields"*] (Tokyo: Inpakuto Shuppankai, 1995).

Kapur, Nick. *Japan at the Crossroads: Conflict and Compromise after Anpo* (Cambridge, MA: Harvard University Press, 2018).

Kariya Haruo. *Edo no seibyō* [*Sexually Transmitted Diseases during the Edo Period*] (Tokyo: Sanichi shobō, 1993).

Kato, H., K. Kanou, Y. Arima, F. Ando, S. Matsuoke, K. Yoshimura, T. Matano, T. Matsui, T. Sunagawa, and K. Oishi. "The Importance of Accounting for Testing and Positivity in Surveillance by Time and Place: An Illustration from HIV Surveillance in Japan." *Epidemiology & Infection* vol. 146, no. 16 (December 2018), pp. 2072–78.

Kato Yōko. *Chōheisei to kindai Nihon, 1868–1945* [*The Conscription System and Modern Japan, 1868–1945*] (Tokyo: Yoshikawa Kobunkan, 1996).

Katz, Leo J. *The Rhythm of Sterility and Fertility in Women: A Discussion of the Physiological, Practical, and Ethical Aspects of the Discoveries of Drs. K. Ogino (Japan) and H. Knaus (Austria) Regarding the Periods When Conception is Impossible and When Possible* (Chicago, IL: Latz Foundation, 1934).

Kawabata Yasunari. *Yukiguni* [*Snow Country*], trans. Edward Seidensticker (Tokyo: Tuttle, [1956] 2017).

Kawamura Hiroki. "The Relation Between Law and Technology in Japan: Liability for Technology-related Mass Damage in the Cases of Minamata Disease, Asbestos, and the Fukushima Daiichi Nuclear Disaster." *Contemporary Japan* vol. 30, no. 1 (2018), pp. 3–27.

218   Bibliography

Kawamura Kunimitsu. *Seisen no ikonogurafi: Tennō to heishi, senshisha no zusō, hyōshō* [*The Iconography of Holy War: Emperor and Soldiers, Pictures of War Dead, Commendations*] (Tokyo: Seikyūsha, 2007).

Sekushuariti no kindai [*Sexuality and Modernity*] (Tokyo: Kōdansha, 1996).

Kawasaki Masako. *Kōshō seido teppai no zehi* (Tokyo: Fujin Shinpō-sha, 1926).

Keller, Nora Okja. *Comfort Woman: A Novel* (New York: Penguin, 1998).

Kim-Gibson, Dai Sil. *Silence Broken: Korean Comfort Women* (San Francisco, CA: Center for Asian American Media, 1999).

Kimi Rito. *The History of Hentai Manga* (Tokyo: FAKKU, 2021).

Kimura, Maki. *Unfolding the "Comfort Women" Debates: Modernity, Violence, Women's Voices* (New York: Palgrave Macmillan, 2016).

Kinsella, Sharon. "Cuteness, *josō*, and the Need to Appeal: *otoko no ko* in Male Subculture in 2010s Japan." *Japan Forum* vol. 32, no. 3 (2020), pp. 432–58.

Kinski, Michael. "Japanische Kindheiten und Kindheitsbilder: Zur Einleitung" [Japanese Childhoods and Images of Childhood: An Introduction]. In *Kindheit in der japanischen Geschichte* [*Childhood in Japanese History*], ed. Michael Kinski, Harald Salomon, and Eike Grossmann, pp. 1–32 (Wiesbaden: Harrassowitz, 2015).

Kirino Natsuo. *Grotesque: A Novel*, trans. Rebecca Copeland (New York: Knopf, 2007).

Kitano Hiromi. "Dokusha e no onegai!" [A Request to Readers!]. *Sei no Kenkyū: Tokubetsugō – Baiin kenkyū* [*Sex Research: Special Issue – Prostitution Research*], January 1, 1919, n.p.

Klemperer-Markman, Ayala. "Art, Politics and Prostitution in Occupied/ Contemporary Japan: The Voice of a Sex Worker." In *Postgender: Gender, Sexuality and Performativity in Japanese Culture*, ed. Ayelet Zohar, pp. 229–49 (Newcastle upon Tyne: Cambridge Scholars Publishing, 2009).

Koch, Gabriele. *Healing Labor: Japanese Sex Work in the Gendered Economy* (Stanford, CA: Stanford University Press, 2020).

Koga, Yukiko. *Inheritance of Loss: China, Japan, and the Political Economy of Redemption after Empire* (Chicago, IL: University of Chicago Press, 2016).

Koizumi, Masumi. "Environment Minister Shinjiro Koizumi Challenges Japan's Workplace Norms with Decision to Take Paternity Leave." *Japan Times*, January 15, 2020, www.japantimes.co.jp/news/2020/01/15/national/shinjiro-koizumi-paternity-leave/#.Xrtw1sZlC7M

Konishi Shigenao. *Shōwa joshi shin kyōikugaku* [*Shōwa New Pedagogy for Girls*] (Kyōto: Nagasawa Kinkōdō, 1937).

Kōseishō Imukyoku. *Isei Hachijūnen-shi* (Tokyo: Insatsukyoku Chōyōkai, 1955).

Kotani Tsunao. "Shigoto ni mukau taido" [Attitude toward Work], *Himawari*, March 30, 1949, pp. 28–29.

Kovner, Sarah. "Base Cultures: Sex Workers and Servicemen in Occupied Japan." *Journal of Asian Studies* vol. 68, no. 3 (2009), pp. 777–804.

Occupying Power: Sex Workers and Service Members in Postwar Japan (Stanford, CA: Stanford University Press, 2012).

Krauss, Friedrich Solomon. *Das Geschlechtsleben in Glauben, Sitte, Brauch und Gewohnheitsrecht der Japaner* [*The Sex Life in Japan's Beliefs, Customs, Conventions, and Common Law*] (Leipzig: Ethnologischer Verlag, [1907] 1911).

Bibliography 219

Krauss, Friedrich S. and Tamio Satow. *Japanisches Geschlechtsleben: Abhandlungen und Erhebungen über das Geschlechtsleben des japanischen Volkes* [*Japanese Sex Life: Analyses and Surveys on the Sex Lives of the Japanese People*] (Hanau am Main: Folkloristische Studien, with Tamio Satow, [1907] 1911).

Kurihara Harumi. "Consuming Domesticity in Post-Bubble Japan." In *Consuming Life in Post-Bubble Japan: A Transdisciplinary Perspective*, ed. Katarzyna J. Cwiertka and Ewa Machotka, pp. 107–27 (Amsterdam: Amsterdam University Press, 2018).

Kuronuma Susumu. "Olympic Sexism Row Pushes Japan toward Work Discrimination Treaty." *NikkeiAsia*, March 10, 2021, https://asia.nikkei.co m/Politics/International-relations/Olympic-sexism-row-pushes-Japan-toward-work-discrimination-treaty

Kushner, Barak. *The Thought War: Japanese Imperial Propaganda* (Honolulu: University of Hawai'i Press, 2007).

Kuwabara Shisei. *Kuwabara Shisei Shashinshū: Minamata Jiken* [*Kuwabara Shisei's Photograph Collection: The Minamata Incident*] (Tokyo: Fujiwara Shoten, 2013).

"Lady Police: Popular Asset to the Metropolitan Force." *Japan* vol. XI, no. 2 (1973), p. 9.

Lamarre, Thomas. "Platonic Sex: Perversion and Shōjo Anime (Part One)." *animation: an interdisciplinary journal* vol. 1, no. 1 (2006), pp. 45–59.

Lazopoulos, George. "Japanese History, Post-Japan." *Cross-Currents: East Asian History and Culture Review* vol. 3, no. 1 (May 2014), pp. 245–52.

LeBlanc, Robin. *The Art of the Gut* (Berkeley: University of California Press, 2010).

Lebra, Takie Sugiyama. *Above the Clouds: Status Culture of the Modern Japanese Nobility* (Berkeley: University of California Press, 1993).

Linhart, Sepp. "Interpreting the World as a *Ken* Game." In *Japan at Play*, ed. Joy Hendry and Massimo Raveri, pp. 35–56 (London: Routledge, 2005).

"Warum sind die Holzschnitte Japans zum Lachen?" [Why Laugh about Japanese Woodblock Prints?]. In *Neue Geschichten der Sexualität: Beispiele aus Ostasien und Zentraleuropa 1700–2000* [*New Histories of Sexuality: Examples from East Asia and Central Europe, 1700–2000*], ed. Franz X. Eder and Sabine Frühstück, pp. 117–43 (Vienna: Turia+Kant, 1999).

Lukacs, Gabriella. "The Labor of Cute: Net Idols, Cute Culture, and the Digital Economy in Contemporary Japan." *positions: east asia cultures critique* vol. 23, no. 3 (2015), pp. 487–513.

Ludovico, Alessandro. "Eine neue Perspektive auf die Do-it-yourself-Kultur" [A New Perspective on the Culture of Do-It-Yourself], *springerin* vol. 1 (2015), pp. 38–41.

Lunsing, Wim. *Beyond Common Sense: Sexuality and Gender in Contemporary Japan* (London: Routledge, 2001).

"Confessions of a Problem: A Roundtable Discussion with Male Prostitutes." In *Queer Voices from Japan: First-Person Narratives from Japan's Sexual Minorities*, ed. Mark McLelland, Katsuhiko Suganuma, and James Welker, pp. 69–80 (Lanham, MD: Lexington Books, 2007).

"Japan: Finding Its Way?" In *Global Emergence of Gay and Lesbian Politics: National Imprints of a Worldwide Movement*, ed. Barry D. Adam, Jan

220   Bibliography

Willem Duyvendak, and André Krouwel, pp. 293–325 (Philadelphia, PA: Temple University Press, 2009).

Lusk, Jeniece. "Japanese Millennials and Intersex Awareness." *Sexuality and Culture* vol. 21, no. 2 (2017), pp. 613–626.

Maeda Ai. *Kindai dokusha no seiritsu* [*The Emergence of Modern Readers*] (Tokyo: Chikuma Shobō, 1989).

Maerkle, Andrew. "All Too Human." *ART iT*, April 12, 2013, www.art-it.asia/en/u/admin_ed_itv_e/ysx8xtnygdjws7orl0zc

Mackie, Vera C. *Feminism in Modern Japan* (Cambridge: Cambridge University Press, 2003).

"From Hiroshima to Lausanne: The World Congress of Mothers and the Hahaoya Taikai in the 1950s." *Women's History Review* vol. 25, no. 4 (2016), pp. 671–95.

Maree, Claire. "'LGBT Issues' and the 2020 Games." *Asia-Pacific Journal: Japan Focus* vol. 18, issue 4, no. 7 (2020), pp. 1–7.

"Queer Women's Culture and History in Japan." In *Routledge Handbook of Sexuality Studies in East Asia*, ed. Vera Mackie and Mark McLelland, pp. 230–43 (London: Routledge, 2015).

queerqueen Linguistic Excess in Japanese Media (Oxford: Oxford University Press, 2020).

"The Un/State of Lesbian Studies: An Introduction to Lesbian Communities and Contemporary Legislation in Japan." *Journal of Lesbian Studies* vol. 11, no. 3–4 (2007), pp. 291–301.

Marran, Christine L. *Poison Woman: Figuring Female Transgression in Modern Japanese Culture* (Minneapolis: University of Minnesota Press, 2007).

Martin, Fran, Peter A. Jackson, Mark McLelland, and Audrey Yue. *AsiaPacifiQueer: Rethinking Genders and Sexualities* (Urbana: University of Illinois Press, 2008).

Masahiro Yamada. "The Growing Crop of Spoiled Singles." *Japan Echo* (June 2000), pp. 49–53.

Masuda Sayo. *Autobiography of a Geisha*, trans. G. G. Rowley (New York: Columbia University Press, [1957] 2003).

Mathews, Gordon. "Finding and Keeping a Purpose in Life: Well-Being and *Ikigai* in Japan and Elsewhere." In *Pursuits of Happiness: Well-Being in Anthropological Perspective*, ed. Gordon Mathews and Carolina Izquierdo, pp. 167–86 (New York: Berghahn Books, 2009).

Matsubara Yōko. "The Eugenic Border Control: Organized Abortions on Repatriated Women, 1945–1948." *Japan Forum* vol. 32, no. 1 (2020), pp. 1–20.

Matsui Eiichi and Watanabe Tomosuke. *Nihon seigo daijiten: Ingo jiten shūsei 21* [*Dictionary of Japanese Sexual Words: Collected Dictionaries of Secret Words 21*] (Tokyo: Ōsora-sha, [1928] 1997).

Matsunaga, Louella. "Bodies in Question: Narrating the Body in Contemporary Japan." *Contemporary Japan* vol. 27, no. 1 (2015), pp. 1–11.

Maxson, Hillary. "From 'Motherhood in the Interest of the State' to Motherhood in the Interest of Mothers: Rethinking the First Mothers' Congress." In *Rethinking Japanese Feminism*, ed. Julia C. Bullock, Ayako Kano, and James Welker, pp. 34–49 (Honolulu: University of Hawai'i Press, 2018).

Bibliography

McDonald, Kate. *Placing Empire: Travel and the Social Imagination in Imperial Japan* (Oakland: University of California Press, 2017).

McKnight, Anne. "At the Source (Code): Obscenity and Modularity in Rokudenashiko's Media Activism." In *Media Theory in Japan*, ed. Marc Steinberg and Alexander Zahlten, pp. 250–84 (Durham, NC: Duke University Press, 2017).

McLelland, Mark. "Death of the 'Legendary Okama' Tōgō Ken: Challenging Commonsense Lifestyles in Postwar Japan." *Asia-Pacific Journal: Japan Focus* vol. 10, issue 25, no. 5 (2012), pp. 1–9.

"Introduction." In *Edges of the Rainbow: LGBTQ Japan*, Michel Delsol and Haruku Shinozaki, pp. 6–9 (New York: New Press, 2017).

Queer Japan from the Pacific War to the Internet Age (Lanham, MD: Rowman & Littlefield, 2005).

"Sex, Censorship and Media Regulation in Japan: A Historical Overview." In *Routledge Handbook of Sexuality Studies in East Asia*, ed. Mark McLelland and Vera Mackie, pp. 402–13 (Abingdon: Routledge, 2014).

McLelland, Mark, Katsuhiko Suganuma, and James Welker, ed. *Queer Voices from Japan: First Person Narratives from Japan's Sexual* (Lanham, MD: Lexington Books, 2007).

McLelland, Mark and Romit Dasgupta, ed. *Genders, Transgenders, and Sexualities in Japan* (London: Routledge, 2005).

McLelland, Mark and Vera Mackie, ed. *Routledge Handbook of Sexuality Studies in East Asia* (London: Routledge, 2014).

Meyerowitz, Joanne. *How Sex Changed: A History of Transsexuality in the United States* (Cambridge, MA: Harvard University Press, 2009).

Mieko Kawakami. *Breasts and Eggs*, trans. Sam Bett and David Boyd (New York: Europa Editions, 2020).

Miller, J. Berkshire. "The Abe Statement of Japan's War Guilt: Regional and Historical Implications." *EastWest.ngo*, June 25, 2015, www.eastwest.ngo/idea/abe-statement-japan%E2%80%99s-war-guilt-regional-and-historical-implications

Mishima Yukio. *Confessions of a Mask*, trans. Meredith Weatherby (New York: New Directions, 1958).

Miyagi Kikuko. *Himeyuri no shōjo: Jūrokusai no senjo* [*The Himeyuri Girls: Battlefields at the Age of Sixteen*] (Tokyo: Kōbunken, [1995] 2002).

Miyatake Gaikotsu. *Hannannyokō* [*Thoughts on Hermaphroditism*, 1922]. In *Miyatake Gaikotsu Chosakushii* vol. 5, ed. Tanizawa Eiichi and Yoshino Takao (Tokyo: Kawade Shobō Shinsha 1986).

Moen, Darrell. "Sex Slaves in Japan Today." *Hitotsubashi Journal of Social Studies* vol. 44, no. 2 (2012), pp. 35–53.

Molony, Barbara. "The Quest for Women's Rights in Turn-of-the-Century Japan." In *Gendering Modern Japanese History*, ed. Barbara Molony and Kathleen Uno, pp. 463–92 (Cambridge, MA: Harvard University Asia Center, 2005).

Mori Rintarō. *Eiseigaku Daii* (Tokyo: Hakubunkan, 1907).

Rikugun eisei kyōtei [*Army Hygiene Manual*] (Tokyo: Rikugun no Igakkō, 1889).

Zwei Jahre in Korea [*Two Years in Korea*]. In *Ōgai zenshū dai nijūhachi-kan* [*Ōgai Collected Works vol. 28*] (1889), ed. Midorikawa Takashi (Tokyo: Iwanami Shoten, 1989), pp. 161–213.

222 Bibliography

Moriyama Shigeki and Nakae Kazue. *Nihon kodomo-shi* [*History of Japan's Children*] (Tokyo: Heibonsha, 2002).

Morris-Suzuki, Tessa. "Ever-Shifting Sands of Japanese Apologies." *East Asia Forum*, February 22, 2016.

"You Don't Want to Know about the Girls? The 'Comfort Women,' the Japanese Military and Allied Forces in the Asia-Pacific War." *Asia-Pacific Journal* vol. 13, no. 31 (2015), pp. 1–21.

Murakami Haruki. *Norwegian Wood*, trans. Jay Rubin (New York: Vintage, 2000).

Murakami Takashi. *Little Boy: The Arts of Japan's Exploding Subculture* (New Haven, CT: Yale University Press, 2005).

Murata Sayaka. *Convenience Store Woman*, trans. Ginny Tapley Takemore (New York: Grove Press, 2019).

Mysorekar, Sheila. "Homosexuality Is Not a Disease." *Development and Cooperation*, January 8, 2019, www.dandc.eu/en/article/world-health-organization-considers-homosexuality-normal-behaviour

Nagai Yoshikazu. *Fūzoku eigyō torishimari* [*Control of Sex Industry Establishments*] (Tokyo: Kōdansha, 2002).

Naikakufu. *Zenkoku yoron chōsa no genkyū* [*Current Research on National Public Opinion*], 2017, https://survey.gov-online.go.jp/genkyou/h27/h26-genkyou/index.html

Napier, Susan. "Where Have All the Salarymen Gone? Masculinity, Masochism and Technomobility in Densha Otoko." In *Recreating Japanese Men*, ed. Sabine Frühstück and Anne Walthall, pp. 154–75 (Berkeley: University of California Press, 2011).

Nara Shiyakusho. *Nara-shi shōgakkō jidō shintai kensa tōkeihyō* [*Statistical Tables of Nara City Elementary School Students' Physical Exams*] (Nara: Shiyakusho, 2019).

Natori Toshiya. "Baishun bōshi-hō ihan" [Violations of the Anti-Prostitution Law]. In *Fūzoku sei hanzai* [*Crimes of Morals and Sex*], ed. Fujinaga Yukiharu, pp. 124–92 (Tokyo: Hōrei Shuppan, [1996] 2005).

Nemoto, Kumiko, Makiko Fuwa, and Kuniko Ishiguro. "Never-Married Employed Men's Gender Beliefs and Ambivalence toward Matrimony in Japan." *Journal of Family Issues* vol. 34, no. 12 (2012), pp. 1673–95.

Ngai, Mae M. "Promises and Perils of Transnational History." *Perspectives on History* vol. 50, no. 9, December 1, 2012.

Nogawa Motokazu, Tessa Morris-Suzuki, and Emi Koyama. *Umi o wataru ianfu mondai: Uha no rekishisen o tou* [*The Comfort Women Issue Crosses the Ocean: Interrogating the Right's History War*] (Tokyo: Iwanami Shoten, 2016).

Norgren, Tiana. *Abortion before Birth Control: The Politics of Reproduction in Postwar Japan* (Princeton, NJ: Princeton University Press, 2001).

Norma, Caroline. "Demand from Abroad: Japanese Involvement in the 1970s' Development of South Korea's Sex Industry." *Journal of Korean Studies* vol. 19, no. 2 (2014), pp. 399–428.

Nottage, Luke. *Product Safety and Liability Law in Japan: From Minamata to Mad Cows* (London: Routledge, 2004).

Nussbaum, Martha. "Toward a Globally Sensitive Patriotism." *Daedalus* vol. 137, no. 3 (2008), pp. 78–93.

Bibliography 223

Ochiai, Emiko and Barbara Molony, ed. *Asia's New Mothers: Crafting Gender Roles and Childcare Networks in East and Southeast Asian Societies* (Folkestone: Global Oriental, 2008).

OECD. "Economic Survey of Japan 2019." www.oecd.org/japan/

OECD iLibrary. "OECD Labour Statistics." www.oecd-ilibrary.org/docserver/ 5842cc7f-en.pdf?expires=1600803684&id=id&accname=ocid195703b&check sum=757F5EC0839C27EDD152CD9701E69BB4

Office of Gender Equality. *The Present Status of Women and Measures: Fifth Report on the Implementation of the New National Plan of Action toward the Year 2000* (Tokyo: Office of Gender Equality, 1996).

Oikawa Kenji. "Tōgō Ken, the Legendary *Okama*: Burning with Sexual Desire and Revolt." In *Queer Voices from Japan: First-Person Narratives from Japan's Sexual Minorities*, ed. Mark McLelland, Katsuhiko Suganuma, and James Welker, pp. 263–69 (Lanham, MD: Lexington Books, 2007).

Okamoto Kazuhiko. "Taishū no gaku toshite no seikagaku no tenkai" [The Turning Point of Sexology as Science of the Masses]. *Gendai Seikyōiku Kenkyū* no. 14 (1983), pp. 108–18.

"Only 10% of Firms in Japan Have Addressed LGBT Issues, Survey Finds." *Japan Times*, June 13, 2020.

Onoo Chieko, ed. *Kaisetsu: Seidōitsu seishōgai-sha seibetsu toriatsukai tokureihō* [*Commentary: Special Law Concerning How to Sexually/Genderwise Distinguish Individuals with Gender Dysphoria*] (Tokyo: Nihon Kajo Shuppan, 2004).

Orbaugh, Sharalyn. "Gender, Family, and Sexualities in Modern Literature." In *The Columbia Companion to Modern East Asian Literature*, ed. Joshua S. Mostow, Kirk A. Denton, Bruce Fulton, and Sharalyn Orbaugh, pp. 43–51 (New York: Columbia University Press, 2003).

Propaganda Performed: Kamishibai in Japan's Fifteen-Year War (Leiden: Brill, 2014).

Ortner, Sherry B. *Making Gender: The Politics and Erotics of Culture* (Boston, MA: Beacon Press, 1997).

Osaki Tomohiro. "LDP Lawmaker Mio Sugita Faces Backlash after Describing LGBT People as 'Unproductive.'" *Japan Times*, July 24, 2018, www .japantimes.co.jp/news/2018/07/24/national/politics-diplomacy/ldp-lawmaker-mio-sugita-faces-backlash-describing-lgbt-people-unproductive/

"Vagina Artist Pleads Not Guilty to Obscenity Charge." *Japan Times*, April 15, 2015, www.japantimes.co.jp/news/2015/04/15/national/crime-legal/vagina-artist-pleads-not-guilty-to-obscenity-charge/

Oshida Nobuko. *Heishi no aidoru: Maboroshi no imon zasshi ni miru mō hitotsu no sensō* (Tokyo: Junpōsha, 2016).

Ōsugi Sakae. *The Autobiography of Ōsugi Sakae*, trans. with an introduction by Byron K. Marshall (Berkeley: University of California Press, 1992).

Ōta Tenrei. *Nihon sanji chōsetsu hyakunenshi* (Tokyo: Shuppan Kagaku Sōgō Kenkyūsho, 1976).

"Otera de dōsei kekkonshiki, Bukkyō no oshie, dare shi mo shiawase ni: Saitama Saimyōji." *Mainichi Shinbun*, June 9, 2020, https://mainichi.jp/articles/ 20200609/ddl/k13/040/003000c

224 Bibliography

Our World in Data. "Representation of Women in Low-Paying Jobs." https:// ourworldindata.org/economic-inequality-by-gender#representation-of-women-in-low-paying-jobs

Outright Action International. "Japan: Psychiatrists Remove Homosexuality from List of Disorders." https://outrightinternational.org/content/japan-psychiatrists-remove-homosexuality-list-disorders

Ozawa-de Silva, Chikako. "Beyond the Body/Mind? Japanese Contemporary Thinkers on Alternative Sociologies of the Body." *Body & Society* vol. 8, no. 2 (2002), pp. 21–38.

Pandora, ed. *Kau otoko, kawanai otoko* [*Men Who Buy, Men Who Don't*] (Tokyo: Gendai Shokan, 1995).

Parreñas, Rhacel Salazar. *Illicit Flirtations: Labor, Migration and Sex Trafficking in Tokyo* (Stanford, CA: Stanford University Press, 2011).

Pennington, Lee K. *Casualties of History: Wounded Japanese Servicemen and the Second World War* (Ithaca, NY: Cornell University Press, 2015).

Plath, David W. *Long Engagements: Maturity in Modern Japan* (Stanford, CA: Stanford University Press, 1980).

Pflugfelder, Gregory M. *Cartographies of Desire: Male–Male Sexuality in Japanese Discourse, 1600–1950* (Berkeley: University of California Press, 2007).

Porath, Or. "The Flower of Dharma Nature: Sexual Consecration and Amalgamation in Medieval Japanese Buddhism" (PhD dissertation, Department of Religious Studies, University of California at Santa Barbara, 2019).

"Nasty Boys or Obedient Children? Childhood and Relative Autonomy in Medieval Japanese Monasteries." In *Child's Play: Multi-sensory Histories of Children and Childhood in Japan*, ed. Sabine Frühstück and Anne Walthall, pp. 17–39 (Oakland: University of California Press, 2017).

Rabson, Steve. "Yosano Akiko on War: To Give One's Life or Not – A Question of Which War." *Journal of the Assocation of Teachers of Japanese* vol. 25, no. 1 (April 1991), pp. 45–74.

Raymo, James M. "Later Marriages or Fewer? Changes in the Marital Behavior of Japanese Women Author(s)." *Journal of Marriage and Family*, vol. 60, no. 4 (1998), pp. 1023–34.

Raymo, James M. and Akihisa Shibata. "Unemployment, Nonstandard Employment, and Fertility: Insights from Japan's 'Lost 20 Years'." *Demography* vol. 54, no. 6 (December 2017), pp. 2301–29.

Reichert, James. *In the Company of Men: Representations of Male–Male Sexuality in Modern Japan* (Stanford, CA: Stanford University Press, 2006).

Rich, Motoko. "After Leader's Sexist Remark, Tokyo Olympics Makes Symbolic Shift." *New York Times*, February 18, 2021, www.nytimes.com/2021/02/18/world/asia/yoshiro-mori-tokyo-olympics-seiko-hashimoto.html

Rich, Motoko and Hisako Ueno. "Woman Wins High-Profile #MeToo Case in Japan against TV Journalist." *New York Times*, December 18, 2019, www.nytimes.com/2019/12/18/world/asia/japan-metoo-shiori-ito-rape.html?login=email&auth=login-email

Rimer, J. Thomas and C. Van Gessel, eds. *The Columbia Anthology of Modern Japanese Literature, Volume 2: From 1945 to the Present* (New York: Columbia University Press, 2005).

Bibliography

Roberson, James E. and Nobue Suzuki, eds. *Men and Masculinities in Contemporary Japan: Dislocating the Salaryman Doxa* (London: Routledge, 2001).

Roberts, Glenda S. "Leaning Out for the Long Span: What Holds Women Back from Promotion in Japan." *Japan Forum* vol. 32, no. 4 (2020), pp. 555–76.

Robertson, Jennifer. "Gendering Robots: Post-Human Traditionalism in Japan." In *Recreating Japanese Men*, ed. Sabine Frühstück and Anne Walthall, pp. 284–309 (Berkeley: University of California Press, 2011).

"Introduction: Sexualizing Anthropology's Fields." In *Same-Sex Cultures and Sexualities: An Anthropological Reader*, ed. Jennifer Robertson, pp. 1–11 (London: Blackwell, 2005).

Robo Sapiens Japanicus: Robots, Gender, Family, and the Japanese Nation (Berkeley: University of California Press, 2017).

Robertson, Jennifer. ed. *Same-Sex Cultures and Sexualities: An Anthropological Reader* (Oxford: Blackwell, 2004).

Takarazuka: Sexual Politics and Popular Culture in Modern Japan (Berkeley: University of California Press, 1998).

"From Tiramisù to #MeToo: Triangulations of Sex, Gender and Sexuality in Heisei Japan." In *Heisei Japan in Retrospect (1989–2019)* (Abingdon: Routledge, in press).

"Yoshiya Nobuko: Out and Outspoken in Practice and Prose." In *Same Sex Cultures and Sexuality: An Anthropological Reader*, ed. Jennifer Robertson, pp. 196–211 (London: Blackwell, 2005).

Rochel, Johan. "Protecting Japan from Immigrants? An Ethical Challenge to Security-based Justification in Immigration Policy." *Contemporary Japan* vol. 30, no. 1 (2018), pp. 164–88.

Roden, Donald. "Taishō Culture and the Problem of Gender Ambivalence." In *Culture and Identity: Japanese Intellectuals during the Interwar Years*, ed. J. Thomas Rimer, pp. 37–55 (Princeton, NJ: Princeton University Press, 1990).

Rokudenashiko. *What Is Obscenity? The Story of a Good-for-Nothing Artist and Her Pussy*, trans. Anne Ishii (Toronto: Koyama Press, 2016).

Rosenbluth, Frances McCall. "The Political Economy of Low Fertility." In *The Political Economy of Japan's Low Fertility*, ed. Frances McCall Rosenbluth, pp. 3–36 (Stanford, CA: Stanford University Press, 2008).

Rowley, G. G. "Prostitutes against the Prostitution Prevention Act of 1956." *U.S.–Japan Women's Journal: English Supplement* vol. 23 (2002), pp. 39–56.

Rubin, Jay. *Injurious to Public Morals: Writers and the Meiji State* (Seattle: University of Washington Press, 1984).

Ryall, Julian. "Korean 'Comfort Women' Statue in Berlin Angers Japan." *Deutsche Welle*, October 1, 2020.

Saga Junichi. *Memories of Silk and Straw: A Self-Portrait of Small-Town Japan*, trans. Garry O. Evans (Tokyo: Kōdansha International, 1987).

Sakata Kiyo. *Onna no mita senjo [Battlefields Women Have Seen]* (Nagoya: Arumu, [1942] 2002).

Sakurazawa, Erica. "Nakamura Shidō, atarashii mei to tomo ni/SHIDO NAKAMURA, NEW BORN." *Harper's Bazar* (May 2018), p. 277.

226   Bibliography

Sanders, Holly. "*Panpan*: Streetwalking in Occupied Japan." *Pacific Historical Review* vol. 81, no. 3 (2012), pp. 404–31.

Sarkeesian, Anita. "Ms. Male Character." *Feminist Frequency*, November 18, 2013, www.youtube.com/watch?v=eYqYLfm1rWA

"Women as Background Decoration: Part I – Tropes vs. Women in Video Games." *Feminist Frequency*, June 16, 2014, www.youtube.com/watch?v=4ZPSrwedvsg

Sasaki Yōko. *Sōryokusen to josei heishi* [*Total War and Female Soldiers*] (Tokyo: Seikyūsha, 2001).

Sasakibara Gō. "Kizu tsukeru sei, dankai no sedai kara otaku sedai e: Gyarugē-teki sekushuariti no kigen" [Sex That Injures from the Baby Boom Generation to the Otaku Generation]. In *Shingenjitsu* vol. 2, ed. Ōtsuka Eiji, pp. 101–28 (Tokyo: Kadokawa Shoten, 2003).

Sato, Barbara. "Commodifying and Engendering Morality: Self-Cultivation and the Construction of the 'Ideal Woman' in 1920s Mass Women's Magazines." In *Gendering Modern Japanese History*, ed. Barbara Molony and Kathleen Uno, pp. 99–130 (Cambridge, MA: Harvard University Asia Center, 2005).

Satō Koka. *Nihon seiteki fūzoku jiten* [*Dictionary for Japan's Sexual Morals and Customs*] (Tokyo: Bungei Shiryō Kenkyūkai, 1929).

Sawabe Hitomi. "'Wakakusa no Kai': The First Fifteen Years of Japan's Original Lesbian Organization." In *Queer Voices from Japan: First-Person Narratives from Japan's Sexual Minorities*, ed. Mark McLelland, Katsuhiko Suganuma, and James Welker, pp. 167–80 (Lanham, MD: Lexington Books, 2007).

Schad-Seifert, Annette. "Dynamics of Masculinities in Japan – Comparative Perspectives on Men's Studies." In *Gender Dynamics and Globalisation: Perspectives from Japan within Asia*, ed. Claudia Derichs and Susanne Kreitz-Sandberg, pp. 33–44 (Münster: Lit Verlag, 2007).

"Japans Single-Gesellschaft – Der Trend zu Partnerlosigkeit in Umfragen des National Institute of Population and Social Security Research" [Japan's Single Society – The Trend toward Being Single in Surveys of the National Institutes of Population and Social Security Research]. In *Japan in der Krise* [*Japan in Crisis*], ed. Annette Schad-Seifert and Nora Kottmann, pp. 75–97 (Wiesbaden: Springer Fachmedien, 2019).

"J-Unterschicht: Japans junge Generation im Zeitalter der gesellschaftlichen Polarisierung" [J-Underclass: Japan's Young Generation in the Age of Social Polarization]. In *Japan Lesebuch IV – J-Culture* [*Japan Reader IV – J-Culture*], ed. Steffi Richter and Jaqueline Berndt, pp. 86–105 (Tübingen: Konkursbuch Verlag, 2008).

"Makeinu und arafō – Die discursive Production von weiblichen Verlierer- und Gewinner-Images im aktuellen japanischen Fernsehdrama" [Makeinu and arafō – The Discursive Production of Female Loser and Winner Images in Current Japanese TV Dramas]. In *Frauenbilder – Frauenkörper: Inszenierungen des Weiblichen in den Gesellschaften Süd- und Ostasiens* [*Women's Images – Women's Bodies: Orchestrations of Femininity in South and East Asian Societies*], ed. Stephan Köhn and Heike Moser, pp. 417–36 (Wiesbaden: Otto Harrassowitz, 2013).

Bibliography

"Väter am Wickeltisch in Japan" [Fathers at the Changing Tables in Japan], *Bildung und Erziehung* vol. 67, no. 2 (June 2014), pp. 203–18.

"Womenomics: A Model for a New Family Policy in Japan?" In *Family Life in Japan and Germany: Challenges for a Gender-Sensitive Family Policy*, ed. Uta Meier-Gräwe, Miyoko Motozawa, and Annette Schad-Seifert, pp. 157–76 (Wiesbaden: Springer, 2019).

Schwind, Martin. "Japanische Raumnot und Kolonisation" [Japan's Lack of Space and Colonization]. *Mitteilungen der Deutschen Gesellschaft für Natur- und Völkerkunde Ostasiens* vol. XXXII, part C (1940), pp. 2–17.

Scott, George Riley. *Far Eastern Sex Life: An Anthropological, Ethnological, and Sociological Study of the Love Relations, Marriage Rites, and Home Life of the Oriental People* (London: Gerald G. Swan, 1943).

Screech, Timon. *Sex and the Floating World: Erotic Images in Japan 1700–1820* (London: Reaktion Books 2009).

Seigle, Cecilia Segawa. *Yoshiwara: The Glittering World of the Japanese Courtesan* (Honolulu: University of Hawai'i Press, 1993).

Seaman, Amanda C. *Writing Pregnancy in Low-Fertility Japan* (Honolulu: University of Hawai'i Press, 2017).

Setoguchi Torao, Masako Izumo Marou, Ranko Otoki, and Reporter for Ōkē magazine. "Confessions of a Problem: A Roundtable Discussion with Male Prostitutes" trans. Wim Lunsing. In *Queer Voices from Japan: First-Person Narratives from Japan's Sexual Minorities*, ed. Mark McLelland, Katsuhiko Suganuma, and James Welker, pp. 69–80 (Lanham, MD: Lexington Books, 2007).

Shida Yōko. "Rokudenashiko saiban – saikō saiban-ketsu wa nani o sabaita no ka – keijibatsu wa makoto ni hitsuyō na koto ni shiborubeki" [Rokudenashiko's Trial]. *Yahoo Nyūsu Japan*, July 17, 2020, https://news .yahoo.co.jp/byline/shidayoko/20200717-00188461/

Shigematsu Setsu. *Scream from the Shadows: The Women's Liberation Movement in Japan* (Minneapolis: University of Minnesota Press, 2012).

Shimada Keizō. "The Adventures of Dankichi." In *Reading Colonial Japan: Text, Context, and Critique*, ed. Michele M. Mason and Helen J. S. Lee (Stanford, CA: Stanford University Press, 2012).

Shimizu Kan. "Meijiki ni okeru guntai to shōgaisha mondai: Chōheisei oyobi rikugun chōjitai o chūshin ni" [The Military and the Issue of Disability in the Meiji Period: Focusing on the Conscription System]. *Shōgaisha Mondai Kenkyū* vol. 36 (1984), n.p.

Shin, Mitch. "South Koreans Welcome Decision to Maintain 'Comfort Women' Statue in Berlin." *The Diplomat*, December 7, 2020.

Shiohara Tamiji. *Joshi shūshinkun* (Kyōto: Shiohara Gakuen Kenkyūjo, 1935).

Shiozaki Toshio. "Shikyūnai ninshin kagu ni kansuru kenkyū: Toku ni Ōta ringu to rūpu to no hikaku kenkyū." *Nihon Sanka Fujin Kagakkai Zasshi* vol. 25, no. 1 (1973), pp. 1–9.

"Shiritsu Meiji jogakkō shinnyū seito boshū" [Recruitment of New Students at the Private Meiji Girls' School]. *Jogaku Zasshi* no. 260, April 11, 1891, inside cover.

Shoji Kaori. "Historical Truths Can Take Decades to Unearth." *Japan Times*, February 15, 2017, www.japantimes.co.jp/culture/2017/02/15/films/histor ical-truths-can-take-decades-unearth/

228 Bibliography

Shōheisha. *Chōhei kensa* [*The Conscription Exam*] (Tokyo: Tosho Shuppan Kyōkai, 1902).

Shufu no tomo-sha, ed. *Fujin eisei jiten* [*Dictionary of Women's Hygiene*] (Tokyo: Shufu no Tomo-sha, 1933).

  ed. *Shufu no Tomo nigaku-gō furoku: Ninshin to ansan to ikujihō* (Tokyo: Shufu no Tomo-sha, 1937).

Simone, Gianni. "Building a Monument to Nothing: A Fantastic Interview with Makoto Aida." *SFAQ/NYAQ/AQ: International Art and Culture*, September 29, 2014, www.sfaq.us/2014/09/building-a-monument-to-nothing-a-fantastic-interview-with-makoto-aida/

Siripala, Thisanka. "Japan's Supreme Court Upholds Surgery as Necessary Step for Official Gender Change." *The Diplomat*, February 5, 2019, https://thediplomat.com/2019/02/japans-supreme-court-upholds-surgery-as-necessary-step-for-official-gender-change/

Smith, Robert J. and Ella Lury Wiswell. *The Women of Suyemura* (Chicago, IL: University of Chicago Press, 1982).

Soh, C. Sarah. *The Comfort Women: Sexual Violence and Postcolonial Memory in Korea and Japan* (Chicago, IL: Chicago University Press, 2009).

Sontag, Susan. *Regarding the Pain of Others* (New York: Picador, 2004).

Soto-Laveaga, Gabriela. *Jungle Laboratories: Mexican Peasants, National Projects, and the Making of the Pill* (Durham, NC: Duke University Press, 2009).

Stanley, Amy. *Selling Women: Prostitution, Markets, and the Household in Early Modern Japan* (Berkeley: University of California Press, 2012).

Steger, Brigitte. "Geburtshilfe – vom unreinen Gewerbe zum Karriereberuf oder: Die Dissemination staatlicher Kontrolle ins Private" [Midwifery – from Impure Occupation to Professional Career or: the Dissemination of State Control in the Private Sphere]. In *Getrennte Welten, gemeinsame Moderne? Geschlechterverhältnisse in Japan* [*Gender Relations in Japan*], ed. Ilse Lenz and Michiko Mae, pp. 150–78 (Opladen: Leske und Budrich, 1997).

  "From Impurity to Hygiene: The Role of Midwives in the Modernisation of Japan." *Japan Forum* vol. 6, no. 2 (1994), pp. 175–87.

Stratz, Carl Heinrich. *Die Körperformen in Kunst und Leben der Japaner* [*Body Shapes in Japanese Art and Life*] (Erlangen: Ferdinand Enke, 1903).

Sugita Naogeki, "Seibyō to seishinbyō no kankei" [The Connections of Sexually Transmitted Diseases to Mental Illnesses]. *Kakusei* vol. 14, no. 8 (1924), pp. 17–19.

Summerhawk, Barbara, Cheiron McMahill, and Darren McDonald, eds. *Queer Japan: Personal Stories of Japanese Lesbians, Gays, Bisexuals and Transsexuals* (Norwich: New Victoria Publishers, 1998).

SWASH (Sex Work and Health), ed. *Sekkusu wāku sutadīsu: Tōjisha shiten de kangaeru sei to rōdō* [*Sex Work Studies: Considering Sex and Work from the Perspective of the People Concerned*] (Tokyo: Nihon Hyōronsha, 2019).

Sylvester, Sara. "Drawing Dangerous Women: The Monstrous Feminine, Taboo and Japanese Feminist Perspectives on the Female Form." *Feminist Encounters: A Journal of Critical Studies in Culture and Politics* vol. 4, no. 1 (2020), pp. 1–16.

Tai, Eika. *Comfort Women Activism* (Hong Kong: Hong Kong University Press, 2020).

Taiwan Sōtokufu Bunkyōkyoku Gakumuka, *Shōwa ninendo Taiwan sōtokufu gakkō seito jidō shintai kensa tōkeisho* (Taipei: Taiwan Sōtokufu Bunkyōkyoku, 1929).

Taishō rokunendo Taiwan sōtokufu gakkō seito oyobi jidō shintai kensa tōkeisho (Taipei: Taiwan Sōtokufu Naimukyoku, 1919).

Takeda Hiroko. *The Political Economy of Reproduction in Japan: Between Nation-State and Everyday Life* (New York: Routledge Curzon, 2005).

Takeuchi-Demirci, Aiko. *Contraceptive Diplomacy: Reproductive Politics and Imperial Ambitions in the United States and Japan* (Stanford, CA: Stanford University Press, 2018).

Takeyama, Akiko. "Intimacy for Sale: Masculinity, Entrepreneurship, and Commodity Self in Japan's Neoliberal Situation." *Japanese Studies* vol. 30, no. 2 (2010), pp. 231–46.

Staged Seduction: Selling Dreams in a Tokyo Hostess Club (Stanford, CA: Stanford University Press, 2016).

Tanaka, Yuki. *Japan's Comfort Women: Sexual Slavery and Prostitution during World War II and the US Occupation* (London: Routledge, 2002).

Tanizaki Junichirō, *Naomi* (New York: Vintage, 2001).

"Tokyo Prosecutors Seek Fine in Trial against 'Vagina Artist' Megumi Igarashi," *Japan Times*, February 1, 2016, www.japantimes.co.jp/news/2016/02/01/national/crime-legal/tokyo-prosecutors-seek-fine-in-trial-against-vagina-artist-megumi-igarashi/

Taniguchi, Hiroyuki. "Japan's 2003 Gender Identity Disorder Act: The Sex Reassignment Surgery, No Marriage, and No Child Requirements as Perpetuations of Gender Norms in Japan." *Asia-Pacific Law & Policy Journal* vol. 14, no. 2 (2013), pp. 108–17.

Thomas, Julia Adeney. "Why Do Only Some Places Have History? Japan, the West, and the Geography of the Past." *Journal of World History* vol. 28, no. 2 (June 2017), pp. 187–218.

Tierney, Robert Thomas. *Tropics of Savagery: The Culture of Japanese Empire in Comparative Frame* (Berkeley: University of California Press, 2010).

Tōgō Ken. *Jōshiki o koete: Okama no michi* [*Overcoming Common Sense: The Gay Man's Path*] (Tokyo: Potto Shuppan, 2002).

Tokuda Shūsei. *Arakure* [*Rough Living*, 1915], trans. Richard Torrance (Honolulu: University of Hawai'i Press, 2001).

"Tokyo Prosecutors Seek Fine in Trial against Vagina Artist Megumi Igarashi." *Kyodo News*, February 1, 2016, www.japantimes.co.jp/news/2016/02/01/national/crime-legal/tokyo-prosecutors-seek-fine-in-trial-against-vagina-artist-megumi-igarashi/

Tomoda Yoshitaka. *Seikō Jiten* [*Dictionary of Human Relations*] (Tokyo: Buyōdō, 1932).

"Trostfrauen-Statue darf vorerst doch bleiben" [The Comfort Women Statue May Stay for Now]. *Berliner Morgenpost*, October 13, 2020, www.morgenpost.de/bezirke/mitte/article230658630/Trostfrauen-Statue-soll-weg-Mitte-beugt-sich-Tokios-Druck.html

Tsunoda, Yukiko. "Sexual Harassment in Japan." In *Directions in Sexual Harassment Law*, ed. Catharine A. MacKinnon and Reva B. Siegel, pp. 618–33 (Oxford: Oxford University Press, 2003).

230   Bibliography

Uchiyama, Benjamin. *Japan's Carnival War: Mass Culture on the Home Front, 1937–1945* (Cambridge: Cambridge University Press, 2020).

Ueno Chizuko, Araragi Shinzō, and Hirai Kazuko, eds. *Sensō to seibōryoku no hikakushi e mukete* [*Toward a Comparative History of War and Sexual Violence*] (Tokyo: Iwanami Shoten, 2018).

Uenoda Setsuo. *Japan – Yesterday and Today: Sketches and Essays on Japanese City Life* (Tokyo: Tokyo News Service, 1956).

Uno Chiyo. *The Story of a Single Woman*, trans. Rebecca Copeland (Doncaster: Bailgate Books, 2003).

Uno, Kathleen. "Womanhood, War, and Empire: Transmutations of 'Good Wife, Wise Mother' before 1931." In *Gendering Modern Japanese History*, ed. Barbara Molony and Kathleen Uno, pp. 493–519 (Cambridge, MA: Harvard University Asia Center, 2005).

"Unsei handan: Zenkyūhyaku gojūsan-nen no kekkon no aite o shiru hō" [Fortune Telling: Methods for Recognizing the Ideal Marriage Partner in 1953]. *Sutairu* 1953.

Vogel, Ezra F. *Japan as Number One: Lessons for America* (Cambridge, MA: Harvard University Press, 1979).

Japan's New Middle Class: The Salary Man and His Family in a Japanese Suburb (Berkeley: University of California Press, 1967).

Walthall, Anne. *The Weak Body of a Useless Women: Matsuo Taseko and the Meiji Restoration* (Chicago, IL: University of Chicago Press, 1998).

Watkins, Susan. "Which Feminisms?" *New Left Review* (January–February 2018), pp. 5–76.

Weiss, Suzannah. "Meet Rokudenashiko, the Artist Arrested for Making a Boat Out of Her Vagina." *Glamour*, June 19, 2017, www.glamour.com/story/rokudenashiko-japanese-artist-arrested-for-vagina-art

White, Merry Isaacs. *Perfectly Japanese: Making Families in an Era of Upheaval* (Berkeley: University of California Press, 2002).

Wieseltier, Leon. *Against Identity* (New York: William Drenttel, 1996).

Wilson, Sean Michael and Akiko Shimojima. *The Minamata Story: An Eco Tragedy* (Berkeley, CA: Stone Bridge Press, 2020).

Yamada, Amy. "Kneel Down and Lick My Feet," trans. Terry Gallagher. In *Monkey Brain Sushi: New Tastes in Japanese Fiction*, ed. Alfred Birnbaum, pp. 187–203 (Tokyo: Kodansha International, 1991).

Yamaguchi Tomomi. "Feminism, Timelines, and History-Making." In *A Companion to the Anthropology of Japan*, ed. Jennifer Robertson, pp. 50–59 (Oxford: Blackwell, 2005).

"'Gender Free' Feminism in Japan: A Story of Mainstreaming and Backlash." *Feminist Studies* vol. 40, no. 3 (2014), pp. 541–72.

"The 'History Wars' and the 'Comfort Woman' Issue: The Significance of Nippon Kaigi in the Revisionist Movement in Contemporary Japan." In *Japanese Military Sexual Slavery: The Transnational Redress Movement for the Victims*, ed. Pyong Gap Min, Thomas Chung, and Sejung Sage Yim (Berlin: De Gruyter, 2020).

"The 'History Wars' and the 'Comfort Woman' Issue: Revisionism and the Right-Wing in Contemporary Japan and the U.S." *Asia-Pacific Journal: Japan Focus* vol. 18, issue 6, no. 3 (March 15, 2020), pp. 1–23.

Bibliography

"Japanese Women and Work: Holding Back Half the Nation." *The Economist*, March 29, 2014.

"The 'Japan Is Great!' Boom, Historical Revisionism, and the Government." *Asia-Pacific Journal: Japan Focus* vol. 15, issue 6, no. 15 (March 2017), pp. 1–6.

"Japan's Right-Wing Women and the 'Comfort Women' Issue." *Georgetown Journal of Asian Affairs* vol. 6 (2020), pp. 45–54.

"'Loser Dogs' and 'Demon Hags': Single Women in Japan and the Declining Birth Rate." *Social Science Japan Journal* vol. 9, no. 1 (2006), pp. 109–14.

The Mainstreaming of Feminism and the Politics of Backlash in Twenty-First-Century Japan." In *Rethinking Japanese Feminisms*, ed. Julia C. Bullock, Ayako Kano, and Japanese Welker (Honolulu: University of Hawai'i Press, 2017), pp. 68–87.

Yamaguchi Tomomi, Nogawa Motokazu, Tessa Morris-Suzuki, and Koyama Emi. *Umi o wataru "ianfu" mondai: Uha no "rekishisen" o tou* [*The Comfort Women Issue Crosses the Ocean: Interrogating the Right's History War*] (Tokyo: Iwanami Shoten, 2016).

Yamakawa Kikue. *Waga sumu mura* [*Our Village*] (Tokyo: Sankoku Shobō, 1943).

Yamamoto Poteto. "'Waisetsu hyōgen' kisei to josei sabetsu kokufuku wa kankei nai? Kenpō gakusha Ishida Yōko-shi intabyū." *Wezzy–Gendai o shian suru seikai no nai WEB magajin*, December 27, 2016, https://wezz-y.com/archives/39102/3

Yamasaki Hiroshi. "Kindai dansei no tanjō" [The Birth of the Modern Man]. In *Nihon no otoko wa doko kara kite, doko e iku no ka?* [*Where Have Japanese Men Come From? Where Are They Going?*], ed. Asai Haruo, Itō Satoru, and Murase Yukihiro, pp. 32–53 (Tokyo: Jūgatsusha, 2001).

Yamashita Chikako. "Dōseikon gōhōka, 8-wari ga kōteiteki Dentsū chōsa no 20–50-dai." *Asahi Shinbun Dejitaru*, January 12, 2019, www.asahi.com/art icles/ASM1C52Z7M1CUTIL025.html

Yamashita Iwao. "Kasei" [Household Finances]. *Jogaku Zasshi* no. 260, April 11, 1891, pp. 20–21.

Yamazaki Tomoko. *Sandakan Brothel No. 8: An Episode in the History of Lower-class Japanese Women*, trans. Karen Colligan-Taylor (New York: M. E. Sharpe, [1972] 1999).

Yanagita Kunio. *The Legends of Tōno*, trans. Ronald A. Morse (Tokyo: The Japan Foundation, [1910] 1975).

Yokuni Masumi and Yokuni Hideyuki. "LGBT ni tsuite kangaeru" [Thinking About LGBT]. Fukujitsugen-tō ōen TV, June 11, 2019, www.youtube.com/watch?v=2q-sWTQJOxE&feature=youtu.be

Yoneyama, Lisa. *Cold War Ruins: Transpacific Critique of American Justice and Japanese War Crimes* (Durham, NC: Duke University Press, 2016).

Yosano Akiko. *Travels in Manchuria and Mongolia*, trans. Joshua Fogel (New York: Columbia University Press, 2001).

Yoshii Kaneoka. "Eiseijō kara mitaru kōshō mondai" [The Prostitution Problem Viewed from the Perspective of Hygiene]. *Kakusei* vol. 30, no. 1 (1940), pp. 38–39.

Bibliography

Yoshimi Yoshiaki. *Comfort Women: Sexual Slavery in the Japanese Military During World War II*, trans. Suzanne O'Brien (New York: Columbia University Press, [1995] 2000).

Yoshimoto Banana. *Kitchen*, trans. Megan Backus (New York: Washington Square, 1987).

Yoshinaga Michiko. *Sei dōitsusei shōgai: Seitenkan no ashita* [*Gender Disphoria: The Future of Sex Change*] (Tokyo: Shūeisha, 2000).

Sesidō issei shōgai (Tokyo: Shūeisha, 2000).

Yoshiya Nobuko. *Yellow Rose*, trans. Sarah Frederick (Los Angeles, CA: Expanded Editions, 2016).

Yuen, Shu Min. "Unqueer Queers – Drinking Parties and Negotiations of Cultural Citizenship by Female-to-Male Trans People in Japan." *Asian Anthropology* vol. 19, no. 2 (2020), pp. 86–101.

Yukiko Tanaka, ed. *To Live and to Write: Selections by Japanese Women Writers, 1913–1938* (Seattle, WA: Seal Press, 1987).

Ziomek, Kirsten. *Lost Histories: Recovering the Lives of Japan's Colonial Peoples* (Cambridge, MA: Harvard Asia Center, 2019).

Index

Abe Isoo, 62, 124, 131
Abe Sada, 174
Abe Shinzō, 20, 37, 39, 111, 114, 153, 160
abolitionists, 125, 129, 131
abortion, 81, 202, *see also* reproduction
abuse, sexual, 103, 179
acquired immunideficiency syndrome
(AIDS), 137, *see also* human
immunodeficiency virus (HIV)
activism, 139, 183, 188, 202, *see also* queer
identities
activists, 6, 57–61, 71, 101, 118, 124, 137, 185
Adelman, Jeremy, 13
Adonis, 150
adoption, 147, 158
advertising (ads), 48, 55, 73
agency, 81–82, 139
Ai Haruna, 162
Ai Weiei, 185
Aida Makoto, 169, 177–78
All Out, 18
Alliance for Women's Suffrage, 124
amnesia, 106–15
ancestry, common, 82
androgyny, 28
anime, 179–81, 185, 188
Annarino, John, 108
Anzai, Sadako, 31, 102, 105
apparel (clothing), 81, 169
articles, 34, 53, 55, 74, 81, 167
Asahi Gurafu (Asahi Graph), 197
Association for the Lesbian and Gay
Movement (OCCUR), 152
Athlete Ally, 18
audiences, 173, *see also* viewers, *see also*
readers
authentic encounters, 88
authority, 4, 6, 14, 23, 88, 144, 178
patriarchal, 49, 82
autobiographies, 29
autonomy, 41, 95, 136
avatars, 187

babies, why have?, 64–68
*Babysan's World: The Hume'n Slant on
Japan*, 107, 109
Badinter, Elisabeth, 72
bar girls, 127
bars, 124, 130, 134, 150, 202
Basic Law for a Gender Equal Society
(1999), 92
battles, recreations of, 28
beautiful boys, 144
*Beautiful Fighting Girl (Sentō bishōjo no
seishin bunseki)*, 181
Being Lesbian, 151
belligerency, states right of, 7, 33
Berlin's Third Sex (Berlins drittes Geschlecht),
149
birth control, 48, 52–53, 57, 79, 84, 125,
195, *see also* reproduction
birth rates, 36, 63, 65, 93, 158
Blender, 177
Bluestockings, 58, 79
bodies, female, 93, 168, 170, 175–77, 181
Boissonade, Gustave Emile, 145
Bolton, Christopher, 180
bombs, atomic, 38, 87, *see also* nuclear
weapons
books, 19, 35, 74, 84, 94, 167, 175, 192
Borges, Jorge Luis, 202–3
Boyce, Bret, 173
brochures, 66, 195
brothels, 100–1, 103, 105, 107, 122, 127,
131
"Brother, Do Not Give Your Life," 83
Bubu De la Madeleine, 108, 111, 137–38
Buckley, Edmund, 192
Bungei Shunjū, 130
Bureau for Gender Equality, 38
burials, 26, 31, 50

cafés, 130–31, 134, 202
campaigns, 25, 38, 40, 47, 67, 125, 138,
197

233

234 Index

care facilities, 66, 204
castration, 182
Cather, Kirsten, 175–76
censorship, 61, 146, 148–49, 170, 173, 175–76, 188, 193
Charles E. Tuttle Co. & Publishers, 107
chastity, 79, 81
child pornography, 178
Child Welfare Act (1947), 135
childbearing, 68
childbirth, 50, 52, 63, 67–68, 90, 93, 156
childcare, 40, 52, 67–68
childhood, 4–5, 38, 87
childrearing, 39–40, 52, 68, 74
children, 4–5, 26–27, 39, 49, 63, 66–67, 71, 76, 78, 93, see also reproduction, see also womanhoods
visual culture, 145, 167–68, 172, 177, 180
citizens (citizenship), 9, 16, 34, 59, 71–72, 75, 95, 143, 177
civilians, 28, 47, 105–6, 113
civilization, 197
clubs, 124, 135–36, 202
codes, 6–9
coercion, 100, 112
collaborations, 111, 152, 188, 195
colonialism, 2, 32, 48, 71, 103, 105, 197
colonies, 26, 32, 57, 81–82, 98
combatants, 28–29, 32, 113
female, 31
comfort bags, 171
comfort stations, 103–4, 106, 111–12
comfort troupes, military, 29
comfort women, 103, 106, 111–13, 116
comics, 13, 108, 188
commemorations, global, 114–19
commodification, 171–72, 177, 180–81, 187
communities, 5, 8, 11, 17, 52, 115, 138, 189, see also queer identities
modern manhood, 28–29, 45
company men, 32–37, see also salarymen
condoms, 47, 58, 65, 102–3
Confucianism, 72, 170
consciousness, 92, 115, 204
conscript identity, 25
conscription, 5, 99
conscription (conscripts), 19, 21–22, 24–25, 45, 99, see also soldiers
Conscription Decree (1872), 21
conspicuous consumption, 32, 81
consumer culture, mass, 81
contraception, 54, 57, 61, 65
contraceptives, 48, 53, 57–63, 65

Convention on the Elimination of All Forms of Discrimination Against Women (1985), 92
cooperation (noncooperation), 32, 83, 116
corporations, 156
Council for Gender Equality, 92
COVID-19, 36
crashes, asset bubble, 36, 38
Crenshaw, Kimberlé, 14
crime, organized, 134
crimes, 1, 113–14, 118, 126, 137, 141, 145
Criminal Code (1907), 172
crises, 20, 41, 90, 152
demographic, 48, 65
financial, 36
culture, cute, 182
culture, queer, 142–49
customers, 136–38
cuteness, 48, 94, 186, 188, see also visual culture, sexing of

dance halls, 130–31
data, 22, 24, 26, 127, 183, 185
"Dawn of the East Asian Race, The," 197
De Becker, J.E., 129
debts, 128, 132
Deguchi Yonekichi, 192
democratization, 21
demon hags, 93
Densha otoko (Train Man), 35
deregulation, 132, 183
desires, male sexual, 65, 99
desires, women's, 75, 186, 189
disability, 22–23, 50, 62, 178
disasters, see triple disaster
discrimination, 18, 150, 154, 156, 158, 160–61, 201
diseases, 62, 148, see also venereal diseases
"Diver and the Octopus, The," 169
diversification, 7, 44, 71, 134, 162
diversity, sexual, 150, 158, 161
divorce, 34, 38, 130, 199
Djerassi, Carl, 64
doctors, 62, 65
Dog, 177
Dōi, Keijo, 195
domination, 23, 90, 121
dōseiai, 146

earnings, 94
earthquakes, 36, see also triple disaster
Ebihara Yuri, 186
Edible Artificial Girls, Mimi-chan, 177
education (schooling), 26–27, 60, 71, 73, 75–76, 82, 92, 95, 128

Index

education, girls', 72, 75, 125
education, history, 115
Ehrlich, Paul, 195
elderly, 66
elders, 65
elites, political, 197
EMA (Equal Marriage Alliance) Japan, 158
employers, 82, 130
employment, 43, 66, 75, 86, 93, 95, 201
  discrimination, 18
EMPOWER, 137
English (language), 76
enslavement, 101, 104, 114
entertainment world, 150–51, 162
Equal Employment Opportunity Law
  (1986), 92
equal rights, 71
equality, 34, 70, 72–74, 81, 85, 92, 152–53,
  159
equality, gender, 96, 177
erotica, 171, *see also* visual culture, sexing of
eroticism, 99, 193
ethics, 73
ethnicity, 82
ethnology, sexual, 192
Eugenic Protection Law (1948), 62
eugenics, 61–63, 130
Eurocentrism, 13
European Human Rights Court, 159
everydayness, 88
examinations, health, 101–2
examinations, medical, 102
examinations, physical, 22
exemptions, military conscription, 25
expectations, 22, 41, 43, 92, 160
experts, law, 185
experts, medical, 99
expression, sexual, 174

factories, 82
families, 3–6, 100
  modern manhood, 34, 38
  queer identities, 158
  reproduction and motherhood, 61, 66–67
  sexual labor, 125, 128, 133
  womanhoods, 76, 94
family planning, 48, 50–52, 61, 81
family values, traditional, 66
fantasy, 181
farmers, 59, 78
fathers, 39, 67
female bodies, 171, 179, 204
femininity, 32, 38, 81, 189
feminism, 58, 90–96, 115, 177, 183, 185,
  see also girls: modern

Ferrante, Elena, 205
fertility, 66
festivals, 185
Field Nurse (Yasen kangofu), 102
film, 175
films, 46, 98, 174, 176, 179
Flower Tales (Hana monogatari), 147
freedom of speech, 173
freedom, sexual, 79
freedoms, 71
Freud, Sigmund, 99
Fukuda, Hideko, 79
Fukui prefecture, 66
Fukuzawa, Yukichi, 22, 48, 71
Funeral of Roses (Bara no sōretsu), 141
furītā, 43

Gaikotsu, Miyatake, 148–49, 162, 203
games, 27
Gamson, Joshua, 203
gay boom, 150–51
geisha, 50, 127, 133
gender, 9–12, 191, 199, 201, *see also* queer
  identities
gender equality, 41, 44, 92, 158
Gender Equality Bureau Cabinet Office, 67
Gender Identity Disorder Act (2003), 159
gender relations, 34, 38
gender rights, 201
Geneva Conventions (1949), 113
Germany, 116
Ghidorah, The Three-Headed Monster (San
  daikaijū, Chikyū saidai no kessen),
  169
"Giant Member Fuji versus King Gidora,
  The", 169
girls, 29, 31, 168
  modern, 79–84
Girls Ethics Instructions (Joshi shūshinkun), 73
Global Network of Sex Work Projects
  (NSWP), 137
globalization, 21
Goldstein-Gidoni, Ofra, 94
government, national, 158
"Governors Are Pregnant, The" (Chiji ga
  ninpu ni), 40
grandparents, 67
*Great Mirror of Male Love (Nanshoku
  Okagami)*, 144
Greater Learning for Women (Onna daigaku),
  71

Halberstam, Jack, 202
Happiness Realization Party, 161
happiness, men's, 41

236 Index

Hara Takashi, 22
Harada Satsuki, 81
hardship, 49, 59, 100, 111, 128
Harper's Bazaar, 41
Hashimoto Ryūtarō, 20, 37–38
Hata Sahachirō, 194–95
Hatakeno Tomato, 121
healing, 35
health checks, 126
health clubs, fashion, 121–22, 124
health examination system, school, 26
health examiners, military, 24, *see also* masculinity
health, family, 61, 74
health, maternal, 65
health, men's, 101
health, mothers' and babies, 55
health, sexual, 138
healthcare, 52, *see also* public health
healthcare services, 202, *see also* medical care
hermaphroditism, 141, 148, 203
heroism, 32
Himawari, 86
Hino Ashihei, 29
Hiratsuka Raichō, 59, 62, 70, 79, 83, 85–87, 129, 131
Hirohito, Emperor, 84, 100
Hirschfeld, Magnus, 149, 193–94
Hokusai Katsushika, 169
homelessness, 37
homosexual love, 193
homosexuality, 146, 148, 151–52, 194, 201
honor, 51
Hosoda Tomoya, 154
hospitals, field, 26
hospitals, military, 102
hotlines, 157
Household Health, 129
household systems, 125
housekeeping, 39–40, 68, 74
Housewife's Companion, The (Shufu no Tomo), 53, 54, 56
housewives, 94
Human Form in Japanese Art and Life, The, 168
human immunodeficiency virus (HIV), 64, 121, 138, 152
human rights, 48, 86, 92, 113, 125, 130, 152, 156, 159
Human Rights Watch, 18, 159
Hume, Bill, 107
humor, 183, 186
hygiene, 55
hypocrisy, 193

Ichikawa Fusae, 131
identities, shifting, 160
identity, middle-class, 75
Igarashi Megumi, 166–67, 181, 183–84
Ihara Saikaku, 144
Iijima Ginjirō, 59
Ikumen Campaign, 39
Ikumen Passport, 39
Ikuta Hanayo, 195
Illouz, Eva, 139
imagery, 94, 100
immigration, 66
imperialism, 48, 58, 131
impurity, 50
In the Realm of the Senses (Ai no korrida), 174, 176
incomes, 34, 43, 55, 75, 93, 137, 186, *see also* wages
independence, economic, 68, 74
individuality, 95
industrialization, 71
industries, sex, *see* sexual labor
inequality, 6, 8, 43, 58, 96
infanticide, 49, 52, 58
infantilization, 37, 88
Inoue Tetsujirō, 125
International Lesbian and Gay Association Japan (ILGA), 152
International Women's Day (2018), 95
International Women's Year (1975), 92
Internet, 186–89
intersectionality, 14, 115, 141, 157
intra-uterine device (IUD), 57
Introduction to Men's Studies (Danseigaku nyūmon), 38
Irisawa Tatsukichi, 195
Ishihara Shintarō, 19, 37
Ishikawa Fusae, 195
Ishimoto Shizue, 61–62, 84, 195
Itō Hirobumi, 27
Itō Kimio, 38
Itō Noe, 79

J-ALL, 18
Japan, 88
Japan Federation of Women's Organizations, 87
Japan Mothers' Congress, 87
Japan Times, The, 34
Japan's Army, 19
Japanese Birth Control Federation, 62
J-humanity, gendered, 199–205
Johnston, Captain James D., 167
journals, 197
justice, 60, 201

Index

Kabuki interlude, 166
Kaibara Ekken, 71
Kamikawa Aya, 154
Kanasugi Eigorō, 125
Kanmonkō Port, 90
Katayama Tetsu, 125
Kim Eun-Sung, 116
Kim Hak-sun, 104, 111
Kim Seo-Kyung, 116
Kinsella, Sharon, 183
Kishida Toshiko, 75
Knaus, Hermann, 52
knowledge, 60, 142–49, 191, 193, 197
Koch, Gabriele, 135, 139
Koizumi Junichirō, 41
Koizumi Shinjirō, 41
Kondo Marie, 94
Konishi Shigenao, 73
Kōno Statement, 111, 113
Korea Verband, 116
Krauss, Friedrich Solomon, 146, 193–95
Kurihara Harumi, 94

Label X, 157
labor, 66, 88, 92, 96
labor forces, 95, 156
labor, emotional, 186, 189
laborers, 5, 37, 59, 107, 128, *see also*
    workers
laughter pictures, 169
Law Regulating Entertainment Businesses,
    135
law, international, 99
lawmakers, 95, 167
laws, 6–9, 73
leave, maternity, 94
leave, parental, 39
leave, paternity, 40–41, 67
legacies, 106–15
legislation, 18, 51, 59, 102, 130, 134, 156,
    185, 188, 204
  children, 4
Leigh, Carol, 137
lesbian, gay, bisexual, transgender, queer
    and/or questioning, intersex, asexual/
    agender (LGBTQIA+), 141, 143–44
lesbianism (lesbians), 11, 138, 150–51
"Let's Change Japan," 161
liberation, women's, 87–90
life satisfaction, 75
lifetime employment, 35
literature, 98, 176
lithographs, pornographic, 171
*Little Boy: The Arts of Japan's Exploding
    Subculture*, 37

localism, 88
loser dogs, 93
love, 29, 47, 58, 79, 125, 174, *see also* queer
    identities
  womanhoods, 72–73, 76, 79
love, romantic, 4, 98
loyalty, 73
lust, women's, 174

MacArthur, General Douglas, 38, 132
magazines, 88, 108, 127, 146, 152, 179,
    197
  reproduction and motherhood, 53–54
  womanhoods, 73, 75–76, 83, 85–86
Majima Yutaka, 60, 62
male bodies, 22, 27, 55, 204
male desire, 179
manga, 179–81, 185, 188
manhood, modern, 19–21
  changing tables, 37–45
  company men, 32–37
  hegemonic masculinity, 21–32
manuals, hygiene, 102
marginalization, 23, 50, 118, 187
marriage, 199, *see also* womanhoods
  modern manhood, 34
  queer identities, 142, 147, 158
  reproduction and motherhood, 67–68
  sexual labor, 125
Married Life (Fūfu Seikatsu), 85
masculinity, 20, 100
  hegemonic, 21–32, 44
  modern manhood, 32, 35–36, 38
mass culture, 27, 29, 81, 86, 107, 180, 183
Masuda Sayo, 50, 133–34, 138
Maternal Protection Law (1996), 63
maturity, 26, 38, 43–44
media, 31, 41, 88, 93, 150–52, 172, 183,
    185, 189
medical care, 128, 133
medical systems, 51–52
Meiji state (government), 51–52, 144, 171
memoirs, 29
memorials, 118
men
  military, 5, 28, 105
  young, 19–20, 23–24, 34
  modern, 41, 43, 45
*Men Who Buy and Men Who Don't Buy
    (Kau otoko, kawanai otoko)*, 137
men, young. *see also* soldiers
Men's Center Japan, 38
Men's Lib, 38
Men's Network, 38
menstrual cycles, 52, 57

238 Index

mental illness (conditions), 24, 29, 62, 102
mercury poisoning, 64
midwifery (midwives), 50, 52, 68
migration, 57, 126
military ideals, 25
military service, 25, *see also* masculinity
Minamata Disease, 64
minors, 6, 135
Misago Chizuru, 93
Miscellaneous People's Association, 150
misconduct, sexual, 29
misunderstandings, cultural, 108
Miwa Akihiro, 162
Miyagi Kikuko, 31
Miyake Koichi, 195
Miyazaki Tsutomu, 180
Miyazawa Kiichi, 111
mobility, upward, 41
modern girls, 130, *see also* womanhoods
modernity, 12–13
moga, 81–82
monuments, 116
moral degeneration, 193
morality (morals), 49, 167, 172–73, 194
    sexual, 2, 6
Mori Arinori, 27, 72
Mori Art Museum, 177–78
Mori Ōgai, 22, 145
motherhood, 47–49, 72, 79, 87
    contracepting imperialism, 57–63
    revolutionizing birth, 49–57
    why have babies?, 64–68
mothers, 29, 72, 93
Mun P'il-gi, 104
Murakami Takashi, 37
murder, 49
Muta Kazue, 177

Nakahara Ichigorō, 125
Nakamura Ataru, 163
Nakamura Shidō, 41
Nakano Chūzō, 98
Napier, Susan, 181
nation building, *see* manhood, modern
National Eugenics Law (1941), 59, 62, 131
National Institute of Population, 39
National League for Pure Blood, 131
nationalism, 15, 32, 94
New Basic Shōwa Pedagogy for Girls (Shinsei junkyo Shōwa joshi kyōikugaku), 73
new halves, 121
New Marilyn Club, 124
new women, 79, 81–84
New Women's Higher Learning (Shin onna daigaku), 71

newspapers, 27, 54, 83, 133, *see also* media
Night Porter, The, 174
non-citizens, 23
Not engaged in or seeking Education, Employment, or Training (NEET), 43
nuclear meltdown, 36, *see also* triple disaster
nuclear weapons, 87
nudity, female, 168
nudity, public, 167, 171
nurses, 29
Nussbaum, Martha, 33

obedience, 70
objectification, 172, 186–87
obscenity, *see also* visual culture
    queer identities, 150, 184
    sexual labor, 122
Ogino Kyūsaku, 52
Ōguma Shigenobu, 22
Okano Yayo, 177
On the Improvement of the Japanese Race (Nihon jinshu kaizōron), 61
oppression, 203
organizations, men's, 38, 41
Orientalism, 86
Ōsawa Mari, 92
Ōshima Nagisa, 174–76
Ōta Tenrei, 57, 62
overpopulation, 59

pacifism, 84–87
pamphlets, 67
parasite singles, 93
parenthood, shared, 40
Parreñas, Rhacel Salazar, 138
partners, matrimonial, 58
Pasolini, Pier Paolo, 175
pastimes, 81
patriarchy, 70, 81–82
patriotism, 32–33, 115
pay, high, 136
penises, 191–99
People Against Pornography and Sexual Violence (PAPS), 177–79
phallicism, 192
photography (photographs), 176, 195
pills, contraceptive, 64, *see also* babies, why have?
players, female, 186
pleasure, 10, 81, 123, 135, 147, 160
    female, 169
    male, 167, 174, 184
poems, 169
poisoning, mercury, 64

Index

239

police forces (raids), 130, 137, 144, 171, 183
political parties, 95
popular culture, 35, 48, 86, 94, 107
Popular Medicine (Tsūzoku Igaku), 55
population norms, 24
populations, 36, 38
pornography, 166–67, 188
poverty, 26, 43, 59, 87, 133–34
power, 3, 48, 131, 176–77, 186, 188, 197
  military, 5, 21
  political, 23, 203
power relations, 6, 191
practitioners, medical, 57
predictability, 35
pregnancy harnesses, 40
prices, contraceptive, 55
prisoners of war, 107
productivity, 35
professionalization, 52
professionals, female, 88, 90
professions, 71
prohibitions, 125–26
  queer, 153–62
promiscuity, female, 64
propaganda, 53
property, 6, 34, 85, 122
Proposed Law on the Promotion of the
  Elimination of Discrimination based
  on Sexual Orientation and Gender
  Identity, 156
prostitutes, 100–1, *see also* sexual labor
prostitution, 81, 87, 111, 113, 122
Prostitution Prevention Law (1956), 132,
  134–35
protests, citizen, 177
psychological standards, 24
public culture, 197
public health, 52, 129
public opinions (sentiment), 154, 156
public trust, 64
publications, 38, 61, 85, 115, 149, 151,
  157, 173
publishers, 173
Purity (Kakusei), 101, 125
Purity Society, 125, 131

queer identities, 141–42, *see also*
  conscription (conscripts)
  culture and knowledge, 142–49
  does trans transform society?, 162–63
  prohibitions and rights, 153–62
  spaces, 149–53

radical ordinariness, 160
rape, 63, 65, 99, 104, 106–7, 113, 177, 187

Ravensbrück National Memorial, 118
readers, 175
Recreation and Amusement Association
  (RAA), 131
recruitment, 104, 112–13, *see also*
  masculinity
redemption, 3–6
refugees, 118
Regarding the Pain of Others, 176–81
relations, gender, 1, 125, 129–30
religion, 160
repatriation, 32, 107
reproduction, 47–49, 161, 174
  contracepting imperialism, 57–63
  revolutionizing birth, 49–57
  why have babies?, 64–68
reputations, 115
research, 13, 52, 102, 114, 170, 177, 192,
  197
researchers, 57
resistance, 70, 167, 176–81
restoration, 35
Robertson, Jennifer, 17, 204
robotics, 66, 186, 204
Rokudenashiko, 181, 183
roles, males, 38, 44
Roosevelt, Eleanor, *80*, 86

Saebōgu/Saeborg, 142
Saga Junichi, 50
Saitō Tamaki, 181
Salaryman Kintarō (Sararīman Kintarō), 35
salarymen, 34, 36, 45
Salò, or the 120 Days of Sodom, 175
Salvarsan 606, 195
Salvation Army, 124, 128
sameness, 82
samurai, 25, 36, 144, 170, 193
Sanger, Margaret, 61
Sarkeesian, Anita, 186
Sasakibara Gō, 188
Satō Tamio, 194–95
Sato Vivienne, 163–64
Sawabe Hitomi, 151
scanning, prenatal, 63
scholars, 192, 202
School Ordinance (1887), 27
schools, 156, *see also* education (schooling)
Schwind, Martin, 57
Screech, Timon, 170
security, 35
seibetsu, 143
self-cultivation, 75
Self-Defense Forces (SDF), 19, 33
self-determination, 70

240 Index

self-help groups, 157
self-isolation, 43
self-realization, 95
self-redefinement, 82
self-sacrifice, 34
seniority principle, 35
senses, dangers in, 173–76
service members, 32
sex, 9–12, 191, *see also* queer identities
sex change, 159, 204
Sex Life in Beliefs, Morals, Customs and Common Law of the Japanese, The (Das Geschlechtsleben in Glauben, Sitte, Brauch und Gewohnheitsrecht der Japaner), 193
sex markets, 107, 127
Sex Research (Sei Kenkyū), 127
sex work, *see also* sexual labor, *see* prostitution
Sex Work and Sexual Health (SWASH), 138
Sex Work: Writings by Women in the Industry, 137
Sex Workers! Encourage, Empower, Trust and Love Yourselves! (SWEETLY), 138
sexual freedom, 79
sexual harassment, 177, 187
sexual labor, 121–23
   liberating protitutes, 123–27
   renewing the oldest profession, 127–34
   work of sex today, 134–39
sexual mapping, 199–205
sexual media, 179
sexual violence, 5, 99–106, 138, 188, *see also* visual culture, sexing of, *see also* wars
sexuality, 9–12, 167, 191
sexuality, female, 17, 146, 174, 181, *see also* lesbianism (lesbians)
sexuality, male, 74, *see also* homosexuality
sexualization, 177, 180–81
sexually transmitted diseases, 131
Shibahara Urako, 59
Shibusawa Eiichi, 125
Shimada Saburō, 125
Shimada Yoshiko, 108, 111
Shimizu Toyoko, 75
Shincho 45, 161
Shindō Hiroshi, 22
Shinobu, 136
shut-ins, 43
slavery, sexual, 100, 103, 105, 111, 113, 115, *see also* wars
social mobility, 82

social protest, 167
Social Security Research Institute, 39
social status, 7, 75
Society of Christian Women, 124–25, 131
society, aging of, 65
Soeda Jūichi, 125
Soil and Soldiers (Tsuchi to heishi), 84
soldiers, 21, 26, 28–29, 171, *see also* conscription (conscripts)
solidarity, 40, 115
sons, 4, 22, 25–26, 28, 74
Sontag, Susan, 176
Sorry for Being a Genius: Monument for Nothing, 177
South Manchurian Railway Company, 83
spring pictures, 171
state violence, 88
Statue of Peace, 118
statues, 116
status, state (empire), 125
status, women's, 49
   Germany, 74
sterilization, 59, 62, 131
Stratz, Charles Heinrich, 168
structures, social, 39
studies programs, 92
Style (Sutairu), 86
submission, 70, 83, 121
subordination, 23, 187
subversion, 171
suffrage, women's, 72, 79, 84–87, 125
Suga Yoshihide, 160
Sugi Kōji, 22
Sugita Mio, 161
Sunflower (Himawari), 86
suppression, 167, 170, 197
surgery, sex-change, 151, 159
surrender, declaration of, 32
surveillance, 52
surveys, 8, 60, 75, 128, 154
Suzuki Bunji, 125
Suzuki Fumi, 50
syphilis, 195, *see also* venereal diseases

Tajima Kazuko, 90
Takamure Itsue, 126, 133
Takeyama, Akiko, 136
taxes, 94
technologies, reproductive, 48
television, 35, 150, 161, *see also* media
textbooks, 72, 113
textbooks, school, 27
Thoughts on Hermaphroditism (Hannannyokō), 141, 149, 162

Index

241

Tōgō Ken, 150–51
Tōkyō Asahi Shinbun (Tokyo Asahi Newspaper), 79
Tokyo Gay and Lesbian Pride Parade (1994), 153
Tokyo Olympics, 18
Tokyo War Crimes Trial, 114
tourism (tourists), 66, 134, 194
training, 75
transgender issues, 121
transmigration of souls, 49
Treaty of Kanagawa, 167
trials, 175–76, 184
triple disaster, 36, 94, 135
Tsuda Umeko, 86
tsunami, *see also* triple disaster
tsunamis, 36

US–Japan Mutual Cooperation and Security Treaty, 87
Ueki Emori, 48
Ueno Chizuko, 92, 177
Uenoda Setsuo, 34
unions, trade, 133
United Nations (UN), 92
Unno Yukinori, 61
urbanization, 71

vaginas, demystifying of, 181–86
veneration, 26
venereal diseases, 55, 59
  sexual labor, 124, 129–31
  wars, 101–3, 107
veterans, 30, 32
Viagra, 65
video games, 179, 186–89
videos, 40, 179
viewers, 176, 180
violation, 186
violence, 197
Violence Against Women in War–Network Japan (VAWW-NET), 114
violence, sexual, 113, 175, 177, *see also* visual culture, sexing of, *see also* wars
violence, state, 87
virtual sexism, 186
visual culture, 26
visual culture, sexing of, 166–67
  dangers in the senses, 173–76
  demystifying the vagina, 181–86
  erotic woodblock prints, 167–72
  females in video gaming, 186–89
  modern morals, 172–73
  Regarding the Pains of Others, 176–81
Vita Sexualis (Wita sekushuarisu), 145–46

Volunteer Military Service Law, 31
voyeurs, 169

wages, 92, 133, *see also* incomes
waitresses, 130
Wakamatsu Shizu, 75
warriors, 25
wars, 87, 98–99
  amnesia and legacies, 106–15
  global commemorations, 115–19
  systematic, military sexual violence, 99–106
Watkins, Susan, 135
weapons, nuclear, 87
welfare, 60
What Is Obscenity? How I Became a So-Called Artist (Waisetsu tte nan desu ka: "Jishō geijutsuka" to yobareta watakushi), 29, 182
What Is X Gender? (X jendā tte nani?), 157
Wheat and Soldiers (Mugi to heishi), 84
Wicked City, 180
Wieseltier, Leon, 203
Wiswell, Ella, 128, 197
wives, 28
Woman's Magazine, The (Jogaku Zasshi), 73–74
womanhoods, 70–71
  mainstreaming feminism and backlash, 90–96
  new women, modern girls, 79–84
  rights and roles, 71–79
  suffrage and pacifism, 84–87
  women's liberation, 87–90
women, 31, 38, 48, 55, 58, *see also* new women
Women Against Sexual Violence, 177
Women in Parliament, 95
Women of the Mito Domain, 199
women, young, 29, 168
Women's Action Network, 177
women's bodies, 54, 85
Women's Eros (Onna Erosu), 88
Women's Friendship (Onna no Yūjō), 147
women's health
  reproduction and motherhood, 57
Women's Hygiene Dictionary, The, 53
Women's International War Crimes Tribunal on Japan's Military Sexual Slavery, 114
Women's National Defense Association, 28, 31
women's rights, 74
women's roles, 4, 28, 48, 70, 79, 94, *see also* womanhoods

242　　Index

women's studies, 191, 197
woodblock prints, 166–72
workers, 35–36, 43, 59, 76, 82, 90, 137–38,
    150, 201, *see also* sexual labor
  factory, 75–76, 82, 100
working hours, 41
work–life balance (WLB), 40–41
workplaces, 75, 128, 130, 156
World Congress of Mothers, 86
World Health Organization, 159
World of Women's Learning, The (Jogaku Sekai), 75

Yamada Waka, 79, *80*
Yamakawa Kikue, 81, 199
Yamamoto Senji, 60–61

Yamamura Gunpei, 126
Yanagita Kunio, 50
Yasukuni Shrine, 31
Yayutz, 98
*Yearbook of Sexual Intermediate Types
    (Jahrbuch für sexuelle Zwischenstufen)*,
    149
Yosano Akiko, 79, 83
Yoshida Sumiko, 132
Yoshimi Yoshiaki, 106, 111
Yoshinaga Michiko, 157
Yoshiya Nobuko, 147–48,
    163
young women, 48

Ziomek, Kirsten, 98

New Approaches to Asian History

1 Judith M. Brown, *Global South Asians: Introducing the Modern Diaspora*

2 Diana Lary, *China's Republic*

3 Peter A. Lorge, *The Asian Military Revolution: From Gunpowder to the Bomb*

4 Ian Talbot and Gurharpal Singh, *The Partition of India*

5 Stephen F. Dale, *The Muslim Empires of the Ottomans, Safavids, and Mughals*

6 Diana Lary, *The Chinese People at War: Human Suffering and Social Transformation, 1937–1945*

7 Sunil S. Amrith, *Migration and Diaspora in Modern Asia*

8 Thomas David DuBois, *Religion and the Making of Modern East Asia*

9 Susan L. Mann, *Gender and Sexuality in Modern Chinese History*

10 Tirthankar Roy, *India in the World Economy: From Antiquity to the Present*

11 Robin R. Wang, *Yinyang: The Way of Heaven and Earth in Chinese Thought and Culture*

12 Li Feng, *Early China: A Social and Cultural History*

13 Diana Lary, *China's Civil War: A Social History, 1945–1949*

14 Kiri Paramore, *Japanese Confucianism: A Cultural History*

15 Robert Peckham, *Epidemics in Modern Asia*

16 Craig Benjamin, *Empires of Ancient Eurasia: The First Silk Roads Era, 100 BCE – 250 CE*

17 John W. Chaffee, *The Muslim Merchants of Premodern China: The History of a Maritime Asian Trade Diaspora, 750-1400*

18 Michael H. Fisher, *An Environmental History of India: From Earliest Times to the Twenty-First Century*

19 Felix Wemheuer, *A Social History of Maoist China: Conflict and Change, 1949–1976*

20 Steven B. Miles, *Chinese Diasporas: A Social History of Global Migration*

21 Chiara Formichi, *Islam and Asia: A History*

22 Jeremy Brown, *June Fourth: The Tiananmen Protests and Beijing Massacre of 1989*

23 Toby Lincoln, *An Urban History of China*

24 Gurharpal Singh and Giorgio Shani, *Sikh Nationalism: From a Dominant Minority to an Ethno-Religious Diaspora*

25 Sabine Frühstück, *Gender and Sexuality in Modern Japan*